PAPERS ON ISLAMIC HISTORY **Volume 5**

PAPERS ON ISLAMIC HISTORY

Thomas Naff and Roger Owen, eds.
STUDIES IN EIGHTEENTH CENTURY ISLAMIC HISTORY
G.H.A. Juynboll, ed.
STUDIES ON THE FIRST CENTURY OF ISLAMIC SOCIETY

PAPERS ON ISLAMIC HISTORY

Studies on the First Century of Islamic Society

Edited by G.H.A. JUYNBOLL

Published under the auspices of
The Near Eastern History Group, Oxford
and
The Middle East Center, University of Pennsylvania

SOUTHERN ILLINOIS UNIVERSITY PRESS
Carbondale and Edwardsville

Library of Congress Cataloging in Publication Data
Main entry under title:

Studies on the first century of Islamic society

(Papers on Islamic history; v. 5)
Papers presented at a colloquium held at Oxford in 1975.
"Published under the auspices of the Near Eastern History Group, Oxford and the Middle East Center, University of Pennsylvania."
Bibliography: p.
Includes index.
1. Islam--History--Addresses, essays, lectures.
2. Islamic Empire--History--622-750--Addresses, essays, lectures. I. Juynboll, G. H. A. II. Near Eastern History Group, Oxford. III. University of Pennsylvania. Middle East Center. IV. Series.
BP55.S88 297'.09 81-21225
ISBN 0-8093-1062-7 AACR2

Printed in the United States of America
Production supervised by Kathleen Giencke

CONTENTS

PREFACE

This is the fifth volume in the series of Papers on Islamic History, prepared in connection with a number of colloquia sponsored jointly by the Near Eastern History Group at Oxford and the Middle East Center of the University of Pennsylvania. The first four volumes dealt respectively with The Islamic City, Islam and the Trade of Asia, Islamic Civilization 950-1150, and Studies in Eighteenth Century Islamic History. The fifth colloquium, of which the present volume is the product, was held in Oxford in 1975. A sixth colloquium, on the Mongol period in Islamic history, was held, also in Oxford, in 1977, and it is hoped to publish the papers written for it.

The grateful thanks of all those concerned wih the colloquium and the book go to Dr. G.H.A. Juynboll, who kindly agreed to edit the volume, and without whose tireless efforts it would not have been produced.

ABBREVIATIONS

AIUON	*Annali dell' Istituto Universitario Orientali de Napoli*
ARCH OR	*Archiv Orientalni*
BGA	Bibliotheca Geographorum Arabicorum
BSOAS	*Bulletin of the School of Oriental and African Studies*
EI, 1 and 2	*Encyclopaedia of Islam*, first and second edition
GAS	Fuat Sezgin, *Geschichte des Arabischen Schrifttums*
GCAL	Georg Graf, *Geschichte der Christlichen Arabischen Literatur*
IBLA	*Revue de l'Institut des Belles Lettres Arabes, Tunis*
IJMES	*International Journal of Middle East Studies*
ISL	*Der Islam*
JAOS	*Journal of the American Oriental Society*
JESHO	*Journal of the Economic and Social History of the Orient*
JQR	*Jewish Quarterly Review*
JSS	*Journal of Semitic Studies*
MUSJ	*Mélanges de la Faculté Orientale de l'Université St Joseph de Beyrouth*
MW	*Muslim World*
PPTS	Palestine Pilgrims' Text Society
REI	*Revue des Études Islamiques*
RHR	*Revue de l'Histoire des Religions*
RIMA	*Revue de l'Institut des Manuscrits Arabes*
SI	*Studia Islamica*
ZDMG	*Zeitschrift des Deutschen Morgenländischen Gesellschaft*

INTRODUCTION

G.H.A. JUYNBOLL

From 4 to 7 July 1975 the Near Eastern History Group of Oxford University, an informal association of Oxford scholars who share a mutual interest in the Middle East, organized its fifth colloquium, thereby continuing a hitherto highly successful series of international mini-congresses. This time the general theme was the formative period of Islamic history. Some seventeen papers were read before an invited audience of about fifty persons who all participated in the discussions.

Along with their invitation the participants received a concise statement drawn up by the organizing body in which it outlined several ideas in the expectation that the colloquium in its discussions would centre on these. Let me quote from this the following passage:

"Islamic civilization originated in a 'barbarian' conquest of lands with ancient cultural traditions. Unlike other such conquests, this one did not end with the conquerors being absorbed into the societies they ruled, but led to the creation of a new social and intellectual framework within which the cultures of the conquered peoples could be reinterpreted and developed. This process can be said to have occurred in the century and a half which lie between the conquests and the firm establishment of Abbasid rule (roughly, the second half of the seventh and the whole of the eighth century). The way in which it took place is by no means clear. The existing cultures of the Middle East, which provided most of the raw materials of the new civilization, are reasonably well-known to us, and so is the end-product, the 'classical' Islamic civilization. But since the conquerors took some time to settle down, their own version of the process by which the new society and culture were created is a belated one and open to considerable doubt. If we rely on it alone, we shall form a picture of a discontinuity between the pre-Islamic and Islamic worlds which strains the imagination; if on the other hand we begin by assuming that there must have been some continuity, we need either to go beyond the Islamic sources or to reinterpret them."

Furthermore, the organizers expressed the hope that the subject would be looked at in a number of different ways, from the point of view of the conquered as well as that of the conquerors, and they added the following directives: the different areas should be duly distinguished from one another, different forms of government should be dealt with, and also the emergence of different aspects of Islam in these areas. The different forms in which these phenomena were expressed as well as the reshaping of already existing forms of expression in poetry, prose and art should be studied.

Did the colloquium realize its objectives as formulated in the above? I think in some ways it did and in other ways it did not.

As is often the case, the organizers found to their consternation that only a few of the contributors who had been invited to read a paper on a given subject did just that. The majority of contributors limited themselves to dealing with a section of the subject allotted to them, went far beyond it, or read papers on entirely different subjects. Assessing the success of a colloquium such as this is therefore all the more difficult. Would it have been more successful if the directives of the Near Eastern History Group had been followed to the letter, or did the unsolicited material lift the colloquium to a higher level of scholarly effort? Weighing the one against the other is well-nigh impossible and it seems fit, therefore, to let the reader judge for himself.

In any case, the most important question which we tried to answer collectively was: what sources do we have at our disposal and how do we interpret them? This question cropped up time and again in the papers collected here and also in those that will be published elsewhere. The answers provided were as diverse as the papers themselves.

The question concerning the sources was perhaps most successfully raised in Brock's paper. For the first time in our lives many of us became acquainted with the outlook of non-Arab, non-Muslim historians on the conquests and its perpetrators. His paper, and to a certain extent also that of Morony, were thought-provoking in this respect. The tendentious Islamic historiography was placed in a new perspective. Most of those present were to varying extents versed in Arabic sources and differed considerably from one another at times in interpreting them. The colloquium helped in bridging certain gaps between various interpretations as even the most vociferous participants will have to admit. This confrontation with Syriac and Hellenistic source material for once neatly pricked the balloons of such Islamic historians as swear exclusively by Arabic sources.

But certain other papers were sometimes thought to lean too heavily and too exclusively on non-Arabic sources. In the contributions of Crone and Cook the initial premise was one that differed radically even from the one generally accepted among Islamic historians since Wellhausen. Their contributions are, however, not included in this anthology since the material was subsequently to be incorporated in full in their Hagarism. The formation of the Islamic world (Cambridge: Cambridge University Press, 1977). Hawting's paper on the origins of the Muslim sanctuary at Mecca constitutes another wholly original look at the breeding ground of Islamic concepts. In his initial premise, as in that of Crone and Cook, the earliest history of Islam is again to be traced to Jewish/Judaic influences rather than allowing for a development of originally Arab/Islamic ideas. He argues that the various, seemingly contradictory, references to the sanctuary and its constituent elements, such as the Maqām Ibrāhīm, the Ḥijr and the Rukn with the Black Stone seem to point to Jewish/Judaic sanctuary ideas having served as model for the Islamic sanctuary rather than an originally pagan Arab sanctuary which preserved its original appearance but was in the course of time simply reinterpreted in Islamic terms.

The main emphasis of the colloquium lay, I think, on the social history of the period as may appear from the description of the following five papers. For once the conquered received just as much attention as--if not more than--the victorious conquerors. But taking into account that the conquered vastly outnumbered the conquerors this should not surprise us at all.

Lapidus depicts the background of the pre-Islamic Arabian bedouin society and juxtaposes that to the Sasanian and Byzantine societies, the "empire societies" as he calls them. But he argues that the pre-Islamic urban society of Mecca had already developed many features similar to those of the empire societies, which led to the conquests being achieved more smoothly. As he puts it: ". . . the conquests rose out of the process of religious and political consolidation in Arabia."

In his paper Morony gives a survey of how the conquered territories in Iran received, and eventually adopted, Islam and Arabism. But he also outlines to what extent the conquerors adapted themselves to the law of the land and were eventually assimilated.

Well within the hitherto generally accepted interpretation of Islam, Kister's paper is of a more general nature on the evolution of Islam, but it offers a deluge of new material culled from the earliest sources (many of which are still only available in manuscript). In his paper Kister shows how certain features of early Muslim ritual and law were in constant transition and how this is reflected in the earliest ḥadīth collections. He does not broach the subject of the chronology of his material but he presents a kaleidoscopic view of the activities of ḥadīth collectors, or, the case being so, ḥadīth forgers, in mitigating or modifying rules and regulations concerning religious rites and day to day behaviour, which in the course of time were felt to be too rigid or too severe. Judging from the majority of Kister's sources these activities took place for the greater part before the second century was over.

The sects of Islam formed the subject of the following papers. Van Ess's contribution describes the transition of discussions on political matters to a gradually evolving form of dialectics of an increasingly dogmatic tenor. He pictures the evolution of Muslim theology (kalām) in various areas of the Islamic world. Syria and Ḥijāz witnessed discussions on qadar and jabr which only to a lesser extent occupied the minds in Iraq. Here theorizing on still purely political issues initiated by various Shīʿite groups, and on a different level by the Murji'ites, gave way only gradually to dialectics of a more speculative theological nature wih the Muʿtazilites. In the third area discussed, Iran, the emergence of the Jahmiyya constituted a beginning of dogmatic reasoning. Later Muʿtazilites incorporated these ideas, and all this culminated in the miḥna. The paper ends with a tentative appraisal of the social position of the earliest mutakallimūn sent out first by the Ibāḍīs to proselytize, an example followed eventually by the Muʿtazilites.

The Ibāḍīs are a separate subject of discussion in Wilkinson's paper. He depicts the early development of the movement and divides their history into two stages. The first of these began with the secession of the Ibāḍīs from the main body of the Khawārij in A.H.64, while the second stage covered the expansion into south-western Arabia, where they attained considerable political power. What eventually remained were the imamates in ʿUmān and Ḥaḍramawt. A brief chronological survey of the successive leaders of the movement serves as a framework on which the history is depicted.

The last paper on Islamic sects, which is at the same time the first of two on historiography, deals exclusively with those Shīʿites who later became known as the Imāmiyya. In it Kohlberg combines a brief survey of the origins of this movement during the Umayyad caliphate with the views the Imāmiyya formulated themselves in due course on their own history. It is obvious that, given the doctrine of infallibility eventually imputed to the imāms, harmonization of political reality with this infallibility proved an almost insurmountable task. Kohlberg reaches the conclusion that a truly motivated historian can write any sort of history provided he uses the right words. This paper demonstrates how Imāmī historians proved to be capable of this.

Historiography is also the subject of discussion in Juynboll's paper on the origins of Arabic prose. After enumerating the various genres of prose writing of the earliest Arabic literature, he deals with the people who produced it and dwells especially on the position of the mawālī among them. In connection with this he speculates on authenticity and historical reliability and reaches the conclusion that, on the whole, precious little historical evidence can be gleaned from isnāds.

In this anthology also, one contribution on political theory is included written by Nagel who was himself not present at the colloquium but whose paper would have loosened many tongues. Nagel investigates such terms as malik, amīn, khalīfa and assesses their semantic development in an attempt at reconstructing the basis on which the authority held by the Prophet, the khulafāʾ al-rāshidūn and the Umayyads was founded. He also emphasizes in what respects the organization of the young community in Medina as a rival ḥaram of Mecca had its roots in the Jāhiliyya.

The atmosphere during the daily sessions grew very tense. The discussions following each paper were lengthy and sometimes heated. When it was all over I personally felt as if I had participated in an overloaded crash course on early Islamic history during which the breathless students were force-fed with a dozen or so standard works on the subject. Such was the collective concentration on each paper and so unexpected sometimes the channels through which criticism was levelled that many a contributor felt as if he had passed through a clothes wringer. Only the most stubborn will not have benefited from this criticism; only the most obstinate might not be willing to admit that he/she has learned a great deal in a short time.

As may be concluded from what I have said so far I think the colloquium was a successful one. In certain respects it had its shortcomings though, which show in this anthology. It proved impossible to illustrate in four days more than just a few facets of this complex period. Many subjects were not touched upon at all and if something not explicitly dealt with in the papers cropped up during the discussions, this will not be reflected in the following pages. Naturally, we did not reach any firm conclusions, but the mass of work being done on the period in various centres of learning, especially Germany, gives cause for optimism. Regrettably, a few contributors had planned to publish their papers elsewhere. Apart from the contributions of Crone and Cook mentioned above, H. Djaït's paper, "Les Yamanites à Kūfa au 1er siècle de l'Hégire," can be found in JESHO, XIX, 1976, pp. 148-181. G. Makdisi, who read a paper on the early development of Islamic education, will include this in a forthcoming general study on Islamic education. Also I.A. Shahid ("Early development of Islamic poetry") plans to publish elsewhere eventually, likewise A.A. Duri ("Arab (Islamic) culture -- an approach through Iraq"). Finally O. Grabar and K. Brisch, who both read papers on certain aspects of Islamic art under the Umayyads, will include these in forthcoming publications. This was, unfortunately, unavoidable since the high costs did not permit the reproduction of illustrations indispensable to any communication on art. In an attempt to compensate partly for all this, I sought the cooperation of Tilman Nagel as alluded to above. I am grateful for his response.

As I have already pointed out, the difficulty with which we all wrestled most and which became sadly obvious during the colloquium is the lack of good, reliable, and early sources. Many disputants had to resort, therefore, to educated guesses rather than referring to unequivocal evidence. And the sources presently at our disposal can only be handled with the utmost caution. Not everybody was equally felicitous in this. It is true that at times pictures were conjured up that were felt to be tantalizingly close to the truth; at other times the opposite was the case, a situation not always conducive to congenial unanimity, but sometimes flaring up in wrangles. The Ikhwān al-Ṣafā had a better solution. In their Rasā'il, in the chapter on the truth or falsehood of historical data (Cairo 1928, IV, p. 417), they say: "Fa-in aradta maʿrifat dhālika fa'nẓur ilā 'l-dalīl wa-huwa 'l-qamar fa-ini 'ttaṣala bi-kawkab fī watad fa'l-khabar ḥaqq wa-ini 'ttaṣala bi-kawkab sāqiṭ fa-huwa bāṭil wa-bi 'l-ḍid min dhālik." If only we had had it so easy! I think many of us realized during those four days that trying to lift a corner of the veil is much more difficult than in many a comparable area or period of Islamic studies.

If the present anthology, when read as a whole, conveys an atmosphere of collective and continuous groping, then it may serve a useful purpose: it may arouse curiosity in others to help in finding the right answers. Only combined efforts may be deemed capable of this. The time when individuals singlehandedly tried to grasp an entire field of study, such as was described in the general motto of this colloquium, is definitely over. The source material --even for the first 150 years of Islam -- has become too plentiful and too varied for that.

Finally, also on behalf of my colleagues who attended the colloquium, I should like to extend my gratitude to the Near Eastern History Group which, with generous financial aid from the Middle East Center of the University of Pennsylvania, organized this happening, especially to Albert Hourani and Derek Hopwood. I personally thank the Group for conferring upon me the honor of editing this volume. I am grateful to my Exeter colleague I.R. Netton for his assistance in brushing up the English style of several papers (including my own) and my gratitude also goes to Ms Susan E. Thompson for typing -- and sometimes retyping -- a number of difficult manuscripts. In addition, I would like to thank Margaret Owen for her meticulous editorial work and Vernon Daykin for preparing the final typescript.

1

SYRIAC VIEWS OF EMERGENT ISLAM

S.P. Brock

I

It requires a strenuous effort of the imagination in order to counteract the advantage of hindsight that we enjoy in looking at the events of the seventh century. How did contemporaries view them? When did the people of Syria and Mesopotamia begin to realize that the Arabs were there for good? How did they reconcile this realization, once attained, with their total world view? How aware were they of the religious background of the conquests?

It is questions such as these that the Syriac sources,[1] sometimes contemporary with the events themselves, can help to answer. Here we have the expression of an articulate and often highly sophisticated section of that part of society which provided the continuum, as it were, in the shifting sands of the seventh century.

On 24 December 633, at a monastery outside Damascus, a sumptuous Gospel manuscript was completed,[2] miraculously to survive the turbulent events of the next few years, to give us some hint of the lack of awareness of the storm clouds over the horizon.

On Christmas day, a year later, the Patriarch Sophronios preached in Jerusalem, and saw in the Arab occupation of Bethlehem a punishment for sin that could be easily remedied: "We have only to repent, and we shall blunten the Ishmaelite sword . . . and break the Hagarene bow, and see Bethlehem again."[3]

It was not long before things began to take on a different look: in a letter dated between 634 and 640 Maximos the Confessor speaks of a "barbaric nation from the desert" as having overrun a land not their own, and hints that the appearance of Anti-Christ is at hand.[4] The Doctrina Jacobi nuper baptizati, of much the same date, fits contemporary events into the apocalyptic scheme of the four beasts of Daniel chapter 7, but Rome is still the fourth beast, simply humiliated by the succession of horns.[5] It is not until the end of the century, with the

Armenian Sebeos, that we find a radical reinterpretation of the beasts, with the Ishmaelites replacing Rome as the fourth beast.[6]

II

In assessing the Christian reactions to the conquests of the seventh century, it is essential to take into account the ecclesiastical allegiance of the various sources, since each of the three main communities, Chalcedonian, Monophysite and Nestorian, came to provide their own particular interpretation of these events. Since I shall be concentrating on Syriac sources, this means that the viewpoints that we shall be given are mainly Monophysite and Nestorian; here and there, however, we can cast a glance at the more scanty Chalcedonian texts (both monothelete and dyothelete) on the topic, mostly in Greek.

Two main types of evidence will be employed, the world chronicles and the apocalyptic literature. As we shall see the division between these two genres is not always as clear-cut as one might have expected. The three world chronicles which have most to say about the seventh century all happen to be products of the Syriac "renaissance" of the twelfth and thirteenth centuries, namely the chronicles of the patriarch Michael, the anonymous writer *ad annum* 1234, and Bar Hebraeus.[7] Thanks, however, to the fact that these works relied very heavily on much earlier sources, two in particular, Jacob of Edessa (who died in 708) and Dionysios of Tellmaḥre (who died in 845),[8] we can recapture from them something of the attitudes of two great scholars and thoughtful men who lived much closer to the events themselves, and who were both active in the general area of Syria and western Mesopotamia.

Before looking in greater detail at these chronicles, however, it is worth stressing that the early decades of the seventh century had already been exceedingly turbulent for the populace of Syria-Mesopotamia; the area had served as the fulchrum of Persian-Byzantine hostilities, and the Byzantine reconquest under Heraklios had brought with it vicious persecution of the dominant Monophysite community by the Byzantine (Chalcedonian) authorities. In view of this background, the sense of relief at the change of rule, from Byzantine to Arab, that we find in these Monophysite chronicles is hardly surprising. The Arab invasions are seen primarily as a punishment for Byzantine ecclesiastical policy. In a famous passage we find the following analysis:

> Heraklios did not allow the orthodox (i.e, Syrian Orthodox, or Monophysites, as I shall call them to avoid confusion) to present themselves before him, and he refused to hear their complaints about acts of vandalism committed on their churches (i.e. by Chalcedonians). This is why the God of vengeance, who has power over the kingdom of men on earth, giving it to whom he wants and raising up to it the lowliest of men,[9] seeing the overflowing measure of the wickedness of the Romans--how they used every means to destroy our people and our church, so that our (religious) community was almost annihilated--(this is why) he roused up and brought the Ishmaelites from the land of the South--the most despised and insignificant of the peoples of the earth--to effect through them our deliverance. In this we gained no small advantage, in that we were saved from the tyrannical rule of the Romans. . . .[10]

This sort of sectarian theological interpretation would appear to have been the standard one in Monophysite circles, and John of Nikiu applies it equally to the Egyptian situation.[11] Mutatis mutandis we find interpretations based on ecclesiastical lines among the Nestorians and Chalcedonians as well. Thus the Chalcedonian Anastasios[12] sees the Arab successes as a punishment for Constans II's pro-monothelete policy and his treatment of Pope Martin.[13] The revival of dyothelete theology under Constantine IV, on the other hand, effects peace between the two empires, and civil war among the Arabs. The monothelete author of a Syriac life of Maximos,[14] in contrast, saw the Arab successes in Africa as a sign of God's wrath, bringing punishment on every place that had accepted Maximos' error (i.e. dyothelete theology). To the Nestorian John of Phenek, to whom we shall come back later, the Arabs were sent by God as a punishment for heresy (i.e. Chalcedonian and Monophysite).

III

Syriac writers are generally much better informed on the religious teachings of Islam than are Byzantine writers, and one of the interesting things that the chronicles have to say concerns the links between Muḥammad and the Jews.

On Muḥammad's early career it is only a few late chronicles that provide any details, and these are of no special interest to us here.[15] Much more important is a section in our Monophysite chronicles, deriving from Dionysios of Tellmaḥre, which describes Muḥammad's contacts with Jews in Palestine.[16] Impressed by their monotheism and the excellence of the land of Palestine "that had been given to them (i.e. the Jews) as a result of their belief in a single God," Muḥammad returned home and promised to those who accepted his new religious teaching that "God would give them a fine land flowing with milk and honey."[17]

In this section we are also given a brief outline of the Prophet's teaching, where it is specifically stated that he accepted the Torah and the Gospels, apart from the crucifixion narrative.[18] Muslim acceptance of the Torah is also a point made in a mid seventh century document, the colloquium between the Monophysite patriarch John and an unnamed emir.[19]

Further hints of Jewish ideology lying behind the early conquests are perhaps to be found in the anonymous chronicler's account of Abū Bakr's address to the four generals on their departure for Syria, where the phraseology is reminiscent of Deuteronomy 20: 10 ff, recording Moses' instructions to the Israelites.[20] Likewise ʿUmar's alleged building of the Dome of the Rock on the site of the temple of Solomon is specifically described in one chronicle as the rebuilding of the temple.[21] The anonymous chronicler again reflects Deuteronomy (this time 17: 16 ff) in the section on ʿUthmān and his "perversion of the law and modest manner of the kings who preceded him."[22] (Incidentally this chronicler, alone of the Syriac writers, knows of ʿUthmān as the collector cum editor of the Qur'ān.)[23]

IV

Although the chronicles generally present rather dry and bare lists of events, we do find an occasional anecdote included that is intended to illustrate some aspect of the change of regime. In that these probably represent popular attitudes, they should be judged worthy of our attention.

Bar Hebraeus retails the story that, in the face of Arab successes, Heraklios gathered some bishops and clergy and enquired how they viewed the situation. After they had all made their own observations, the emperor himself volunteered a statement: "As far as their way of life, manners and beliefs are concerned, he said, I see this people as the faint glimmer of first dawn--when it is no longer completely dark, but at the same time it is not yet completely light."

Asked to elucidate further, he went on: "Yes, they have indeed left darkness far behind, in that they have rejected the worship of idols and worship the One God, but at the same time they are deprived of the perfect light, in that they still fall short of complete illumination in the light of our Christian faith and orthodox confession."[24]

The story itself is no doubt apocryphal: this is obvious, if for no other reason, from the fact that the judgment pronounced has a theological rather than political concern behind it. The positive attitude to Islam is interesting,[25] and it finds a close parallel in the writings of Timothy I, the Nestorian patriarch.[26] The story probably represents a reflection later in date than the seventh century, since sources best anchored in the seventh century suggest that there was greater awareness that a new empire (malkuta) had arisen, than that a new religion had been born. One Chalcedonian (monothelete) source from the end of the century can still openly speak of "paganism."[27]

Another anecdote concerns precisely this transfer of power, from the Persians to the Arabs; it also says something of the attitudes of Christian Arabs. As we shall see it has a surprising ancestry. In the course of Yezdegerd's final struggle with the Arabs, the Persian army was encamped on the Euphrates near Kūfa, and a spy, a man from Ḥirta d-Naʿman, was sent to the Arab encampment. When the spy arrived he saw a Maʿadd tribesman outside the encampment, who urinated, sat down to eat and then proceeded to remove the fleas from his clothing. They got talking and, asked what he was doing, the tribesman replied: "As you see, I am introducing something new, and getting rid of something old; and at the same time I am killing enemies." The spy, having puzzled over the matter, eventually came to the conclusion that this signified that "a new people was coming in, and an old one departing and that the Persians would be killed."[28]

The interesting thing about this story is the way it portrays the dawning of an awareness, on the part of the Christian Arabs, that the invaders were there to stay, and that their present masters, the Sasanids, were already doomed. Actually we have here, adapted to a totally new setting, a slightly modified version of an anecdote about an encounter between Homer and some Arcadian fishermen who, when questioned by the poet as to what they were doing, made a very similar reply.[29] Homer, unfortunately, was not as quick-witted as the spy from Ḥirta, and he died of frustration at not being able to solve the riddle.

V

We should now turn briefly to the terminology used in the Syriac texts dealing with the seventh century. If we can identify the conceptual framework into which Syriac-speaking Christians tried to fit the new situation of their times, we can perhaps learn something of the way in which they regarded their new overlords.

All the Syriac writers of this period, including those active in the middle of the century, would appear to be writing with sufficient hindsight for them to be aware that Byzantine and Persian rule was at an end, and that the Arabs were there to stay, representing a new empire, or "kingdom." The caliphs, and Muḥammad himself, are regularly described as "kings," and the malkuta, kingdom of the Arabs, is seen as the direct heir of the "kingdoms" of Byzantium and Persia. No doubt behind this terminology lies the influence of the book of Daniel, with its picture of successive world empires. We have already seen how, from a very early date, this book played an important role in the process of fitting the new state of affairs into an already accepted conceptual framework.

For Muḥammad the title "prophet" is not very common, "apostle" even less so.[30] Normally he is simply described as the first of the Arab kings,[31] and it would be generally true to say that the Syriac sources of this period see the conquests primarily as Arab, and not Muslim. There is, however, one interesting term used of Muḥammad that turns up in both Monophysite and Nestorian sources, namely mhaddyana, "guide,"[32] a term that has no obvious ancestry, although the related haddaya is a Christological title in early Syriac literature.

The term caliph occurs only once, in a Syriacized form, in the texts covering the seventh century, and this is in direct speech, addressed to ʿUthmān.[33] Here, as we have seen, "king" is the normal term employed, although Ishoʿyahb, writing in the middle of the century, uses the term shalliṭa rabba.[34] For local governors the Syriac sources either take over the Arabic term amira,[35] or use the colourless words shalliṭa (Ishoʿyahb) or risha, neither of which had served as part of the technical vocabulary for officials of the Byzantine and Sasanid empires in earlier Syriac sources.

As is well known, the Arabs are generally referred to in Syriac sources as Ṭayy. As far as their identity and origin were concerned, seventh century writers already had available a tradition going back to Eusebios, according to which the Arabs had been classified as the descendants of Ishmael and Hagar. The term Ṭayy itself has no religious overtones, and could imply pagan, Christian or Muslim. Where it was thought necessary to specify them as Muslim the term used in early texts is mhaggraye,[36] which can also be used alone. In origin the term would appear to be connected with muhājirūn, but to most Syriac writers it probably came to be more or less synonymous with bnay Hagar, "sons of Hagar." This latter term, howevery, could evidently (to judge by a couple of passages in Michael the Syrian)[37] bear pejorative overtones, presumably not present in another term, "sons of Ishmael," also commonly found.[38] The pejorative overtones in Michael's Chronicle certainly fit in with Sozomen's statement that the Sarakenoi disguised their servile origins by calling themselves Ishmaelites, rather than Hagarenes.[39]

VI

Of the east Syrian, or Nestorian, sources John of Phenek, writing in the 690s, is the most important, but before turning to him we should first glance at a few passages in the correspondence of the Catholicos Isho'yahb III, who died in 659.[40] As a background to these two writers two things need to be kept in mind. First, and most obviously, the Nestorian church, living under the Sasanid empire, had problems very different from those that faced the Monophysites under Byzantine rule. Secondly, the seventh century saw the expansion of the Monophysite church into north Mesopotamia at the expense of the Nestorians. We shall see that both these factors colored our author's attitudes.

Isho'yahb takes a very positive attitude towards the events of his time.[41] To him there was no doubt that God had given dominion (shulṭana) to the Ṭayy.[42] What is more, he describes them as "commenders of our faith," who honor the clergy, the churches and the monasteries. Writing in the same letter (addressed to Shem'un, bishop of Rev Ardashir) about the wholesale apostasy of the Christian Community in Mazon, or Oman, he says that there was no question of pressure to convert being exerted, only of temporal financial disadvantage, and he upbraids his correspondent for the laxity of his clergy in the whole shameful affair.[43]

Others of Isho'yahb's correspondents had also tried to use the Arab invasions as an excuse for their own failures. Thus the clergy of Nineveh (Mosul) evidently attributed the Nestorian losses to the Monophysites in north Mesopotamia to the fact that the new rulers favored the Monophysites. Utter nonsense, says Isho'yahb, it is quite untrue that the ṭayyaye mhaggraye helped the Theopaschites (i.e. Monophysites), the losses are entirely your own fault.[44]

Some of his correspondents evidently looked back to Sasanid rule with a certain degree of nostalgia, which we are also to find later in John of Phenek,[45] but this only brings a sharp rebuke from the Catholicos.[46]

Isho'yahb was evidently on excellent terms with the Arab authorities, and they supported his case when some of his clergy in Kerman revolted against his authority and appealed unsuccessfully to the "chief shalliṭa, chief of the officials of the time."[47] Isho'yahb's attitude is found spelt out even more explicitly in the writings of one of his most famous successors on the patriarchal throne, Timothy I (died 823). Timothy writes that "the Arabs are today held in great honor and esteem by God and men because they forsook idolatry and polytheism, and worshipped and honored the One God." "God honored Muḥammad greatly, and subdued before his feet two powerful kingdoms, of the Persians and of the Romans; in the case of the Persians God effected this because they worshipped creatures instead of the Creator, in that of the Romans, because they had propagated the theopaschite doctrine."[48]

John of Phenek, writing some decades later than Isho'yahb, is no less convinced that the "sons of Hagar" were divinely called:

> We should not think of their advent as something ordinary, but as due to divine working. Before calling them, God had prepared them beforehand to hold Christians in honor; thus they also had a special commandment from God concerning our monastic station, that they should hold it in honor.[49] . . . How otherwise, apart from God's help, could naked men, riding without armor or shield, have been able to win:[50] God called them from the ends of the earth in order to destroy, through them, a sinful kingdom (Amos 9:8), and to humiliate, through them, the proud spirit of the Persians.[51]

As proof texts of the divine calling of the Arabs, John adduces Zechariah 3:2, Deuteronomy 32:30 and

Genesis 16:12.

John also sees the advent of the Arabs as a punishment for Christian laxity, apparently chiefly in matters of doctrine (i.e. failure to oppose Monophysites and Chalcedonians sufficiently vigorously). Because of the bloodshed of the conquests John sees the Arabs as themselves punished by a divided rule. In contrast to Monophysite writers, who tend to view the rule of Abū Bakr and ʿUmar in idealistic terms, John sees only division until the reign of Muʿāwiya, in whose time there was unprecedented peace, "such as our forefathers had never experienced."[52]

John specifically states that all the new rulers required was payment of taxes, and that otherwise there was complete religious freedom. Moreover he definitely sees the new rulers in ethnic and not religious terms: "among the Arabs are not a few Christians, some belonging to the heretics (i.e. Monophysites), and some to us (i.e. Nestorians)."[53]

The peace brought by Muʿāwiya, however, only led to further laxity--in particular allowing the Monophysites to spread eastwards. It is in punishment for this that there followed the troubled times under Muʿāwiya's successors. Yazdin (i.e. Yazīd) is castigated for his immorality, which is contrasted with (Ibn) Zubayr's zeal against the "sinful westerners." (Ibn) Zubayr's death John regards effectively as the collapse of the Arab "kingdom": "from that time on the kingdom of the Ṭayy was no longer firmly established."[54]

To top the political turmoil comes the plague of A.H.67 (A.D.686/7), and it is at this point in his narrative that John begins to strike an apocalyptic note: "the end of the world has arrived." The only thing lacking so far is the advent of the Deceiver (i.e. Antichrist);[55] we are in fact experiencing the beginnings of the eschatological birthpangs. John specifically sees the successes of the "captives" liberated by Mukhtār as a sign of the coming destruction of the Ishmaelites and the end of Ṭayy rule.[56]

John of Phenek was not alone in seeing the turmoils of the last decades of the seventh century as the beginnings of the end, and his work serves as an excellent bridge to the last work we should consider, the Apocalypse attributed to Methodios, dated to the second half of the seventh century. This work was written in Syriac, but was soon translated into Greek, and thence into both Slavonic and Latin, the last being a language in which it won its greatest popularity. I shall base myself in what follows on the original Syriac, surviving complete in a single, as yet unpublished, manuscript,[57] since the Greek and Latin versions have both been considerably reworked in places.

The Apocalypse attributed to Methodios was evidently written in the region of Sinjar,[58] about A.D.690, in any case (as we shall see) before 692. After a highly individual account of the pre-Christian empires, the author makes it quite clear that, in contrast to the kingdom of the Persians, already uprooted, that of the Greeks, being Christian, will never be completely dominated by any other. God has brought the "barbaric" Ishmaelites into the kingdom of the Christians, not out of any love he had for them, but because of the sins of the inhabitants (especially in the matter of sexual licence). The oppressive rule of the "tyrants" will last ten apocalyptic "weeks" (i.e. seventy years), after which the Greek king will suddenly rise up and destroy the unsuspecting Ishmaelites: he himself will attack the desert of Yathrib from the Red Sea, while his sons will finish off those Ishmaelites who are left in the "land of promise."[59]

There follows a period of the "last peace," in which apostates will receive their reward, and priests no longer be subject to taxation. Next, the nations enclosed by Alexander in the gates of the north will burst out, only to be destroyed by an archangel in the plain of Joppa, after wreaking havoc for one "week." Thereupon the king of the Greeks will enter Jerusalem for 1½ "weeks" (here also specified as 10½ years), after which the "false Christ" will appear. The Greek king will then go to Golgotha, place his crown on the cross, and commit the kingdom to God. Both crown and cross are raised to heaven, thus fulfilling Psalm 68:31.[60]

This psalm actually speaks of Kush as "stretching out her hands to God," and it is clear that some of the author's contemporaries understood this to mean that a savior would appear from Kush. Our author, however, is at pains to refute this, and he does so by providing an elaborate genealogy for the Greek kingdom, going back to Alexander's Kushite mother.[61] In this way he is able to claim that it is really the Greek kings who are meant by Kush here.[62]

The author regards the tyranny of the Arabs as coming to an end at the conclusion of the tenth "week," in other words after seventy years, which would be 692.[63] He himself is quite clearly living in the final "week," thus between 685 and 692--precisely the period that John of Phenek was describing as the "last days." John specifically mentions the "plague" of A.H.67 (A.D.686/7) as adding to the miseries; "plague" is among the ills mentioned by Pseudo-Methodios, but what he finds really oppressive is the tax system:[64] "even orphans, widows and holy men will have to pay poll tax," he writes. And in this statement we have, I believe, the key to the precise dating of the Apocalypse: it must belong to the period immediately before (or possibly during) the census of ʿAbd al-Malik, on the basis of which the tax system in Mesopotamia was reformed. The Chronicle of Pseudo-Dionysios gives A.G.1003 as the year of this reform, i.e. A.D.691/2.[65] I would suggest that the Apocalypse of Methodios should be dated to 690 or 691, at a time when rumors about the new tax laws were rife: in antiquity, as today, a census always gave rise to strong feelings. 690-1 was significantly also a time when hopes of a Byzantine recovery could be nurtured without too great a degree of improbability: 678 had seen a major Byzantine victory, and ten years later, in 688, ʿAbd al-Malik had renegotiated humiliating peace terms with Justinian II. The tension between these two factors--rumors of vastly increased taxes, and Byzantine military recovery--thus provided an ideal hotbed for eschatological ideas. As products of this ferment we have, not only John of Phenek and Pseudo-Methodios, but also another, shorter, Syriac apocalypse that goes under the name of the Apocalypse of John the Less.[66]

Eschatological speculations seem indeed to have been rife in the late seventh and early eighth centuries, focusing on the recapture of Jerusalem among Christians, and on the destruction of Constantinople among Muslims and Jews,[67] and it is against this wider background that these Syriac texts need to be viewed. John of Phenek and the Apocalypse of John the Less show no interest in the revival of Byzantine power, and this makes Pseudo-Methodios stand out all the more sharply in contrast, for here is an apparently Monophysite writer looking to the re-establishment of Byzantine power--in complete opposition to what was evidently the standard Monophysite attitude that we saw in Michael the Syrian. Pseudo-Methodios is in fact much more in line with what seems to have been the Chalcedonian attitude in Syria, where in the early eighth century John of Damascus was writing hymns which pray for deliverance, at the hands of the Byzantine emperor, from the enemies of Christ, the Ishmaelites.[68] One wonders whether Pseudo-Methodios may not in reality have been a Chalcedonian, whose work (unobjectionable Christologically to the

Monophysites) happens to have been transmitted in Syriac by Monophysite scribes; the fact that the work is also quoted by Nestorian writers perhaps lends support to this suggestion. Such a hypothesis would also explain how the work came to be translated into Greek--an honor achieved by no other Syriac text in this period, as far as I know.[69]

With this piece of speculation, perhaps we could try to draw together the various strands. One thing is quite clear: after only a short period, perhaps just a decade, of uncertainty, people became aware that a new, Arab, empire (malkuta) had arrived on the scene, replacing the Sasanid entirely, and half the Byzantine. In such times the Christian population resorted to the book of Daniel to find divine backing for these major upheavals, and it is this that would seem to be the reason why the seventh century texts use the terms malka, malkuta, of Arab rule, and not because the new rulers corresponded in any obvious way to either the Sasanid or the Byzantine emperors. This explanation of the choice of terminology would be supported by the fact that the Syriac writers were clearly at a loss to describe other figures in the new power structure: since they did not correspond obviously to anything with which they were already familiar, these writers resorted either to colorless terms, such as risha, head, or to the Arabic ones, duly Syriacized, such as amira.

To writers of every ecclesiastical body there was, without any doubt, some theological reason to be sought for the demise of the two former world empires and the concomitant ills suffered by Christians as a result of the Arab invasions. To the Nestorian and Monophysite communities there was a ready-made answer, based on inter-church relationships: for the Monophysites, the Byzantine defeat was simply a punishment for Chalcedonian arrogance and the persecution under Heraklios, while the Nestorians saw in the hardships they endured divine punishment for the Monophysite successes in northern Mesopotamia, or, alternatively moving to a wider viewpoint, the Arab conquest of the Sasanids was understood as a punishment for Zoroastrianism. The Chalcedonians, on the other hand, were faced with a problem:[70] as long as the Arab presence seemed only temporary, the general laxity and sins of the Christian community could be blamed, but this was a bit drastic when the Byzantine armies bade Syria their final "farewell"; and the monothelete/dyothelete controversy could not continue to be the scapegoat for very long.

It is thus probably the Chalcedonian

community's dilemma, as well as in the worsening conditions for Christians during the second civil war, and fears aroused by the census, that led to the rise of the apocalyptic literature, around 690, which found a ready audience in all three religious communities.

It was perhaps only with Dionysios of Tellmaḥre (died 845) that we really get a full awareness of Islam as a new religion. Earlier observers had not always been able to distinguish the religion of the Arabs from paganism, although Christians who came into direct contact with the new rulers, such as the patriarchs John and Isho'yahb, certainly knew better, and perhaps it is the story about Heraklios and the first dawn that would best reflect the viewpoint of the majority of Christians under Arab rule--that is, of those who bothered to think about the matter at all.

2

THE ORIGINS OF THE MUSLIM SANCTUARY AT MECCA

G.R. Hawting

This paper is concerned with the question of how the pre-Islamic sanctuary at Mecca became the Muslim sanctuary.[1] I intend to put forward some of the evidence which has led me to think that the way in which the question is usually answered, both in the traditional Muslim literature and in works of modern scholarship, produces an inadequate account of the origins and development of the Muslim sanctuary, and I wish to propose the outlines of an alternative way of envisaging the islamization of the Meccan sanctuary.[2]

The traditional view emphasizes continuity of development and places the adoption of the Meccan sanctuary by Islam in the context of the career of the Prophet Muḥammad in the Ḥijāz. It seems that Muḥammad adopted the Meccan sanctuary, after an initial attraction towards Jerusalem, because it was the religious centre of the society in which he had grown up. The process of islamization is not seen to involve any radical changes in the organization of the sanctuary, nor in the ceremonies associated with it. The one important concomitant of Muḥammad's takeover of the Meccan sanctuary, the destruction of its idols, is seen as a reimposition of the monotheism for which it had been founded by Abraham, a purification of the sanctuary from the abuses which had been introduced in the Jāhiliyya. Generally, the features of the Muslim sanctuary at Mecca and the ceremonies which are performed there are explained as a continuation of those which had existed in pagan times but which had originated in the time of Abraham.[3] In spite of some extensive modifications to this traditional account proposed by modern scholars, what seem to be its essential features have not been disputed. Scholars such as Wellhausen and Lammens have suggested that the islamization of the Meccan sanctuary involved changes in its organization and rituals which were rather more significant than one would gather from the traditional Muslim literature,[4] and western scholars in general, of course, have been unable to accept that the islamization of the sanctuary was merely the restoration of its original monotheism. Nevertheless, the Muslim sanctuary at Mecca continues to be seen as basically a continuation of the sanctuary of pagan times in the same place, and the islamization of that sanctuary continues to be associated with the prophetic career of Muḥammad.

Now, in so far as the theme of this colloquium is concerned, this stress on continuity of development in the Muslim sanctuary implies, conversely, that the Muslim sanctuary is an element of discontinuity for the Middle East as a whole in the transition from Late Antiquity to the Islamic period. According to the generally accepted account just summarized, the Muslim sanctuary at Mecca is to be seen as a legacy of the origins of Islam in the pre-Islamic Ḥijāz, not connected with the pre-Islamic history of the wider Middle East outside Arabia. In this respect Islam is to be seen as something brought out of Arabia by the Arab conquests and accepted by the conquered peoples at the hands of their new rulers. The traditional account of the origins of the Muslim sanctuary, then, supports the view that the coming of Islam marks an almost complete break in the history of the Middle East.

The evidence which I wish to concentrate upon in this paper, and which I think is difficult to reconcile with the generally accepted version of the islamization of the Meccan sanctuary, is provided by the use in the Muslim literature of certain terms or names which are connected with the sanctuary at Mecca. There are certain names and terms which, with reference to the Muslim sanctuary at Mecca, have fixed and precise meanings but which sometimes occur in the traditions, in the Qur'ān and in the poetry in a way which conflicts with their usual meanings, or at least suggests that they are being used with a different sense. It seems likely that these cases date from a time before the Muslim sanctuary became established at Mecca in its classical form, the form in which we know it, since I can see no way in which the sort of material which I will discuss could have originated once the Muslim sanctuary had taken its final shape. These names or terms, it must be emphasized, are now applied to some of the most important features of the Muslim sanctuary at Mecca, but the evidence seems to show that they originated independently of that sanctuary and only later came to be used to designate features of it. Furthermore, in some cases it is possible to indicate the likely source of the name or term in question or to suggest its probable original associations, and when we can do this it is to Judaism that we have to look. It appears that certain Muslim sanctuary ideas and certain names which Islam applies to its sanctuary at Mecca originated in a Jewish milieu, in the context of Jewish sanctuary ideas, and that they were then taken up by Islam and applied to the Meccan sanctuary.

This evidence, as already said, is very difficult to reconcile with the usual version of how the Meccan sanctuary was adopted by Islam. When scholars have recognized that certain features of Islam parallel those of Judaism or are to be explained as having their origins in Judaism, they have generally had recourse to two distinct theories in order to explain the phenomenon. The usual explanation is that the Prophet or the Muslims "borrowed" beliefs, rituals or institutions from Judaism and elsewhere as Islam came into contact with other religions. Such "borrowing" would have been possible, according to the traditional accounts of the origins of Islam, either in Medina in the time of the Prophet where there existed a significant Jewish community, or after the conquests outside Arabia when the Muslims came into contact with the Jews and others in ʿIrāq and elsewhere. The other theory which has been used is that parallels between Judaism and Islam are to be explained by the fact that both are descendants of one hypothetical "Semitic Religion", the religion of the Semitic people before it became dispersed into the various groups which are known in historical times. In other words, there is a mentality or stock of religious ideas which is common to the various Semitic peoples and which explains why so many Muslim ideas and institutions seem to be related to those of the Old Testament and of Judaism.

Regarding the sanctuary at Mecca, both theories have been used by scholars to explain obvious points of contact between it and sanctuary ideas found in the Old Testament, in Judaism and sometimes in other "Semitic" religions like Syriac Christianity.[5] But it seems that neither theory can be used to explain the sort of material to be discussed here. On the one hand, the sort of contacts between Muslim and Jewish sanctuary ideas with which we are concerned are more than simply parallels of a general kind. They indicate a close historical contact between the two religious traditions, the Muslim sanctuary ideas growing directly out of those of Judaism, and thus the theory of an underlying "Semitic Religion" cannot provide an adequate explanation of them. On the other hand, the traditional version of the origins of Islam does not really allow for the "borrowing" of ideas from Judaism in the period before the Meccan sanctuary became the Muslim sanctuary, which is what must have happened in the cases to be discussed in this paper. According to the traditional accounts, Muḥammad made the Meccan sanctuary the Muslim sanctuary early in the Medinan period of his career, and there is nothing in the traditional accounts which would explain how he could have "borrowed" ideas from Judaism in the period before the Hijra. In the case of the material to be discussed here, therefore, if one wanted to maintain the theory of "borrowing" in the way in which it is usually used, one would have to postulate some way in which Muḥammad could have become conversant with and adopted Jewish sanctuary ideas while still at Mecca, for which there is no supporting evidence in the sources.

Only one scholar has attempted to argue in detail that this happened: the Dutch scholar R. Dozy in his work Die Israeliten zu Mekka (1864). Impressed by the points of contact and parallels between the Muslim sanctuary at Mecca and its rituals and the sanctuary ideas of the Old Testament and Judaism, Dozy thought that the Muslim sanctuary had to be seen as a development of those ideas. But at the same time Dozy accepted the traditional Muslim version of the origins of Islam in the Ḥijāz at the beginning of the seventh century A.D. In order to reconcile his conviction with the traditional information, therefore, Dozy put forward his hypothesis that there had been a number of migrations of Jews to Mecca, beginning even before Jerusalem had become established as the Israelite sanctuary, and that the sanctuary of Mecca had been founded originally by these Jewish immigrants to Mecca. In the course of time many of the original practices and beliefs had become deformed and it was in this form that they were taken over by Muḥammad as he grew up in Mecca. In particular, Dozy argued that the tradition that the Meccan sanctuary had been founded by Abraham was current in Mecca in the lifetime of Muḥammad and had been accepted by him even before his Hijra.

C. Snouck Hurgronje's Het mekkaansche Feest (1880) was intended largely as a refutation of Dozy's work and was so successful that since its publication scholars have generally rejected Dozy's ideas or have ignored them. Snouck Hurgronje's argument, which has become one of the most widely accepted ideas of modern scholarship on the beginnings of Islam, was that the adoption of the Meccan sanctuary by Muḥammad has to be seen as a reaction to the rejection of him by the Jews of Medina. Only in the face of this rejection, according to Snouck Hurgronje, did Muḥammad move towards the arabization of his religion, a move in which the adoption of the Meccan sanctuary was an important step. And only at this time did Muḥammad begin to formulate the doctrine that the Meccan sanctuary had been founded by Abraham, an idea which grew out of his contact with the Jews of Medina.[6] This thesis, therefore, rules out direct borrowing from Judaism in the period before the Hijra and restricts the influence of Judaism on Islam to a period after the adoption of the Meccan sanctuary by Islam. In cases where it is not possible to use this explanation, it seems one has to fall back on the theory of the underlying common "Semitic Religion". Accepting the traditional version of the islamization of the Meccan sanctuary as it is expressed in the thesis of Snouck Hurgronje, therefore, scholars who have discussed the parallels and points of contact between the Muslim sanctuary and Jewish and Old Testament sanctuary ideas have used now one, now the other explanation, according to the material under discussion.

If, then, neither of the theories offers an adequate explanation of the sort of material to be discussed here, how can we explain it without introducing a hypothesis that would seem as improbable as that put forward by Dozy? It seems that it is possible to propose an alternative scheme for the islamization of the Meccan sanctuary which would allow for Muslim "borrowing" of Jewish sanctuary ideas before the Meccan sanctuary became established as the Muslim sanctuary, a scheme which has been suggested in part by the evidence to be discussed in this paper. There is other evidence too which seems to support the scheme I wish to propose, but it is not possible to discuss it all here. The scheme can, of course, only be envisaged in its broad outlines, and precise details, in particular the question of chronology, remain unclear, but it does seem that the general scheme which will now be outlined makes sense of and is in accordance with the evidence to be discussed.

It seems that the Muslim sanctuary at Mecca is the result of a sort of compromise between a pre-existing pagan sanctuary and sanctuary ideas which had developed first in a Jewish milieu. I envisage that Muslim sanctuary ideas originated first in a

Jewish matrix, as did Islam itself. At a certain stage in the development of the new religion the need arose to assert its independence, and one of the most obvious ways in which this could be done was by establishing a specifically Muslim sanctuary. The choice of sanctuary would have been governed by already existing sanctuary ideas and when a suitable sanctuary was fixed upon these sanctuary ideas would themselves have been modified to take account of the facts of the sanctuary which had been chosen. It seems likely that the Meccan sanctuary was chosen only after the elimination of other possibilities--that in the early Islamic period a number of possible sanctuary sites gained adherents until finally Mecca became established as the Muslim sanctuary. And it also seems likely that one reason for the adoption of the Meccan sanctuary was that it did approximate to the sanctuary ideas which had already been formed--although they had to be reformulated, the physical facts of the Meccan sanctuary did not mean that already existing notions and terminology had to be abandoned. The precise details of this process, as I have said, are still unclear, especially with regards to chronology. It does seem likely, however, that it took longer than is allowed for by Muslim tradition and that it was only concluded at a relatively late date in the Islamic period, not at its beginning as has been generally accepted. If this theory, which can be supported by evidence other than that which is to be discussed here, is accepted, then the Muslim sanctuary at Mecca should no longer be regarded as simply a remnant of Arab paganism. In part at least, it is a continuation of ideas which had developed in non-Arab circles before the conquests.

One of the most striking characteristics of the traditional Muslim material on the sanctuary is the surprising degree of change and movement within the Meccan sanctuary which it allows for. I have already indicated that the traditional version of the islamization of the Meccan sanctuary suggests an essential continuity between the sanctuary of the Jāhiliyya and that of Islam, but, in spite of this, one would gather from the Muslim traditions that the sanctuary or features of it were continually subject to rebuilding and changes of position. The Kaʿba itself is frequently said to have been demolished and rebuilt.[7] The Black Stone is on a number of occasions removed from the Kaʿba and then restored to its place.[8] The stone called Maqām Ibrāhīm is moved around by floods and by human actions.[9] The well of

Zamzam is "discovered" on two separate occasions.[10] Al-Masjid al-Ḥarām, explained as the mosque containing the Kaʿba at Mecca, is several times rebuilt and enlarged.[11] It is true that in the way in which they are presented these details do not conflict with the essential continuity between the Jāhilī and Muslim sanctuaries: the reports about changes in the organization or form of the sanctuary, or aspects of it, refer to specific occasions in the Jāhiliyya and early Islam and to features of the Meccan sanctuary as it is known in its Muslim form, so that they do not necessarily indicate that the traditional version has to be revised in the way I am suggesting. Nevertheless, the preservation of so much detail, much of which is self-contradictory, does seem to be noteworthy and possibly to indicate that even Muslim tradition recognized that the history of the sanctuary and its incorporation by Islam could not be presented as a simple, straightforward development.

Furthermore, the traditional material on the history of the sanctuary is hardly of a sort to inspire confidence in it as a record of historical events. Sometimes we find the same basic material being made to refer to two allegedly separate events: compare, for example, the accounts of the demolition and rebuilding of the Kaʿba by Ibn al-Zubayr with those of its earlier demolition and rebuilding by al-Walīd b. Mughīra,[12] or the traditions about the fire which is said to have damaged the Kaʿba in the Jāhiliyya with those about the fire which destroyed the Abyssinian church of al-Qallīs at Ṣanʿāʾ.[13] Elsewhere we find a sort of overlapping of material --two allegedly distinct features of the sanctuary having the same or related traditions attached to them. The overlapping of the material on the Black Stone and the Maqām Ibrāhīm will be discussed later, and a similar phenomenon occurs in the material on the well of Zamzam and the hollow (bi'r or jubb) which is said to have existed inside the Kaʿba.[14]

Even if we could discount the information which is obviously legendary or unhistorical in character, then, the contradictions, overlapping and duplications which occur in the traditions about the history of the Meccan sanctuary would make it a hazardous, in my view, impossible, undertaking to write a straightforward narrative history of the sanctuary and its islamization. If there is a historical basis to the traditions, it seems likely that it is to be sought in their general presentation rather than in the specific details which they present. On this level the details about change and movement within the sanctuary seem to be suggestive. They seem to prepare the way for a hypothesis which envisages even more radical developments in the process which led to the adoption of the Meccan sanctuary by Islam. If we now look more closely at the use of a number of important names or terms in the traditions, it appears that on some occasions it is only with difficulty that they can be understood in the sense in which they are now used with reference to the Muslim sanctuary at Mecca. It seems that they have been redefined at some stage so that they have come to be used in a sense which is not their original one.

a. Maqām Ibrāhīm. In the Muslim sanctuary at Mecca the name Maqām Ibrāhīm is given to a stone which is situated a little distance from the north-east wall of the Kaʿba. The stone has a place in the pilgrimage rituals, two rakʿas being made there at the end of the ṭawāf. Muslim tradition preserves a number of different explanations for the sanctity of the stone and the reason for the application to it of the name Maqām Ibrāhīm. The traditional material on the stone has been summarized most fully in a recent article by Professor Kister.[15] With the Maqām Ibrāhīm, as with most other aspects of the sanctuary and its rituals, the main concern of modern scholarship has been to explain its significance for the religion of the Jāhiliyya, to detach it from the Muslim traditions which associate it with Abraham and to explain it as a relic of paganism. Wellhausen suggested that it was a pagan sacrificial stone, a suggestion which Gaudefroy-Demombynes supported by reference to the indentation or hollow which it contains; Lammens preferred to see it as a bethel.[16]

The most obvious reference which seems at odds with the idea that the Maqām Ibrāhīm is the sacred stone bearing that name at the Muslim Sanctuary is the Qur'ānic verse 2:125: "Take for yourselves a place of prayer from the Maqām Ibrāhīm" ("wa'ttakhidhū min Maqāmi Ibrāhīma muṣallan"). In connection with this verse the exegetes give a number of different explanations of what is meant by Maqām Ibrāhīm. In addition to the view that the name here refers to the stone which is now so called, it is also said to indicate the whole of the ḥaram or various extended areas within the ḥaram.[17] The context seems to require explanations such as these since it is necessary to explain away the preposition min as a redundant particle if it is desired to see the Qur'ānic reference as to the stone which is now called Maqām Ibrāhīm.[18] On the whole, therefore, the verse seems inconsistent with the usually accepted signification of the name Maqām Ibrāhīm.

Furthermore, in some traditions and verses of poetry the name Maqām Ibrāhīm, or more frequently simply al-Maqām occurs in contexts which suggest that we are dealing with something other than the stone which now bears the name. In one tradition there is reference to Quraysh sitting in the "groups" (scil. "in the Maqām").[19] In a verse of Hudhayfa b. Ghānim included in Ibn Hishām's Sīra, ʿAbd Manāf is said to have "laid bare (?) Zamzam by the Maqām" ("ṭawā Zamzam ʿinda al-Maqām").[20] This latter reference is typical of several in that it seems to give the Maqām undue prominence if it is envisaged that the name refers to the sacred stone which is now called Maqām Ibrāhīm. On evidence of this sort Lammens argued that al-maqām was a synonym for al-kaʿba,[21] and he also cited in support of this view a verse of ʿUmar b. Abī Rabīʿa which refers to the pilgrims making the takbīr at the Maqām: "lā wa'lladhī baʿatha al-nabiyya Muḥammadan bi'l-nūri wa'l-Islām . . . wa-bimā ahalla bihi al-ḥajīju wa-kabbarū ʿinda al-Maqāmi wa-rukni bayti al-ḥarām. . . ."[22] Although the verse does not support Lammens's contention fully, it is easy to see how he formed the opinion that al-Maqām here means the Kaʿba: this is another example of the use of the word al-Maqām where, if we have the Muslim sanctuary at Mecca in mind, we might expect from the context some expression broadly synonymous with "the sanctuary," such as al-kaʿba or al-bayt. Possibly another example of the same sort would be Azraqī's statement that the Prophet used the Maqām as a qibla while he was in Mecca (fa-kāna yuṣallī ila'l-Maqām mā kāna bi-Makka").[23]

At this stage I am concerned only to indicate the difficulty in attaching the references to the Muslim sanctuary at Mecca as we know it. As yet it is not possible to say what the names al-Maqām and Maqām Ibrāhīm do refer to in the sort of examples cited above, but one thing that should be borne in mind, and which discussion so far has ignored, is the possibility that references to al-Maqām are not always to Maqām Ibrāhīm, whatever the latter indicates. Sometimes it seems that a gloss has been inserted into a text in order to make it clear that al-Maqām does mean Maqām Ibrāhīm, and it may be wondered why such glosses, which affect the continuity of the text, were considered necessary. For example, Azraqī reports that when al-Mahdī came to Mecca to make the ḥajj, ʿUbayd Allāh b. ʿUthmān came to him where he was staying in the Dār al-Nadwa bringing with him al-Maqām Maqām Ibrāhīm.[24] In the section dealing with Quraysh's rebuilding of the Kaʿba, Azraqī has two versions of a tradition describing in almost identical terms the fear of Quraysh in face of the serpent which God had caused to dwell in the bayt. According to one version, Quraysh withdrew ʿinda al-Maqām, according to the other ʿinda Maqām Ibrāhīm.[25] The possibility is obvious that the latter is a standardizing gloss.

Leaving this question on one side, however, it seems clear that, whether the references are to al-Maqām or Maqām Ibrāhīm, there is frequently some difficulty in reconciling the references with the Meccan sanctuary as we know it, or some suggestion that they are not to the stone which now bears the name Maqām Ibrāhīm. Since it seems impossible that such references could have originated after the Muslim sanctuary had become established at Mecca in the form in which we know it, it seems to follow that they must date from an earlier period when the name Maqām Ibrāhīm meant something else. The name has then been reinterpreted and applied to the stone which is now so called.

Such material, I agree, is frequently somewhat ambiguous, and it is often not possible to say with certainty that al-Maqām or Maqām Ibrāhīm does not refer to the sacred stone of the Muslim sanctuary at Mecca. The attempt to reconcile the Qur'ānic reference with the facts of the Meccan sanctuary, however, seems obviously forced, and when the evidence is taken as a whole it does seem to indicate a development of the sort suggested. In general, it seems likely that the literary sources we have for early Islam represent the outcome of a long process of editorial amendment and revision made necessary by the gradual development of the new religion. If this is accepted, then it seems probable that the remnants of the earliest traditions which would survive would be those which have escaped the editorial process precisely because of their ambiguity: it was not impossible to reconcile them with later ideas and so it was not necessary to remove or alter them. The survival of references like those above which indicate that the Maqām Ibrāhīm was not originally a sacred stone at Mecca, I suggest, can often be attributed to their ambiguity. In the case of the Qur'ānic reference, where the contradiction between its conception of Maqām Ibrāhīm and that of later Islam is more clear, amendment of the text would not have been so easy for obvious reasons. In this case the necessary reconciliation was attempted in the tafsīr literature rather than by alteration of the text itself.

b. Al-Ḥijr. A similar development, I think, has occurred in the case of this term. At the Muslim sanctuary at Mecca the name al-Ḥijr designates the semi-circular area adjacent to the north-west wall of the Kaʿba. The area is regarded as of special sanctity, and the pilgrims perform the ritual circumambulations (ṭawāf) around the whole of the area covered by the Kaʿba and al-Ḥijr, not just around the Kaʿba.[26] The special status of the Ḥijr is explained in Muslim tradition in a number of ways: at various times it is said to have been included in the Kaʿba, but ultimately its sanctity derives from its association with Hagar and Ishmael. Most frequently the Ḥijr is explained as the place where Ishmael and his mother are buried.[27] Modern scholarship has again concentrated on the question of the significance of the Ḥijr in the religion of the Jāhiliyya, rejecting the association with Ishmael and Hagar. Lammens argued that it was originally an independent pagan sanctuary which Islam subordinated to the Kaʿba, others have given it some place in the performance of sacrifices in or near the Kaʿba.[28]

Again, however, there are references to al-Ḥijr which suggest that it has changed in meaning. For example, there is mention of Quraysh meeting in al-Ḥijr in the Jāhiliyya and in the lifetime of the Prophet,[29] something which would hardly have been possible in the rather small area which now bears the name. This is reminiscent of the tradition about Quraysh in their "groups" in the Maqām, and just as the name al-Maqām sometimes occurred where we might expect a term indicating "the sanctuary," so too al-Ḥijr is sometimes used apparently interchangeably with al-bayt or al-kaʿba. Ibn al-Zubayr, having taken refuge from the Umayyad Caliph Yazīd I, it is said, in Mecca, is usually reported to have taken the title ʿā'idh bi'l-bayt because he was claiming sanctuary at the Kaʿba.[30] In Ibn ʿAsākir's version, however, Ibn al-Zubayr is described as "clinging to al-Ḥijr (lazima bi'l-Ḥijr),[31] and the title ʿā'idh bi'l-Ḥijr can be found in ḥadīth as a variant of ʿā'idh bi'l-bayt.[32] ʿĀ'isha too is said to have taken refuge in al-Ḥijr when, after the murder of ʿUthmān, ʿAlī was recognized as amīr al-mu'minīn: "nazalat ʿalā bāb al-masjid fa-qaṣadat li'l-Ḥijr fa-suttirat fīhi."[33] Al-Ḥijr is also named in some traditions as the place where Muḥammad was sleeping when he was miraculously taken on his Night

Journey,[34] and too as the place where his grandfather, ʿAbd al-Muṭṭalib, was sleeping when he experienced his dream in which the place of the hidden Zamzam well was revealed to him.[35] In these cases it would not be impossible to see al-Ḥijr as the area adjacent to the Kaʿba but the material suggests that we are dealing with a different concept. Lammens suggested, on the evidence of these traditions, that the religious practice of incubation was performed in the independent sanctuary called al-Ḥijr in the Jāhiliyya.[36]

There are some indications of a dispute about the status of al-Ḥijr. The inclusion of al-Ḥijr inside the bayt is the most striking feature of the sanctuary constructed by Ibn al-Zubayr and, similarly, the exclusion of al-Ḥijr appears to be the chief alteration made by al-Ḥajjāj when he destroyed and rebuilt the sanctuary after his defeat of Ibn al-Zubayr.[37] Ibn al-Zubayr's decision is said to have been justified by reference to a ḥadīth transmitted by ʿĀʾisha, according to which Muḥammad said that, if it had not been for the fact that Quraysh (?ahluki) had only recently given up polytheism or unbelief (shirk or kufr), he would have demolished the Kaʿba and rebuilt it to include al-Ḥijr.[38] In a related tradition ʿĀʾisha is said to have been encouraged by the Prophet to pray in al-Ḥijr because it was a part of the sanctuary (al-Ḥijr min al-bayt).[39] Against this, however, Muḥibb al-Dīn al-Ṭabarī reports that ʿUmar b. al-Khaṭṭāb "invoked God against a woman who prayed in al-Ḥijr" ("aʿzimu bi'llāh ʿala ʾmraʾatin ṣallat fi'l-Ḥijr"),[40] and in spite of Ṭabarī's denial, this seems to be a clear reference to ʿĀʾisha. A tradition given by Azraqī, apparently citing non-Qurʾānic divine revelation, says that al-Ḥijr is a gate of Paradise,[41] but Maqdisī cites a prohibition of the use of al-Ḥijr as a qibla.[42]

From material of this sort, then, it seems that al-Ḥijr sometimes designates an entity rather different from that which is so called at the Muslim sanctuary at Mecca, and again it is difficult to see how such material could have originated after the term had become established in its application to the sanctuary at Mecca. The possible earlier associations of some of the material in which the name al-Ḥijr occurs will be discussed shortly.

c. Al-Ḥaṭīm. Unlike the two previous terms, there does not seem to be any generally accepted definition of what is meant by the name al-Ḥaṭīm at the Muslim sanctuary at Mecca. Apparently most frequently it is taken to refer to the semi-circular wall which marks the boundary of the area adjacent to the Kaʿba called al-Ḥijr, but the name is also explained as a synonym for al-Ḥijr, as referring to the wall of the Kaʿba beneath the water-spout (<u>mīzāb</u>), and sometimes as designating that part of al-Ḥijr beneath the water-spout. Other, fuller definitions say that al-Ḥaṭīm is the area "between al-Rukn, al-Maqām, Zamzam and al-Ḥijr," or "between the door and the corner (<u>rukn</u>, to be discussed shortly) in which is the stone." There does not seem to be any satisfactory explanation of the meaning of the word, most attempts at an etymology connecting it with the root ḤṬM with the sense "to break, to smash."[43] Lammens, of course, suggested that al-Ḥaṭīm was a bethel, "un nouveau rokn, non encore catalogué."[44]

Again we find that there are references to al-Ḥaṭīm in the traditions which suggest that none of these conflicting definitions is adequate.

Ibn al-ʿAbbās is reported to have attempted to forbid the mentioning of al-Ḥaṭīm "because in the Jāhiliyya men swore oaths and threw down their whips, shoes or bows (there)."[45] In particular the Khārijite Ibn Muljam is said to have taken at, by or near (<u>ʿinda</u>) al-Ḥaṭīm his oath to kill ʿAlī.[46] One isolated tradition calls into question the conception of al-Ḥaṭīm as a place or area and explains it as the name of a destroyed idol.[47] It was this last tradition which was decisive in forming Lammens's view that al-Ḥaṭīm was a pre-Islamic bethel which had been abolished by Islam.[48]

This lack of consensus regarding the meaning of the name distinguishes the case of al-Ḥaṭīm from those of Maqām Ibrāhīm and al-Ḥijr. The last two are well known as the names of features of the Muslim sanctuary at Mecca, but traces of what we have suggested are earlier, superseded meanings for them are occasionally to be found in the literary material. With al-Ḥaṭīm, however, the name really seems superfluous with regard to the Meccan sanctuary[49] and I suggest that here we are dealing with a remnant of early Muslim sanctuary ideas which it has not proved possible to attach definitively to any feature of the sanctuary when it was islamized.

There must remain some doubt about the earlier meaning of al-Ḥaṭīm or its source, but the view that it was an idol or sacred stone of some sort is not convincing. The majority of the traditions seek to explain it as the name of an area and it is difficult to see why they should do so if it was an object of limited size. Presumably Lammens would have seen the various definitions of al-Ḥaṭīm which have been given above as called forth by embarrassment on the part of Muslims at the memory of this remnant of the pagan past of the Meccan sanctuary. This view, which underlies most of Lammens's efforts to explain the inconsistencies which he had noted in the Muslim traditions,seems wrong. There is no reason why the Muslims should seek to hide the pagan past of the sanctuary, and indeed it is a prominent feature of the Muslim sanctuary traditions. The pagan deities and ceremonies are explained as aberrations which had been introduced in the period after Abraham had founded the sanctuary.[50] It seems that it is necessary, in order to provide a satisfactory explanation of the material which has been noted here, and much of which was adduced by Lammens, to go beyond the traditional version of how the Meccan sanctuary was incorporated into Islam, a version which Lammens's explanations accept, and to envisage instead an attempt to apply sanctuary ideas to a sanctuary to which they did not originally refer.

d. Al-Masjid al-Ḥarām. In the Islamic period al-Masjid al-Ḥarām designates the mosque at Mecca with the Kaʿba at its centre. Since Muslim tradition attributes the origin of this mosque to the caliphate of ʿUmar, and since there are a number of references to al-Masjid al-Ḥarām in the Jāhiliyya and the lifetime of the Prophet, however, it is necessary for Muslim tradition to allow for the existence of al-Masjid al-Ḥarām before the existence of the building which now bears that name. In traditions referring to the earlier period, then, the name is taken to indicate the empty space around the Kaʿba even though this was not yet enclosed by a wall, covered with a roof, or dignified architecturally or decoratively. The walls of this pre-Islamic al-Masjid al-Ḥarām, it is said, were no more than the walls of the houses which enclosed the empty space, and its gates (abwāb), which are frequently named, were merely the main streets between the houses giving on to the empty space. In the early Islamic period, beginning with ʿUmar, the empty space is said to have been several times enlarged, enclosed with walls, and covered with a roof to form the mosque which now bears the name.[51]

It may seem that the data already require a surprising amount of accompanying explanation which is not entirely satisfying. In addition to this, however, it is possible to find in the Qurʾān and traditions a number of examples where the name al-Masjid al-Ḥarām occurs and does not seem to coincide with either of the definitions already given.

Sometimes it is necessary for Muslim tradition to see al-Masjid al-Ḥarām as a synonym for the Kaʿba. This interpretation appears most often in connection with Qur'ān 2:139, 144 and 145, the qibla verses: "Turn your face towards al-Masjid al-Ḥarām." These verses are said to have been revealed when Jerusalem was superseded as the Muslim qibla, and since it is the Kaʿba, or even more specifically a particular part of the Kaʿba, which is the Muslim qibla, it is necessary to see al-Masjid al-Ḥarām here as a reference to the Kaʿba rather than to the space around it.[52] The same interpretation sometimes occurs in commentaries on Qur'ān 3:96-7: "the first bayt established for the people was that at Bakka." The bayt at Bakka is seen as a reference to the Kaʿba at Mecca and sometimes in this connection a ḥadīth is cited in which it is said that al-Masjid al-Ḥarām was founded a certain amount of time before al-Masjid al-Aqṣā (understood here as the Jerusalem Temple).[53] Again, therefore, we have the equation of al-Masjid al-Ḥarām with the Kaʿba.

Sometimes, however, we find a very different interpretation: al-Masjid al-Ḥarām means the whole of the ḥaram, an area bigger than that of Mecca itself. This appears most frequently concerning Qur'ān 17:1, the isrā' verse: "Praised be He who transported His servant by night from al-Masjid al-Ḥarām to al-Masjid al-Aqṣā. . . ." Several of the traditions about Muḥammad's miraculous Night Journey, to which the Qur'ānic verse is seen as an allusion, contain information about its starting point which would conflict with the Qur'ān if al-Masjid al-Ḥarām in 17:1 were seen as a reference to the empty space around the Kaʿba. Of these traditions, perhaps the most common is that which says that Muḥammad was sleeping in the house (dār) of Umm Hāni' when Gabriel came to take him.[54] Whatever the house of Umm Hāni' might be, it was clearly not possible to locate it in al-Masjid al-Ḥarām if that is understood as a designation of the empty space around the Kaʿba (or of the Kaʿba itself). In commentaries on the isrā' verse, therefore, it is frequently stated that al-Masjid al-Ḥarām means the whole of the ḥaram, such an interpretation allowing the house of Umm Hāni' to fall within it.[55] This extended interpretation of the expression also occurs, for example, in commentaries on Qur'ān 9:28 which prohibits the mushrikūn from entering al-Masjid al-Ḥarām. Several traditions make it clear that it is the whole of the ḥaram, not just the mosque or the Kaʿba, which is forbidden to the mushrikūn.[56]

I do not wish here to enter on a discussion of what al-Masjid al-Ḥarām might have meant originally, merely to make the point that, if we accept the traditional version of the history of the Meccan sanctuary, there seems no satisfactory reason for the fluctuation in the meaning of the name in the ways illustrated. If al-Masjid al-Ḥarām always meant what it now means at the Muslim sanctuary at Mecca, why would it be used in the Qur'ān and the traditions in ways which can only be made to coincide with that meaning with some difficulty? It seems more satisfactory to try to dissociate the name from the Muslim sanctuary at Mecca in cases like those mentioned, to try to make sense of the material without using the concepts of later Islam to interpret it. It seems, for example, that the need to equate al-Masjid al-Ḥarām with the Kaʿba in connection with the qibla verses only arises if we accept the traditional Muslim exegesis of these verses and the traditional accounts of the institution of the qibla. If, as seems more likely, it is considered that the practice of facing the Kaʿba at Mecca in prayer developed independently of these Qur'ānic verses and that the scriptural support for the practice was only provided later, then it is possible to try to reach some understanding of what al-Masjid al-Ḥarām means in the Qur'ān without prejudging the outcome. Again, therefore, I suggest that we have a term which has been adapted in order to provide it with some application to the Meccan sanctuary but which probably originated in a different context.

e. Al-Rukn. This term is explained in two senses: it can mean either the Black Stone which is fixed in the south-east corner of the Kaʿba, or the corner itself which contains the Stone. Sometimes al-Rukn al-Aswad occurs, also with this possible dual meaning. Sometimes the name al-Ḥajar al-Aswad is used, but only with reference to the Stone, not the corner containing it. The plural form, al-Arkān, is also found in connection with the sanctuary, and is explained as referring to the four corners of the Kaʿba.[57] We have, then, one name (al-Rukn) which can refer to two different things, and two names (al-Rukn and al-Ḥajar) which are used to refer to one thing, the Black Stone.

Lammens noted that the Arkān are sometimes mentioned in contexts where it seems inappropriate to envisage them merely as the four corners of the Kaʿba, and he suggested, again, that they were bethels, not necessarily four in number, which at some time in the Jāhiliyya were fixed in the walls of the Kaʿba; the Rukn he saw as the most important of these bethels, the Black Stone. Again he explains the application of the name al-Arkān to the four corners of the sanctuary by reference to Muslim embarrassment and concern to obscure the pagan significance of the Kaʿba and its attachments.[58]

There is some evidence, however, that, as with the other terms which have been mentioned above, the name al-Rukn has been subjected to a redefinition aimed at bringing it into line with later Muslim sanctuary concepts, a redefinition of a sort rather different to that proposed by Lammens.

In some cases it seems that al-Rukn cannot be either the Black Stone or the corner containing it. For example, in the accounts of Ibn al-Zubayr's rebuilding of the sanctuary it is reported that he placed the Black Stone (variously al-Ḥajar al-Aswad or al-Rukn) in an ark (tābūt) while the bayt was demolished and then ceremoniously replaced it in the south-east corner of the new building.[59] Other traditions relating to this rebuilding, however, mention that Ibn al-Zubayr dug in al-Ḥijr and found there a stone.[60] In some of the traditions this stone appears as a foundation stone, for its uncovering causes all of Mecca to tremble, and one of the traditions refers to it as a rukn min arkān al-bayt.[61] A further series of traditions concerns a text which was found, either during the demolition of the Kaʿba by Ibn al-Zubayr or that by Quraysh in the Jāhiliyya, containing a divine promise of sustenance for the people of the sanctuary.[62] These traditions are adduced à propos of Abraham's request to God as given in Qur'ān 14:40/37: "Oh my Lord, I have settled some of my offspring in an unfruitful valley by your sacred House. . . . Provide them with fruits that they may be grateful." The traditions, which give the text with only relatively minor variants so that it is clear they are referring to the same phenomenon, variously report that the discovery was made "in al-Maqām," "in a stone of the foundations (ḥajar min al-asās) of Abraham," "in a stone (ḥajar) of al-Ḥijr," "fī baʿḍi al-zabūr,"[63] "in the well (bi'r) of the Kaʿba," and finally, "in al-Rukn." In these traditions, then, the Rukn seems to be something buried or hidden, and it seems likely that there is a degree of overlap between the traditions about the stone discovered by Ibn al-Zubayr, the foundation stone, and those about the stone with the text--we seem to be talking about the same stone in both cases, and the word rukn is used in connection with each.

Such a connection might help to explain a report of Masʿūdī which perplexed Gaudefroy-Demombynes.[64] According to this report, Ishmael was buried in al-Masjid al-Ḥarām in the place where the Black Stone (al-Ḥajar al-Aswad) was. As we have mentioned, Ishmael is most frequently said to have been buried in al-Ḥijr, while the Black Stone is usually said to have been found in the hill called Abū Qubays. It may be that al-Masʿūdī or his source had in mind the stone found in al-Ḥijr, which one tradition says marked the grave of Ishmael and another calls al-Rukn, and that the later generally accepted identification of the term al-Rukn with the Black Stone of the Kaʿba led to the substitution in the report of al-Ḥajar al-Aswad for al-Rukn. There are other cases where it can be shown that this has happened.[65]

One of the traditions regarding the burial of certain sanctuary objects in the Zamzam well by the last Jurhumī chief of Mecca before the tribe was expelled says that the Ḥajar al-Rukn was among the articles which were buried.[66] As Caetani has noted, it seems unlikely that this is a reference to the Black Stone: there is no mention that the Black Stone was missing from the Kaʿba in the period following the expulsion of Jurhum, and it would be difficult to account for the persistence of the cult without it.[67]

A tradition of Ibn Saʿd mentions that Ishmael was buried "between al-Rukn and al-bayt."[68] This makes no sense if the bayt is identified as the Kaʿba and the Rukn as the Black Stone in its corner.

It is hoped to show that it is possible to go further in discussing the significance of the term al-Rukn before it came to be used to designate the Black Stone of the Meccan sanctuary. The way in which the term was redefined and developed seems a sort of paradigm for the development of the Muslim sanctuary at Mecca.

If we look beyond the evidence provided by the Muslim literature, in some cases it is possible to relate names and ideas, which are now attached to the Muslim sanctuary at Mecca, to certain Old Testament passages and Jewish traditions associated with them. While we cannot be as precise as we would like, it looks from the evidence as though at least some of the sanctuary ideas and terminology of early Islam had developed first in a Jewish milieu and that they were then, as already said, adapted and redefined so that they could be attached to features of the Meccan sanctuary. I have already indicated why the usual theories of "borrowing" by Islam from Judaism or of the common underlying "Semitic Religion" cannot be used to account for the relationship between Muslim and Jewish ideas and traditions in this case. I wish to illustrate the relationship, as far as possible, with regard to the Maqām Ibrāhīm, al-Ḥijr and al-Rukn.

Sidersky suggested, on general grounds, that there may be a link between the name Maqām Ibrāhīm in Qur'ān 2:125/119: "And take for yourselves a place of prayer from the Maqām Ibrāhīm," and a passage in the Babylonian Talmud, Berakhot 6b.[69] In that passage the Talmud recommends that each believer should have a fixed place (māqōm) for his prayer, and in support reference is made to Abraham's practice of keeping a fixed place for his prayer. As evidence of Abraham's practice, there is cited Genesis 19:27: "And Abraham got up early in the morning to the place (māqōm) where he had stood." This māqōm was the place where Abraham had previously stood asking for God's mercy on Sodom, and the Talmud makes it clear that by "stood" is meant "prayed."[70] From the wording and ideas of the Talmudic passage, therefore, it does not seem far to the Qur'ānic passage mentioning the maqām of Abraham.

Nevertheless, the Qur'ānic passage is clearly not just a variant of the Talmudic--where the latter is simply recommending a fixed place for prayer, the former uses the expression Maqām Ibrāhīm, apparently, as a proper name, possibly as the name for the sanctuary or a part of it.[71] It seems possible, therefore, that the Qur'ānic Maqām Ibrāhīm is not derived from the Talmudic passage as such but rather from the Genesis passage to which it refers. In Genesis 18:22 ff. Abraham stands before the Lord in the māqōm which is referred to in 19:27, and this indication that the māqōm had been visited by God may have been strengthened by the later use of the word māqōm to refer to God, a usage which seems to fit some of the occurrences of the word maqām in the Qur'ān.[72] It may be, therefore, that the association of the place with the divinity suggested the designation Maqām Ibrāhīm for the sanctuary and maybe it was considered that the place where Abraham prayed was the site of the sanctuary he had founded. Some support for this may be found in the Muslim traditions which describe Abraham's journey to found the bayt in the company of three heavenly beings, one of which is named as the sakīna, a word used by the Rabbis for the Divine Presence.[73] This is reminiscent of Abraham's three visitors in the Genesis story, one of whom could be identified with the Lord before whom Abraham ministered in the māqōm.[74]

The associations here are rather imprecise and one cannot point to the occurrence of the expression Maqām Ibrāhīm in pre-Islamic Jewish sources. Nevertheless, there does seem to be enough to suggest that the name Maqām Ibrāhīm arose first in the context of elaborations on the Genesis passages, and I can see no obvious alternative explanation for the use of the term in the way in which it occurs in the Qur'ān and some of the other material cited above. I envisage, therefore, that the name first arose as a designation for the sanctuary because it was there that Abraham had stood in the presence of God; when the Meccan sanctuary was taken over, for reasons which are not clear, Maqām Ibrāhīm could no longer be used as a name for the sanctuary as a whole and so it became attached to the stone which now bears the name, a literal interpretation of the root from which maqām is derived giving rise to the story which is most commonly used to explain why the stone is called Maqām Ibrāhīm: it is a stone on which Abraham had stood while building the bayt. I would agree that this proposed scheme goes beyond the evidence provided by the sources, but it does make sense of the evidence in a way which the traditional accounts do not.

In the case of al-Ḥijr, it is possible to establish in rather more detail a link between some of the Muslim material and the account of Jacob's dream in Genesis chapter 28 as it was elaborated in Jewish traditions. I have not, however, been able to find any connection between the name al-Ḥijr itself and the traditions concerning Jacob's dream.

As we have seen, al-Ḥijr often occurs in the Muslim traditions where we might expect a term indicating the sanctuary--in classical Islam al-bayt or al-ka'ba. Indeed al-Ḥijr sometimes appears as a variant for al-bayt or al-ka'ba. Now, in Jewish traditions the place where Jacob experienced his dream of the heavenly ladder is regarded as the site of the sanctuary: it is the very same place where Abraham prepared to sacrifice Isaac and later the Temple was to be built there.[75] The possibility that the Muslim traditions about Muḥammad's Night Journey have been in part influenced by or derived from the story of Jacob's dream of the heavenly ladder has sometimes been suggested,[76] but in this connection the significance of the names given for the starting point of the Night Journey seems to have been overlooked: one of the most common versions says that he was sleeping in al-Ḥijr at the time.[77] The possibility that the Night Journey was a dream is allowed for by Muslim tradition.[78]

In Genesis 28:17, Jacob awakes from his dream and exclaims "There is none other than the house of God, and this is the gate of heaven." Reference has already been made to Azraqī's tradition according to which God revealed to Ishmael that he would open for him a gate of heaven in al-Ḥijr, and in the traditions about the Night Journey al-Ḥijr functions as a gate of heaven--from there Muḥammad goes up through the seven heavens. The idea, of course, is part of the Navel of the Earth circle of ideas,[79] but the important point is that in Muslim tradition it is associated particularly with al-Ḥijr rather than with the sanctuary in general, and, if we accept the traditional explanation of the meaning of al-Ḥijr, there seems no reason for this.

The phrase "the land whereon thou liest" in Genesis 28:13 could be taken to mean that Jacob was buried in the place where he had experienced his dream, the site of the sanctuary. God's promise that He would give "the land whereon thou liest" to the descendants of Jacob is taken to be a divine promise of the whole of Palestine for Israel since at that time Palestine was reduced in size to the spot where Jacob was sleeping.[80] As mentioned before, the sanctity of al-Ḥijr in Muslim tradition derives in part from the fact that Ishmael is buried there, and the descendants of Ishmael possess the Muslim sanctuary.[81]

It seems, then, that some of the Muslim traditions about al-Ḥijr developed out of Jewish traditions which had grown up around the narrative of Jacob's dream and that they originated independently of the Meccan sanctuary. I cannot see any way in which the name al-Ḥijr itself may have originated in the traditions about Jacob's dream, but, if we now come to discuss the possible meanings of the term al-Rukn before it became fixed as the Black Stone or the corner containing it, the link between Muslim sanctuary ideas and the traditions associated with Jacob's dream becomes even stronger.

In the story in Genesis, Jacob erects a stone in the place where he had slept: this is the stone which had served for his pillow, and Jacob calls it "Gods house." The stone is, naturally, made much of in the elaborations on the story: it is identified with the Eben Shetiya, the corner stone of the Temple and the pivot on which the whole world is balanced; after Jacob had set it up, God cast it down into the abyss where it serves as the corner stone for the whole world.[82] It seems that al-Rukn was originally, before it became the Black Stone, the name for this Eben Shetiya or a development of it.

In at least one of the traditions about the stone which Ibn al-Zubayr turned up in al-Ḥijr, and the uncovering of which caused all of Mecca to tremble, the stone is referred to as a rukn. Evidently in this guise it is a foundation stone. A similar stone is said to have been unearthed when Quraysh demolished the Kaʿba in the Jāhiliyya: when they attempted to move it, all of Mecca shook and the stone gave out a blinding light.[83] Although the term rukn does not appear in this latter version, it is obvious that we are dealing with the same phenomenon as in the tradition about Ibn al-Zubayr--the two traditions are variants.[84]

The blinding light which the stone gives out in the tradition about Quraysh's discovery is a further indication that we are dealing with the Rukn and a further link with the Eben Shetiya. One of the most common traditions about the Black Stone or al-Rukn is that it was originally dazzlingly bright and that, if God had not effaced it, it would have illuminated everything between east and west.[85] Muslim tradition ascribes the blackness of the stone sometimes to pollution by sin, sometimes to the action of the several fires which have engulfed the Kaʿba.[86] In Jewish tradition the first ray of light which illuminated the whole world issued from the Eben Shetiya,[87] and the Eben Shetiya also parallels the Rukn in that it is said to have come down to earth from heaven and is one of the few things of heavenly origin in this world.[88]

The idea that the Rukn was buried, like the Eben Shetiya, seems well established. In addition to the stone which Ibn al-Zubayr and Quraysh found in al-Ḥijr, we have al-Masʿūdī's reference to the Black Stone buried in the same place as Ishmael,[89] and the tradition of the burial of the Ḥajar al-Rukn by the last Jurhumī chief of Mecca.[90] Even the traditions about the bringing down of the Black Stone from Abū Qubays by Ishmael and Abraham sometimes say that they had to dig it up.[91] This feature seems too persistent to be insignificant, and again it appears to link the three apparently separate objects--the Eben Shetiya, the stone in al-Ḥijr and the Black Stone.

In Jewish tradition the Eben Shetiya is stamped with the name of God;[92] the inscription which, according to Muslim tradition, was found on the stone discovered in al-Ḥijr or elsewhere begins: "I am Allah, the Lord of Bakka . . ." ("innanī Allāh Dhū Bakka").[93]

If we simply had to explain parallels between the Black Stone and the Eben Shetiya, it might be possible to do so by reference to a borrowing by Islam of Jewish material and the application of it to Muslim institutions in the period when Islam came into contact with "foreign" religions--the usual form of the "borrowing" theory in fact. But any explanation of this sort seems to be belied by the fact that, as I have argued, in Muslim traditions the name al-Rukn may refer to two stones which are in theory quite distinct, that the material on the Eben Shetiya which was "borrowed" is applied to the stone buried beneath the sanctuary as much as to the Black Stone embedded in the wall of the Kaʿba. If the traditions about the Eben Shetiya were "borrowed" in the way which is usually envisaged, there would not seem to be any way in which the stone beneath the sanctuary, overlapping with both the Black Stone and the Eben Shetiya, could be explained. Again the most satisfactory explanation is to see the Rukn as a remnant in Muslim tradition of the Jewish sanctuary ideas out of which the earliest Muslim ones arose. The Rukn was originally the corner stone of heavenly origin buried beneath the sanctuary. When the Meccan sanctuary was taken over by Islam, the name and some of the ideas associated with it came to be applied to the stone of that sanctuary, the Black Stone. But, since the name al-Rukn (pillar, support, foundation) means something more than merely "stone," the name was also applied to the corner containing the stone. This development, I suggest, typifies that whereby the earliest Muslim sanctuary ideas were modified and adapted to take account of the facts of the Meccan sanctuary when it was taken up as the Muslim sanctuary.

But it is not only the Black Stone and the stone buried beneath the sanctuary which seem to share some of the same traditional material. Overlapping occurs too between the material on the Rukn (in both senses) and that on the stone now called Maqām Ibrāhīm, and this suggests that the redefinition of terms which accompanied the islamization of the Meccan sanctuary took some time to achieve.

Some sources report that on the stone called Maqām Ibrāhīm there is an inscription in "foreign" characters.[94] The historian al-Fākihī reports that he saw this inscription when the stone was being restored in 256/870, and he reproduces the foreign letters as far as he could read them. It seems that this inscription, as it is given in Arabic in the sources, is basically a variant of that found by Ibn al-Zubayr and Quraysh when they demolished the Kaʿba, the text promising sustenance to "its people." Introducing his discussion of the text on the Maqām Ibrāhīm, al-Fākihī specifically says that it was found by Quraysh in the Jāhiliyya.[95] It will be remembered that the traditions about the discovery of that text give several different versions of where it was found, including "in a stone in al-Ḥijr," "in al-Rukn," and "in al-Maqām."[96] One of the traditions about Quraysh's discovery, one which names al-Rukn as the place where the text was found, says that it was a kitāb written in Syriac which Quraysh got a Jew to read for them.[97] Al-Fākihī says that the inscription was in Hebrew or Himyaritic, although one of his informants offered a translation on the basis of his many years study of al-Barābī.[98]

Finally, al-Fākihī cites a tradition from Ibn al-ʿAbbās mentioning that there is an inscription (kitāb) in the Maqām Ibrāhīm which could be read if it were washed. Notwithstanding, Ibn al-ʿAbbās gives the text of the kitāb, and it is another variant on the other texts promising sustenance to "its people."[99] It seems, then, that Muslim tradition applied the story of the inscription to the stone called Maqām Ibrāhīm as well as to the Rukn.

Several other traditions give broadly similar information about the stone called Maqām Ibrāhīm and the Black Stone. Both are said to have come down to earth from heaven and both were originally dazzlingly bright.[100] Both were brought down from Abū Qubays when Abraham was building the Kaʿba.[101] The two stones are also linked in eschatology: on the Last Day they will both appear as big as Abū Qubays, both will have eyes and lips, and both will testify in favour of those who visited them.[102]

The information about the inscription which is applied both to the Maqām Ibrāhīm and the Rukn suggests that there is more to this than merely a desire to link two important features of the sanctuary. Provisionally, I suggest that this overlapping of material is evidence that the redefinition of terms involved in the adoption of the Meccan sanctuary by Islam took some time to carry through. It seems possible that, before the Rukn finally came to be identified with the Black Stone and then with its corner, there was a tendency to attach some of the ideas about the Rukn, and perhaps the name too, to the stone which eventually came to be called Maqām Ibrāhīm. Possibly the fact that the stone now called Maqām Ibrāhīm did bear an inscription led to application of traditions about the Rukn to it.[103]

I have, of course, left many questions about the

terms and institutions discussed in this paper unanswered, but should like to conclude by saying again that I think the evidence put forward is difficult to make sense of if the usual version of the adoption of the Meccan sanctuary by Islam is accepted, and that the alternative scheme suggested here seems to me necessary to account for the evidence I have presented.

3

THE ARAB CONQUESTS AND THE FORMATION OF ISLAMIC SOCIETY

I.M. Lapidus

Preface

The Arab conquests were an epochal and cataclysmic event. Not only historians, but all peoples, of east and west, have been mystified by the sudden and mass migration and conquest by Arab nomadic peoples, and the defeat of refined and civilized societies by vigorous "barbarians." We are fascinated to see a new religion triumph over old faiths, corrupted empires be displaced by a new regime, and old civilizations die to serve the birth of a new. How are such sudden and extraordinary changes to be explained?

The facts are well known. Historians agree that a complete understanding of these events must include an account of Arabian history, the rise of Islam, the conquests, and the early history of Arab-Islamic civilization. Most historians emphasize one of several themes. Some stress the history and the institutions of pre-Islamic society so that we may better understand the subsequent contribution of Arab civilization to the development of the Middle East. Hence the emphasis is placed upon bedouin poetic and linguistic accomplishments, the structure of bedouin social life, the religions and monarchies of South Arabia, and Meccan commerce and religion. Other writers analyze the conjunction of social, political and religious conditions which make intelligible the rise of Islam. Still others deal with the mechanisms by which great tribal confederations are formed, how they were able to overwhelm the defenses of established empires, and why conquering peoples were assimilated into the polity and culture of the conquered peoples. Yet despite the impressive scholarship, the rise of Islam and the conquests still seem arbitrary developments in terms of Arabian and Middle Eastern history. Arabian history is portrayed as chaotic until the rise of Islam. In terms of the history of the Middle East, the Arab conquests are taken as an historic accident, a diversion from the true course of Middle Eastern developments.

I think that we can improve our perspective on these matters, and better comprehend the rise of Islam and the conquests, in their intrinsic relation to the development of Arabian society, and in their relation to the history of the conquests and the formation of a new civilization, by considering the conquests as an integral part of the relationship between Arabia and the Middle Eastern societies. For this we do not need new facts, but an interpretation of the historical process as a whole. This process was the joint and interrelated evolution of two types of societies--the empire type societies of the Middle East, Byzantine and Sasanian, and the "peripheral" society of Arabia. The genesis of the Arab conquests was profoundly influenced by the character of the environing civilization, just as the transformation of late Roman and Persian civilizations and the rise of Islamic civilization in the Middle East were influenced by the Arab conquests. The pre-conquest phase of this history involved the development within Arabian society of the very same types of institutions and forms of culture which were already established in the empire societies, a transformation which created the internal conditions for the rise of Islam and the Arab conquests. The post-conquest phase of this history entailed the integration of the conquering peoples and their home territories into a comprehensive new civilization. The conquest itself helped to complete the assimilation of the conquering peoples, begun in Arabia, into general Middle Eastern society, while the injection of new peoples and new values representing a variant but related form of Middle Eastern culture introduced an Arab and Islamic identity for Middle Eastern peoples.

This point of view turns our attention from the drama of the rise of Islam and the Arab conquests and brings to light the slow, lengthy, elaborate history by which Arabian and Middle Eastern empire societies were amalgamated. The epochal events associated with the rise of Islam and the Arab conquests are best understood, not as a purely Arabian development, nor as an imposition of an Arabian society upon the rest of the Middle East, but as an evolutionary process by which several Middle Eastern societies became more highly integrated and more highly developed.

Arabia and the Middle East

The key to this larger historical process lies in the long-term relationship between Arabia and the rest of Middle Eastern society. The two regions had developed in very different ways. In the empire Middle East the development of civilization was marked by several critical features. First was the development of an agricultural economy. Second was the emergence of complex forms of social organization superimposed on the small family or clientele groups which were the earliest forms of human society. The first complex societies in the Middle East were city societies, which were different from smaller groups in that they were characterized by non-familial forms of political leadership, social stratification, division of labor and new forms of cultural achievement including writing and monumental architecture. In ancient Mesopotamia, where the first cities took shape in the late fourth millenium B.C., the crucial development was the growing authority of priests and the increasing role of temple worship and temple structures in the life of agricultural communities. Temples absorbed numerous small clans into a new community. Priestly managers regulated the distribution of resources in the larger community, and, in the interests of the temple, favored the growth of specialized artisan, merchant, and farming activities outside the basic clan groups.

From the middle of the third millenium B.C. empires succeeded cities as the most extensive and complex form of social organization. Empires were regimes which dominated numerous smaller communities --families, tribes, cities, temples and regional states. They were commonly formed by conquerers who devised new means of military domination and administration to control their territories. Empires, however, must be understood not only as a type of political regime, but also as a form of society and culture. The formation of an empire had profound social consequences. Like the formation of the temple city, the formation of empires burst asunder the earlier forms of community. Empires detached individuals from the matrixes of clans and temples. To fight, to administer, to serve at court, to trade, to colonize distant lands, men were torn from their homes. Resources once committed to local communities were taxed or confiscated and redistributed in the interests of the state. Empires thus stimulated specialization of functions in society. Priests lost their administrative authority and became religious functionaries. Artisans and merchants were set free to work for the market. In turn, the increased scale of society, and the increased individualism implied by specialization and mobility, required new modes of cultural integration. Empires thus favored common languages, common laws, and common religions to forge bonds between ever more numerous and diverse individuals and communities over ever greater reaches of territory.

The empire type of society also fostered the development of new religious mentalities. In the ancient Middle East the archaic pantheon remained in force, but greater emphasis was placed upon the celestial gods and the supreme lord of the pantheon, for the gods of the wider heavens symbolized the larger and more impersonal order of the empire. At the same time, the breakdown of small communities allowed a sentiment of individuality to develop and to be expressed in the worship of personal gods with whom men stood in an intimate emotional relationship. The larger the empire, the greater the freedom of the individual; the wider the heavens, the more intimate the gods. Men assumed a personal relationship to the gods, and a personal responsibility for upholding the impersonal order of society and cosmos.

A late but crucial development in the religious mentality of the ancient Middle East was, of course, the birth of the monotheistic religions. Judaism, Zoroastrianism, Christianity, and later Islam represented a new conception of God, of man, and of human society. For these religions, the true reality was not within this world but transcended it utterly; man's destiny was not within the fabric of temple or empire but was, rather, his salvation beyond.

The new kind of religions not only represented a new mentality; they had profound social and political consequences. Archaic religion and early empire religions were cultic religions in the hands of specialists, closely identified with the political elite. The new religions, however, formed congregations, or churches, which assigned all believers an active religious role and united them as brothers in a common religious life regardless of other familial, tribal, communal, or political loyalties. In principle, the churches embraced mankind as a whole, though in fact they continued to represent the collective identity of particular peoples or regions. Thus, the formation of churches marked a differentiation of religious and political communities, of religious and political elites, and of secular and religious values.

By the seventh century, Middle Eastern empire societies, Roman and Sasanian, Christian and Zoroastrian, were characterized by agricultural and urban forms of economic production, citied societies, monotheistic religions and imperial regimes. Arabia was not part of these developments. For various reasons, primarily because of the prevailing climatic and ecological conditions, Arabia remained at a state of development which resembled the ancient rather than the evolved condition of the rest of the Middle East. In Arabia the primary communities--the bedouin clans --remained especially powerful, while urban, religous and royal institutions, though not absent, were relatively less developed. Whereas the empire world was predominantly agricultural, Arabia was primarily pastoral. While the empire world was citied, Arabia was the home of camps and oases. Whereas the empire peoples were committed to the monotheistic religions, Arabia was largely pagan. While the empire world was politically organized, Arabia was politically fragmented.

At the same time, Arabia was always in close contact with and strongly under the influence of the empire regions. There were no physical boundaries between Arabia and the Middle East proper. No rigid ethnic or demographic frontier isolated Arabia from the rest of the region; nor did great walls or political frontiers. Arabian peoples migrated slowly into the Middle East and themselves made up much of the population of the North Arabian desert and of Syria. Arabs in the fertile crescent region shared political forms, religious beliefs, economic connections, and physical space with the societies around them. Arabia was further connected to the rest of the region by itinerant preachers, who introduced monotheism into the largely pagan peninsula; by merchants who brought textiles, jewelry, and foodstuffs such as grain and wine into Arabia, and stimulated the taste for the good things of life; and by the political agents of the empire powers who intervened diplomatically and politically to extend their trading privileges, protect sympathetic religious populations, and advance their strategic interests. The Byzantines and the Sasanians disputed control of the Yemen, and both were active in creating spheres of influence in North Arabia. They also exported military technique to the Arabs. From both the Romans and the Persians the Arabs obtained new arms, and learned how to use mail coats of armor. They learned new tactics, and the importance of discipline. This seepage of military technique came through the Lakhmid and the Ghassanid states, sometimes through the enrollment of other Arabs as auxiliaries in the Roman or Persian armies, and sometimes through the unhappy experience of being repulsed by superior forces on the frontiers of the empires. This passing on of military ability was of great importance for the Arab conquests for it gradually equalized the quality of forces on either side of the frontier.

The civilization of the Middle Eastern empires was seeping into Arabia as happened everywhere where developed empires maintained frontiers with the politically and culturally less organized societies. Military expansion, trade, or missionary activities induced social change in still undeveloped societies. The need to mobilize the power and resources required to maintain political autonomy, or to carry on trade with empires, stimulated in less developed societies the same processes of stratification, specialization, and of community and identity formation by which the empires had themselves come into being. They generated in peripheral areas just those conditions which allowed for the eventual amalgamation of empire and outside areas into a single society.

The Basic Structures of Arabian Society

By the late sixth century, however, these inducements to evolutionary change had not gone so far as to absorb Arabia into the general civilization of the Middle East or to inspire in it the birth of a new civilization. The outbreak of the Arab movement and the subsequent mutual assimilation of Arabian and Middle Eastern empire societies seem to come suddenly in the early seventh century. How is this to be explained? The key to understanding this lies, I think, in a close study of the history within Arabian society of the relationship between the basic parochial small group bedouin society and the elements of urban, religious and royal institutions which represented the more evolved type of Middle Eastern society.

The nomadic pastoral clan was the most fundamental institution of Arabian society. It goes back at least to the beginning of camel domestication and the occupation of the Central Arabian desert in the thirteenth and twelfth centuries B.C. Bedouin peoples lived in tightly knit kinship groups, in patriarchal families formed of a father, his offspring and their families, living in a few tents. These families were further grouped into clans of about 100-300 tents which migrated together, owned their pasturage in common, and politically drew one line. Each clan was fundamentally an independent unit. All loyalties were absorbed by the group which acted as a collectivity to defend its individual members and to meet their responsibilities. If a member was harmed the clan would revenge him. If he did harm they would stand responsible with him for money, or indeed, for forfeiture of life. As a consequence of this ʿaṣabiyya, the bedouin clan regarded itself as a complete polity and recognized no authority outside of the group. The clans were led by a sheikh who was usually selected by the elders of the group from one of the aristocratic families, and always acted in accord with this council. He settled internal disputes according to the traditions of the group. His office was the embodiment of the clan tradition, and respect and willingness to follow his lead depended on the conviction of the tribesmen that the sheikh represented the true tradition, and that he epitomized the virtues of the clan. The sheikh had to be wealthy and generous to the needy and to his supporters, a man of tact and prudence, forebearing, resolute and practical, with the good judgment to avoid antagonizing the sensitive among his followers.

The mental universe of the bedouin was entirely defined by the clan. Poetry expressed his fundamental devotion to the prestige and security of the group; without the clan, the individual bedouin had no status, no place in the world, no life of his own. As Chelhod has pointed out, there is no way to express individuality or personality in the language of the bedouin. The term wajh, face, which applied to the chief, was a concept designating the persona of the group, rather than the individuality of the sheikh.

In certain conditions, these primary communities could be integrated into more inclusive, often stratified, bodies. At the points of contact between the fertile parts of Arabia and the desert, at oases, in Yemen, and in the northern margins where the Arabian desert touches the fertile crescent, the relationships between bedouin and sedentary peoples involved regular cooperation for the exchange of agricultural for pastoral products and for the organization of the caravan trade. Cooperation could lead to trade agreements and treaties among autonomous participants, and it could also lead to the formation of political confederations. Such confederations were formed by the domination of one tribe over others or through the recognition of an aristocratic family as leader of a confederation of clans. Though such groups did not show any of the ceremonial trappings or conceptions of political authority transcending the tribal or familial context which we usually associate with the development of full-fledged monarchies, their integrative functions were still important.

The integration of different groups could also occur on a religious basis. The formation of a ḥaram, a common sanctuary, allowed for worship of the same gods, economic exchange, sociable contact and political bargaining.

Only in the peripheral zones did monarchs and kingdoms, at times, prevail. In South Arabia, royal authority was first established about 1000 B.C. and lasted until Muslim times. In Yemen, the political elite was drawn from aristocratic tribes and controlled landed estates. Temples also had extensive holdings, while the common people were organized into clans which were obliged to provide agricultural and military services to the elites. Tributary and vassal tribes extended the power of the Yemeni kingdoms well into the interior of Arabia. In the north, kingdoms were less fully institutionalized. For example, the ancient Nabatean kingdom was ruled by a king who claimed a divinely given authority and had some centralized administration but really depended on the support of a coalition of clan and tribal chiefs.

Historical Tension and Change

The degree to which the individual bedouin clan was the predominant historical actor and the degree to which confederated or large scale societies were dominant was historically variable. The main factor regulating this balance was the degree to which sedentarized forms of economy and society imposed upon or were overwhelmed by pastoral forms. The history of Arabia was governed by the tension between the settled areas and the pastoral areas. From about 1000 B.C. until about A.D. 300 stable political organizations in the settled areas--Yemen, the Ḥijāz and on the northern periphery--successfully organized the interior of the peninsula and kept bedouin life subordinate to the agricultural and commercial economies of the settled kingdoms.

Settlement in Yemen dates back to the tenth century B.C. to the kingdoms of Saba', Maʿīn, Qitbān and Ḥaḍramawt, which were agricultural and trading societies active in the international spice and incense trade along the coasts of Arabia. By the fifth century B.C., Yemen was organized into kingdoms which had monarchical institutions, a stratified landed elite, a religious pantheon and organized temple worship of the gods, and encompassed agriculture, trading, and pastoral peoples. By 115 B.C., the Himyarites united the south. By A.D. 300 the union of southern kingdoms was still in force.

In the North Arabian desert, the first evidence of small kingdoms or confederations dates to the ninth and eighth centuries B.C. In the north, the influence of Middle Eastern empires and religions was important from earliest times. From the middle of the eighth to the middle of the seventh century B.C., Assyrian kings attempted to subdue the Arabs, secure the caravan routes, and extract tribute from the desert peoples, but permanent order was beyond their reach. By the early sixth century B.C., the Nabateans were in the course of forming a kingdom. Nabatean monarchical institutions and religious pantheon were derived from Syrian examples. By 587 B.C., they had replaced earlier peoples in North Arabia; by the end of the fourth century B.C., Petra was founded; and by the second century B.C. the Nabatean kingdom was fully established. By 85 B.C., the new kingdom had control of much of Jordan and Syria. Its business was the caravan trade with Yemen in the south and Egypt and Damascus and the coastal cities of Palestine. The kingdom lasted until A.D. 106 when it was destroyed by the Romans. Palmyra succeeded Petra, and extended monarchical control over the deserts and surrounding bordering areas. Urbanized capitals, elaborate temples, wide commercial networks, and strong Hellenistic culture marked Palmyran supremacy.

These kingdoms, northern and southern, maintained economic and political order in the peninsula as a whole, integrating the bedouins of the desert interiors into the political and cultural frameworks of the border states. The nomads functioned in peninsula-wide trade, linked settled places, and were absorbed in political coalitions sponsored by the northern and southern powers.

The phase of the border kingdoms did not last. The opening of sea routes for international trade in the first century B.C. proved to be a financial and political disaster for Yemen. Political power in the south weakened with the failure of overland routes; bedouin troops interfered in internal conflicts in South Arabia, pushed in against agricultural areas, and cut off Yemeni influence in the Ḥijāz and in central Arabia. In A.D. 328, Imru' al-Qays b. ʿAmr, king of the Arabs, took control of Najrān. In the north, Palmyra was destroyed in A.D. 271, the victim, as were the Nabateans, of Roman efforts to incorporate North Arabia directly into the empire. By the end of the third century, the grip of the old order was shattered.

However, the effort to re-establish the border kingdoms and to extend peripheral power throughout Arabia resumed. The period from early fourth century to the end of the sixth century represents a phase of efforts to re-establish the dominance of border kingdoms in the peninsula. From the beginning of the fourth century, the old kingdoms were being replaced by "middle period kingdoms" which tried to restore or to keep order in the desert and to protect trade and oasis cultivation. In Yemen, the Himyarite kingdom was restored, but not with effective powers of old. The lessened authority of kings, the increased power of "feudal" families and independent tribes, the decline of the economy, and the breakdown of the old cultural identity of the pagan archaic society under Jewish and Christian competition made it impossible fully to restore the old order. Still, in the fifth century, Yemeni influence extended over the bedouins of the Ḥijāz and central Arabia, mediated by the tribal confederation of Kinda. Kinda came into being in the fifth century and lasted about one hundred years. The authority of the Kinda family, however, was entirely personal and very limited. The confederation blossomed so long as the heirs to the chieftainship of Kinda were able men whom the bedouins of other tribes would respect, and the confederation managed to keep together on this uncertain basis for about four generations. No permanent state could be established without institutions of a more sophisticated and durable kind.

In the same period, the Yemen was severely disrupted by internal religious struggles and foreign invasion. In 512, Abyssinians invaded the country to restore Christian influence after the rise to power of a Jewish ruler, Dhū Nuwās. In 525 they succeeded in capturing control of the Yemen; in 535 they attacked central Arabia and in 570 penetrated the Ḥijāz. The South Arabian economy crumbled, and political unity was completely lost. In 572 the Sasanians took control of Yemen from the Abyssinians.

Similar efforts were made under Roman and Persian auspices to re-establish order on the northern borders of the Arabian desert. After the destruction of the kingdoms of Petra and Palmyra, Romans assimilated the old kingdoms as provinces of the empire and attempted to defend these provinces by recruiting Arab confederates to guard against other Arabs and against the Sasanians. The Banū Ṣāliḥ served as Roman auxiliaries throughout the fifth century and were replaced at the end of the century by the Ghassanids. The Ghassanids were an Arab Christian-Monophysite people. Their duty was to prevent the penetration of the bedouins from the desert into Syria and Palestine, to police and keep order on the frontiers between the Roman Empire and the desert, and to defend the Empire against the Persians and their clients. The Sasanian Empire also sustained a buffer state--the Kingdom of Lakhm--from A.D. 328 to A.D. 604. Along the border between Iraq and the desert the tribes of the area were organized into a new confederation under the leadership of the house of Lakhm whose capital was at Ḥīra, on the lower reaches of the Euphrates. Most of these peoples were Arameans and Nestorian Christians.

However, the new competitors were not so powerful as their predecessors. Kinda and Ghassan represented tribal confederations rather than kingdoms. While the Lakhmids at Ḥīra had an urban capital, a developed monarchy, differentiated from its tribal base of support, and were strongly supported by the Sasanians, they were severely hampered by Sasanian controls and Arab competition. In the north, by the end of the century, the Romans and the Persians both removed their vassals from power and attempted to absorb North Arabia into their respective empires. Ghassan was deprived of Roman backing in 584 and the Lakhmids were replaced by Sasanian governors in 602. The middle period confederations were destroyed by outside powers who could not replace even their ephemeral contributions to political and economic order.

In the sixth century, only Mecca stood out against the trend to political and social fragmentation. Mecca was a religious sanctuary, founded to serve the worship of the gods. From the fifth century, if not earlier, the shrine of Mecca, the Kaʿba, attracted pilgrims from all over Arabia. Mecca became the repository of the various idols and tribal gods of the peninsula, and the locus of an annual pilgrimage. The pilgrimage was also a period of truce which served not only for religious worship, but also for the arbitration of disputes, settlements of claims and debts, and of course, for trade. The Meccan fairs gave the Arabian tribes what sense they had of a common identity, and gave Mecca a kind of moral primacy in much of western and central Arabia.

These fairs were probably the origin of Mecca's commercial interests. The people called the Quraysh, who had taken control of Mecca in the fifth century, became a skilled retailing population, and in the sixth century international developments gave them a place in the spice trade as well. In the sixth century, difficulties with other routes diverted a good deal of traffic to the overland Arabian route. Byzantine sea power in the Red Sea and the Indian Ocean was on the decline. Piracy was endemic in the Red Sea. At the same time, the route from the Persian Gulf up the Tigris-Eurphrates rivers was harrassed by Sasanian exploitation, and was frequently disrupted by Lakhmid, Ghassanid, and Persian-Roman wars. By the middle of the sixth century, Mecca had become, as the heir to Petra and Palmyra, one of the important caravan cities of the Middle East. The Meccans carried from Yemen to Syria goods coming from Africa or the Far East--spices, aromatics, leather, drugs, cloth, and slaves--and imported into Arabia money, weapons, cereals and wine. The trade required treaties with Byzantine officials, and with the bedouins, to assure safe passage of the caravans, protection of water and pasture rights, and guides and scouts. Such arrangements eventually gave Mecca a sphere of political as well as commercial influence among the nomads and created a rough confederation of client tribes. With the decline of Abyssinia, Ghassan and Lakhm, a loose Meccan diplomatic hegemony in association with Tamim tribes was established. Mecca became crucial as the center of latter day efforts to maintain large scale economic and political organization in Arabia. Combining elements of tribal confederation with caravan city business organization and religious communal loyalties, Mecca attempted to maintain commercial and political order in the west and north of Arabia.

In most of Arabia, however, the failure of the border powers to restore effective control over the center of the peninsula resulted in progressive, but not uninterrupted, bedouinization. The discipline imposed by the settled peoples upon the desert weakened. Bedouin communities were set free of the political and commercial controls once exerted by the border Kingdoms. As early as the third century, bedouin groups made inroads upon the settled areas of South Arabia. By the fourth and fifth centuries and continuing into the sixth, large scale migrations of bedouin peoples in the North Arabian desert and to the margins of the fertile crescent were under way.

Within Arabia, violent conflict between clans and tribes became more frequent. Progressively, pastoral interests overcame agricultural interests. Bedouin migrations turned marginal regions in Yemen and on the borders of Iraq and Syria back to pasturage. The trade routes were increasingly harrassed by marauders, and the sedentary population drifted into pastoral activities as it became too difficult to sustain agricultural life and as commercial opportunities were lost. The "bedouinization of Arabia," of course, did not happen all at once. It was a gradual and cumulative process, shifting the ever-delicate balance between organized polities and clan society in favor of the latter. The predominant trend of the past centuries had been toward strengthening the bedouin clan, at the expense of economic prosperity and political security. Yet the tension between the interests of small groups and Mecca's political and religious confederacies remained high. The contrary trends would contribute explosively to the outbreak of the Arab conquests.

Bedouin Religion, Meccan Religion and Monotheism

The confrontation between strengthened small communities and trading and religious confederacy was reflected in the cultural as well as the political life of Arabia in the late sixth century. The religious culture of Arabia reflected the different levels of social organization of the bedouin tribe, the Meccan confederacy and the influence of the imperial powers. Just as the political realm was beset by the tension among different types of political and economic organization, cultural life was beset by incompatible visions of human life, human society, and conflicting concepts of the cosmos and the gods.

The poetic and religious culture of the clans remained a constant and fundamental element in bedouin life. By and large, the Arabian bedouin was a pagan, a polytheist, and an animist who believed that all natural objects and events were living spirits who could either be helpful or harmful to man. The universe of the Arabs was peopled with jinn--demons who had to be propitiated or controlled and defeated by the use of magic. By magical practices, the bedouin might determine his fate or coerce these forces, but he had no sympathetic relation with them. They were another tribe, not his own, though they invested his existence. The bedouins were also ancestor worshippers, worshippers of moon and star gods, and also of gods in the form of stones or trees placed in protective santuaries, or *ḥarams*. Otherwise the religiosity of the bedouin *did* not extend to the formation of a cult, nor to the cultivation of emotionally based spiritual capacities. Nor was his religion a philosophic or religious vision of the universe. Still, his religious beliefs were important in the bedouin's life. They expressed his sense of the sacred vested mysteriously in the plethora of forces which dominated the natural world and the being of man.

The religions of the politically more complex confederations and kingdoms were also pagan and polytheistic, but expressed a more differentiated concept of the divine, the natural and the human world. The tribal *ḥarams* or the temples of archaic kingdoms were devoted to regularized cultic worship. The Meccan Kaʿba, for example, the center of a pilgrimage, was the sanctuary of numerous gods arranged in a hierarchy. These gods were no longer simply identified with nature; they were considered to be distinct persons separate from the natural forces which, as willful beings, they controlled. Such gods had to be propitiated by sacrifices; one could communicate with them as persons, and the shrines in Mecca had a regular priesthood to assure their proper worship.

In an environment of shared sanctuaries, new conceptions of collective identity emerged. The annual trade and religious fairs at Mecca and other places of pilgrimage, which brought the numerous families and tribes of the peninsula together, focused the worship of tribal peoples upon common cults, allowed them to observe one another's mores, and standardized the language and customs by which they dealt with each other. Awareness of common religious beliefs and that the tradition of each clan was similar to the life ways of others, recognition of aristocratic tribes and families, agreed institutions regulating pasturage, warfare, and commerce, alliance and arbitration procedures, a poetic *koine* and poetic forms used by reciters throughout Arabia--marked the development of a collective identity transcending the individual clan. Von Grunebaum has argued that cultural integration in Arabia had proceeded so far as to create a single Arabian people, and Chelhod in *Sociologie de l'Islam* has argued the existence of an Arabian national culture, indeed an Arabian nation without a political state, before the time of Muḥammad.

In another sense there was a profound similarity

between the cultic confederation of Mecca and the fragmented life of the bedouin clans. The bedouin mentality and Meccan polytheism presented the same view of the person, society, and the universe. This view afforded no coherent conception of the human being as an entity. In ancient Arabic there is no single word corresponding to the soul. Qalb, rūḥ, nafs, wajh were the several terms in use; there was no conception of a self-conscious integrated personality. Also the plurality of the gods reflected and symbolized a fragmented view of the nature of society and of the forces which governed the cosmos. In the pagan view the self was without a center, society without wholeness, and the universe barren of overall meaning.

The monotheistic religions stood for something other. They were introduced into Arabia by foreign influences. Jewish and Christian settlements in Arabia, travelling preachers and merchants, the political pressure of the Byzantine empire and Abyssinia insinuated new ideas into the peninsula. By the sixth century, monotheism already had a certain vogue. Many non-believers understood the monotheistic religions; others, called ḥanīf in the Qur'ān, were believers in one God but not adherents of any particular faith. Others, in small oasis populations, had adopted Judaism or Christianity. Yemen and the border regions in the north, Lakhm and Ghassan, were officially Christian. Alongside of primary groups and pagan societies, Christianized societies reflecting larger Middle Eastern developments had formed. Their adherents were in the minority, and yet they were profoundly influential and, to many people, deeply appealing, both by the force of their teaching and by force of representing what was felt to be a more powerful, more sophisticated, and more profound civilization. The new religions taught that there was a single God who created the moral and spiritual order of the world; a God who made men individually responsible for their actions and faith; a God who made all men brethren, whatever their race or clan, and who made their salvation possible. Thus, they differed profoundly from the pagan in their sense of the unity of the universe and the meaningfulness of personalized experience. Whereas the one could only see a fragmented world composed of numerous, disorderly and arbitrary powers, the other saw a universe as a totality grounded in, and created and governed by a single being who was the source of both the material and spiritual order of the cosmos. Whereas the pagan world envisaged a society in which people were divided by clan and locality, each with its own community and its own gods, the monotheistic religions imagined a society in which common faith made men brothers in the quest for salvation. Whereas in the pagan view the human being was a concatenation of diverse forces without any moral or physical center a product of the fates, in the view of the monotheistic religions he was a moral, purposive creature whose ultimate object was redemption. In the view of the high religions, God, the universe, man, and society were part of a single and meaningful whole.

The monotheistic religions offered not only a new concept of the nature of man, God and the universe but also suggested new forms of communal and social organization. The possibilities were barely manifest, but in exceptional cases, such as the Christian community of Najrān, a new type of political organization in conjunction with new religious identifications was in evidence. Najrān was governed by three leading officials: a sayyid who acted as military commander and handled foreign relations; an ʿaqīb who dealt with internal affairs; and the bishop in charge of the church and the monastic communities. In Najrān, religion implied not only a different religious, but also a different political order, with recognition of the distinction between religious and secular authorities and communities. Similarly, Arabic speaking Nestorians of Ḥīra formed a congregation which coupled religious with tribal identity. Such communities were an image of developments which the higher religions inspired in Middle Eastern society at large and of the potentialities for further evolution within Arabian society itself.

Mecca was the center of diverse cultural tensions much as it was the focus of diverse political and social arrangements. Like the rest of Arabia, Mecca had its elements of conservative clan society, but it was also the focus of bedouin pilgrimage and of foreign religious influences. Mecca was therefore the most complex and heterogeneous place in Arabia. Here society had grown beyond the limitations of the clan and tribe and afforded some complexity of political and economic ties outside the confines of clan relationships. Mecca had a council of clans called a mala', which held a moral authority though it had no right to coerce any of the members or to enforce any council decisions without the co-operation of each individual clan. Mecca was also one of the few places to have a floating non-tribal population of individual exiles, refugees, outlaws, foreign merchants, and settlers. The very presence of different peoples, of different clans, of people who belonged to none of the clans, of foreigners, of people with diverse religious convictions, of people with differing views of life's purposes and values, moved Meccans away from the old tribal religions and moral conceptions. New conceptions of personal worth and social status, new social relationships were fostered by the development of a more complex society. On the positive side, the imperatives of commercial activity, and Arabian-wide contacts and identifications, set individual personalities free from the traditions of their clans, set free self-conscious, critical spirits, capable of experimenting with new values, who might conceive a universal God and ethical obligations. On the negative side, society suffered from economic competition, social conflict and moral confusion. Commercial activities brought social stratification on the basis of wealth, and morally unassimilable discrepancies between individual ambitions and the imperatives of clan loyalty. The Qur'ān condemned the displacement of tribal virtues by the ambition, greed, arrogance, and hedonism of the new rich.

Thus, as compared with the Middle East which had centuries earlier reached an equilibrium of cultural, religious and political institutions, Arabia was a transitional society. Elements of a regressive economy, strong parochial community life, and pagan religious mentality were balanced by tendencies toward political, cultural and religious unification and by the development of new forms of religious and political order. Widening mental horizons were coupled with resistance to new forms of sociocultural organization. Arabia was in ferment. A society in the midst of constructive political experiments was threatened by anarchy. Strong clan and tribal powers threatened to overwhelm the fragile forces of agricultural stability, commercial activity and political cohesion. Arabia was a society touched by imperial influences but without a central government, marked by the monotheistic religions but without embracing churches, transparent to the radiation of Middle Eastern ideas but not permeated by them. Arabia had yet to find its place in the Middle Eastern world.

The Conquests and the Assimilation of Arab Peoples into Empire Society

From this vantage, we can interpret the meaning of

the Arab conquests and their place in the evolution of Arabian society. They no longer appear as a sudden, unexpected, or accidental development, but as one which rose directly out of the conflict of different forms of religious, social and political organization in Arabia. In previous centuries the influence of the Middle East upon Arabia created conditions favorable to the development of elements of large-scale socio-political organization and for the development of monotheistic religious life in Arabia. Arabian society had reached a stage of development which brought intense political, social and moral conflict among alternative political and religious possibilities. With conflict came the potentiality for revolutionary change, a potentiality realized through the inspiration and leadership of the Prophet Muḥammad. Through the revelations of the Qur'ān, and his career as moral exemplar and politician, Muḥammad found the solution in principle to the conflicts within Arabian society. He could begin to integrate the otherwise anarchic small clans into a larger confederacy on the basis of religious loyalty, build a state structure through which political and economic order might eventually be achieved, and resolve the conflict of bedouin familial and Meccan commercial values in a new religious point of view. Muḥammad fused tribal society, the monotheistic religious mentality, with religious community, trading confederacy and political organization to create a new society built upon a "church"-like religious community and incipient imperial organization. Out of the manifold elements of the old order Muḥammad helped to generate a new dispensation for Arabia which gave it an institutional and cultural structure, parallel to, and on a par with, that of the larger Middle East. Under the aegis of Muḥammad, Arabia became a Middle Eastern type society in which parochial and tribal groups were integrated into a monotheistic community.

The Arab conquests were the result of the formation of the new community. They began as a result of the Muslim effort to build an Arabian-wide political and religious regime, and to impose its vision of the human and social order on Arabia. There is a good deal of uncertainty about how early and how clearly this objective was formulated. Muḥammad himself attempted to extend his religious and political influence throughout the Ḥijāz; Watt argues that his ambition extended to the Christian tribes on the borders of Syria; Shoufani in a recent book on the Riddah argues that from the time of the capitulation of Mecca, Muḥammad aspired to an Arabian and Syrian empire. In any case, within a year after Muḥammad's death, the leaders of the new community had decided to extend its boundaries beyond the tribes who had already submitted to Muḥammad's authority and to incorporate the whole of Arabia under the rule of Medina and Mecca. Whether the attacks on Syria and Iraq were decided in advance or whether they were a natural outgrowth of the fighting in Arabia--the result of splinter movements of tribes seeking to compensate themselves elsewhere for losses in Arabia --whether planned, or whether determined by events and responses to events, the construction of a new commercial, religious, and then political confederation in the Ḥijāz in disequilibrated and unsettled times, and in a vacuum of established powers, led to the conquest of much of the Middle East. The conquests began in reconnaissance and booty raids, but the early victories opened the way for a great flood of peoples to enter the fertile crescent, riding on the wave of initial successes. With the defeat of the Byzantine and the Sasanian Empires, a frontier between populations broke down; Arabian people moved into the lands of the Middle East.

Thus the conquests rose out of the process of religious and political consolidation in Arabia. In turn they set the stage for two crucial, interconnected developments. One was the completion of the historic process of transforming Arabian society and assimilating it into the larger society of the Middle East; the other was the reciprocal integration of Middle Eastern peoples into a new political and religious identity which marks the origin of a new Middle Eastern civilization in the wake of the nomadic conquests.

The first part of this double process--the integration of Arabian peoples into the general Middle Eastern society--was a function of the conquests and the migration of masses of Arabians into the fertile crescent and other parts of the empire Middle East. The migrations created two new arenas for the assimilation of Arabian peoples into the citied, religious and imperial institutions of the empire societies. In the courts of the Arab caliphs, Arabian and Middle Eastern political institutions and ideologies would be integrated, the Islamic religion bolstered and its repertoire of expression expanded by the assimilation of previous religious attainments of the Middle East, and a new cultural style, literary, artistic and scientific, elaborated on the basis of Middle Eastern precedents. The process by which a distinctive

Islamic cultural style, yet one which was based upon the past achievements of Middle Eastern civilizations, took shape has been frequently described and does not require further attention here. But there is another aspect of the integration of Arabian people into Middle Eastern society and culture which is less fully appreciated. In the great centers of Arab settlement, especially such garrison towns as Baṣra, Kūfa, and Fusṭāṭ, bedouin peoples were finally integrated into the general Middle Eastern society. They were citified, truly instructed in monotheistic religion and subjected to imperial regimes. In the villages and towns which the Arabs settled, the institutions of a new mass society were forged. In these settlements the pressures generated by sedentarization and urbanization, by the teachings of Islam, and by contact with other Middle Eastern peoples weakened the old tribal society, fostered new group and communal structures, intensified the stratification of society and the division of labor, and brought about the Islamic cultural developments which together amounted to a new stage in the history of Arab society.

Baṣra is the best known example of these developments. In Baṣra the traditional structure of the bedouin clan was disrupted. The exigencies of settlement and the requirements of military and fiscal administration led to the organization of the Arab settlers into new groups, which were clans and tribes in name only. To make uniform regiments and pay units, big clans were subdivided and smaller ones combined. The composition of these military units was also changeable. Newcomers had to be integrated into older units; with the settlement of Marw in 681, the remaining groups had to be reorganized. Clan solidarity was disrupted; new groups were created; only very small units of the older sort remained viable.

Another source of pressure on bedouin society was the breakdown of the barriers between the Arab and non-Arab populations of Iraq. Baṣra was flooded with non-Arabs. As the Arabs made use of defeated armies to recruit manpower for further advances, Iranian regiments were enlisted en masse. Arab governors brought back troops from the east to serve as police and bodyguards. Mercenaries came to the towns looking for work and wanting to throw in their lot with the conquerors. So did scribes, tax-collectors, clerks, estate managers, and even village chiefs and landowners. In addition, merchants in long distance trade and menial workers (including bath attendants, weavers, and spinners) also came to Baṣra; finally, itinerant construction and naval workers, fugitive peasants, migrant laborers, and slaves flooded the city. This non-Arab population was extremely diverse. Aside from Indians, Malays, Gypsies, Negroes, Turks, who came in small numbers from remote areas, the non-Arab population was mainly Iranian and Aramean, Nestorian Christian, with some Jews. Many kept their religions, but others converted to Islam. Some were taken into Arab clans as mawālī, others were not.

The absorption of this migrant population had important repercussions on the clans. As they absorbed mawālī, clans became less and less kinship groups and more and more political and economic groups built around a kinship core. In some cases, the mawālī even began to outnumber the Arabs. Not only was kinship weakened, but class distinctions came to be introduced. The mawālī themselves constituted an inferior class; furthermore, they affected the stratification of Arab clans. The gap between aristocratic and other clans widened as the influx of mawālī changed the relative power of the clans. For example, one tribe, the Tamīm, acquired former Persian cavalry units as its clients, while another, the Ḥanẓala, had slave laborers and weavers as its clients.

Within clans, the emergence of class distinctions was even more profound. We can see a growing differentiation on a class basis between the sheikh and the rest of the tribesmen. The sheikhs had always had higher status within the group, but in the city their administrative and military functions and other opportunities to prosper widened the gulf between the chiefs and their followers. Tribal chiefs became landowners, sometimes of lands granted to them by the caliphate, and formed a new aristocracy, taxed at favorable rates, whose interests diverged from the general interest of the city Arabs in a uniform revenue administration and in a steady supply of income for stipends. Lists of the residences or palaces of notables and tribal leaders, apart from the dwellings or quarters of their clans, and lists of agricultural estates owned privately by the chiefs and not as part of the collective pasture reserves of the clan, suggest that the notables were living apart and enjoying wealth, privileges, and a style of life not consistent with the ancient bedouin mores. Sedentarization broke up the social unity of the tribes. Class distinctions emerged in what once had been cohesive and integrated groups. Tribal society was breaking down in favor of a society stratified on the basis of class and power.

Under pressures of urbanization and contact with settled peoples, Arab society was also evolving into a more specialized, urbanized occupational structure. In Baṣra the Arabs had created a camp town, but settlement soon made it an important manufacturing and trading center. New international routes connected Baṣra with Iran and India. Baṣra was also a nodal point for trade with the Ḥijāz and Yemen. The city became a center for the importation and exportation of oriental luxuries, weapons, and money; also a city of regional importance in manufacturing, especially of cloth goods, and in banking, as a center for money changing. With the retirement of Arab townspeople from active military duty at the end of the seventh century, the working and commercial population must have been strengthened. Similarly, the new religion of Islam offered opportunities for social mobility through what we may call careers in religion--teaching, scholarship, and legal administration. While Arab clans remained the crucial unit of society, Islam, urbanization and interaction with non-Arab peoples converted a clan-based society into a more highly differentiated urban type of society.

These tendencies point to a post-conquest evolution of Arab society which repeated the process of social change by which previous Middle Eastern societies--stratified, specialized societies, culturally identified by allegiance to a monotheistic religion--had been established. The first century of Islam brought about just those changes which mark the emergence of an empire type society. In this period we see the formation of Arab-Islamic political institutions, the progressive differentiation of political and religious life, the birth of a new religious culture, and the spawning of a stratified, occupationally specialized mass society in an urban setting.

One further aspect of this evolution should be mentioned, though we cannot explore it--that is the reciprocal influence of Arab peoples upon the Middle East as a whole. The formation of an "Arab-empire type society" did not occur within Arabia itself, in isolation from the rest of the Middle East, but within the former empire provinces in conjunction with the reciprocal assimilation of Middle Eastern peoples into a shared Arabic and Islamic culture. The overall effect of the historic transformation of Arabian peoples under the influence of Middle Eastern society was not to generate a new and parallel civilization, but to merge the Arabian and Middle Eastern peoples into a single new civilization. Just as Arabian peoples were assimilated into the urbanized world of the Middle East, they in turn absorbed Middle Eastern peoples into the cultural identity of Islam and the political affiliation of the caliphate. In the formation of a new civilization the Arabs were absorbed into the economic and social structures of the Middle Eastern empire societies while lending to those societies a new cultural and political identity. From this point of view, the Arab conquests were not a "barbarian" invasion but a crucial moment in the process of interaction between peoples by which an "outside" people acquired the institutional and cultural forms--not the particular style--of empire peoples, and in the course of doing so forged, in conjunction with empire peoples, a new form of civilization.

Summary and Conclusion

What is the significance of the Arab conquests? What do they tell us about the relationship between outside and empire peoples? My argument has been that the case of Arabia and the Middle East is one in which outside peoples were in the process of an historic evolution which paralleled and recapitulated the historical sequences by which the empire civilizations themselves had come into being. In the course of this transformation, the influence of empire peoples upon outside peoples was a crucial factor. In Arabian history this influence manifested itself in the development of archaic political, commercial, and religious institutions and later in the diffusion of the higher religions through the peninsula. In Arabian history, however, the process of induced social change was never completed, but led rather to an historical crisis, the crisis of the sixth century in which the several unintegrated levels of Arabian society--bedouin groups, archaic religious and commercial communities, and monotheistic religious culture--were fused into a new and into the first Arabian-wide society. This new society conquered the empires and thereby moved the terrain of its own internal evolution into more intimate contact with the empire peoples. In the new Arab settlements, the process of social change, induced by Islamic religious identifications, and by contact with empire peoples, led to the integration of tribes into larger communities, the specialization and stratification of society, and the differentiation of religious and political institutions so that Arabian society at last acquired all of the institutional features of empire civilization. In the course of these developments a reciprocal Arab influence upon empire peoples led to changes which served to fuse Arabian and empire peoples into a single civilization.

At the same time, it is worth noting that no evolutionary development is ever complete. Each stage bears with it the marks of past levels of organization. In Arab-Islamic society, the power of the family and the clan remained potent both as a social institution and a cultural ideal. Other features of archaic society and culture remain embedded in the new order. The later history of Islamic societies, like the history of Arabia, may also be described in terms of the imminent tensions between successive levels of institutional and cultural development. In the maturation of a society, as in the growth of a person, the past is never lost, but lives on as an active force embedded in the present.

4

CONQUERORS AND CONQUERED: IRAN

M.G. Morony

It seems most appropriate to center a discussion of the relationships between the conquerors and the conquered in Iran following the Arab-Muslim conquest on three related conceptual issues which are embedded in this subject.[1] While these issues do not necessarily exhaust the possibilities they may have some application to other parts of the early Islamic empire. In the first place, the assumption of a relationship between conquerors and conquered implies contacts which ultimately served as the basis of mutual assimilation. Secondly, such contacts occurred according to differing modes of interaction among the people involved which depend, thirdly, on the establishment and recognition of the categories into which people are divided for the purpose of describing their interaction. It is best to approach these issues in reverse order although they will remain somewhat interwoven.

The first kind of category which presents us with difficulties is geographical. What do we mean by Iran in the seventh and eighth centuries? In practice the use of this term is perhaps even less definite than Syria and would appear to include those parts of the Islamic empire north and east of Iraq which included the conquered Sasanian empire plus parts of Transoxania and Afghanistan, to say nothing of northern India, which were not parts of the Sasanian empire but were incorporated into the Islamic empire. While an Iranian cultural region may thus be defined as the entire <u>mashriq</u> neither the geographical region of the Iranian plateau nor the territory of the modern state corresponds to the ethnic Iranian presence in this period. There were Iranians outside of Iran such as the Soghdians in Transoxania, Hephthalites in Afghanistan, Kurds and Persians in Iraq, Persians and Soghdians in the Ḥijāz, and a general post-conquest diaspora of Persians in the western parts of the Islamic empire. Nor was the Iranian plateau inhabited exclusively by

Persians. The Arabs established relationships with non-Persians such as Armenians, Indians, Indonesians, Qufīchīs, and Turks, and with other non-Persian Iranians such as Daylamis and the "Kurds" of Fars, Khūzistān, the Jibāl and Azerbaijan.

While the use of ethnic categories yields a set of bilateral relationships among Arabs and the various non-Arab peoples in Iran, religious distinctions are equally useful in defining relationships in post-conquest Iran. Ideally relations among Muslims and non-Muslims should include all the other religions present in Iran: Magians of every kind, Manichaeans (including Mazdakis), Buddhists, pagans, Jews and Christians. One should also acknowledge regional differences within the Iranian plateau which tended to be increased by local terms of capitulation at the time of the conquest and by differing modes of Arab settlement in different parts of Iran.

One also suspects that behind the categories of conquerors and conquered lurks the assumption that they are equivalent to rulers and subjects, Arabs and non-Arabs, or Muslims and non-Muslims. Perhaps this was less true in Iran than in other parts of the early Islamic empire and Persians participated as members of the ruling/conquering society in three different ways. First, Persian defectors, nobles, volunteers, mawālī, and conscripts were present in Muslim armies. Units of the Sasanian army from western Iran participated in the conquest of the eastern provinces of the Sasanian empire and in pushing the borders of the Islamic empire further east. By the eighth century non-Arab elements were being used to balance and neutralize Arab forces in Umayyad armies, and to swell the size of armies for conquest. Qutayba ibn Muslim was joined by the dahāqīn of north-eastern Iran and formed a special unit of ten thousand archers from the Soghdian, Hephthalite, and Khurāsānī nobility. There was also a unit of mawālī in the army by this time, but the conscripts levied for Qutayba in Khurāsān, Bukhārā and Khwārizm by the local dahāqīn for seasonal service were present in the army as subjects and as an aspect of their servitude.

Secondly, local Sasanian notables survived as part of the ruling class of the early empire by virtue of agreements they made with the Muslim Arabs to submit at the time of the conquest in return for paying tribute at Nihāvand, Iṣfahān, and briefly at Rayy in the Jibāl, at Zarang in Sīstān, at Nīshāpūr, Nasa, Abivārd, Ṭūs, Marv, Marv-al-Rūd and Herat in Khurāsān, and at Bukhārā in Soghdia. The tributary agreements recognized and perhaps increased the powers that local notables exercised over the rest of the population. They served as intermediaries between the Arab military organization and the tax-paying subject population, assessing and collecting taxes according to the Sasanian system in their own districts and turning them over to the Arabs with a minimum of interference. As non-Muslim members of the ruling class, by the eighth century they were practising tax discrimination against native converts to Islam and collecting taxes from demilitarized Arabs at Marv. Collaboration with the Arabs could be vindictive and at Iṣfahān, where the defense had been weak and divided at the time of the conquest, the local notable who came to terms with the Arabs claimed the people of the city deserved what he had done with them.[2] Arab governors usually collected taxes through such local authorities and as early as 39/659 we hear of widespread tax revolt in the Jibāl, Fars, and Kirmān.[3]

Non-Arabs also served as administrators and advisors for Arab generals and governors: people such as al-Ḥasan al-Baṣrī who was secretary for the governor of Khurāsān and set up the dīwān of kharāj for the governor of Sīstān,[4] or Ḥayyān al-Nabaṭī and his son Muqātil in Khurāsān.[5] In general, unlike the dahāqīn, mawālī who acted as administrators did so as part of the central administration, were supposed to be part of Arab tribal society, and operated without any roots in the local population.

While Persians might thus be part of the ruling class, conversely, Arabs were not always rulers but might be rebels such as the tribal bands that ravaged Sīstān during the first civil war, or most often the Khawārij. During the Umayyad period Khārijī activities in southern Iran were an extension of conflicts in Iraq into Khūzistān, Fars, Iṣfahān, Kirmān, and Sīstān. Khārijī rebels might catalyze local feelings of resentment against taxation and central control, often enjoyed support in rural areas, and were sometimes joined by native non-Muslims and mawālī attracted by their equalitarian outlook and regard for the rights of non-Muslims. The brief independence they enjoyed meant that taxes were spent locally, but also made them liable to double taxation and government reprisals. Kirmān, which served as a refuge and restaging area for the Khawārij during the second civil war, is a case in point. In 68/687-8 the Azraqī rebel Qaṭarī extorted money from the local Kirmānīs to finance his return to Khūzistan and is said to have "devoured the land."[6] Natives who got involved with the Khawārij could find themselves compromised when the government forces eventually arrived, so they might go over to the government side at the proper moment for the sake of expediency and help to suppress the Arab rebels.

Local opposition to control by the central government of the Islamic empire was also expressed in isolated risings and disorders such as those at Istakhr in 659-60, Badhghis, Herat and Pushang in 661-2, or at Nīshāpūr and Zarang during the first civil war. Sometimes they were led by the local notables as was the revolt of the marzban Qārin in Khurāsān in 653 that spread to Qūhistān, Nīshāpūr, and Balkh. Many of these revolts were part of the conquest itself and amounted to attempts to throw off the tributary arrangements local notables had concluded with the Arabs and perhaps regarded as only temporary expedients. Several places had to be subdued by the Arabs twice or more before a final settlement was reached but in the Arabic sources the opponents of the Muslims in places that had once agreed to tribute are described as "rebels." Local revolts were also more likely to occur when the Arabs were proccupied with their own conflicts, especially during the two civil wars of the seventh century, and the attempt to throw off Arab Muslim rule was repeated in Khurāsān in the 680s.

Rebellion, raiding and baditry were the usual expressions of opposition to any control by the rural tribes of the mountains and deserts such as the Qufīchīs of Baluchistan who assisted refugees from Kirmān. Kurds were likely to take advantage of any disorder. In 18/639 the Kurds of Fars attacked Hurmuzān when he was defending Ahwāz against the Muslims and then, in 23/644 they joined the revolt of Fayrūz in Khūzistān against Abū Mūsā. In 38/658-9 they joined the Khawārij in the mountains of Rāmhurmuz along with the peasants (ʿulūj) and in 77/696 when the Kurds around Ḥulwān and other local people joined the Khawārij the Kurds occupied Ḥulwān. It is not surprising to find Khārijī attitudes surviving among the Kurds as a consequence of such involvement. At the beginning of the eighth century the Kurds of Fars also joined Ibn al-Ashʿath after he had been driven out of Iraq.[7]

Some regions were never permanently controlled but offered sources of booty and slaves through raiding the territory of autonomous or independent Iranian rulers. The Daylimis of Gilan were raided from Qazvīn and Azerbaijan while the pagans of Ghūr provided slaves for the markets of Herat and Sīstān. The Soghdian captives taken by Qutayba at Bukhārā were taken back to Marv. The terms of submission for most places in Iran included the provision that the inhabitants were not to be enslaved, and while defeated, captured Khawārij might be enslaved, most slaves came from the advancing edge of the conquest as it moved east and north. Slaves were part of the booty and the traffic moved them west and south, first to the frontier settlements and garrisons, then to the amṣār in Iraq where Khurāsānī and Sīstānī captives were taken, and even to the Ḥijāz where Soghdian captives were taken in the 680s. The fate of such captives and the relation between master and slave varied widely. Some became administrators, such as Ṣāliḥ ibn ʿAbd al-Raḥmān whose parents were taken captive at Nashrudh in Sīstān in 653 and who converted the tax accounts in Iraq from Persian into Arabic as the secretary of Ḥajjāj and then rose to be ʿāmil of the Sawād in the reign of Sulaymān (715-17). Others became military slaves. ʿUbaydallāh b. Ziyād, who raided Paikand and Ramitin in the territory of Bukhārā in 673-4, kept four thousand (or two thousand) prisoners as his own slaves and settled them in Baṣra as a corps of archers.[8] In tragic contrast to this is the fate of the eighty Bukhāran hostages taken back to Medina by Saʿīd ibn ʿUthmān in the reign of Yazīd I (680-3) where he forced them to do agricultural labor so they killed him and committed mass suicide.[9]

The treatment of captive women and children varied just as widely. Most became domestic servants and concubines in Muslim Arab households, but we are told of two women belonging to the highest Persian aristocracy taken captive in Khurāsān in 37/657-8 who were entertained by a dihqān in Iraq who fed them from golden dishes on silken cloth (freed them?) and returned them to Khurāsān.[10] The treatment of the Soghdians at Paikand again stands out in contrast, perhaps because of the stiffer resistance the Arabs met in Transoxania. About 706 Qutayba's amīr at Paikand, Warqāʿ ibn Naṣr, is said to have appropriated the two beautiful daughters of one of the residents for himself and the distraught father's attack on the governor set off a revolt there. To suppress it Qutayba loosed his troops on the town, everyone capable of fighting was killed and the rest enslaved. But the merchants of Paikand who had been off trading with China at the time of the revolt were able to ransom their women, children, and relatives after they returned.[11]

Muslim Arabs also interacted with the native population in Iran as neighboring settlers and landowners in towns and villages. At first the main mode of Arab settlement was the establishment of military colonies as garrisons in fortified administrative districts or new suburbs of existing cities, or in villages on their outskirts. Arab military enclaves were often segregated from the local population for the purposes of security, defense and control and interactions between them on a non-official level were to some extent affected by whether the Arabs confined themselves to a walled citadel district as at Rayy or Bukhārā or were dispersed throughout a city and its environs as at Nīshāpūr, Marv, Balkh, or Iṣfahān. But even where Arab garrisons were settled outside of cities, in new suburbs or old villages, they tended to be separated from the native population, as at Qumm where one of the villages was garrisoned in 644, or might be pulled back within the city for greater protection and control, as the Iraqi tribesmen settled in villages around Balkh were moved inside the city in 725. Initial settlement patterns were overlaid by the migration of successive groups of Iraqi Arabs sent to Iran as military reinforcements or who came as the relatives and retinues of new governors.

The other main type of settlement was the result of the unofficial migration of Iraqi Arabs most of whom established themselves as land-owners in western Iran. By the early eighth century, especially after the failure of the revolt of Ibn al-Ashʿath, Iraqis fleeing the oppression of Ḥajjāj sought refuge and new economic opportunities in Iran.

Arab settlers interacted with the native population in a number of ways. Where Arabs settled in new suburbs and villages and brought new land under cultivation the disruption was minimal although they had the effect of reorienting urban life to new internal centers, increasing the size of cities, and competing for resources, especially water, for agriculture. In some places, such as Kirmān and Bukhārā, the native population was actually displaced to provide houses and lands for the Arab settlers. At Bukhārā, where the Arab garrison settled inside the town, it was the natives who had to give up their houses to them who built a new suburb outside the city.[12] At Kirmān many people fled to Mukrān, Sīstān, or overseas at the time of the conquest in 650 leaving their dwellings and lands to be divided among the Arabs who settled there, cultivated the land and paid the tithe on it.[13] Such displacement sent a reverse current of Persian emigrants to the Arab garrison cities in Iraq.

In addition to whatever disruption they caused, the establishment of a new class of Arab landlords in western Iran set up complex relationships between themselves and their Persian neighbors and a landlord-tenant relationship between themselves and the native Persian peasants on their estates. Land was acquired in a number of ways. At Kirmān abandoned lands were seized while at Qazvīn lands were assigned for the support of the five-hundred-man garrison established there in 645. New Arab landlords were also created by the land-grants made by ʿUbaydallāh ibn Ziyād for governors in Iran about 680. When Sharīk ibn al-Aʿwar al-Ḥārithī was appointed governor of Kirmān ʿUbaydallāh granted him land there and likewise granted Kathīr ibn Shihāb many villages from the state domains in the Jibāl when he was made governor of that province. Kathīr built his fortress in Dīnawar and four generations later his great-great-grandson Zuhra is said to have held many estates at Masabadhan.[14] Some land was purchased from its native owners at Qazvīn by later settlers, at Qumm, and in Azerbaijan where Arab settlers from Iraq and Syria bought land from Persians and acquired villages the inhabitants of which became their tenant farmers.[15] Sharīk sold the land granted to him in Kirmān to Ḥarb b. Ziyād from Baṣra while Idrīs b. Maʿqil al-ʿIjlī, a sheep-trader and preparer of perfumes, settled with his relatives at a village near Hamadhān in the 730s where they used their wealth to acquire many villages.[16] Finally, land was acquired by gift as at Qumm where the Persian notable, Yazdanfādhār, who owned the village of Abarishtjan gave land to the Ashʿarī Arab settlers from Kūfa in the early eighth century.[17]

Qumm actually provides the clearest example of the kinds of interactions and tensions that developed between the new Arab settlers and landowners and their Persian neighbors. The hospitality extended to the first settlers wore thin as new settlers arrived and the development of their lands by the Arabs competed for local resources. The Arabs are said to have constructed over twenty new underground water channels and began to introduce new crops which led to a dispute with the people of neighboring villages over the Arabs' share in the water rights. The issue was decided by force. The Arabs destroyed their neighbors' dams, forced them to concede one third of the water to the settlement at Qumm and emerged from the conflict in control of the distribution of river water and owning a majority of the channels.

Economic interactions were not limited to landlord-tenant relationships or the purchase and sale of land. They also included the collection of taxes and the taking of booty that served to redistribute the wealth, concentrate it in the hands of the new ruling and landholding class, and to a certain extent diverted some of the wealth of the Iranian plateau to the Arab garrison cities of Iraq. Arabs were also involved in trade with the native population either to purchase provisions for the army (ʿUbaydallāh ibn Abī Bakra used the opportunity for profiteering as governor of Sīstān in 697) or to engage in the international transit trade through the Soghdian merchants at Marv.[18] While it is natural to think of the native population as the sellers and the Arabs as the buyers in most transactions, Arabs seem to have made their contribution to organizing economic activity. We hear of a trading-post on the eastern frontier of Sīstān that was set up by the Bakr ibn Wā'il that was so valuable that Bakr and Tamīm clashed over its control a total of twenty-four times during the second civil war. Likewise, Idrīs ibn Maʿqil brought his skills as a perfumist and sheep-trader to Hamadhān. Commercial transactions also led to creditor-debtor relationships between the natives and Arabs that could have differing consequences. The Soghdian merchants who loaned money to finance Bukayr's expedition against Transoxania from Marv in 696 were later given special treatment by him because of the great favor he owed them. In contrast there is the story that Idrīs ibn Maʿqil once attacked and throttled a merchant who owed him money.[19]

By all indications the Arabs who settled in Iran tended to assimilate to the local population once they abandoned their exclusively military status and entered into the local economic life. The Arabs who settled at Kirmān were lost to the army, but in most places assimilation was mitigated by the preservation of an Arab identity and Arab genealogies by the settlers even though their descendants came to speak Persian. The result was a mixed but still fairly distinct society. In the tenth century Yaʿqūbī describes towns in the western Jibāl such as Hulwan, Saimara, and Sirawan inhabited by mixed populations of Arabs, Persians and Kurds but where everyone spoke Persian.[20]

Apart from considerations based on ethnic distinctions among Arabs and non-Arabs interactions among Muslims and non-Muslims also illustrate post-conquest relationships. Normally, at first, all non-Muslims paid tribute but suffered losses in varying degrees to Islam either through captivity or conversion.

Muslims had already dealt with Magians in Yaman

and Bahrayn as well as Iraq by the time they reached the Iranian plateau, and it had been decided that they were eligible to pay tribute in return for protection just as Jews and Christians were although they had no revelation or prophet. As a result of contacts with Magians in Iraq the legal scholars also eventually decided that a Muslim should not marry Magian women or eat animals slaughtered by Magians. But from a religious point of view Magians as such were largely ignored at the time of the conquest. The priesthood was not recognized as representing a religious community and there was little interference in the cult. The only specific arrangement made at the time of the conquest was the Muslim agreement not to interfere with the dances of the people of Shiz in Azerbaijan.[21] In some places fire-temples were converted into mosques as the result of Arab settlement and Magian evacuation or, later on, as a result of conversion by the local population.

The first serious attempt at suppression, intervention, and apparently even conversion of the Magians came in the reign of Muʿāwiya when Ziyād sent his kinsman ʿUbaydallāh ibn Abī Bakra of Baṣra to destroy the fire-temples in Fars and Sīstān, confiscate their wealth, and suppress the priesthood. He seems to have been only successful in Fars where he destroyed the fire-temple of Kariyan near Darabjird while the hirbadh of Sīstān escaped with his temple at Karkuya intact.[22] Later we hear that Ḥajjāj destroyed the fire-temple in a Magian village at Qumm.[23] Other extinctions occurred even later. The fire continued to burn at a pre-Islamic temple at Idhaj on the border between Khūzistān and Iṣfahān until the reign of al-Rashīd (786-809).[24] Still later suppressions were carried out by the Turk Barun at the turn of the tenth century who destroyed the pre-Islamic fire-temple at al-Fardajan near Iṣfahān in 895,[25] and destroyed the last fire-temples of the village of Jamkaran at Qumm in 901.[26] This means, by the way, that there were Magians at all of these places up to the time of destruction and even afterwards we hear of Magians venerating the sites where fire-temples had been.

The loss of state support and the liability to intermittant persecution brought by the Muslim conquest had several consequences for Magians. First was the loss of members through conversion to Islam or Christianity. There seems to have been an official attempt at converting Magians in Sīstān by persuasion and force in the reign of Muʿāwiya, and we are told that "many" Magians became Muslims there.[27]

However, the practical consequences of conversion for Magians included changes in inheritance patterns, the abandonment of exposure for the burial of the dead, and the abandonment of endogamy (although traces of it survive in Islamic literature).[28] So severe was the change that all indications are that conversions from Magianism to Islam were minimal in the Umayyad period and for some time afterwards. Secondly, the beginning of persecution and the destruction of part of the structure of the cult and priesthood in the time of Muʿāwiya may be linked to a Magian eschatological calculation that would make the year 661 the end of the tenth millenium, marked by calamities and awaiting the arrival of a savior.[29] Thirdly, the attack on the fire-temples in the time of Ziyād may have been responsible for the decline of the priestly order of hirbadhs who had controlled the cult in the late Sasanian period, allowing the mobadhs to recapture it although it is not entirely clear whether this is to be connected to the suppression of Zurvanism and the rise of the "new orthodoxy" of Mazdaism. The conversion of urban notables and dihqāns was also a factor in the decline of Zurvanism while the mobadhs emerged as leaders of the Magians because they kept their hold over members in smaller towns and villages.[30] Nevertheless, the decline of the hirbadhs and the rise of the mobadhs seems connected to the gradual extinction of pre-Islamic fires and the export of the fires of Shiz and Kariyan (which must have been restored after the time of Muʿāwiya) to other fire-temples.[31] The escape of the hirbadh at Karkuya, likewise, meant the survival of fire-priests there down to the eleventh century making the detailed description of their cult by Qazwīnī possible.[32] Lastly, the treatment of Magians may have been a factor in the emigration of Persians from Iran in the Umayyad period.

Judging by conditions in the tenth century either the decline of Magianism and losses through conversion following the conquest have been exaggerated or Magians experienced a spectacular revival in the eighth and ninth centuries. In the tenth century Magians with fire-temples, some of them said to be pre-Islamic, are to be found all over Iran and in regions to the east. The temple at Shiz in Azerbaijan remained an important center. There was a large number of Magians in Iraq and a monumental fire-temple on the west bank of the Tigris opposite Madā'in. There were a few Magians in Khūzistān with several fire-temples at the sacred village of Hudijan. Magians were numerous in the Jibāl and we hear of a fire-temple in a Kurdish village, of Magian villages near Qumm, and of fire-temples in almost every district, town, and village of Fars where there were more Magians than anywhere else. Magians survived in the mountains outside Kirmān until the middle of the eighth century, in significant numbers as late as the tenth century in Qūhistān and Khurāsān where there were fire-temples at Nīshāpūr and Herat and a village of Magian donkey-drivers outside of Marv, and at Karkuya outside Zarang in Sīstān as late as the eleventh century. Magians also survived at Bukhārā with the fire-temples they built after moving to the suburbs until at least the ninth century, and there were Magians living in villages in Turkish territory as far as the Chinese border in the early tenth century.[33]

There was also a remarkable degree of assimilation between Muslims and Magians in Fars by the tenth century where the markets were decorated for non-Muslim festivals and Muslims joined in the celebration of Nawrūz and Mihrijān and used the Persian solar calendar.[34] Although we do not know when it started or how long it had been going on, this is most probably to be taken as an indication of how Persian converts to Islam preserved their own native culture.

There is less evidence of interactions among Muslims and Manichaeans and Mazdakis in the early Islamic period. It is generally supposed that the failure of the Muslims to make specific distinctions among adherents of the various Iranian traditions allowed the survival and perhaps encouraged the revival of both Manichaeans and Mazdakis in Iran although only the Manichaeans seem to have been organized. By the eighth century ideas associated with both of them were beginning to affect sectarian forms of Islam, as Zindīqs they were persecuted by the early ʿAbbāsids, and they may have contributed to dualist revolts against the Islamic state.

Buddhists and pagans figure in this period largely as the objects of raids and attacks for plunder such as the cult of Zūn in Afghanistan or the Buddhist temple-monastery of Naw-Bahār at Balkh looted in 663. It might be suggested that the atmosphere of conflict with people using images in their religion helped to confirm or intensify the original Muslim objection to the religious use of images along the eastern frontier. We are told of a flourishing semi-annual idol market which survived at the village of Makh near Bukhārā until the tenth century even after a mosque had been built on the site of the local fire-temple.[35] Apart from contributing to attitudes that helped to justify jihād in the east it is hardly surprising that such conditions led Persian Muslims to call idolatry bōt-parastī ("Buddha worship") and an idol temple, and by symbolic extension a tavern, a bōt-khaneh ("house of Buddha"). On the other hand, it has been suggested that contacts along the eastern frontier may have resulted in influence by the Buddhist form of the Hindu world-view on the universal symbolism of Manşūr's Round City at Baghdad,[36] or Hindu influences on early Iranian Sūfism.[37]

The relationship between Muslims and Jews in Iran was basically that between rulers and subjects. The people of Yahudiyya at Işfahān surrendered on terms during the conquest. But in one important case Muslims also had to deal with Jews as rebels and suppress the Messianic rising of Abū ʿĪsā al-Işfahānī probably between 685 and 692. Abū ʿĪsā's anti-rabbinic rising betrays both Christian and Muslim (possibly Khārijī) influences in its syncretism, may have exercised a reverse influence on the early development of Shīʿism, and certainly contributed to the general millenial expectations towards the end of the seventh century.[38] Apart from a sect that survived down to the tenth century this movement left a rather interesting legacy in the piece of Muslim eschatology that makes the arrival of an army of seventy thousand Jews from Işfahān one of the signs of the end of the world.

As subjects of the Islamic state Christians in Iran fared much the same as Jews, but compared to the relative wealth of information about Christians in Sasanian Iran we know little about them after the Muslim conquests. The information in the Syriac sources seems to recede to Iraq giving the impression of a loss of interest and possibly control in the affairs of their Church on the Iranian plateau on the part of the Nestorian authors. Lists of bishops that include the plateau are no longer available after the early seventh century until the latter part of the eighth century. In the interval, what we have indicates a concentration of interest in the problems of the Church in Iraq and the Persian Gulf. The best early evidence for what was happening in Iran is provided in a letter written by the Catholicos Ishōʿyahb III (647-59) to Simeon the metropolitan bishop of Rev-Ardashir in Fars in which he complained that in spite of the lack of persecution by the Arabs many Christians in Fars and Kirmān had converted to Islam to escape paying taxes.[39] To find this so soon after the settlement of Arabs in Kirmān supports the view that conversion tended to be the result of social contact and interaction with Muslims and was greater wherever they settled.

In fact, conversion to Islam served as the main means for the assimilation of the non-Muslim population of Iran to their Muslim rulers just as Islam also provided a vehicle for the integration of Arab tribesmen. Although the state often discouraged the conversion of the non-Arab population the establishment of an Islamic presence by the building of mosques, the appointment of qāḍīs, and bringing preachers, teachers and traditionists to provincial centers to improve the Islam of the settlers had the opposite effect of encouraging conversion. There may also have been a policy favoring conversion in exposed frontier districts in the interests of security and local solidarity as in Sīstān in the reign of Mu'āwiya or at Bukhārā under Qutayba. We are told that in order to control Bukhārā, Qutayba settled an Arab garrison there, built a mosque on the site of the fire-temple in the citadel, required the people to worship there, punished those who did not and paid those who did a two-dirham reward. At first the Qur'ān was recited in Persian while the worshippers were given instructions on performing their prostrations in Soghdian by a man who stood behind them. The main result was that the poor of Bukhārā were attracted to Islam giving old class differences a new context and leading to a riot between poor, urban Muslims and rich, suburban non-Muslims.[40] In this case the distinction between Muslim and non-Muslim expressed social and economic differences that are the opposite of what is usually assumed. The second main mode of contact for conversion was through unofficial preaching as at Bukhārā after Qutayba or through the Arab settlers at Ardabil.[41] Thirdly, captives, slaves, and mawālī usually converted to Islam.

On the other hand, the assimilation of Arabs with non-Arabs was mainly a matter of Arabs being introduced to Persian customs and ways of doing things by the Persians themselves. At the siege of Tustar during the conquest the local notable called Sīna who offered to help the Muslims take the city in return for his own safety and that of his family, children, and property, got the Muslim spy, al-Ashras ibn 'Awf, into the city past the guards by putting a ṭaylasān on him and having him walk behind him as his servant.[42] Contacts in the army do not seem to have been very fruitful beyond showing Arabs how to use military slaves and heavy cavalry tactics. By the eighth century the segregation of the <u>mawālī</u> in their own unit in the army of Khurāsān tended to minimize such contacts although it encouraged a group identity among the <u>mawālī</u> for the first time.

Much more significant and successful in the long run for the transfer of values and attitudes was the way members of the Persian upper classes approached their conquerors and new rulers in the same ways and with the same expectations as they had been used to approaching native Persian rulers or each other. These contacts were effective largely because both groups shared common interests in terms of maintaining their status and control. One of the clearest examples is in the giving of gifts. The Persian notable called Dīnār who was taken captive by Simāk ibn ʿUbayd al-ʿAbsī at the city of Nihavand offered the latter anything he might ask in return for sparing his life and afterwards often brought Simāk gifts.[43] Similarly, we are told that the people of Balkh offered presents to the Muslim governor who collected taxes in 652 because they were used to offering presents at <u>Nawrūz</u> and <u>Mihrijān</u>.[44] Such customs were easily appreciated and adopted by Arab governors in the east as an added source of income and there is a detailed description of the <u>Mihrijān</u> gifts presented to Asad ibn ʿAbdallāh in 737 and of the speech made to him by the <u>dihqān</u> of Herat on that occasion describing some of the qualities a ruler was expected to have.[45] In the same way a Magian <u>dihqān</u> gave the governor of Sīstān advice on rulership and ethics.[46]

As a result of such contacts Arab governors in the east tended to adopt the local customs of court ceremonial and to approximate to their subjects' concepts of what a ruler ought to be. A successful governor, such as Ziyād in Fars, might be compared to Anūshirvān while an unpopular one might be called a frog. The real cement was common interest, however, and when Ibn al-Ashʿath told the people of Sīstān in 699 that he would attack the enemies who had been raiding them he was joined not only by the Arab soldiers but by "all the people of the market."[47]

Thus the effective modes of interaction and contact among Arabs and Persians, Muslims and non-Muslims were those among rulers and subjects as taxpayers, rebels or bandits, between master and slave or client, neighboring settlers and landowners, landlords and tenants, parties to commercial transactions, creditors and debtors, fellow administrators, and comrades-in-arms. Assimilation was the outcome of all these interactions, usually as a blending of opposite, mutually friendly or hostile acts. But their immediate impact was less important than the long term transformations. Arab settlers eventually learned Persian, while a growing number of Persians learned Islam.

5

ON 'CONCESSIONS' AND CONDUCT

A STUDY IN EARLY ḤADĪTH

M.J. Kister

Traditions about early ritual practices and customs reported on the authority of the Prophet, of his Companions (ṣaḥāba) or their Successors (tābiʿūn) are often divergent and even contradictory. Early compilations of ḥadīth occasionally record these traditions in separate chapters with headings which point out their differences; they also enumerate the scholars who held these divergent views. So, for example, the chapter "Man kāna yutimmu l-takbīr" is followed by the chapter "Man kāna lā yutimmu l-takbīr"; the chapter "Man qāla laysa ʿalā man nāma sājidan wa-qāʿidan wuḍū'" is followed by "Man kāna yaqūlu idhā nāma fa-l-yatawaḍḍa'." Traditions arranged under headings "Man kariha . . ." followed by "Man rakhkhaṣa fī . . ." are of a similar type. It is obvious that these diverse traditions reflect differences in the opinions of various circles of Muslim scholars and indicate that in the early period of Islam many ritual prescriptions were not yet firmly established.

The rukhaṣ or "concessions," i.e., the changes in ritual prescriptions designed to soften their harshness, were indeed an efficient tool in adapting the prescriptions to the real conditions of life and its changing circumstances. They established practices that were in keeping with the new ideas of Islam. Yet it is evident that the concession, rukhṣa, had to acquire authoritative sanction and legitimacy; this could be achieved only through an utterance of the Prophet. As a matter of fact, the following ḥadīth is attributed to the Prophet: "Truly, God desires that His concessions be carried out [just] as He desires His injunctions to be observed" ("inna llāha yuḥibbu an tu'tā rukhaṣuhu kamā yuḥibbu an tu'tā ʿazā'imuhu").[1] This tradition was interpreted in manifold ways. According to one interpretation it implies a whole view of life; al-Shaybānī (died

189/805) states that the believer who restricts himself to the most basic means of subsistence acts according to the prescriptions, whereas pleasant life and delights are for him a concession, a rukhṣa.[2] The purchase of the arable kharāj land in Iraq by Muslims was approved by ʿUmar b. ʿAbd al-ʿAzīz on the ground of a rukhṣa interpretation of a Qur'ānic verse; grants of land in the Sawād, given to Muslims, were also based on rukhṣa precedents.[3] The Prophet is said to have denied believers permission to enter baths, but later granted them a rukhṣa to enter them, provided they wore loincloths, ma'āzir.[4] There were in fact two contradictory attitudes in the matter of baths: the one disapproving[5] and the other recommending them.[6] Accordingly scholars are divided in their opinion as to whether the water of the bath can be used for ritual washing, ghusl, or whether, on the contrary, ghusl has to be performed for cleaning oneself from the very water of the bath.[7]

The knowledge of rukhaṣ granted by the Prophet is essential for the proper understanding of the faith and its injunctions. The misinterpretation of the verse: "Those who treasure up gold and silver, and do not expend them in the way of God--give them good tidings of a painful chastisement . . ." (Qur'ān 9:34) by Abū Dharr is explained by the fact that Abū Dharr met the Prophet and heard from him some injunctions of a severe character("yasmaʿu min rasūli llāhi [ṣ] l-amra fīhi l-shiddatu"); he then left for the desert. The Prophet, in the meantime, alleviated the injunction ("yurakhkhiṣu fīhi") and people adopted the concession. But Abū Dharr, unaware of this, came back and adhered to the first (scil. severe) injunction.[8] In later periods of Islam the practice of rukhaṣ was presented as the attitude of the first generations of Islam. The righteous predecessors (al-salaf), argues Abū Ṭālib al-Makkī, were in the habit of alleviating (yurakhkhiṣūna) the rules of ritual impurity, but were strict in the matter of earning one's living by proper means alone as well as in the moral aspects of behavior like slander, futile talk, excessive indulgence in rhetoric etc., whereas contemporary scholars, Abū Ṭālib continues, are heedless in problems of moral behavior, but are rigid (shaddadū) with regard to ritual impurity.[9] Sufyān al-Thawrī speaks about rukhṣa in the following terms: "Knowledge in our opinion is merely [the knowledge of] a rukhṣa [reported on the authority] of a reliable scholar; the rigid, rigoristic practice can be observed by everyone."[10] The pious ʿAṭā' al-Sulaymī asked for the traditions of rukhaṣ; they might relieve his grief, he said.[11] The rukhaṣ-traditions were of great importance for the strengthening of belief in God's mercy for the believers ("ḥusnu l-ẓanni bi-llāh").[12] Sulaymān b. Ṭarkhān asked his son to tell him rukhaṣ-traditions in order to come to the Presence of God (literally: to meet God) with hope for God's mercy.[13]

In a wider sense rukhaṣ represent in the opinion of Muslim scholars the characteristic way of Islam as opposed to Judaism and Christianity. The phrase ". . . and he will relieve them of their burden and the fetters that they used to wear" (Qur'ān 7:157) is interpreted as referring to the Prophet, who removed the burden of excessively harsh practices of worship[14] and of ritual purity.[15] The rigid and excessive practices of worship refer to Jews and Christians alike. The Prophet forbade his believers to follow the harsh and strict way of people who brought upon themselves destruction. The remnants of these people can be found in the cells of monks and in monasteries; this, of course, refers to Christians.[16] These very comments are coupled with the ḥadīth about the rukhaṣ mentioned earlier: "inna llāha yuḥibbu . . ." It is thus not surprising to find this rukhaṣ tradition together with an additional phrase: ". . . fa-qbalū rukhaṣa llāhi wa-lā takūnū ka-banī isrā'īla ḥīna shaddadū 'alā anfusihim fa-shaddada llāhu 'alayhim."[17]

The rukhṣa tradition is indeed recorded in chapters condemning hardship in the exertion of worship and ritual practices,[18] stressing the benevolence of God for His creatures even if they commit grave sins, reproving cruelty even towards a cat,[19] and recommending leniency, moderation and mildness towards the believers. Rukhṣa is rukhṣatu llāh, God's concession for His community; it imposes on the believers kindness and moderation towards each other. Rukhṣa is in this context associated with rifq, yusr, samāḥa and qaṣd.[20]

In a different context a concession, rukhṣa, is meant to ease the burden of the decreed prescription (al-ḥukm) for an excusable reason (li-'udhrin ḥaṣala); the acceptance of rukhṣa is almost obligatory in such a case (yakādu yulḥaqu bi-l-wujūb); the believer must act according to the rukhṣa, subduing his pride and haughtiness.[21] Breaking the fast of ṣawm al-dahr is such a rukhṣa; continuing the fast is stubbornness.[22] Commenting on the ḥadīth "The best of my people are those who act according to the rukhaṣ," al-Munāwī stresses that the rukhaṣ apply to specific times only; otherwise one should follow the incumbent prescription.[23] The ḥadīth "He who does not accept the concession of God will bear a sin as heavy as the mountains of ʿArafāt"[24] was quoted in connection with a concession according to which it is recommended to break the fast when on a journey. The core of the discussion was whether the breaking of the fast during a journey is obligatory or merely permitted. Some scholars considered it as a rukhṣa.[25] The phrase in Qur'ān 2:187 ". . . and seek what God had prescribed for you" ("fa-l-āna bāshirū-hunna wa-btaghū mā kataba llāhu lakum") indicates, according to one interpretation, God's concession concerning the nights of Ramaḍān.[26] The phrase in Qur'ān 2:158 ". . . fa-lā junāḥa ʿalayhi an yaṭṭawwafa bihimā . . ." (". . . it is no fault in him to circumambulate them . . ."), referring to the circumambulation of al-Ṣafā and Marwa, gave rise to the discussion whether it indicated an order or a concession.[27] The bewailing of the dead by hired women, the niyāḥa, is forbidden; but the Prophet granted the afflicted relatives the rukhṣa to mourn the dead and to weep over a dead person's grave.[28]

In some cases the choice between the prescription and the rukhṣa has been left to the believer: such is the case of the ablution of the junub. Three traditions about how the Prophet practised wuḍū', ablution, when in the state of janāba contain contradictory details: two of them state that he, being a junub, performed the wuḍū' before he went to sleep, while the third one says that he went to sleep without performing wuḍū'. Ibn Qutayba, trying to bridge between the contradictory traditions, states that in a state of janāba washing before one goes to sleep is the preferred practice (afḍal); by not washing the Prophet pointed to the rukhṣa.[29] The believer may choose one of the two practices.

In some cases the rukhṣa completely reverses a former prohibition. The Prophet forbade the visiting of graves, but later changed his decision and granted a rukhṣa to visit them: "nahā rasūlu llāhi [ṣ] ʿan ziyārati l-qubūri thumma rakhkhaṣa fīhā baʿdu."[30]

Cupping during a fast was forbidden by the Prophet; both the cupper and the person whose blood was drawn were considered to have broken their fast. The Prophet, however, changed his decision and granted a rukhṣa; cupping did not stop the fast.[31]

Lengthy chapters contain discussions of the problem as to whether kissing one's wife while fasting is permitted. Some scholars considered kissing or touching the body of the wife as breaking the fast, others considered it permissible. Both parties quote traditions in support of their arguments. The wives of the Prophet, who testified as to their experience, were not unanimous about the problem. ʿĀʾisha's evidence was in favor of kissing. The statement that old and weak people may kiss their wives, while young men may not, is an obvious attempt at harmonization.[32]

A similar problem was whether kissing one's wife imposes wuḍūʾ. Scholars were divided in their opinions. ʿĀʾisha testified that the Prophet used to kiss his wives and set out to pray without performing ablution. Many scholars stated that kissing or touching one's wife does not require wuḍūʾ, but others argued that it does. Some scholars found a compromise: wuḍūʾ is required if the kiss is accompanied by a feeling of lust.[33]

The rukhaṣ, apparently, were exploited by scholars attached to rulers and governors. As usual precedents of wicked court-scholars in the period of banū isrāʾīl were quoted: they frequented the courts of kings, granted them the required rukhaṣ and, of course, got rewards for their deeds. They were happy to receive the rewards and to have the kings accept their concessions. The verse in Qurʾān 3:189 "Reckon not that those who rejoice in what they have brought, and love to be praised for what they have not done--do not reckon them secure from chastisement . . ." refers, according to one tradition, to these scholars.[34] Orthodox, pious scholars fiercely criticized the Umayyad court-jurists and muḥaddithūn.[35] The fuqahāʾ seem to have been liberal in granting rukhaṣ, as can be gauged from a remark of the pious Sulaymān b. Ṭarkhān (who himself very much appreciated the granted rukhaṣ, see above note 13) that anyone who would adopt every rukhṣa of the fuqahāʾ would turn out a libertine.[36] In order to assess the actions of rulers it became quite important to find out to what extent they had made use of rukhaṣ. ʿUmar is said to have asked Muhājirs and Anṣārīs in his council what their opinion would be if he applied rukhaṣ in some problems. Those attending remained silent for a time and then Bishr b. Saʿīd said: "We would make you straight as we make straight an arrow." ʿUmar then said with approval: "You are as you are" (i.e., you are the proper men).[37] When al-Manṣūr bade Mālik b. Anas to compile the Muwaṭṭaʾ he advised him to stick to the tenets agreed upon by the Muslim community and to beware of the rigoristic opinions of Ibn ʿUmar, the rukhaṣ of Ibn ʿAbbās and shawādhdh (readings of the Qurʾān) of Ibn Masʿūd.[38]

Many a rukhṣa indeed served to regulate relations between people, establish certain privileges for the weak and disabled, to alleviate some rigorous practices and, finally, in some cases, to turn Jāhilī practices into Muslim ones by providing them with a new theoretical basis. Al-Ḥākim al-Naysābūrī[39] says that the Prophet's command to Zayd b. Thābit to learn the writing of the Jews (kitābat al-yahūd) in order to be able to answer their letters, serves as the only rukhṣa permitting the study of the writings of the People of the Book. Weak and disabled people were given special instructions on how more easily to perform certain practices during the pilgrimage.[40] The Prophet enjoined that the ritual ablution (wuḍū') should start with the right hand; but a rukhṣa was granted to start from the left.[41] The cutting of trees and plants was forbidden in the ḥaram of Mecca, but the Prophet allowed as a rukhṣa the idhkhir rush (schoenantum) to be cut since it was used in graves and for purification.[42] A special rukhṣa was given by the Prophet to take freely the meat of animals sacrificed by him; the nuhba (plunder) of sugar and nuts at weddings was also permitted by the Prophet.[43] A rukhṣa was issued by the Prophet allowing use of gold and silver for the embellishment of swords, for the repair and fastening of damaged cups and vessels, for a certain treatment in dentistry and for the restitution of a cut nose.[44] The Prophet uttered a rukhṣa about the nabīdh of jars;[45] the use of jars for nabīdh (steeping of dates) was forbidden before that. The muttering of healing incantations, the ruqya, a current practice in the Jāhiliyya period, was forbidden by the Prophet. Later he fixed the formulae of these healing incantations for various kinds of illnesses, bites from snakes and scorpions, and the evil eye, giving them an Islamic character.[46] This was, of course, a rukhṣa of the Prophet.

It is also a rukhṣa to denounce Islam in case of danger to one's life. Two Muslims were captured by a troop of Musaylima and were ordered to attest the prophethood of Musaylima. One of them refused and was killed; the other complied and saved his life. When he came to the Prophet, the Prophet said that he had chosen the way of the rukhṣa.[47]

The discussion of a rukhṣa could, in certain circumstances, turn into a bitter dispute. ʿUthmān disapproved of the tamattuʿ pilgrimage.[48] ʿAlī, who was at the council of ʿUthmān, opposed this opinion fiercely, arguing that tamattuʿ was a sunna of the Prophet and a rukhṣa granted by God to his servants. ʿUthmān excused himself saying that he had merely expressed his personal opinion which anybody could accept or reject. A man from Syria who attended the council and disliked ʻAlī's argument said that he would be ready to kill ʻAlī, if ordered to do so by the Caliph, ʻUthmān. He was silenced by Ḥabīb b. Maslama[49] who explained to him that the Companions of the Prophet knew better the matter in which they differed.[50] This remark of Ḥabīb b. Maslama is a projection of later discussions and represents the attitude of orthodox circles which recommend refraining from passing judgment on the contradictory arguments of the ṣaḥāba. However the passage also reflects the contrasting ways in which the pilgrimage was performed. It is noteworthy that Ibn Qayyim al-Jawziyya wrote lengthy passages in which he examined in a thorough manner the contradictory opinions of the scholars about the tamattuʻ pilgrimage.[51]

Close to the concept of rukhṣa was the idea of naskh, abrogation, total change, referring to ḥadīth. Such a case of naskh is the practice of wuḍū' after the consumption of food prepared on fire. The Prophet is said to have uttered a ḥadīth: "tawaḍḍa'ū mimmā massat al-nār." A great number of traditions assert that the Prophet later used to eat cooked food and immediately afterwards prayed without performing the wuḍū'. The traditions concerning this subject are found in some of the compendia arranged in two separate chapters, recording the opinions and deeds of the righteous predecessors who respectively practised wuḍū' or objected to it.[52] The arguments brought forth by the partisans of both groups and the traditions reported by them may elucidate some aspects of the problem under discussion. According to a tradition, reported by al-Ḥasan b. ʻAlī, the Prophet was invited by Fāṭima and was served the shoulder of a ewe. He ate and immediately afterwards started to pray. Fāṭima asked him why he had not performed the wuḍū' and the Prophet answered, obviously surprised, "[To wash] after what, o my daughter?" She said, "[To wash] after a meal touched by fire." Then he said, "The purest food is that touched by fire."[53] A similar tradition is recorded on the authority of ʻĀ'isha. When she asked the Prophet why he did not perform the wuḍū' after eating meat and bread he answered, "Shall I perform the wuḍū' after the two best things: bread and meat?"[54] There is a tradition on the authority of Umm Ḥabība, the wife of the Prophet, who had ordered the performance of wuḍū' after having eaten gruel of parched barley (sawīq) on the grounds of the ḥadīth: "Tawaḍḍa'ū mimmā massat al-nār,"[55] but traditions recorded on the authority of Ṣafiyya, Umm Salama and the Companions of the Prophet affirm that the Prophet prayed after eating cooked food without performing the wuḍū'.[56] The scholars who deny the obligation of wuḍū' after the consumption of meals state that the principle established by the Prophet was that wuḍū' is obligatory after what comes out (of the body) not after food taken in.[57] Ibn ʿAbbās, who authoritatively stated that there is no injunction of wuḍū' after food prepared on fire, argued that fire is a blessing; fire does not make anything either forbidden or permitted.[58] On the authority of Muʿādh b. Jabal, a Companion of the Prophet and a very indulgent person in matters of ablutions, who stated that no ablution is needed in case of vomiting, bleeding of the nose or when touching the genitalia, the following philological explanation is given: people had indeed heard from the Prophet the utterance: "tawaḍḍa'ū mimmā massat al-nār," but they did not understand the Prophet's meaning. In the time of the Prophet people called the washing of hands and mouth wuḍū'; the Prophet's words simply imply the washing of hands and mouth for cleanliness (li-l-tanẓīf); this washing is by no means obligatory (wājib) in the sense of ritual ablution.[59] There are in fact traditions stating that the Prophet ate meat, then rinsed his mouth, washed his hands and started to pray.[60] Another tradition links the abolition of the Prophet's injunction of this wuḍū' with the person of Anas b. Mālik, the servant of the Prophet, and puts the blame for the persistence of wuḍū' after the consumption of cooked food on authorities outside Medina. Anas b. Mālik returned from al-Iraq and sat down to have his meal with two men of Medina. After the meal he came forth to perform the wuḍū'. His companions blamed him, asking: "Are you following the Iraqi way?"[61] This story implies that in the practice of Medina no wuḍū' was observed after eating cooked meals. The emphasis that Anas's practice was Iraqi is noteworthy. It can hardly be conceived that the Iraqis stuck to the earlier practice of the Prophet which was later abrogated by him. It is more plausible to assume that Anas adopted an Iraqi usage observed there since the Sasanian period. The severe reproach which Anas faced seems to indicate that it was a foreign custom, considered as a reprehensible innovation by the Muslim community.[62]

The lenient character of the abrogation of wuḍū' after eating food prepared on fire is exposed in a tradition reporting that the Prophet ate roast meat, performed the wuḍū' and prayed; later he turned to eat the meat that was left over, consumed it and set to pray the afternoon prayer without performing wuḍū' at all.[63] It is evident that his later action (ākhiru amrayhi) is the one to be adopted by the community, as it constitutes an abrogation, naskh, of the former tradition, although some scholars consider it as rukhṣa.

The problem of "wuḍū' mimmā massat al-nār" was left in fact to the inventiveness of the fuqahā' of later centuries; it becomes still more complicated by an additional ḥadīth according to which the Prophet enjoined wuḍū' after the consumption of the meat of camels, but did not regard wuḍū' as necessary after eating the meat of small cattle (ghanam).[64] The two chapters in the Muṣannaf of Ibn Abī Shayba about wuḍū' after consuming the meat of camels, contradictory as they are, bear additional evidence to the diversity of practice and usage, and to the divergencies in opinions held by the scholars of ḥadīth. No less divergent are the views of the scholars about the wuḍū' before the consumption of the food,[65] the confinement of wuḍū', as an obligatory act, before prayer only, the question whether ablution before every prayer was obligatory for the Prophet only,[66] and whether the wuḍū' may be replaced as a concession by cleaning the mouth with a toothpick.[67]

The great number of diverse traditions, merely hinted at above, clearly indicate that the formation of a normative code of ritual and usage began relatively late.

A survey of some traditions about the ṭawāf, the circumambulation of the Kaʿba, and certain practices of the ḥajj may shed some light on the peculiar observances and customs followed in the early period and may explain how they were later regulated, transformed or established.

The ṭawāf was equated by the Prophet with prayer (ṣalāt). In an utterance attributed to him the Prophet said, "The ṭawāf is indeed like a prayer; when you circumambulate diminish your talk."[68] In another version of this ḥadīth the Prophet, making ṭawāf equal to prayer, bade the faithful confine their conversation to good talk. During the ṭawāf the Prophet invoked God saying, "Our Lord, give to us in this world and in the world to come and guard us against the chastisement of Fire" (Qur'ān 2:201). This verse was recited as in invocation by some of the Companions.[69] Some of the invocations were extended and included praises of God, assertions of His oneness and omnipotence as they were uttered by the angels, by Adam, Abraham and the Prophet while they went past various parts of the Ka'ba during the ṭawāf.[70] The pious Ibn 'Umar and Ibn 'Abbās are said to have performed the ṭawāf refraining from talk altogether.[71] Ṭāwūs and Mujāhid circumambulated in solemnity and awe "as if there were birds on their heads."[72] This was, of course, in the spirit of the imitatio prophetarum; Wahb b. Munabbih reported on the authority of Ka'b that three hundred Messengers (the last among whom was Muḥammad) and twelve thousand chosen people (muṣṭafan) prayed in the ḥijr facing the maqām, none of them speaking during the ṭawāf except to mention the name of God.[73] When 'Urwa b. al-Zubayr approached Ibn 'Umar during the ṭawāf, asking him to give him his daughter in marriage, Ibn 'Umar did not reply. After some time 'Urwa came to Medina and met 'Abdallāh b. 'Umar. The latter explained that he had not been able to answer him because he "conceived that he faced God" during the ṭawāf ("wa-naḥnu natakhāyalu llāha 'azza wa-jalla bayna a'yuninā"). Now he replied and gave him his daughter in marriage.[74] Merriment and joviality were, of course, forbidden and considered as demeaning. Wahb b. al-Ward,[75] while staying in the ḥijr of the mosque of Mecca, heard the Ka'ba complain to God and Jibrīl against people who speak frivolous words around it.[76] The Prophet foretold that Abū Hurayra would remain alive until he saw heedless people playing; they would come to circumambulate the Ka'ba, their ṭawāf would, however, not be accepted.[77]

The concession in the matter of speech granted during the ṭawāf was "good talk."[78] Pious scholars used to give guidance, exhort, edify and recount ḥadīths of the Prophet.[79] Common people made supplications during the ṭawāf, asking God to forgive them their sins and to grant them Paradise, children, and wealth. It was however forbidden to stand up during the ṭawāf, and to raise one's hands while supplicating. "Jews in the synagogues practise it in this way," said 'Abdallāh b. 'Amr (b. al-'Āṣ) and advised the man who did it to utter his invocation in his council, not to do it during the ṭawāf.[80] The fact that large crowds were gathered during the ṭawāf was, however, exploited by the political leaders. Ibn al-Zubayr stood up in front of the door of the Ka'ba and recounted before the people the evil deeds of the Umayyads, stressing especially the fact that they withheld their payment of fay'.[81] 'Alī b. al-Ḥusayn cursed al-Mukhtār, after his death, at the door of the Ka'ba.[82]

Some traditions narrate details of the behavior of certain persons in the ṭawāf who did not conform to this requirement of awe and solemnity in the holy place. Saʿīd b. Jubayr used to talk during the ṭawāf and even to laugh.[83] ʿAbd al-Raḥmān b. ʿAwf was seen to perform the ṭawāf wearing boots and singing ḥidā' tunes. When rebuked by ʿUmar he replied that he had done the same at the time of the Prophet and so ʿUmar let him go.[84] Al-Fākihī records certain frivolous conversations which took place during the ṭawāf, which may indeed be considered coarse and were certainly out of place in the sanctuary.[85] But groups of people engaged in idle talk during the ṭawāf were reprimanded. ʿAbd al-Karīm b. Abī Mukhāriq[86] strongly reproved such talk; al-Muṭṭalib b. Abī Wadāʿa[87] was surprised when he came to Mecca after a period of stay in the desert and saw people talk during the ṭawāf. "Did you turn the ṭawāf into a meeting place," he asked.[88] The "arabization" of the ṭawāf is evident from an utterance attributed to the Prophet making it unlawful to talk in Persian during the circumambulation. ʿUmar gently requested two men who held a conversation in Persian during the ṭawāf to turn to Arabic.[89] Reciting verses of the Qur'ān during the ṭawāf in a loud voice was disliked and considered a bad innovation (muḥdath); the Prophet is said to have asked ʿUthmān to turn to dhikru llāh from his qirā'a. Nevertheless certain groups of scholars permitted the recitation of verses from the Qur'ān.[90]

The problem of the reciting of poetry during the ṭawāf is complicated. The Prophet is said to have told Abū Bakr who recited rajaz verses during the circumambulation to utter allāhu akbar instead. This injunction of the Prophet seems to have been disregarded. Ibn ʿAbbās, Abū Saʿīd al-Khudrī, and Jābir b. ʿAbdallāh used to talk during the ṭawāf and recite verses.[91] A report on the authority of ʿAbdallah b.ʿUmar says that the Companions used to recite poetry to each other (yatanāshadūn) during the circumambulation.[92] The argument in favor of the lawfulness of the recitation of poetry during ṭawāf was based on the precedent of ʿAbdallāh b. Rawāḥa who had recited his verses during the Prophet's ṭawāf in the year A.H.7 (ʿumrat al-qaḍā'): "Khallū banī l-kuffār ʿan sabīlih . . ."[93] Also during the ṭawāf ʿĀ'isha discussed with some women of Quraysh the position of Ḥassān b. Thābit and spoke in his favor, mentioning his verses in defense of the Prophet;[94] Ḥassān, some traditions say, was aided by the angel Jibrīl in composing seventy verses in praise of the Prophet.[95]

Al-Nābigha al-Ja'dī recited his verses in the mosque of Mecca, praising Ibn al-Zubayr and asking for his help at a time of drought.[96] Ibn al-Zubayr asked, during the ṭawāf, a son of Khālid b. Ja'far al-Kilābī to recite some verses of his father against Zuhayr (b. Jadhīma al-'Absī). "But I am in a state of iḥrām," argued the son of Khālid. "And so am I," said Ibn al-Zubayr and urged him to recite the verses. He responded and quoted the verse: "And if you catch me, kill me . . . ." ("Fa-immā ta'khudhūnī fa-qtulūnī: wa-in aslam fa-laysa ilā l-khulūdi"). Ibn al-Zubayr sadly remarked that this verse suited his position in relation to the Banū Umayya.[97] Sa'īd b. Jubayr recalled having heard during the ṭawāf the verses of a drunkard who prided himself on the fact that he would not refrain from drinking wine even in old age.[98] An old woman recalled verses composed about her beauty in her youth.[99] There are moving verses composed by devoted sons, who carried on their backs their old mothers during the ṭawāf and supplications by women asking God to forgive them their sins. Poets had the opportunity to watch women doing their ṭawāf and composed verses extolling their beauty.[100] The wearing of a veil by women performing the ṭawāf was the subject of a heated discussion among scholars who used as arguments the contradictory utterances attributed to the Prophet and quoted as precedents the ṭawāf of his wives.[101] Another important problem was whether men and women could lawfully perform the ṭawāf together. According to one tradition women used to perform the ṭawāf together with men in the early period. The separation of women from men was first ordered by Khālid b. 'Abdallāh al-Qasrī.[102] Al-Fākihī remarks that this injunction was received with approval and people conformed to it until al-Fākihī's own time. Two other decrees of al-Qasrī continued to be observed by the people of Mecca: takbīr during the ceremony of ṭawāf in the month of Ramaḍān and a special arrangement of rows of men around the Ka'ba.[103] The separation between men and women in the mosque of Mecca was carried out by the governor 'Alī b. al-Ḥasan al-Hāshimī as late as the middle of the third century by drawing ropes between the columns of the mosque; the women sat behind the ropes.[104] At the beginning of the third century (about 209) the governor of Mecca under al-Ma'mūn, 'Ubaydallāh b. al-Ḥasan al-Ṭālibi,[105] ordered a special time to be set apart for the women's ṭawāf after the afternoon prayer; men were not allowed to perform the ṭawāf at that time. This regulation was implemented again by the governor of Mecca, Ibrāhīm b. Muḥammad about A.H. 260.[106] These changes in the ceremony of the ṭawāf seem to point to a considerable fluctuation of ideas and attitudes among the rulers and the orthodox in connection with the sanctuary and the form of the ṭawāf.

The new arrangements, which were apparently meant to grant the ḥaram more religious dignity and sanctity and to turn the ṭawāf into a solemn ceremony with fixed rules, may be compared with some peculiar customs practised in the early ṭawāf, as recorded by al-Fākihī. The passage given by al-Fākihī begins with a rather cautious phrase: "wa-qad zaʿama baʿḍu ahli makkata," which clearly expresses a reservation on the part of the compiler. In the old times (kānū fīmā maḍā) when a girl reached the age of womanhood her people used to dress her up in the nicest clothes they could afford, and if they were in possession of jewels they adorned her with them; then they introduced her into the mosque of Mecca, her face uncovered; she circumambulated the Kaʿba while people looked at her and asked about her. They were then told "This is Miss so and so, the daughter of so and so," if she was a free-born person. If she was a muwallada they said: "She is a muwallada of this or that clan." Al-Fākihī remarks in a parenthetical phrase that people in those times had religious conviction and trustworthiness ("ahlu dīnin wa-amānatin") unlike people of his day, whose manner of belief is obnoxious ("laysū ʿalā mā hum ʿalayhi min al-madhāhibi l-makrūha"). After the girl had finished her ṭawāf she would go out in the same way, while people were watching her. The purpose of this practice was to arouse in people the desire to marry the girl (if she was free-born) or to buy her (if she was a muwallada). Then the girl returned to her home and was locked up in her apartment until she was brought out and led to her husband. They acted in the same way with slave-maidens: they led them in the ṭawāf around the Kaʿba clad in precious dresses, but with their faces uncovered. People used to come, look at them and buy them. Al-Awzāʿī asked ʿAṭā' (apparently Ibn Abī Rabāḥ) whether it was lawful to look at maidens who were led in ṭawāf around the Kaʿba for sale; ʿAṭā' objected to this practice, except for people who wanted to buy slave-girls.[107] This report is corroborated by a story recorded by Ibn Abī Shayba, according to which ʿĀ'isha dressed up a maiden, performed the ṭawāf with her and remarked: "We may perhaps succeed in catching (literally: hunting) a youth of Quraysh" (scil. for the girl).[108] ʿUmar is said to have encouraged the selling of slave-maidens in this manner.[109] All these reports--al-Fākihī's reference to "people with religious conviction and trustworthiness," al-Awzāʿī's inquiry, ʿAṭā''s answer, ʿĀ'isha's story--seem to reflect ṭawāf customs prevailing in the early period of Islam, in all likelihood during the first century of the Hijra. The reports indicate a certain informality and ease of manners. All this was bound to change if the ḥaram was to acquire an atmosphere of sanctity and veneration.

The early informality and intimacy can be gauged from a number of traditions concerned with the daily behaviour of the faithful in the mosque of Mecca. Ibn al-Zubayr passed by a group of people who were eating their meal in the mosque and invoked upon them his benediction. Abū Nawfal b. Abī ʿAqrab[110] saw Ibn ʿAbbās there eating roasted meat with thin bread; the fat dripped from his hands. A broth of crumbled bread used to be brought to Ibn al-Zubayr in the mosque. One day a boy crawled towards it and ate from it; ʿAbdallāh b. al-Zubayr ordered the boy to be flogged. The people in the mosque, in their rage, cursed Ibn al-Zubayr.[111]

A similar problem was whether it is lawful to sleep in the mosque of Mecca. Scholars arguing for it quoted the precedent of the Prophet whose isrā' took place (according to the report of Anas b. Mālik) from the mosque of Mecca where he had slept.[112] Another argument in favor of sleeping in mosques was mentioned by Sulaymān b. Yasār,[113] when questioned by al-Ḥārith b. ʿAbd al-Raḥmān b. Abī Dhubāb:[114] "How do you ask about it, said Sulaymān, knowing that the aṣḥāb al-ṣuffa slept in the mosque of the Prophet and prayed in it."[115] Ibn ʿUmar used to sleep in the mosque (of Medina) in the Prophet's lifetime.[116] When Thābit (al-Bunānī) consulted ʿAbdallāh b. ʿUbayd b. ʿUmayr[117] whether to turn to the amīr in the matter of the people sleeping in the mosque of Mecca, ʿAbdallāh bade him not to do that, quoting the opinion of Ibn ʿUmar who considered these people as ʿākifūn, people praying in seclusion. The pious Saʿīd b. Jubayr used to sleep in the mosque of Mecca. ʿAṭā' b. Abī Rabāḥ spent forty years in the mosque of Mecca, sleeping there, performing the ṭawāf, and praying.[118] In a conversation with his student Ibn Jurayj he expressed a very favourable opinion about sleeping in mosques. When ʿAṭā' and Saʿīd b. Jubayr were asked about people sleeping in the mosque of Mecca and who have night-pollutions they nevertheless gave a positive answer and advised them to continue to sleep in the mosque. In the morning, says a tradition, Saʿīd b. Jubayr used to perform the ṭawāf, wake up the sleepers in the mosque, and bid them recite the talbiya.

These reports quoted from a chapter of al-Fākihī entitled "Dhikru l-nawmi fī l-masjidi l-ḥarāmi wa-man rakhkhaṣa fīhi wa-man karihahu"[119] give some insight into the practices in the mosque of Mecca in the early period of Islam and help us to understand the ideas about ritual and the sanctity of the ḥaram current at that time.

Of special interest are some customs of ṭawāf and ḥajj which include hardships, rigid self-exertion and self-castigation. Tradition tells about people who vowed to perform the ṭawāf while crawling,[120] or fastened to each other by a rope,[121] or being led with a rope threaded through a nose-ring.[122] Tradition reports that the Prophet and his Companions unequivocally condemned these practices, prohibited them and prevented the people from performing the ṭawāf in this way. It is obvious that these usages reflected the Jāhiliyya ideas of self-imposed harshness, of vows of hardship and severe practices. These went contrary to the spirit of Islam which, while transforming it into an Islamic ritual, aimed to give the ṭawāf its own religious values. Ibn Ḥajar is right in tracing back the prohibited forms of ṭawāf to their Jāhilī source.[123]

Similar to these vows of self-exertion during the ṭawāf are the vows of hardship during the ḥajj. The traditions tell about men who vowed to perform the ḥajj on foot. Some women vowed to perform the ḥajj walking, or with their faces uncovered, or wearing coarse garments, or keeping silent.[124]. The Prophet passed censure on these practices, emphasizing that God does not heed (literally: does not need) vows by which people cause harm and suffering to themselves.

These practices recall certain customs observed by the Ḥums which therefore had to be abolished in Islam. It may however be remarked that some early Muslim ascetics or pious men used to perform the ḥajj on foot, or vowed not to walk under a shade during their ḥajj.[125] It is true that the outer form of these practices recalls the old Jāhiliyya ones; there is however a clear line which has to be drawn between them: the devotional practices of the pious Muslims are different in their content and intention; they are undertaken out of a deep faith and performed for God's sake. These practices of the pious gained the approval of the orthodox circles and were considered virtuous. This attitude is clearly reflected in a *ḥadīth* attributed to the Prophet: "The advantage of the people performing the *ḥajj* walking over those who ride is like the advantage of the full moon over the stars."[126]

Fasting on the Day of ʿArafa gave rise to another important controversy. The contradictory traditions and reports are arranged in al-Fākihī's compilation in two chapters: the one encouraging the faithful to fast on this day, the other reporting about Companions who refrained from fasting.[127] According to a tradition of the Prophet the sins of a man who fasts on the Day of ʿArafa will be remitted for a year;[128] another version says two years,[129] a third version a thousand days.[130] The list of persons who did fast includes also ʿĀʾisha, who emphasized the merits of fasting on that day. The opponents who forbade fasting on that day based their argument on accounts and evidence that the Prophet had broken the fast on the Day of ʿArafa.[131] ʿUmar,[132] his son ʿAbdallāh and Ibn ʿAbbās prohibited fasting.[133] In another version Ibn ʿUmar stressed that he performed the pilgrimage with the Prophet and the three first caliphs; none of them fasted on the Day of ʿArafa. He himself did not fast, but did not explicitly enjoin either eating or fasting.[134] The conciliatory interpretation assumed that the prohibition of fasting referred to the people attending ʿArafa; but people not present on that Day of ʿArafa may fast, and are even encouraged to fast.[135] The reason given for not fasting on that day in ʿArafa was the care for the pilgrims, who might be weakened by the fast and prevented from properly performing the *duʿāʾ* and *dhikr*, which are the most important aims of the pilgrims staying at ʿArafa.[136]

The transfer of some rites performed at ʿArafa to the cities conquered by the Muslims is of special interest. This practice was introduced in Baṣra by ʿAbdallāh b. ʿAbbās[137] and by ʿAbd al-ʿAzīz b. Marwān in Fusṭāṭ.[138] On the Day of ʿArafa people used to gather in the mosques to invoke and to supplicate. When Ibn ʿAbbās summoned the people to gather in the mosque he argued that he wished that the supplications of the people may be associated with those attendant at ʿArafa and that God may respond to these supplications; thus they would share God's grace with the attendants at ʿArafa.[139] Muṣʿab b. al-Zubayr introduced this innovation in Kūfa.[140] Some pious Muslims participated in these gatherings, others considered them as <u>bid'a</u>.[141] The <u>ta'rīf</u> in Jerusalem is linked in some sources with 'Abd al-Malik, who is accused of having built the Dome of the Rock in Jerusalem in order to divert the pilgrimage from Mecca to Jerusalem, since 'Abdallāh b. al-Zubayr, the rival caliph in Mecca, forced the pilgrims to give him the oath of allegiance. When the Dome of the Rock was built people used to gather there on the Day of 'Arafa and performed there the <u>wuqūf</u>.[142] So the <u>bid'a</u> of <u>wuqūf</u> in Jerusalem arose. Al-Ṭurṭūshī describes a gathering of the people of Jerusalem and of its villages in the mosque, raising their voices in supplications. They believed that four "standings" (<u>waqafāt</u>) in Jerusalem were equal to a pilgrimage to Mecca.[143] Ibn Taymiyya, of course, strongly censured this innovation.[144]

It is evident that the idea behind the <u>ta'rīf</u> is that it is possible to transfer sanctity from 'Arafa to another sanctuary where the rites of 'Arafa are being performed on the same day, or that one may share in the blessing of 'Arafa through the performance of certain devotions at the same time as they are done at 'Arafa (as is the case with the supplications in the <u>ta'rīf</u> mentioned in note 139 above), or the notion that two sanctities may be combined as indicated in the tradition about Zamzam visiting Sulwān on the night of 'Arafa.[145]

The idea of transfer of sanctity is clearly reflected in a peculiar Shī'ī tradition in which a Shī'ī adherent asks the <u>imām</u> Ja'far al-Ṣādiq whether he may perform the <u>ta'rīf</u> on the grave of Ḥusayn if the opportunity to perform the <u>ḥajj</u> (scil. to Mecca) escapes him. The <u>imām</u> enumerates in his answer the rewards for visiting the grave of al-Ḥusayn on common days and those for visits on feasts, emphasizing that these rewards are multiplied for a visit on the Day of 'Arafa. This visit is equal in rewards with a thousand pious pilgrimages to Mecca and a thousand <u>'umra</u> accepted by God and a thousand military campaigns fought on the side of a prophet or a just <u>imām</u>. The adherent then asked, how he could get a reward similar to that of the <u>mawqif</u> (of 'Arafa). The <u>imām</u> looked at him as if roused to anger and said: "The believer who comes to the grave of al-Ḥusayn on the Day of 'Arafa, washes in the Euphrates and directs himself to the grave, he will be rewarded for every step as if he had performed a <u>ḥajj</u> with all due rites." The transmitter recalls that the <u>imām</u> did say: "and [took part in] a military campaign.[146]

Some changes of ritual were attributed to the

Umayyads and sharply criticized by orthodox scholars. A number of innovations of this kind are said to have been introduced by Muʿāwiya. It was he who refrained from the takbīr on the Day of ʿArafa, because ʿAlī used to practise it.[147] He forbade the loud recitation of the talbiya at ʿArafāt, and people obeyed his order; then Ibn ʿAbbās ostentatiously came forth and uttered the talbiya loudly.[148] It was Muʿāwiya who transformed a place where the Prophet had urinated into a place of prayer,[149] and invented (aḥdatha) the adhān in the ṣalāt al-ʿīdayn.[150] He changed the order of the ceremony of the ʿīd al-aḍḥā and ordered the khuṭba to be delivered before the prayer.[151] He was also the one who banned the tamattuʿ pilgrimages.[152] Changes of this kind were recorded as wicked innovations of the impious Umayyad rulers.

The inconsistencies of the usages, customs and ritual practices of the early period of Islam are reflected in almost every subject dealt with in the early sources of ḥadīth. Opinions divergent and contradictory are expressed about the sutra which has to be put in front of the praying Muslim and whether a dog or a donkey or a woman passing by invalidates the prayer.[153] Scholars differ in their opinions as to whether the form of sitting during the prayer called iqʿāʾ is permitted,[154] whether the prayer by a believer clad in one garment (thawb) is valid,[155] and whether counting of the tasbīḥ by pebbles is allowed.[156]

Some of the subjects dealt with in the early ḥadīths lost their actuality and relevance. It is however a special feature of Muslim ḥadīth literature and ḥadīth criticism that some of these themes reappear and are discussed even in our days. Thus, for instance, the contemporary scholar Nāṣir al-Dīn al-Albānī examines the tradition prohibiting fasting on the Day of ʿArafa for people attending ʿArafa.[157] He carefully analyzes the isnāds, finding out their faults; he harshly reprimands al-Ḥākim for his heedlessness in considering the ḥadīth sound and states that the ḥadīth is in fact weak. He argues that the ḥadīth about the forgiveness of sins for a period of two years for him who fasts on the Day of ʿArafa is a sound tradition; but the attached phrase about the rewards for fasting on every day of Muḥarram is a forged one.[158] An exhaustive scrutiny of ḥadīths about the counting of tasbīḥ by pebbles is included by al-Albānī in the examination of the ḥadīth about the rosary (al-subḥa).[159]

Of interest are certain traditions in which some social and cultural, as well as religious, trends are exposed. Of this kind are the traditions in which the Prophet predicted that his community would erect sumptuous mosques in the manner of Jewish synagogues and Christian churches, adorn them richly and embellish them with inscriptions. This will be the sign of decline of the Muslim community and portend the End of the Days. Traditions of the very early period of Islam reflect the opposition against arched <u>miḥrābs</u>. "Beware these altars" ("ittaqū hādhihi l-madhābiḥ"), followed by an explanatory comment, "he meant the <u>maḥārīb</u>"("ya'nī l-maḥārīb"), says a tradition attributed to the Prophet.[160] "My people will fare well as long as they will not build in their mosques altars like the altars of the Christians," the Prophet foretold.[161] Pious men usually refrained from praying in these <u>miḥrābs</u>.[162] Of the same kind were traditions against the adornment of mosques,[163] prayers in the <u>maqṣūra</u> of the mosque,[164] and against writing Qur'ān verses on the walls of the mosque, or in the <u>qibla</u> of the mosque.[165]

These traditions should, of course, be studied against the background of the reports about the sumptuous buildings which were erected by the impious rulers and their governors and the richly decorated <u>jāmi'</u> mosques in which the delegates of the rulers led the prayer. Many a time a pious Muslim had to ask himself whether he should pray behind them, as can be deduced from the numerous traditions dealing with this subject.

The few traditions reviewed in this paper clearly demonstrate the fluidity of certain religious and socio-political ideas reflected in the early compilations of <u>ḥadīth</u>, as already proved by I. Goldziher. The diversity and divergence of traditions expose the different opinions of various groups of Muslim scholars. The divergent traditions are faithfully recorded in the compilations of the second century of the Hijra with no obligatory conclusions imposed and no prescriptions issued.

This activity reflects a sincere effort to establish the true path of the Prophet, the Sunna, which the believer should follow.

6

EARLY DEVELOPMENT OF *KALĀM**

J. van Ess

The subject "early development of *kalām*" needs clarification. Kalām is understood, in secondary literature, in a broad and in a narrow sense. In the broad sense it means something like "Muslim theology," in contrast to philosophy (*falsafa*) or to jurisprudence (*fiqh*); in the narrow sense it means a technique which became a characteristic of Muslim theological texts, namely the dialogue, be it real or fictitious, with an opponent, on a given problem, proceeding in question and answer, preferably on the basis of alternatives derived from this given problem. The opponent is confronted with a doctrine which he himself considers to be true, or with a statement which draws its authority out of itself, e.g. a verse of the Qur'ān. Then in a series of questions normally put in the form of a dilemma which does not leave him any opportunity for evasive answering, he is forced to admit a consequence which contradicts his own thesis, or the untenable nature of all its implications. The dialogue always aims at a merciless reduction to silence; missionary zeal and the conviction of defending eternal truth, both so characteristic of a religion based on revelation, work together to expel the charm and elegance of Socrates' maieutic method on which this technique is ultimately based.[1]

In this technical sense the word *kalām* is an eloquent term; it reveals its close connection with the corresponding verbal forms *kallama* and *takallama*, "to talk to somebody" and "to talk about something." These words may always possess a terminological meaning, but they are still close enough to their basic connotations to leave our judgment sometimes in suspense. The problem we have to solve is when the transformation took place--the *waḍʿ*, to use a term of later Muslim linguistics--and why it was considered to be so decisive that, for a long time, no other word for "theology" could rival *kalām* in Arabic; *fiqh* was soon restricted to "religious science" in the sense of jurisprudence, *ilāhiyyāt* was confined to philosophy, *ʿilm al-lāhūt* to Christian theology, and only uṣūl al-dīn gained a certain appeal for Ḥanbalī and Ash'arī circles from the fourth century onward.[2] Why and when was Muslim theology characterized in this way? Why was this not according to its subject-matter like Greek theo-logía, but according to its formal structure?

The conventional answer to this question has been repeated over and over again. Let me quote from an article published in 1974: "le premier kalām a été mu'tazilite."[3] The Mu'tazilites, so it is assumed, were the first to develop this kind of argumentation, be it as a methodical tool in real discussions or as a stylistic device for the exposition of their ideas; and they had to develop it because they assumed the task of defending Islam against its numerous intellectual critics from outside, especially the adherents of the dualistic creeds in the area of the former Sasanid empire. Kalām as a technique was understood as an instrument of apologetics. This has turned out to be wrong or at least only partially true. We possess at least one testimony which is earlier than the Mu'tazila, extensive fragments from a treatise against the Qadariyya written about A.H. 75 by a grandson of the Caliph 'Alī, Ḥasan b. Muḥammad b. al-Ḥanafiyya. In this text the kalām t e c h n i q u e is applied with a certain awkward stubbornness, and even the w o r d takallama is used once in its terminological sense. The date and authenticity of the text are, of course, open to discussion; but a paragraph by paragraph comparison with other documents relevant to the Qadarī movement (Ḥasan al-Baṣrī's letter to 'Abd al-Malik written between A.H. 75 and 80; 'Umar II's epistle against some anonymous Qadarites, presumably Khārijites and adherents of Shabīb b. Yazīd al-Najrānī, written about A.H. 100; and the material derived from our ḥadīth collections)[4] seems to demonstrate a certain primitiveness on the part of Ḥasan b. Muḥammad b. al-Ḥanafiyya and an ignorance of later solutions which it would have been difficult to imitate afterwards.[5] Thus the kalām technique was not invented by the Mu'tazilites in Iraq, but dates back at least to the time of 'Abd al-Malik, to an influential member of the House of the Prophet who seems to have spent much of his time in the Ḥijāz.

Once we accept this as fact, we discover that it does not stand completely isolated. In an Ibāḍī source a certain Ṣuḥār al-'Abdī who, in spite of all uncertainty in matters of biographical detail, has to be dated back to the first century of the Hijra, is credited with the following advice concerning the treatment of the Qadarites whom he disliked as much as his contemporary Ḥasan b. Muḥammad b. al-Ḥanafiyya: "Talk with them about (divine) knowledge (kallimūhum fī l-ʿilm)! If they admit it, they contradict (their doctrine); if they deny it they fall into unbelief." This is characteristic in three respects: because of the technical use of kallama in kallimūhum; because of its "if--if not" disjunction, i.e. the alternative or dilemma typical for kalām; and because of its naive assumption that God's foreknowledge means predestination and that the Qadarites therefore cannot deny the latter if they accept the former--a hasty identification of two different concepts which is also found with Ḥasan b. Muḥammad b. al-Ḥanafiyya, but which was already refuted by Ḥasan al-Baṣrī in his letter to ʿAbd al-Malik. The same source mentions as the first mutakallim, obviously within the Ibāḍiyya, a certain Bisṭām b. ʿUmar b. al-Musayyab al-Ḍabbī who had joined Shabīb b. Yazīd al-Shaybānī, the Kharijite rebel against al-Ḥajjāj who had been drowned in the Tigris in A.H. 77--thus another personality of the first century. With this in mind we might perhaps reconsider our sceptical reaction towards some Shīʿī material concerning kalām discussions by their imāms Muḥammad al-Bāqir and Jaʿfar al-Ṣādiq. Although there is no doubt that the danger of projecting and antedating is especially imminent here, we should not overlook the fact that with these reports we are already entering the second century.[6]

In all this, however, there is not only a problem of time, but also of space. The early Shīʿī imāms resided in Medina, and so, probably, did Ḥasan b. Muḥammad b. al-Ḥanafiyya. Kalām, then, obviously did not--or not only--originate in the centres of the pre-Islamic oriental civilizations, in Syria or in Iraq, but in the birthplace of Islam itself. Does this mean that we are dealing with an inner-Muslim development and that all those well-known parallels with Christian vocabulary and technique: the stereotype Greek formula ei dé phate--apokrinoumetha discovered by Von Grunebaum as the counterpart of the Arabic pattern in qultum--qulnā, the equation kalām = dialexis and takallama = dialegesthai etc.,[7] are a mere coincidence or only relevant for a later stage of development? This seems rather hard to accept.

We might, of course, venture the hypothesis that the Shīʿī imāms as well as Ḥasan b. Muḥammad b. al-Ḥanafiyya had frequent contacts with Iraq and that they were not entirely unfamiliar with the circumstances in the capital, Damascus--that they learnt theological argumentation there, at a court where

John of Damascus lived, the author of the well-known Dialexis Christianoū Kai Sarakēnou. Being written in Greek, the text was, of course, not immediately accessible to the Arabs; but its contents and its intention leave no doubt that the Christians used their bilingualism to defend their religious convictions against the "heresy" of their Muslim masters.[8] Nevertheless, this theory sounds somewhat too contrived. Moreover, John of Damascus was not the first Christian to use the method: his Dialexis is a good example of kalām, a dialektos of the kind already practised by Origen in his discussion with Heraclides and the Egyptian bishops,[9] but it was certainly written after A.H. 75, the approximate date when Ḥasan b. Muḥammad b. al-Ḥanafiyya finished his treatise.[10] Moreover, we may be sure that a more thorough analysis of our sources will yield additional names: the same Ibāḍī text referred to before mentions a certain Ṣāliḥ b. Kathīr "min mutakallimī l-muslimīn" (muslimīn here evidently meaning not the Muslims in contrast to Christians and Jews, but the Ibāḍīs who considered themselves the Muslims par excellence), and this man turns out to be also a Medinan, a friend of al-Zuhrī.[11]

What we have thus far failed to consider are two things: first, Medina was at that time--more than in any other period--not a point outside or at the periphery of the civilized world; and secondly, kalām was always applied with the Qur'ān in mind. The Qur'ān, however, uses kalām structures: the Prophet gets divine advice on how to question his Jewish, Christian or pagan opponents, and how to anticipate their answers. This advice is normally introduced by the formula qul (Say); thus, many passages of the Scripture have the character of a manual for argumentation, and controversy becomes an essential part of revelation.[12] This does not mean that the Qur'ān is the ultimate and only source of the kalām technique; we must not expect too much of its i'jāz. It only shows that the Qur'ān, too, was part of a tradition[13] and that Muḥammad's method of argumentation is not essentially different from that of his adversaries who had inherited their dialectical style over the centuries. His successors in spirit--or even in the flesh, like the two Shī'ī imāms I mentioned--would not have had the impression of creating any bid'a when they argued in terms of kalām. Whether they were aware of paying homage to an age-old, pre-Muslim custom is another question.[14] What they had to learn was not the technique itself, but skill in applying it; they had not lived outside the intellectual world of antiquity, only at its periphery.

So much for kalām in its specific and more restricted sense. Whoever talks about kalām would, however, disappoint the expectations of his audience if, in malicious precision, he were to understand kalām only as a technique typical of Muslim theology, and not as Muslim theology itself, i.e. as its content rather than its form. We will then have to put up with the fact that kalām in the sense of "theology" (which is a usage of the term introduced by western Islamicists; a Muslim would either say ʿilm al-kalām or use a completely different expression) does not necessarily manifest itself in the stylistic form called kalām. If we take, for instance, Ḥasan al-Baṣrī's epistle to ʿAbd al-Malik, we are justified in saying that this is an important specimen of early Muslim theology, but as a letter expounding upon request the author's opinion about a certain theological problem, it is, by definition, not kalām. In shifting the accent thus from Formgeschichte to Dogmengeschichte we always have to keep in mind that we are not dealing with a phenomenon restricted to one region, but with the intellectual history of an empire. We have to differentiate, therefore, not only according to problems, but also according to areas.

The main problem in S y r i a and obviously also in the Ḥijāz was qadar, the question of the origin of and responsibility for man's evil actions. This is, of course, no mere coincidence: in the capital man's responsibility tended to be understood as the caliph's responsibility, and evil actions meant the injustice of the ruling establishment and the social iniquity of a rapidly changing world; the theological discussion was loaded with political and revolutionary overtones. But this only accounts for the importance attributed to the problem, not for its origin. The theological discussion precedes the political crisis: about A.H. 75, i.e. several years before the execution of the so-called founder of the Qadariyya, Maʿbad al-Juhanī,[15] Ḥasan b. Muḥammad b. al-Ḥanafiyya refers to a conceptual apparatus of the doctrine which is rather elaborate. One of the key terms seems to have been duʿā', God's "call" to follow his commandments, the "right guidance" (hudā) provided by the prophets. Man is free to accept this hudā or to reject it; evil originates through his giving in to his own whims (hawā) or to the deception (takhyīl) of Satan. This presupposes that man is able to perform something (qadara) and that he possesses a capacity (istiṭā'a) which has been conveyed (wakala) to him by God. In order to find the right direction he needs reason ('aql), and reason is therefore given to everybody, as fiṭra, as his nature by which he becomes a priori aware of God's existence and of his own createdness.[16]

All this does not sound very new. But we should not forget: it is not Mu'tazilite theology but conceived before the last quarter of the first century. And it is not sectarian for only later heresiography treated the Qadariyya as a sect--with all the consequences of such a concept as being a minority and a novelty (bid'a) introduced by a founder. Yet the Qadariyya probably never had a founder; the movement is solidly rooted in a consistent exegesis of the Qur'ān--an exegesis which has been shown to correspond well with the Qur'ān's own intentions in the recent study of H. Räisänen[17]--and rooted to such an extent that its adherents never wholly agreed to accept other authoritative proofs for their view, especially not from ḥadīth.[18] Secondly, there is no evidence that the movement, at that time, reflected only the interest of a minority. It may have become the position of a minority later on because of the resistance of the government and through political escalation (although considering the undisputed success of the early Mu'tazila even this may be subject to doubt, at least for certain areas). But even if the other side represented the majority, they did not have the better theologians; the conceptual apparatus used by Ḥasan b. Muḥammad b. al-Ḥanafiyya is rather primitive. One gets the impression that he is not so much defending a traditional position, as constructing his own stance in reaction to the more elaborate Qadarī system. He is remarkably cautious in his refutation: he never says that God creates evil or is responsible for it; he only insists on the fact that it is always God who initiates actions and events. Instead of the Qadarī notion of du'ā', God's call which leaves the response to man's own decision, he uses tawfīq which leaves the choice to God: those to whom God "grants success" will act righteously, while everybody else will go astray. This is, as he understands it, a token of divine grace; there is no compulsion, jabr or ikrāh, involved.[19] The Jabriyya is a myth created by the heresiographers, and the term is taken over from Qadarite propaganda.[20]

The way the Qadariyya used this term shows the direction which the discussion was going to take:

for them it implies more a political than a religious deviation. Jabriyya means the "tyranny" of the Umayyads from the time of ʿAbd al-Malik onward, that is, of all those who were only recognized as kings (mulūk) after the period of the ideal caliphate. Whoever, according to the Qadariyya, admitted that God may "force" someone to do evil justified the Umayyad jabriyya and identified himself with it. With special delight the Qadarīs brought up the case of Pharaoh, and we may be sure that they did not do so merely as an exercise in Qur'ānic exegesis; Pharaoh was the unjust tyrant par excellence.[21] The other side stressed the idea that man owed his rizq, his livelihood, solely to God, not to his own endeavor; and rizq, in spite of its etymology (from Persian rōzīk), did not only mean the daily bread or the daily ration of a soldier, but also the power given to a caliph, his mulk understood as his milk, and the wealth granted to the Arab aristocrats in contrast to the mawālī. Predestinarianism was seen as a guarantee for the established social order and against the onslaught of the underprivileged. The political and social antagonism involved may explain, together with other, more specific reasons, the execution of Ghaylān al-Dimashqī, a mawlā, who himself was obviously not a revolutionary, but whose ideas concealed a revolutionary element which was set free in the rebellion against Walīd II and the program of Yazīd III.[22]

The situation in I r a q was different. Many Qadarīs lived there, but we do not hear that much about their specific political aspirations. And whereas in Syria our information breaks off with the rise of the ʿAbbāsids, it continues in Iraq at least up to the end of the second century: the continuing predominance of the theological aspect of the problem facilitated the integration of the movement into the new society. The movement was gradually taken over by the Muʿtazilīs who, in spite of differences in their qadar doctrine, came close enough in order to make the merger possible, especially as the predestinarian polemics did not make any efforts to differentiate between them. Whatever remained of the militant wing may appear in our sources as those Muʿtazilites around Bashīr al-Raḥḥāl who, in 145, joined the rebellion of al-Nafs al-Zakiyya.[23]

But the Qadarīs only played a role in Baṣra where they lived in fruitful tension with the Ibāḍiyya who were, for the most part, moderate predestinarians.[24] Kūfa, on the contrary, was held by the Shīʿa and the Murji'a. In this town the activists were attracted by the slogans of a strong pro-ʿAlid community; they could combine their revolutionary energy with the frustrations of the House of the Prophet.[25] Mukhtār had exploited these feelings. When his rebellion collapsed, the expectations which he had raised lived on in a number of millenarian movements whose gnostic superstructure shows the influence of foreign, e.g. Mandean, ideas. These movements were initiated and supported by craftsmen and simple people, members of the lower strata of the population who had frequently come from the countryside. By emancipating the mawālī, Mukhtār had obviously encouraged a wave of religious syncretism where Islam, which was still more or less restricted to the larger towns and the upper classes, came into closer contact with the notions of indigenous religiosity. These ideas had survived Zoroastrian impact and Christian mission, and they could now infiltrate Islam all the more easily as the shape and circumference of the new religion were not yet sufficiently defined. Since these sectarian movements came from social strata which were utterly despised by the new masters, they manifested themselves in a chiliastic form; one waited for the Mahdī to establish justice in this world, or even more than that, one believed in new prophets having come and Paradise having been installed on earth.[26] This utopianism normally exploded in rebellion or terrorist activities; the social injustice in the newly founded towns seemed unbearable to those who came from outside, driven away from their land by an over-demanding tax-policy or by the insecurity caused by the Khawārij.

The wealthy ʿAlids and the Iraqi ashrāf did not show much sympathy for these fantasies. The most impressive attack against the extremists--impressive enough to be repeated over and over again in the political propaganda of the time--came from an ʿAlid, the same Ḥasan b. Muḥammad b. al-Ḥanafiyya whom we mentioned earlier as an opponent of the Qadariyya. Shortly after 73/693 he wrote an open letter to the adherents of his family and to whoever wanted to listen to it, especially in Kūfa, where he severely criticised the "Sabaʾiyya"--not "Kaysāniyya" as they were called later on--and accused them of claiming secret knowledge and distorting the Qurʾān. This was intended as an initiative in favor of ʿAbd al-Malik who tried to restore the religious unity of his empire after the end of Mukhtār's rebellion and the downfall of ʿAbdallāh b. al-Zubayr's anticaliphate. The key term of his letter was irjāʾ, meant as a call for political moderation and prudent abstention from useless discussions about the mistakes of the first civil war. Thus, in a sense, an ʿAlid started a religious movement, the Murji'a, which was later on usually regarded as the ideological legitimation for Umayyad rule.

This is paradoxical only with hindsight. Ḥasan b. Muḥammad b. al-Ḥanafiyya's initiative progressed differently from what he had intended. In spite of the fact that, during the last phase of Mukhtār's rebellion, he himself had joined the revolutionaries--or perhaps just because of this--he could not calm them down now. He did not even succeed in becoming the head of a moderate Shīʿī wing. His idea turned out to have a future, yet not in politics but in theology --like the Qadarī doctrine at Baṣra. He had pleaded for epochē, postponing one's judgement, in the case of the participants of the first civil war, especially ʿUthmān and ʿAlī, i.e. in the case of a limited and well-defined number of people and certain well-known events in the past. Shortly afterwards this was reinterpreted as abstention from judgement about the salvation-status of anyone in the past or present. The decision not to talk about the possible "sin" of ʿUthmān and ʿAlī--who, after all, had been Companions of the Prophet--was changed into the conviction that nobody, be he alive or dead, should be denied the predicate of mu'min as long as had pronounced the shahāda.[27] In spite of this development, however, the basic intention of the movement remained unbroken: i.e. to preserve the cohesion of the community. This created a peculiar atmosphere; for whereas the other movements were mostly interested in elaborating their own standpoint and in contrasting it against other views, the Murji'a tried to define the minimum of beliefs and tenets to which all Muslims should adhere. Instead of refutations, they wrote ʿaqā'id of which the Kitāb al-fiqh al-akbar connected with the name of Abū Ḥanīfa was only the first.[28]

This is how the Murji'ites outlined the limits of the Sunna. Characteristically enough, Abū Ḥanīfa, in his letter to ʿUthmān al-Battī, strongly objects to being called a Murji'ī, which he understands as a derogatory term used by the ahl al-bidaʿ, and prefers, as a self-designation, names like ahl al-sunna or ahl al-ʿadl.[29] The latter term strikingly evokes the pretensions of the Muʿtazila. This observation tallies with the fact that the principle of al-manzila bayna l-manzilatayn, which was so characteristic of Wāṣil b. ʿAṭā''s theology, is not entirely without parallel in Abū Ḥanīfa's thinking.

But for Abū Ḥanīfa a l l people who are not polytheists (mushrikūn) share this manzila, which can only be changed for the better, namely into the status held by the prophets and the ʿashara al-mubashshara, but not for the worse.[30] Wāṣil's thinking, for his part, has also a Khārijī component: when he disapproves of the attempt to restrict general (ʿāmm) statements in the Qur'ān to specific (khāṣṣ) cases,[31] he seems to be attacking the Murji'ī doctrine that the Muslim sinner is exempt from the Qur'ānic prediction of eternal punishment.[32] We may assume that his Kitāb Aṣnāf al-Murji'a[33] contained criticism in addition to mere doxographical description. In the long run, the Muʿtazilīs turned out to be much more exclusive than the Murji'a; their rationalism pushed them in this direction. Abū Ḥanīfa and his followers, on the contrary, seem to have extended their universalist claim also to jurisprudence; it would be interesting to investigate to what extent the Ḥanafī madhhab was meant to be more than just the Iraqi school of law. More than Mālik b. Anas, Abū Ḥanīfa seems to have attracted disciples from everywhere. We have to ask whether this is merely a reflection of the growing influence of Iraq in the first two decades of ʿAbbāsid domination (between 132 and 150, the year of Abū Ḥanīfa's death) or the indication of a conscious effort on his part.[34] Balkh was called by Kūfan scholars Murjiyyābād because of the local predominance of the Ḥanafīs.[35]

Balkh brings us to a new area, I r a n. Here, our information about factions and movements like those in Syria and Iraq is scarce, but we encounter the first systematic theologian of Islam, Jahm b. Ṣafwān. We might venture the statement that theology properly speaking did not exist before Jahm. The early community did not discuss theological issues as such, but its widely diverging views of history, its Geschichtsbild. For what had been really novel in Islam was not its doctrine; Muḥammad's message was to be understood simply as a renewal of the kerygma of the Old and the New Testament. What was novel was its success and its rapid expansion; this development, together with its social and political consequences, was the prime factor requiring an explanation. This is why predestination was seen in connection with political power and "repression." It was only Jahm who changed predestination into a systematic determinism; for him God's power and almightiness were not so much linked with man's action, but with God's entire "otherness."

In spite of this, Jahm was not a completely isolated figure. His formulation that, in view of God's omnipotence, all statements about human actions and worldly events are mere "metaphors" can now be traced back to Ḥasan b. Muḥammad b. al-Ḥanafiyya's treatise against the Qadariyya.[36] He adopts the Murji'ī concept of community together with their definition of îmān, belief. But he is the first to develop a consistent concept of God and His attributes. His "system" (which we have to reconstruct from a few remarks found in the heresiographers) puts strong emphasis on God's transcendence, and we are still unable to decide whether this attitude was simply a formulation of a principle genuinely inherent in Islam as such, or whether it originated out of Neoplatonic ideas,[37] or reacted against divergent views where God was conceived as a body immanent in space, as propounded by a circle of theologians in the Iraqi Shīʿa[38] and presumably also by Muqātil b. Sulaymān, a compatriot of Jahm in Balkh.[39] The problem of Neoplatonism is that we lack any precise information as to the intellectual background against which early Islam could unfold itself in Khurāsān.[40] The Shīʿī "corporealists" in Iraq present us with the difficulty that all of them were probably one generation younger than Jahm. Muqātil, on the other hand, was really a contemporary, for he met Jahm at Marw where he discussed the problem of anthropomorphism with him. Both of them are said to have written books against each other on this topic after their dispute.[41] But the character of Muqātil's *tashbīh* is still a mystery.[42] Possibly their disputation had concentrated on the problem whether God can be located on His throne or whether He is *lā fī makān*; the *Kitāb al-fiqh al-absaṭ*, which seems to have been transmitted in Balkh since the time of Abū Muṭīʿ,[43] attacks some "unbelievers" just for this doctrine.[44]

Muqātil and Jahm were not only opponents in their theological views but also enemies in political affairs. Jahm was executed as a secretary of the anti-Umayyad revolutionary Ḥārith b. Surayj in 128/746 whereas Muqātil had been selected as an expert on the Qur'ān, together with his namesake Muqātil b. Ḥayyān,[45] by Naṣr b. Sayyār, the Umayyad governor, during his negotiations with Ḥārith b. Surayj.[46] Jahm's execution did not hamper the expansion of his theological ideas; they remained prominent in the area where he had lived. The Jahmiyya is explicitly attacked in the *Kitāb al-fiqh al-absaṭ*;[47] and in the *Kitāb al-fiqh al-akbar*, where the attack constitutes only a few lines, they are the only group of opponents mentioned by name.[48] Simultaneously, but in their own way, the muḥaddithūn started to formulate their protest. Ibrāhīm b. Ṭahmān (died 163/747-8), author of one of the oldest collections of ḥadīth preserved,[49] had discussions with the Jahmīs in Nīshāpūr and tried to convert them to Murji'ī views.[50] His Kitāb al-sunan[51] contains a fair amount of traditions which were later on used as key arguments against the Jahmiyya and which may have already been collected by him for this purpose.[52] During the same period Jahm's ideas found their way into Iraq where they influenced the first Muʿtazilī theologian to develop a comprehensive coherent system of his own: Ḍirār b. ʿAmr.[53] Thus some of his concepts were taken over into a Muʿtazilī context--at least for one generation until Abū l-Hudhayl and Bishr b. al-Muʿtamir dissociated themselves from Ḍirār and excluded his "Jahmisms" from the official Muʿtazilī doctrine.[54] The "heresies" were thus set free again to be taken over, now in their Ḍirārian framework, by a non-Muʿtazilī theologian (and jurist) who played an important role during the miḥna under the Caliph al-Ma'mūn: i.e. by Bishr al-Marīsī. Only after this shift did the term Jahmiyya come into use in Iraq.[55]

This tour d'horizon is by no means complete. I have not mentioned dogmatic issues like the pre-existence of the Qur'ān and the character of God's speech[56] or politico-religious movements like the Khawārij.[57] I have passed over theologians like Jaʿd b. Dirham[58] and ʿAmr b. ʿUbayd, and I have only touched on the numerous attempts at installing new prophets, attempts which are so typical of the Umayyad period, not only inside the Shīʿa. We need only remember the enigmatic personality of Ḥārith b. Saʿīd who claimed the gift of prophecy in Syria and Jerusalem during the time of ʿAbd al-Malik.[59] Instead, I would like to add a few final and very tentative remarks about a problem which brings us back to kalām as a technique and as a "profession," i.e. about the social position of the mutakallimūn.

It is well known that Wāṣil b. ʿAṭā' sent missionaries (duʿāt) to different regions of the Muslim oikumene. They distinguished themselves through an ascetic life style and special apparel: they performed nightly supererogatory prayer and clipped their moustaches; they wore a special kind of turban, and some of them may have dressed in wool garments (ṣūf).[60] Moreover they excelled in the art of disputation; one of them, Ḥafṣ b. Sālim who had been sent to Khurāsān, is said to have debated with Jahm b. Ṣafwān in Tirmidh.[61] This last fact leaves no doubt that the missionaries had to function as mutakallimūn. In the same way, however, as kalām turned out not to have been invented by the Mu'tazilīs, so also did the idea of proselytizing not originate with them. We should mention here the Ibāḍīs who had moulded the intellectual atmosphere at Baṣra where the Mu'tazila were to emerge. They had applied the same tactics before Wāṣil b. 'Aṭā'; they called their missionaries ḥamalat al-'ilm.[62] Hishām b. 'Abdallāh al-Dastuwā'ī (died 153/770 or 154/771), a famous muḥaddith[63] of Ibāḍī leanings,[64] offered every bedouin who accepted his teachings a garment from those fabricated by the Ibāḍī community in his native town of Dastuwā in Ahwāz.[65]

There may have been differences in the organizational set-up: Wāṣil's enterprise looks like the idea of one man, whereas the Ibāḍī missionaries followed the instructions of the jamā'at al-muslimīn, the "presbyterian" council of the sect which, in true Khārijī tradition, identified its circle with the community of the only "true" Muslims.[66] But there are many similarities, too. Hishām al-Dastuwā'ī's disciples attracted attention through their supererogatory fasting and their piety[67] as the early Mu'tazilīs did through their nightly prayer. Most Ibāḍī missionaries were merchants who, in connection with the far-flung trade relations of the Baṣran Ibāḍī community, may have combined the pious with the useful. And, strangely enough, Wāṣil b. 'Aṭā' was a spinner (ghazzāl), i.e. a cloth merchant, like those Ibāḍīs who furnished Hishām al-Dastuwā'ī with the garments which served as bait (or as token of identification?) in his mission. Reports which try to interpret Wāṣil's laqab in a less direct way look like attempts at removing from him the blemish of a contemptible profession.[68] His disciple 'Uthmān b. Khālid al-Ṭawīl, a mawlā of the Banū Sulaym whom he sent to Armenia as his emissary, was a rich draper who had apparently belonged to the circle of Ḥasan al-Baṣrī. Following Wāṣil's advice, he introduced himself in Armenia by delivering fatwās according to Ḥasan's principles and met with great success afterwards.[69] It seems that the merchants were the first to give up, for obvious reasons, the exclusiveness of the town-dwellers; here it did not make much difference that the Ibāḍīs were, by descent, genuine Arabs, mostly from the Azd, whereas all the early Mu'tazilīs belonged to the mawālī.[70]

Both movements also resembled each other in the

success they had. In the Maghrib they entered into a competition which lasted for centuries.[71] The Ibāḍīs of al-ʿAṭf in the Mzāb still preserve the cemetery of the Muʿtazilite community whom they gradually superseded from the sixth century of the Hijra onward.[72] The propaganda was aimed at Muslims and non-Muslims alike. There were, of course, lots of unbelievers to be converted, but the missionaries sent by Wāṣil in Medina[73] probably functioned in the context of "inner mission," like Ḥafṣ b. Sālim in his dispute with Jahm b. Ṣafwān.[74] The Umayyad caliphate was generally not interested in the conversion of its non-Muslim subjects and did not set any specific religious ideals for the Muslims either. Consequently, groups which recognized the caliphate only as an inevitable evil like the Ibāḍīs, or a movement like the Muʿtazila, which sprang up at a time when the spiritual weakness of the caliphate had become evident, felt the need and the right to fill the gap.

There is a second point where the Ibāḍiyya tells us something about the relevance of kalām. When ʿAbd al-Wahhāb b. ʿAbd al-Raḥmān b. Rustam, who was Imām of Tāhert between 168/784 and 208/823, fought against the Zenāta berbers who were Muʿtazilīs and dominated the environs of his town, he felt he had to arrange a kalām discussion before the battle.[75] Kalām was thus not only an intellectual pursuit of ivory tower theologians; its polemical character made it suitable for psychological warfare. Something of the battles in rhetoric of the ayyām al-ʿArab seems to have survived here. But since one was fighting for Islam now--or for the better interpretation of Islam --the poets had been replaced by mutakallimūn. There is more material to back up this theory. Ḥārith b. Surayj, who employed Jahm b. Ṣafwān tried, during his battles, to convert his enemies by means of moral and religious arguments.[76] Secret agents of the ʿAbbāsid revolution arranged kalām disputations in order to win adherents for their cause.[77] The ideal situation was, of course, when the general himself was experienced in kalām. Again the Ibāḍīs offer an example: ʿĀṣim al-Sidrātī who came to Baṣra in order to study with Abū ʿUbayda al-Tamīmī, the head of the Ibāḍī scholars in the beginning of the second century A.H., and then returned to the Maghrib where he appears as a general and a preacher of his community in Tripolitania.[78]

Does this mean that the mutakallimūn were a kind of militant clergy or, as has been said recently, "a fundamental political and social institution of Islam"?[79] Certainly only in a limited sense. We should not overlook the fact that all our present examples from the early period deal with anti-Umayyad movements. It is true that ʿAbd al-Malik for some time supported kalām and seems to have used Ḥasan b. Muḥammad b. al-Ḥanafiyya to further his religious peace policy. Thus assuming responsibility for the religious unity of his empire, he may have had in mind, apart from mere political considerations, the example of the Byzantine emperors.[80] And it is true that ʿUmar II invited representatives of different religious movements for discussion in order to win them for the ideal of one jamāʿa under one Sunna.[81] We might add that Jaʿd b. Dirham had been the teacher of Marwān II. But the same Jaʿd b. Dirham was executed at the order of Hishām; kalām had turned out to be an ambiguous instrument. The theological institution created by the Umayyads were not the mutakallimūn but the quṣṣāṣ. Their position had been fixed by Muʿāwiya, and under ʿAbd al-Malik they had been officially established in the mosques.[82] Their functions were sometimes the same as those described above in connection with the mutakallimūn: they had to speak encouraging words and to pray for victory before the battle.[83] This entanglement with government interests, together with a certain theatrical behavior almost inevitable in this profession, exposed them to the reproach of hypocrisy. It also explains why they came quite soon under the attack of the religious opposition and why they obviously did not survive, as an institution, the downfall of the dynasty, at least not in Iraq or in Syria.[84] The mutakallimūn are found, so it seems, rather among the intellectual cadres of the opposition movements. As such they were taken over by the ʿAbbāsids and afterwards achieved a high reputation as court theologians.[85] As members of the new establishment they, in turn, attracted the criticism of the religious idealists. But this carries us beyond the scope of the period we are concerned with here.

7

THE EARLY DEVELOPMENT OF THE IBĀḌĪ MOVEMENT IN BAṢRA

J.C. Wilkinson

The internal view of the development of the Ibāḍī movement[1]

A much repeated image that can be traced back at least to the fifth/eleventh century likens the true religion (al-ʿilm) to a bird. The egg was laid in Medina, it hatched in Baṣra and it flew to Oman (ʿUmān). Parallel with this geographic rationalization is a rather less explicit historical one which traces the political development of the movement through a line of true believers: the original Islamic state of the Prophet and his Companions, then the early Khawārij, who are seen as a more or less monolithic block, then the Ibāḍīs themselves who came into existence with the split up (tafrīq) of the Khawārij in A.H. 64. Their imāma existed in a concealed state (kitmān) under their first "imams" in Baṣra, Abū Shaʿthāʾ Jābir b. Zayd, Abū ʿUbayda Muslim b. Abī Karīma, al-Rabīʿ b. Ḥabīb al-Farāhīdī, Abū Ayyūb Wāʾil b. Ayyūb al-Ḥaḍramī, and finally Abū Sufyān Maḥbūb b. al-Raḥīl, who eventually retired with his family to Oman once the movement was firmly established there. It was under the second of these imams, Abū ʿUbayda, that the movement entered into an expansionist stage so that at the end of Umayyad times a sensational, albeit short-lived, imamate, that of Ṭālib al-Ḥaqq (ʿAbdallāh b. Yaḥyā al-Kindī), was established in south-western Arabia which actually took possession of the Holy Cities. A rump imamate survived for a little time in Ḥaḍramawt whilst a separate one was created in Oman under al-Julandā b. Masʿūd which lasted for a couple of years at the very beginning of the ʿAbbāsid period. Early attempts to establish imamates in North Africa were also short-lived, but during the 160s the Rustamid imamate of Tāhert was founded whilst a couple of decades later the Omani imamate was fully established. Towards the end of the third century both imamates began to collapse; but whilst the North African Ibāḍī movement found itself increasingly weakened and eventually only survived in a few isolated communities, the imamate in Oman had an active, albeit cyclic, history of appearance and disappearance down to the middle of the present century. The Ḥaḍramī imamate, which had always been more or less subservient to that of its neighbor, collapsed when the last and greatest of their imams, Abū Isḥāq Ibrāhīm b. Qays, broke with the Omani imam in the early fifth century of the Hijra, probably over the doctrines of the so-called Rustāq party, and within a short time all traces of Ibāḍism in the Peninsula had been obliterated outside the mountainous heartland of Oman.[2]

So we can see where the somewhat parochial idea of the Ibāḍī bird came from. In this paper we shall only be concerned with the hatching phase.

The Khawārij Beginnings

As Shaban[3] rightly points out there is a sharp distinction to be made between the Khawārij of ʿAlī's time and those we shall be concentrating on here. Our so-called Khārijī school belonged to the Baṣran rather than the Kūfan milieu and its members were not concerned with defending privileges gained from participation in the conquest of Iraq. Nevertheless, there was a certain continuity of the ideology by which the Muḥakkima party had rationalized their position and it is this that led our group also to be known as Khawārij. Their basic principles are contained in the phrase lā ḥukm illā lillāh, a slogan which far transcended the arbitration issue as may be judged by its triple enunciation in the ceremony of electing an imam in Oman.[4] Its fundamental meaning was no government except by what God has ordained, that is by the prescriptions through which government had been conducted until ʿUthmān's time. Hence the basic logic of opposition to subsequent caliphate government summed up in the following little exchange with Muʿāwiya: "I give you allegiance on (the condition of the prescriptions of) God's book and the Sunna of his Prophet," declared Saʿīd b. al-Aswad; "You may make no conditions," replied Muʿāwiya; "And you, no allegiance to you," retorted Saʿīd.[5]

It will be noted that the man held responsible for the betrayal of the true order was ʿUthmān, rather than ʿAlī, because it was he who reversed the policy of precedence in Islam (sābiqa) in favour of the élitism of pre-Islamic sharaf in his ordering of government.[6] For the later Khawārij, no longer concerned with the political issues behind this, it was also important to play down the dispute with ʿAlī and shift as much of the opprobium onto his predecessor for two main reasons. First, by focusing on the events of his caliphate it sometimes became possible to debate fairly openly certain principles of leadership without overtly having to attack the Umayyad dynasty itself. Such discussion seems to have been conducted by the Başran Khawārij on at least three occasions, with Ibn Zubayr, with ʿAbd al-Malik b. Marwān, and with ʿUmar b. ʿAbd al-ʿAzīz. Second, it provided a much more satisfactory starting point than ʿAlī's reign for the doctrine of wilāya and barā'a, association and dissociation, which is the basis of imamate community theory.[7] The fundamental duty to dissociate from the unjust imam who persists in his errors was clearly established when ʿUthmān was removed from office: the dispute with ʿAlī was a degree less serious for here the basic principle was that ʿAlī had reneged his rightful authority (wilāya) by submitting his imamate to arbitration.

A third possible reason is that it potentially offered the olive branch to the shīʿat ʿAlī. ʿAlī was a rightful imam and the only reason that the Khawārij had dissociated from him (bari'a ʿanhu) was that he had allowed himself to be tricked by their common enemies. This line of argument was emphasized by the more moderate Khawārij, through maintaining that it was only the extremists who had attacked the peaceful separatists at Nahrawān and the latter had no particular quarrel with ʿAlī. All that they had done was to elect their own imam, ʿAbdallāh b. Wahb, when ʿAlī had "abdicated" as a result of his submitting to arbitration; and they would have had no objection to his rejoining them after the decision went against him, on condition of course of his recognizing Ibn Wahb as imam. Furthermore, ʿAlī himself subsequently repented (tawba) Nahrawān.[8] Such a compromising attitude which might have permitted the opposition to the Umayyads to reunite,[9] was strongly rejected by the more extremist Khawārij, as witness ʿImrān b. Ḥittān's verses extolling the Khārijī who avenged Nahrawān by murdering ʿAlī.

In this difference of attitudes towards ʿAlī we have an example of the divergence which characterizes the whole history of the Khawārij-Ibāḍī movement, that between compromisers and militants (qaʿada and shurāt). So, in the year between Ḥarūrā' and Nahrawān, a large part of those who had left ʿAlī over the arbitration issue, went back to him, very largely due to the mediation of Ibn ʿAbbās, known to the Ibāḍīs as al-baḥr. And of those who remained estranged, by no means all united under ʿAbdallāh b. Wahb's banner at Nahrawān, for the two thousand Khawārij from Kūfa who were finally dealt with during Muʿāwiya's reign at Nukhayla were Khawārij who had nothing to do with Ibn al-Wahb. On the other hand, the militants must have their martyrs and so the Ibāḍīs present Ḥarūrā', Nahrawān and Nukhayla as a continuity and emphasize how those who lost their lives compromised not only qurrā' (which to them has come to mean Qur'ānic readers, whatever it may have originally signified), anṣār and muhājirūn, but also seventy of those who had fought at the Prophet's side at Badr. And to underline their direct descent from this true beginning the Ibāḍīs emphasize that they are the only Khārijī group to trace their movement back to ʿAlī's true successor, for does not the name "Wahbiyya" derive from Ibn Wahb (ʿAbdallāh b. Wahb)?[10] Such a dubious claim, which in any case would have been hotly disputed by their rivals the Ṣufriyya, is furthered through incorporating Ibn Wahb (who was probably a Bajīla mawlā) into the Rāsib and in turn making this tribe of Azd descent, with the implication that he was of Omani origin.[11]

In contrast with this "true" line of Khawārij is a second type of secession, not recognized by the Ibāḍīs, that of the would-be independent tribal republic. The pattern of such revolts is nonetheless of considerable importance for understanding the development of the movement and can best be discussed by reference to a well-documented prototype dating back to A.H. 38, that of Khirrīt b. Rāshid al-Nājī.[12]

Khirrīt's band was made up of three main elements. At its core were his fellow tribesmen, that is those members of the powerful Banī Nājiyya of Oman who had come to the miṣr of Baṣra when the campaigning centre at Tawwaj was disbanded; there they formed a distinct military and settlement unit (this, of course, is before Baṣra was reorganized into akhmās). Seizing on the chaos following Ṣiffīn to reject the control of central government (incidentally on the excuse that ʿAlī had not accepted the arbitration decision) the clan, in effect, declared itself an independent Muslim tribal republic. That it was able to do so was basically due to the fact that it had a tribal territory to fall back onto in Arabia. And it was this potential territorial independence that made it essential that Khirrīt's revolt be dealt with; for if the Banī Nājiyya could get away with it, then so could other more important tribal groups.

Numerically, the main part of Khirrīt's followers was made up of non-Arabs who had particularly suffered from the Muslim conquest. These, it is to be noted, were not the former Persian land-owning classes, the dahāqīn and the asāwira, who in Iraq at any rate had done well out of the change of regime, but the old subject peasantry and indigenous population (the ahl al-bilād, ʿulūj, etc.); not only had they to bear the brunt of the kharāj tax, but it was they who had suffered most from the collapse of the administration which at least had assured them a basic living in Sasānid times. Thus Khirrīt's policy of remitting their tax obligations, whilst also allowing them to remain in their old religions, obviously drew them to his banner, particularly once he retreated home to Oman. And it is an interesting comment on the early Islamic state to note that, while Khirrīt's Arab followers escaped relatively lightly when he was eventually defeated, exemplary punishment was meted out to these subject peoples who had sought to break their tax obligations.

The third element in Khirrīt's band consisted of the undesirable fortune seekers who were with him for the plunder and other pickings: bedouin raiders from the desert, "Kurdish" brigands from the mountains, ex-Zanj slaves, and urban riff-raff. It was these people who really gave the Khawārij their bad name and led to general support for their ruthless suppression.

Now the importance of these types of Khārijī secession for the Ibāḍīs lies in the fact that they prepared the ground where the seed of the moderates was later to be implanted. And, in so doing these tribal secessionists fertilized it with certain social principles that all their successors had to accept, willy-nilly. Perhaps the most important of these was the idea that the Arab and non-Arab population formed a common social structure.

This drawing together of the conquerors and the conquered, which is one of the features which distinguishes the Baṣran from the Kūfan Khārijī secessions, did not stem just from ideology or the benefits to be gained by mutual support, but from a much deeper rapport which, I believe, had its roots in common experience under Sasānid rule. True, there was an ideal in bedouin society throughout pre-Islamic Arabia of sharing between rich and poor,[13] but this had been extended to cut across race in Sasānid territory, because there the Arabs had been considered as second-class citizens, deprived of the best lands, forced into the Persian marine and generally treated in the same way as the rest of the poor indigenous population.[14] Of this the Ḥijāzīs never ceased to remind them: had it not been for their bringing them Islam, they would still be the hirelings of the people they now ruled, living their repulsive way of life in the coastal lowlands and desert outbacks to which they were relegated by their former Persian overlords; the peoples of the Gulf were animals who did not seek to better themselves and ʿUmān, Sīrāf and Ubulla were the three sinks of the world.[15] So it is not surprising that some of the Gulf tribes reacted by rejecting the ideals on which Ḥijāzī dominance was built, notably Qurashī pretensions to lead the state, the division of Arab society into sharaf and non-sharaf descent, and the distinction between aḥrār and mawālī.

But to move from that position to the ideology that all men and women, ʿabīd, bayāsira and mawālī, Arab and non-Arab, were fully equals, and that precedence only stemmed from the personally achieved quality of ʿilm, was perhaps a bit much for the more conservative elements. Thus women came to be specifically debarred as candidates for the imamate in Oman, whilst in reality throughout Arabia the Khawārij tended to select their imams from the leading Arab tribes of the region. Even so, it is relevant to note that in Oman two of the early imams were probably of peasant background and did much to encourage the development of village life and remove the distinction between Arab and non-Arab settlers.

One of the broader implications arising from the Khārijī doctrine that developed in line with this concept of social organisation was that it provided a general theory of opposition which made particular appeal both to Arabs rejecting Ḥijāzī domination and to non-Arabs resentful of their status; not just the mawālī, but also "national" groups which accepted Islam but not Arab government: it is certainly no coincidence that the man the Ibāḍīs were to choose as their main missionary to the Berbers was a Persian refugee claiming descent from the Sasānid royal line.[16] On a yet more general level Khārijī doctrine must obviously have had potential appeal for the Yamanī party, if Shaban's thesis that this represented those who wished to settle and assimilate the local population in the conquered lands is accepted.

Another aspect of early Khārijī revolts that was later to raise major problems for the movement was that of secession and how to conduct relationships with other Muslims. Khirrīt's revolt, it will be noted, involved full secession; by contrast the groups which separated at Ḥarūrāʾ and met martyrdom at Nahrawān and Nukhayla were not breaking definitively with the rest of the Muslim community but were forced by circumstances to remove themselves from their presence. To the observer of the time such a distinction might not then have appeared particularly significant; more likely what would have struck him is that if a revolt based on Khārijī principles was to succeed then it was necessary to have an independent territorial base. For the Baṣrans two areas offered themselves: either nearby Ahwāz where the local population was always delighted to receive any Khārijī secession which remitted their tax obligations (e.g. Abū Bilāl and then the Azāriqa),[17] or a tribal homeland in the Peninsula (e.g. the Nājiyya, Banū Ḥanīfa etc.).

The Tafrīq of the Khawārij

The crisis which followed the death of Yazīd b. Muʿāwiya officially marks the break-up of the Khawārij and with it the birth of Ibāḍism. Such a rationalization obscures the true evolution of Khārijī activity in Baṣra.

This really begins with the bulldozing of the old settlement and dīwān order and its replacement by enormous new tribal quarters (akhmās) to meet the miṣr's rapid population growth and military importance during the governorships of Ziyād b. Abīhi and later his son ʿUbaydallāh. Some of those already affected began to react in the same way as had the earlier Kūfan Khawārij when their interests were threatened, so that a mass of revolts by splinter groups broke out. Their suppression by Ibn Ziyād was initially generally welcomed in the interests of law and order, but his increasing ruthlessness in dealing with all Khawārij opposition, actual or potential, after the rising of Qarīb al-Azdī and Zuhhāf al-Ṭā'ī,[18] led to a strong reaction amongst the moderates and the secession in A.H. 61 of the highly respected Abū Bilāl Mirdās b. Judayr/Ḥudayr, one of the survivors of Nahrawān. The failure of the qaʿada to respond to his call to join him in Ahwāz and from there to cross over to Oman and prepare to take the Holy Cities, even after his success in defeating the army sent against him, coupled with the story of his eventual "martyrdom", profoundly stirred all who subscribed to the "No government except by what God has ordained" principle, and raised the question of a full secession. Nothing came of this at this stage because "Ibn Ibāḍ" counselled his followers not to join "Nāfiʿ b. al-Azraq." But for generations to come Abū Bilāl remained the prototype Muslim hero and the inspiration for the Ibāḍī shurāt: "I am the shārī man who has made a contract for his soul; he wakes in the morning hoping for death in the good fight after the model of Mirdās," wrote the fifth century Ḥaḍramī imam Abū Isḥāq Ibrāhīm b. Qays in his Dīwān.

Now it is quite clear, from the context in which Ibn Ibāḍ (whether it was really he or not matters little) came to his decision, that the real issue under debate was not simply that of revolt but of secession.[19] This issue finally came to a head in A.H. 64 when the Khawārij of Baṣra were released from prison and began to make common cause with the Banū Ḥanīfa to create a new Muslim state which would reconquer the old. Two fundamental positions quickly emerged; that of the secessionists whose policy was to form a new migration (hijra) and consider all other Muslims as polytheists and their territory as dār al-ḥarb, and that of what I shall call the "unitarians," those who wished to preserve the integrity of the present dār al-Islām and to introduce reform from within. The main proponent of the secessionist school was Nāfiʿ b. al-Azrāq, while the views of the unitarian school were most fully expressed by a minor Tamīmī leader, ʿAbdallāh Ibn Ibāḍ. Ibn Ibāḍ however, is an unimportant figure. He simply happens to have argued with a degree of coherence (subsequent rationalization?) the viewpoint of those who instinctively felt that the extremists' policy would be disastrous for Islam; indeed his name was probably resuscitated at a later stage because it provided a convenient label to contrast with the Azāriqa: the eponym of the third "colour" label, the Ṣufriyya, is probably a complete fabrication. At this stage we simply have two groupings, the secessionists, who are called by the other grouping Khawārij, and the unitarians (Jamāʿat al-Muslimīn) who in the course of the next few decades try to formulate a satisfactory religious rationale for their position. That the political organization of the unitarians was almost non-existent and that it is pointless to label any particular group amongst them as Ibāḍiyya or Ṣufriyya will become clear when we see whom the Ibāḍīs claim as their early members.

The period of "intellectual" development

A study of the list of names given in the second Ibāḍī ṭabaqa[20] shows that, as well as including people claimed by other schools, it figures men whose attitudes and actions are not really reconcilable with

Ibāḍī views, or who can at best only be considered as sympathizers. Chronologically recorded this list starts with the names of some of the pre-tafrīq Baṣran secessionists (notably the followers of Qarīb al-Azdī and Abū Bilāl), and of Ibn Ibāḍ; also from this period is ʿImrān b. Ḥittān, that is the man whom the Ṣufriyya claim as their successor to Abū Bilāl.[21] In fact ʿImrān simply represents the more militant wing of the unitarians; from his early days he was very much a firebrand, as can be judged by his praise of ʿAbd al-Raḥmān b. Muljam (ʿAlī's "executioner," who incidentally also features in the list), and the fact that he was only just dissuaded by family pressure from joining the revolts against Ibn Ziyād; later he was involved with risings in northern Iraq and eventually had to take refuge in Oman (where he found his hero, Abū Bilāl, was much respected): there he died in A.H. 89. Also featuring in this list are the names of the great Tamīmī leader al-Aḥnaf b. Qays, and of ʿUmar II's son ʿAbd al-Mālik. Obviously neither of these can seriously be considered as an Ibāḍī, but it is quite clear from the events of A.H. 64 that the former had a moderating influence on the extremist Khawārij (many of them were in fact Tamīm) and was probably sympathetic to the views of the unitarians, whilst the latter gave the so-called Ibāḍī delegation to his father a particularly sympathetic hearing.

The third group of names is clearly much more "Ibāḍī." First and foremost amongst them is Abū Shaʿthāʾ Jābir b. Zayd (A.H. 18 or 21-93), a Yaḥmadī (Shanūʾa Azd) who originated from interior Oman (Firq near Nazwa in the region called the Jawf). Close friend of his teacher Ibn ʿAbbās, confidant of ʿĀʾisha, acquainted with seventy of those who had been at Badr, he is the real founder of the sect in the Ibāḍī literature. But precisely because he was the tābiʿ from whom the first indisputable Ibāḍīs drew their knowledge of the Prophet's Sunna (rafaʿa al-ʿilm ʿanhu) and thereby lay their claim to be the first sunnī madhhab, I believe Jābir's role has been exaggerated by his Ibāḍī successors. Let us clear away some of the undergrowth that has developed around his name.

Jābir was an Ibāḍī in the sense that he subscribed to the lā ḥukm . . . principle and was a unitarian. His political ideology therefore envisaged bringing the state back into its true Muslim form by the as yet unspecified actions of the right-minded, the Jamāʿat al-Muslimīn (i.e. the unitarians). But he belonged to no particular sub-group, and when schools did begin to form towards the end of his life he refused to be associated with them: when he denied being an Ibāḍī[22] (if indeed he was ever really asked the question), he was not simply disguising his views, he objected to being labelled with the name of one of the nascent political parties which risked splitting the unity of the Jamāʿat al-Muslimīn.

Jābir's political role was one of consultation by the initiated.[23] He was not an imam (at least not outside the sense of a leader in prayer) or president of some Ibāḍī council which ordered the killing of spies like Khardullāh:[24] at most he may have indicated to the more active of his associates that under the particular circumstances the elimination of this dangerous spy might be justifiable. The Jamāʿat al-Muslimīn was simply a loose association of the more learned Baṣrans with a similar viewpoint, who discussed amongst themselves principles and problems. The idea of a formal council with a presumably elected imam is an ex post facto rationalization. The implications of its existence and of Jābir's role in it--and they are only an implication if the early Ibāḍī sources are studied carefully--arise from the need to push back the beginnings of the movement. The embellishment of this early history is, I suggest, largely the work of Abū Sufyān Maḥbūb b. al-Raḥīl (Shammākhī's source), the last Baṣran imam of the first half of the third century A.H.,[25] and his son Abū ʿAbdallāh Muḥammad (d. 260/873).

Jābir's founding role in Ibāḍism has been achieved in several ways, notably:

(a) by rationalizing certain incidents and exaggerating his participation in them. The case of Khardullāh has already been cited; another example is his association with Abū Bilāl. According to the sources it is they together who extract a tawba from ʿĀʾisha for her part in the rising against ʿAlī (thereby also conveniently disposing of this particular awkwardness), whilst later Abū Bilāl is made to consult with Jābir before his secession: to avoid pitfalls Jābir is conveniently found absent in Oman at the time while his opinion is stated in the most ambiguous of terms.

(b) by exaggerating the dangers he ran and invoking taqiyya and kitmān (the doctrines of dissimulation and of the imamate in concealment) to cover up awkward moments. In fact if we examine the reports carefully it will be found that Jābir is claimed to have been in danger only twice. The first time was during Ibn Ziyād's persecutions when everyone was at risk; but whilst others were being tortured and imprisoned Jābir was never more than suspect, as he himself admits to Ibn ʿAbbās. The second occasion is towards the end of Ḥajjāj's government when once again all potential and actual opposition was forcibly dealt with. This time Jābir is exiled to Oman with, significantly enough, Abū Sufyān's own great?-grandfather; in contrast the real leaders of the Ibāḍī movement-to-be, Ḍumām b. Sā'ib and Abū ʿUbayda Muslim b. Abī Karīma are cruelly imprisoned in Baṣra.[26] Such an exile in any case is impossible because on Abū ʿUbayda's own testimony Jābir died at home in Baṣra in A.H. 93.[27] To counteract this difficulty, another date for his death occurs in the sources, A.H. 96, i.e. after Ḥajjāj's death when the real Ibāḍī leaders were released and Jābir might feasibly have returned to Baṣra. But the prolonging of Jābir's life does not end there for reasons that are connected with the "succession" of his "pupil" Abū ʿUbayda.

(c) if Abū ʿUbayda, who it will be shown was the real organizer of the Ibāḍiyya in the period of political activation after ʿUmar II's death, is to succeed Jābir then it would be convenient to have Jābir die at an even later time, hence two other quoted dates for his demise, 103 and 104, plausible enough since he would only be in his eighties, nothing very aged for early Islamic hagiography. This, however, is only part of the manipulation. Its main aspect is the intensification of the relationship between Abū ʿUbayda and Jābir, notably that of pupil-teacher.

Abū ʿUbayda was not a pupil of Jābir's, or at least if he was he was only a minor one. This is not just because he was only a very young man when Jābir was teaching but because the sources, Abū Sufyān himself first and foremost, say that Abū ʿUbayda's main teachers were Ḍumām b. Sā'ib, a much older man and a real pupil of Jābir, Jaʿfar b. al-Sammāk, and Ṣuḥār al-ʿAbdī.[28] Perhaps more serious from the point of Muslim scholarship is the fact that in the Musnad (also known al Al-Jāmiʿ al-ṣaḥīḥ), in which Abū ʿUbayda's successor, Al-Rabīʿ b. Ḥabīb al-Farāhīdī, collected Jābir's transmissions, the chain almost inevitably runs Rabīʿ-Abū ʿUbayda-Jābir. This does not necessarily invalidate their accuracy, for Jābir's transmissions were recorded elsewhere,[29] notably in a somewhat mysterious Dīwān, and in such extant works as the Aqwāl of his pupil Qatāda (died

117-18) and a Ḥifẓ by Abū Ṣufra ʿAbd al-Malik b. Ṣufra of transmissions recorded by Ḍumām, known as the Kitāb Ḍumām. But it does cast a little doubt on the Ibāḍī claim that it is the most important book after the Qur'ān, a fortiori when it is remembered that the version used is in an arrangement (Tartīb) made by Abū Yaʿqūb Yūsuf b. Ibrāhīm al-Warajlānī who died in 570/1174.[30]

(d) another argument which is sometimes used by those unacquainted with the early tribal relationships of the Gulf is to build on Jābir's Azd connections. This is futile, for as will be shown at the end of this paper he belonged to the "establishment" Azd clans who for long bitterly opposed the Ibāḍī revolution. In any case, if Masʿūdī[31] is to be believed, Jābir was only a mawlā of his tribe.

No, the reality of the situation is that Jābir was an apolitical figure, even though a believer in the basic doctrines of unitarian Khārijism. He may have been pious and ascetic, but the fact remains that he drew a comfortable salary from the dīwān, took care to remain on good terms with Ḥajjāj's secretary Yazīd b. Muslim, and was never in serious danger of his life. But whilst he was never president of any council, Ibāḍī or otherwise, he was muftī of Baṣra and a reliable transmitter. It was as a jurist and teacher that he influenced those of his pupils who were to become Ibāḍīs. His was an indirect contribution to Ibāḍism and he most certainly was not the founder of the sect.

Proto-Ibāḍism

But if the key figures of this second ṭabaqa cannot really be considered as Ibāḍiyya there were nevertheless members from a particular milieu bridging the second and third ṭabaqas who were beginning to develop a more specific political ideology from certain general principles of the unitarians that can perhaps be labelled proto-Ibāḍī. The doctrines help explain who these people were.

The first, deriving from the Muḥakkima, was that precedence was in Islam. From this developed the rules of wilāya (and its converse barā'a) determining past and present membership of the community and authority within it. Wilāya is God's friendship which is given to believers (wilāyat Allāh li'l-mu'minīn).[32] Those that have wilāya form the community and its members associate with all who seek the path of Islam.[33] Leadership stems from excellence (faḍl), and the confidence that the community places in its imam to judge by Islamic precepts (al-maʿrūf) established by those with precedence (ʿulamāʾ, ḥamalat al-ʿilm, arbāb al-ḥall wa'l-ʿaqd) constitutes his authority (wilāya). The ḥadīth that the imam is from Quraysh and others of the preferred simply indicates that Quraysh and non-Quraysh are equals, an interpretation reinforced by the Prophet's statement that mawlā ʾl-qawm minhum.[34]

Such doctrine obviously had enormous appeal for the underdog. It is not surprising, therefore, to find that the figures who were starting to formulate it were from the humblest Baṣran background: Jaʿfar b. al-Sammāk, son of a fisherman (variant Sammān, butter merchant), Abū Nūḥ Ṣāliḥ b. Nūḥ al-Dahhān, the painter/greaser who lived in the Ṭayy quarter, Abū ʿUbayda Muslim b. Abī Karīma, a basket weaver (qaffāf) who was a mawlā of the Banī Tamīm.

The second principle, deriving from the basic stance of the unitarians that reform must be within the existing framework of the Islamic state, was that other Muslims were Ahl al-Qibla. This meant that in the expansionist phase of Ibāḍism, the property (so long as this was legally acquired) of those Muslims defeated, as well as their persons, was inviolate, whilst in the defensive the Ibāḍīs could disguise their views and associate with non-members. Such political pragmatism obviously had appeal for those who sincerely desired ordered reform but were not of the mould which makes heroes (shurāt). Hence the early attachment to the nascent movement of members of the Baṣran merchant community, few of whom had reason to love the Umayyads. Apart from the disdain with which the Ḥijāzī élite treated this polyglot mercantile society whose trading organization inherited from the Sasānids stretched from the Gulf to India (the Arḍ al-Hind), they specifically suffered from a law[35] whereby they could only sell Gulf agricultural produce once the state had disposed of its own revenue in kind.

What these proto-Ibāḍīs still lacked, however, was a significant political following. At one time, in the latter part of Ḥajjāj's governorship, they may have made some ground in dissatisfied tribal circles, but the main Yamanī leaders had little need for religious dogma to back their resistance to central government, a fortiori a dogma propagated by their social inferiors who undermined their authority. Such ground as they may have gained was, in any case, largely cut away by the reversal of Ḥajjājian policy when Sulaymān succeeded to the caliphate, whilst under ʿUmar II many of the reforms claimed by the unitarian Khawārij were met; indeed so far did ʿUmar go that Abū ʿUbayda regretted that the Ibāḍī mission to Damascus was not able completely to reconcile itself to him and accord him recognition (wilāya).[36]

The death of ʿUmar b. ʿAbd al-ʿAzīz and the accession to the caliphate by Yazīd II reversed this whole situation. Now the Yaman party was in rout whilst any reconciliation between central government and the proponents of moderate Khārijī reform was henceforth impossible. The time for the two to make common cause had come.

The Organization of the Daʿwa

During the first half of the second century A.H. the Ibāḍī movement began to undergo a profound change and it is probably from this period that its members began to be known by others as Ibāḍiyya.[37] From being a nascent school within the unitarian Khawārij movement it now becomes a daʿwa with a properly defined membership and doctrine and organizing missionary activities.

It had three father figures, Ḍumām b. Sā'ib, Jaʿfar b. al-Sammāk/Sammām and Abū ʿUbayda Muslim b. Abī Karīma. The first, a Baṣran born Omani of bedouin origin, was in fact a much more important figure than the Ibāḍī sources might indicate. He was the main teacher of Abū ʿUbayda, with whom he was imprisoned by Ḥajjāj, and was probably the main Ibāḍī authority for the transmissions of Jābir b. Zayd; he also played an important role in formulating the rules of association and dissociation (wilāya and barā'a) which determined past and present membership of the community.[38] Jaʿfar too was a teacher of Abū ʿUbayda and a member of the proto-Ibāḍī mission to ʿUmar II: a man of humble station, he was considered the main religious authority amongst his contemporaries. These two elder statesmen were later succeeded by Abū Nūḥ Ṣāliḥ b. Nūḥ al-Dahhān as the main religious guiding figure in the movement. But the real jurist who began to develop their ideas into a proto-madhhab and organize a daʿwa was Abū ʿUbayda.[39]

This involved the finding and training of agents who would propagate Ibāḍī ideas and supervise the setting up of Ibāḍī states when the time was propitious. Such missionary activities were most carefully organized. In the case of North Africa recruiters were first sent out; in the cases of southern Arabia, Oman and Khurāsān the material was at hand; the ḥajj was also a suitable occasion for sounding out potential followers. But however recruited, all had to come to Başra for a sound grounding in doctrine. These secretly trained missionaries (ḥamalat al-ʿilm) were the Ibāḍī chicks hatched in Başra. At this stage they were numerous: they flew to Medina and Mecca; to Yemen and Ḥaḍramawt; to Oman, Baḥrayn and even further afield in the Arḍ al-Hind; to Sadarāt, Ghadamès, Nafzāwa and elsewhere in North Africa; and to Mosul, Khurāsān, Khwārizm and even Mişr. These latter places, except perhaps Khurāsān, were never serious centres for propaganda; but they were areas with considerable anti-Umayyad feeling where sympathisers might usefully be recruited.

Such organization obviously required proper financing and this material side of the business was in the hands of Abū Mawdūd Ḥājib, an Omani merchant of Ṭayy origin based in Başra who died in Abū Jaʿfar Manṣūr's reign shortly before Abū ʿUbayda.[40] Two assistants worked tirelessly collecting money for his dīwān which not only had to bear the cost of political activities but also aid the poor of the community. The main source of income was the merchants, in particular those involved in the Gulf trade living in Başra and the monsoon entrepôt of Şuḥār on the Omani coast, but there were also others, including one important Meccan, a gold-dealer (?), trading between Başra and his home town. Although he, and at least one of the Gulf merchants, lost their lives when the Ibāḍī revolts broke out at the end of Umayyad times, these traders were generally not shurāt; they contributed to the cause through financial help and through their trade network which permitted relative freedom of communication when movement outside the period of the ḥajj might have been regarded with suspicion.[41]

Behind this new Ibāḍī organization lay the political unrest which it hoped to organize. Two major areas were selected for preparation, the Berber territory of North Africa, and the Peninsula homelands of the discontented Yamanī tribes. To treat both these areas would be far too lengthy a business but, fortunately, we may eliminate the distinct North African field since this has already been adequately covered by T. Lewicki in numerous articles. At first sight the Arabian picture would appear complex, for certainly in Abū ʿUbayda's time propaganda was directed at Oman, Yaman, Ḥaḍramawt and the Holy Cities themselves, whilst the spectacular success of installing ʿAbdallāh b. Yaḥyā al-Kindī as Ibāḍī imam over the last-mentioned during the ḥajj of 129 resulted from co-operation between Ibāḍīs in all these areas. But the man who recruited ʿAbdallāh and co-ordinated plans during the hajj of the previous year and who led the joint Omani-Ḥaḍramī force which installed him as "Ṭālib al-Ḥaqq" was an Omani, Mukhtār b. ʿAwf. And the dominant role in the history of the Ibāḍī movement always came from Oman; indeed when Ḥaḍramawt finally broke away in the fifth century A.H., it signalled the end of Ibāḍism there. So it is with a study of how the Omanis were recruited to the Ibāḍī cause that this paper will conclude.

The Omani Conversion

To understand the Omani adherence to the Ibāḍī calling it is necessary first to understand something of their tribal and leadership organization.

Within the tribal structure of the Azd of south-east Arabia was a major split which is represented in the outside sources as being between Azd ʿUmān and Azd Shanūʾa, although both were Omanis. It was the latter who provided the paramount leaders through the Julandā clan; but their authority outside the mountain area occupied by their own Shanūʾa following (Awlād Shums and Yaḥmad) and Kinda allies stemmed from an alliance with the Banū Hunāʾa, whose shaykhs claimed leadership over the earlier Azd settlers living in the bajada zone,[42] that is other Mālik b. Fahm tribes and the two major divisions of ʿImrān led by the ʿAtīk. On the other hand Hunāʾī power was limited: it was strongly resented by a grouping from the Mālik b. Fahm led by the Maʿn, whilst those members of the powerful Banū Salīma who lived in Oman tended to look to the Persian Coast where their shaykhs had established control over the strategic centres at the entrance of the Gulf (the Julandā b. Karkar family). Also of importance in the tribal equation was the fact that the Mālik b. Fahm tribes were generally on good relations with the ʿAbd al-Qays, whose own power extended from Baḥrayn (eastern Arabia) to the desert borderlands of Oman, whilst the ʿAtīk were the pivot of a working agreement with the Banū Nājiyya (Sāma b. Luʾay) of northern Oman, the most powerful non-Azd tribe of the country.

Early Omani participation in the wars of conquest was as members of ʿUthmān Ibn Abī al-ʿĀṣī al-Thaqafī's army which campaigned on the Persian coast of the Gulf from Tawwaj: their contingents divided along the lines already indicated, Shanūʾa, Mālik b. Fahm, ʿImrān, Azd Baḥrayn, ʿAbd al-Qays, Banū Rāsib and Banū Nājiyya. Their subsequent settlement in Baṣra followed the same lines, with the leadership of the Azd in the hands of the second-string tribes comprising the Azd power bloc at home, that is the Ḥuddān, a brother clan of the Maʿwilī Julandā, the Jahāḍim, Mālik b. Fahm allies of the Banū Hunā'a, and the ʿAtīk.[43]

The successes of the Baṣran armies in their new campaigns in Persia sparked off a new wave of migration to the miṣr from Oman. These newcomers, for the most part, came from the desert borderlands of south-east Arabia: ʿAbd al-Qays and Mālik b. Fahm badw whose links with the "establishment" tribes had been considerably weakened since the latter had gained control of the villages of Oman after the eviction of the Persian ruling classes with the coming of Islam. Tension between these newcomers, represented as the "Azd ʿUmān," led by a Maʿnī, and the establishment Azd (that is the alliance backing the Shanū'a, now under an ʿAtakī), reached a peak during the events of A.H. 64 when the Maʿnī leader (Masʿūd b. ʿAmr, known as Qamar al-ʿIrāq) tried to seize control over Baṣra and forced ʿUbaydallāh Ibn Ziyād to seek refuge with his old friends, the "establishment" Azd, who had helped save his father some quarter of a century earlier.[44] Following Masʿūd's murder at the hands of a Tamīmī ʿilj Fārsī the whole Azd alliance was dragged to the brink of a full-scale tribal war with the Tamīm, but fortunately the intervention of Masʿūd's half-brother(?),[45] al-Muhallab b. Abī Ṣufra, and the statesmanship of al-Aḥnaf b. Qays on behalf of the Tamīm, saved the day. Shortly afterwards the turbulent Azd ʿUmān found themselves otherwise engaged in al-Muhallab's wars against the Khawārij extremists; their subsequent history remained closely linked with that of the Muhallabites and this kept them pretty well out of Baṣra.

So where then do the Muhallabites fit into this tribal picture?[46] In the first place it must be clearly understood that they were not a shaykhly family. Accounts of the origins of al-Muhallab's father are highly contradictory while the genealogy which tries to place him in ʿAtīk is equally suspect. His enemies were probably telling the truth when they say that Abū Ṣufra was originally a weaver from Kharg island called Beshkharé, who enlisted in Ibn Abī 'l-ʿAṣī's service as a sayce (groom). It was therefore as a warrior that Muhallab's father established his reputation and it was in the same way that his son enhanced it. But the Muhallabites were never true clan leaders and their followers were soldiers of fortune largely recruited from the Omani badw. They had little tribal influence in Başra, where they continued to be resented by the Azd establishment right down to the final collapse of their power.

It was the brusque reversal of the fortunes of Yazīd b. al-Muhallab and his Azd ʿUmān at the beginning of Yazīd II's reign which opened the way for Ibāḍī propaganda. Hitherto the Omanis had had little interest in unitarian Khawārij doctrine; on the contrary their interests lay in supporting the central government regime whose policies, except in the late Ḥajjājian period, had generally brought them fortune. So, whilst the early Muhallabites are quite specifically stated as not belonging to the ṭarīq,[47] some of its later members were recruited, largely through their women-folk (a favourite tactic of the Ibāḍīs).[48]

Three principal figures[49] worked for Abū ʿUbayda to raise support amongst the defeated tribesmen, many of whom had slunk back to Oman which had remained outside central government control ever since ʿUmar II's governor there had handed his office to Ziyād b. al-Muhallab following the caliph's death:

(a) Abū ʿAmr al-Rabīʿ b. Ḥabīb al-Farāhīdī, the man who later succeeded Abū ʿUbayda and probably began the process of formalizing an Ibāḍī school by recording Jābir b. Zayd's transmission in the Musnad. He seems to have been directly active in Oman before the first attempts to establish the imamate. (At the end of his life he was again directly active in propagating Ibāḍism in Oman, having handed over the reins of office in Başra to the Ḥaḍramī Abū Ayyūb Wā'il b. Ayyūb. Rabīʿ b. Ḥabīb died at his home at Ghaḍfān, near Şuḥār, in 170/786, seven years before the decisive battle of Majāza in which the Julandā were finally defeated by the Ibāḍīs.)

(b) Al-Mukhtār b. ʿAwf of the Banū Salīma who came from Majazz, and was to organize the revolt which put Ṭālib al-Ḥaqq as imam over Yaman and, finally, the Holy Cities.

(c) His recruit Balj b. ʿUqba, a Farāhīdī from his home village of Majazz: Balj was to command the Omani contingent which jointed Mukhtār's rising.

All three, it will be noted, came from Mālik b. Fahm tribes that had fought with the Muhallabites, and all three came from the Bāṭina coast of Oman, geographically and economically linked with the Gulf maritime society in which Ibāḍism flourished and removed from the domain of the tribal Julandā, whose real power rested in the mountain interior. It was from this coastal region too, that came the support for the first imam that the Omanis and Khurāsānīs selected after the defeat of Ṭālib al-Ḥaqq, al-Julandā b. Mas'ūd. And it was in his struggle with his kinsmen, in which, as imam, al-Julandā was forced to execute members of the ruling section, that there arose the implacable enmity of the tribal ruling establishment of the interior towards the Ibāḍī regime that was to prevent it from re-establishing their state in Oman for nearly another half century after the imam Julandā's death c. A.H. 133. Only by giving a free hand to the predatory tribes of the Azd 'Umān, and by offering the imamate to the rival Yaḥmad branch of the Julandā in the Shanū'a Azd confederation, were the Ibāḍīs eventually able to build up a tribal alliance which enabled them to defeat the Julandā and establish their government.[50] The hatreds engendered by the ruthless way the Ibāḍīs let loose the anti-Julandā tribesmen in the guise of being shurāt, however, were never completely subdued and were contributory to the events leading to the terrible civil war that marks the real end of the Ibāḍī Golden Age in southern Arabia at the end of the third century.

The Ṣufriyya-Ibāḍiyya Split

Further details of the initial attempts to set up imamates in Abū 'Ubayda's time during the late Umayyad-early 'Abbāsid period and of the eventual success in securing the southern Arabian and Tāhert imamates, as also of the later history of the Baṣran Ibāḍīs and their final withdrawal to Oman, lie outside the scope of this paper. One further aspect of the early expansion of the Ibāḍī movement from Baṣra remains to be touched on, that is the dispute with the Ṣufriyya. As already indicated, the origins of this split reputedly go back to the tafrīq of A.H. 64. Whether in fact some sort of nascent Ṣufrī movement can be traced back in the same way as that of the Ibāḍīs matters little, because early differences in the ideologies of the unitarian Khawārij schools were minor, as is symbolized by the story of how the first Ibāḍī and Ṣufrī dā'īs came to Ifriqiyyā riding the same camel.[51] What really counted is that in their period of political activity the Ibāḍīs and Ṣufrīs began to recruit from rival tribal domains. The virulence of feeling that consequently developed may be judged from the fact that when the remnants of the Ṣufriyya took refuge in Oman from the 'Abbāsid army of Khāzim b. Khuzayma al-Khurāsānī (c. A.H. 133), the Ibāḍīs under al-Julandā b. Masʿūd immediately marched out and slaughtered them.

So it can be seen that while Ibāḍī doctrine may have originated in a non-tribal milieu, it was closely linked with the political ambitions of tribal or national groups in its period of expansion. At a later stage it was able to modify the excesses of the tribal way of life in Oman, but its history was never divorced wholly from tribal politics. Indeed it could not be, for at root the concepts of the imāma and wilāya represented a religious transformation of tribal formulations of political power. Had determination of the organization of this community and of the authority of its leader remained entirely within the province of Islamic precedence, then the Ibāḍī imamate would have forever stayed in kitmān and its membership remained an intellectual society secretly plotting away in cellars in Baṣra. By linking fundamental Islamic principles to the temporal ambitions of particular groups opposed to the existing political regimes, Ibāḍism was able to reach fruition (ẓuhūr). But the cost it paid was that, in Oman at least, the imam's authority remained entirely religious: the execution of "God's laws by which he judged" lay firmly in the hands of the tribal leaders of his community. ʿIlm and ʿaṣabiyya stemmed from two different sources; in the interests of a tribal democracy it was essential that they remained that way.

8

SOME IMĀMĪ SHĪʿĪ INTERPRETATIONS OF UMAYYAD HISTORY

E. Kohlberg

In the very title of his book, Die religiös-politischen Oppositionsparteien im alten Islam,[1] Julius Wellhausen long ago drew our attention to the central role played by anti-government forces in the Umayyad period. Of these forces, none posed a greater threat to the caliphate or were more instrumental in bringing about its ultimate demise than the various Shīʿī groups, or sects. Not all of these groups were equally successful: some suffered quick, ignominious defeats and did not survive the regime which they had vowed to overthrow; others proved to be highly effective, but then disintegrated or were transformed into virtually new entities; while yet others combined durability with relative passivity. To this last category belongs Imāmī Shīʿism--or, more precisely, that Shīʿī sect which constituted the nucleus of the later Imāmiyya. Imāmī Shīʿism cannot be described as having displayed a particularly vigorous opposition to the Umayyads; in fact, during most of the Umayyad period its leaders played no political role whatever. On the other hand, it not only proved to be durable, but attracted in subsequent generations a growing number of adherents, until it came in due course to be regarded as the most important representative of Shīʿism.

The central position of Imāmī Shīʿism in Islam makes it worth asking how the Imāmīs themselves view their role in the Umayyad period. As is only to be expected, Imāmī scholars have always insisted that theirs is the only true Islamic faith, and that all other sects deviated from the Imāmiyya at various points in history. Naturally, this outlook had a direct bearing on the Imāmī interpretation of events. The interpretation was undertaken with two major aims in mind: first, to define and justify the attitudes adopted by the imams towards the Umayyads, and second, to defend the views of the Imāmiyya against attacks by rival Shīʿī groups. We shall begin by looking into the actions and utterances ascribed to the imams and relating directly to the Umayyad rulers, and then briefly focus our attention on relations with some non-Imāmī Shī'īs.

I

The essential historical facts are well known and not generally disputed by either side: five of the twelve imams recognized by the Imāmiyya as legitimate lived during the Umayyad period; the first of them, al-Ḥasan b. 'Ali (died c. 49/669), yielded power to Mu'āwiya; al-Ḥasan's younger brother al-Ḥusayn rose in revolt against Mu'āwiya's successor Yazīd and subsequently fell in the battle of Karbalā' (Muḥarram 61/October 680); 'Alī Zayn al-'Ābidīn (died 94/710-711 or 95/712-713), Muḥammad al-Bāqir (died 114/732 or 117/735) and Ja'far al-Ṣādiq (died 148/765) (the fourth, fifth and sixth imams) retreated to Medina, dissociated themselves from any overt anti-Umayyad activities, and devoted their energies to the consolidation of the Shī'ī heritage.

Yet these very facts confronted the Imāmiyya with some serious problems, the most obvious of which is posed by the fact that Imāmī doctrine holds that all twelve imams are immune from error and sin (ma'ṣūmūn), and serve as the sole guides of the community; their actions and behavior are the model which it is incumbent upon all to follow. Now each of the five imams of the Umayyad period faced the same problem, how to cope with an illegitimate, usurping power. Yet they do not seem to have reacted in the same manner: four of them acquiesced in the Umayyad rule, while al-Ḥusayn raised his sword against it. How can this difference be explained? The question looms largest when applied to the dramatically contrasting actions of al-Ḥasan and al-Ḥusayn. Why did al-Ḥusayn rebel, even though he faced graver dangers than al-Ḥasan? Nor did this question remain purely academic: according to the information in the Firaq al-shī'a of al-Nawbakhtī,[2] it precipitated an early crisis among a group of supporters of the two imams; the lack of a satisfactory answer led them to cast doubts on the validity of the imamate of the two brothers and to renounce Shī'ism.

The most obvious and uncompromising Imāmī reaction to such a question is to dismiss it out of hand by arguing that since the imam is by definition ma'ṣūm, his decisions are always right and may never be questioned, even when the reasoning behind them is not immediately clear.[3] In this context, reference is made to the Qur'ānic story of Moses and one of

God's servants (usually said to be al-Khaḍir) (Qur'ān 8:65(64) ff): Moses berated al-Khaḍir for various seemingly cruel actions, such as boring a hole in a ship and thus endangering the lives of all aboard; only later did Moses realize that al-Khaḍir's actions derived from his possession of secret knowledge.[4] Such an argument, convincing though it may sound to an Imāmī, is obviously not good enough when addressed to adversaries who would challenge the premiss upon which it is based, namely the ʿiṣma of the imam.

More to the point, it is often argued that all actions of the imams have been predetermined by God. This idea is exemplified by a large body of traditions. According to one of these traditions, Gabriel gave Muḥammad a heavenly scroll, which consisted of twelve sections, each sealed by a separate seal. The sections contained the instructions (waṣiyya) for the twelve imams. Whenever one of them assumed the office of imam, he would break open his particular seal and act in accordance with the instructions in the corresponding section. Thus al-Ḥusayn's instructions were: "You will fight, kill and be killed; only you will lead men to martyrdom." Just before his death, al-Ḥusayn ordered the scroll to be passed on to ʿAlī Zayn al-ʿĀbidīn, who was in turn instructed to keep silent, remain at his home and worship his lord. ʿAlī's son Muḥammad al-Bāqir was told to explain the Qur'ān, spread the Shīʿī heritage among the people, and speak the truth regardless of the dangers involved.[5] In other traditions, the Prophet speaks of the future actions of each imam. Thus it is preordained that each imam will be forced to give the bayʿa to the tyrant of his age, except for the Qā'im, who will install a reign of justice.[6] In a Risāla ascribed to Jaʿfar al-Ṣādiq a similar idea recurs: the imams will have to undergo many ordeals and suffer persecution and injustice before they are returned to power.[7] The third of the four representatives (safīrs) of the period of the Small Occultation, Abū 'l-Qāsim Ḥusayn b. Rūḥ, makes a more general statement: God has ordained that His prophets and messengers will not always be victorious, but will also suffer defeat; occasional defeat is necessary so as to teach them the virtue of perseverance in the face of adversity, and in order to prevent people from worshipping them as gods.[8] This statement might be regarded as applying to the imams as well.

In addition to such deterministic arguments, attempts are also made to provide a rational explanation for the behavior of the two imams. In the case of al-Ḥasan, justification is first of all provided by the precedent of both Muḥammad and 'Alī. The Prophet was forced on several occasions in his career to come to terms with the unbelievers or to seek refuge from them. On all these occasions, Muḥammad was deprived of an alternative by his lack of the support of a sufficiently large number of followers.[9] For the same reason, 'Alī had to suffer the usurpation of power by Abū Bakr, 'Umar and 'Uthmān. Thus, when the Shī'īs promised al-Ḥasan that they would obey him, he is said to have reminded them that he could not place his trust in them, since they had been disloyal to his father;[10] subsequent events proved the validity of al-Ḥasan's premonitions. In Shī'ī tradition, those who were ready to heed al-Ḥasan's call for a jihād against Mu'āwiya are described as a mixed lot: except for a hard core of supporters who had previously also helped 'Alī out of a genuine belief in the Shī'ī cause, al-Ḥasan's camp consisted of Khārijīs (who joined only because of their hatred for Mu'āwiya), adventurers propelled by their greed for booty, and men who were merely following the leaders of their tribes and whose motivation was 'aṣabiyya, not the wish to fight for the true faith.[11] It is not surprising that al-Ḥasan did not feel secure with these men; indeed, the Khārijīs soon turned against him, while others sent secret messages to Mu'āwiya, pledging their support and promising to undermine al-Ḥasan's cause from within.[12] These men made an outward show of loyalty to al-Ḥasan and urged him to fight, but only in order to get him embroiled in battle, so that they might then be able to deliver him to Mu'āwiya.[13] On the Day of Judgment, says a Shī'ī tradition, only two men will come forward when the disciples (ḥawārī) of al-Ḥasan are asked to make their appearance.[14]

A different argument is presented regarding the nature of al-Ḥasan's agreement with Mu'āwiya. In Sunnī sources, al-Ḥasan is often described as having willingly renounced all claims, and as having recognized Mu'āwiya as the sole legitimate ruler. For the Shī'īs, on the other hand, it is absurd to claim that al-Ḥasan abdicated, because a Shī'ī imam cannot give up the office which he has been given by God.[15] They therefore maintain that al-Ḥasan's apparent recognition of Mu'āwiya--just like 'Alī's apparent recognition of Abū Bakr--consisted only of the physical act of a handclasp (ṣafqa) and of an outward show of satisfaction, but was not indicative of true consent.[16] Hence it was not a "real bay'a" (bay'a ḥaqīqiyya), but merely a temporary truce (muhādana), which was intended to save the lives of al-Ḥasan's followers.[17] The fact that al-Ḥasan refused to address Muʿāwiya as amīr al-mu'minīn proves that he did not accept him as the ruler.[18] Indeed, when Muʿāwiya asked him to wage a campaign against Khārijī dissidents, al-Ḥasan refused.[19]

As for al-Ḥusayn, a comprehensive analysis of his behavior is provided by the famous Imāmī theologian al-Sharīf al-Murtaḍā (died 436/1044):[20] after al-Ḥasan's death, says al-Murtaḍā, al-Ḥusayn became imam, but he did not openly challenge Muʿāwiya, out of respect for the truce which had been agreed upon between Muʿāwiya and al-Ḥasan. Contrary to the claims of al-Ḥasan's critics, the muhādana was not for an indefinite period, but was to last only for Muʿāwiya's lifetime.[21] After the caliph's death, a growing number of Kūfans appealed to al-Ḥusayn to lead them against the Umayyads. As their appeals and pledges of support grew increasingly insistent, al-Ḥusayn concluded that it was his duty to respond and to fight for his rights. He used his best judgment (ijtihād), and did not think that so many Kūfans would desert him. Nor could al-Ḥusayn foresee his bad luck (al-ittifāq al-sayyi'), epitomised by the killing of his cousin Muslim b. ʿAqīl. When al-Ḥusayn realized that his chances of success were dwindling, he tried to retreat, but was prevented from doing so by al-Ḥurr b. Yazīd. It is therefore unjust to accuse al-Ḥusayn of recklessly sending his men to their deaths. Even during the last desperate hours at Karbalā', al-Ḥusayn would have been ready to come to terms with his enemies; but ʿUbaydallāh b. Ziyād turned down all his proposals, agreeing only to provide him with a safe-conduct. Al-Ḥusayn knew Ibn Ziyād's treachery, could not trust him, and was left with no choice but to fight and be killed as shahīd, together with his closest family and followers. It thus follows that there is no contradiction between the actions of al-Ḥasan and al-Ḥusayn: like their father before them, they both wished to avoid going to war when they realized they faced overwhelming odds; both were ready to come to terms with the Umayyads, except that al-Ḥasan was able to do so while al-Ḥusayn was not.

One aspect of al-Sharīf al-Murtaḍā's apology must have caused discomfort among some Imāmīs, namely the argument that al-Ḥusayn did not know what would happen. This can hardly be reconciled with the doctrine that the imams know future events. An attempt to overcome this hurdle is made by the Shīrāzī scholar ʿAlī Khān b. Aḥmad Ibn Maʿṣūm (died 1120/1708) (who does not say if he is relying on earlier authorities). He draws a distinction between outward knowledge (al-ʿulūm al-ẓāhiriyya), based on known facts and the conclusions which may be drawn from them, and secret knowledge (al-ʿulūm al-ghaybiyya), known only to the imam. The imam may act only in accordance with the outward knowledge, even when he knows through his secret, inner knowledge that such action will prove unwise. For example: when it looked as if the Kūfans were ready to obey al-Ḥusayn, he had to fight for the glorification of God's religion, even though he knew he would be defeated. Conversely, al-Ḥasan agreed to call off the jihād when it seemed as if he and his supporters might otherwise come to harm.[22] Ibn Maʿṣūm does not spell out the reasons for this behavior on the part of the imams; perhaps the idea is that since they wish to conceal their superior knowledge (primarily from enemies, but often also from sympathizers), they must be seen to be acting in an apparently rational manner.

A modern Shīʿī interpretation of the motives of al-Ḥasan and al-Ḥusayn is that of Muḥammad Riḍā al-Muẓaffar in his *ʿAqā'id al-imāmiyya*.[23] Al-Muẓaffar maintains that, in the eyes of both imams, the ultimate interests of Islam took precedence over all other considerations. For that reason, al-Ḥasan made his peace with Muʿāwiya (even though the Hāshimīs had a legitimate case and were ready to fight for it), thus placing the unity of Islam above his own rights. By the time al-Ḥusayn became imam the situation had, however, changed: the Umayyads, who were by then firmly entrenched in power, were proving to be godless and evil; al-Ḥusayn believed that if they were not checked, they would obliterate all traces of Islam. His revolt was therefore meant to draw attention to their unjust rule, and thus to save Islam from final destruction.

With al-Ḥusayn's death, the "active" phase of the early history of the Imāmiyya drew to a close. The political passivity of the imams in subsequent generations (which did not spare them harassment by suspicious rulers) posed some intricate problems for Imāmī polemicists: it became essential for them to justify this passivity, to defend the imams against accusations of cowardice, to define clearly the attitude of the imams towards the reigning caliphs, and above all, to establish conclusively the imams' superiority to the Umayyad rulers.

The problem of the imams' passivity is tackled by arguing that the persecution of the Shīʿīs, coupled with their relatively small numbers, rendered any other policy foolhardy and even suicidal. Under such circumstances, the Imāmīs maintain, it is absurd to accuse the imams of cowardice for having refrained from open revolt. Such accusations, heard in Zaydī circles, were levelled mainly against ʿAlī Zayn al-ʿĀbidīn, whose withdrawn personality contrasted sharply with that of his father. The Imāmīs therefore make a point of stressing his valor. Thus it is said that after Karbalāʾ, ʿAlī Zayn al-Ābidīn told ʿUbaydallāh b. Ziyād that he would not be cowed by threats to his life, since "death [in battle] is customary with us, and martyrdom is a sign of our nobility."[24] When brought before Yazīd, ʿAlī spoke up for the rights of the _ahl al-bayt_ and reminded the caliph that ʿAlī b. Abī Ṭālib had been fighting at Muḥammad's side while the Umayyads were still unbelievers fighting against the Prophet.[25] When Yazīd dared ʿAlī Zayn al-ʿĀbidīn to wrestle with Yazīd's son Khālid, the imam is said to have retorted: "What will be gained by my wrestling with him? Give me a knife and him a knife, and let the stronger of us kill the weaker." Yazīd said: "You snake, son of a snake![26] I bear witness that you are indeed an offspring of ʿAlī b. Abī Ṭālib."[27] After ʿAbd al-Malik's accession, he asked ʿAlī Zayn al-ʿĀbidīn to hand him Muḥammad's sword; but the imam refused and would not yield to the caliph's threats.[28] When criticized by ʿAbbād al-Baṣrī[29] for preferring the gentle rites of the _ḥajj_ to the harshness of _jihād_, Zayn al-ʿĀbidīn answered that only the lack of a sufficient number of true believers prevented him from waging holy war.[30]

A more general point made in this context is that all imams share the same qualities, since they were all created from the same light substance (_min nūr wāḥid_). Yet each imam presented a different aspect of these qualities, in accordance with the exigencies of his particular situation. While ʿAlī and al-Ḥusayn were able to display their courage, the others were not, because they had been ordered by God to protect their lives. However, this does not invalidate the doctrine that each imam is the most courageous person of his generation.[31]

An additional vindication of the political inactivity of the imams is provided by traditions of a deterministic character, which are cited with the avowed aim of showing that the length of Umayyad rule and the manner of its final destruction were preordained. For example, when one of al-Bāqir's supporters voices the hope that God will grant al-Bāqir victory over the Umayyads, the imam is quoted as replying that those who are destined to liquidate the Umayyads are the "sons of fornication," that is, the 'Abbāsids.[32]

As mentioned before, the events at Karbalā' are seen as a watershed. Previously, open rebellion was carried out not only by al-Ḥusayn, but also by men such as Ḥujr b. 'Adī, 'Amr b. Ḥamiq and their followers, all of whom are claimed by the Imāmīs as their own.[33] Such activities tally with the Imāmī viewpoint that jihād against enemies within the Islamic world (who are known as bughāt) takes precedence over jihād against outside forces. Following Karbalā', however, jihād against Muslim enemies is considered to be in abeyance until the arrival of the Mahdī. During that period, the Shī'īs are to abstain from any contact with the rulers. Where such contacts are unavoidable, the imams and their followers may either resort to taqiyya or, when they feel they are not exposing themselves to mortal danger, they may speak out against the existing government.[34] On the question of Shī'ī participation in a Sunnī-led attack on infidels, the answer, ascribed to 'Alī al-Riḍā, is unambiguous: no Shī'ī may participate in an offensive jihād; his only duty is to defend the borders (i.e. ribāṭ). He should engage in actual warfare only when there is a direct threat to the territory of Islam; in such an event he would be fighting for his own personal survival and for the survival of Islam, but not for the Sunnī government which happened to hold power at the time.[35]

The adoption of deterministic views is one factor which makes it easier for the Imāmiyya to accept the fact that their leaders assumed a quiescent posture towards the Umayyads. Other factors are, first, anecdotes in which the superiority of the imams to the caliphs is highlighted; secondly, eschatological traditions; and thirdly, popular Shī'ī literature, in which the imams are vested with real power which they turn against the Umayyads.

The following are typical anecdotes. When Hishām b. 'Abd al-Malik (who is not yet caliph at the time) goes on a ḥajj to Mecca, he is unable to reach the Black Stone because of the crowds; but when Zayn al-'Ābidīn appears, he is shown great respect by all and has no difficulty in reaching the stone. Hishām feigns not to recognize Zayn al-'Ābidīn, but the poet Farazdaq, who happens to be there, immediately embarks on a long poem in praise of the Shī'ī imam.[36] When Hishām returns to Mecca some years later, this time as caliph, he engages in a legal and theological disputation with al-Bāqir, at the end of which even

Nāfiʿ (died 117/735), a mawlā of ʿAbdallāh b. ʿUmar b. al-Khaṭṭāb and a close associate of Hishām, acknowledges al-Bāqir's superior knowledge.[37] According to a story allegedly told by Hārūn al-Rashīd, ʿAbd al-Malik's famous decision to issue an Islamic gold coinage, replacing the Byzantine denarius by a Muslim dīnār, was made at the suggestion of al-Bāqir.[38] The credit for one of ʿAbd al-Malik's major administrative reforms thus goes to a Shīʿī imam.

As for eschatological traditions, these are sometimes based on Qur'ānic passages, and usually include vivid details of the ultimate revenge to be inflicted upon the Umayyads. On the coming of the Mahdī, we are told in one typical account, the Umayyads will seek refuge with the Byzantines, and will even agree to embrace the Christian faith in order to save their skins; yet they will be forced to return and will then be executed for their crimes.[39]

Finally, an example from popular Shīʿī literature: one day, al-Bāqir goes with his disciple Jābir to the Prophet's mosque, takes out of his pocket a thin thread (originally presented to Muḥammad by Gabriel), and hands Jābir one of its two ends. The imam slyly moves his end of the thread, then takes the other end back from Jābir. This movement causes a major earthquake in the town, in which more than 30,000 people die. The Umayyad governor immediately calls on the populace to go to Zayn al-ʿĀbidīn (who is the imam at the time) and repent. Al-Bāqir explains that his action served to cleanse the land of some Umayyads, and to warn the rest to stop harassing the Shīʿa. The imams only refrain from totally liquidating that evil dynasty, says Zayn al-ʿĀbidīn, because the period of Umayyad rule has been predetermined.[40]

Despite their wholesale condemnation of the Umayyads, Shīʿī traditionists sometimes single out particular rulers as less vicious than others. ʿAbd al-Malik, for example, is reported to have ordered al-Ḥajjāj to refrain from molesting members of the ahl al-bayt, since in his view the Sufyānīs were stripped of power as a direct result of their murder of al-Ḥusayn. Indeed, ʿAbd al-Malik is said on occasion to have treated Zayn al-ʿĀbidīn with great respect; Zayn al-ʿĀbidīn on his part informed the caliph that God would prolong his reign because he did not permit persecution of the Hāshimīs.[41]

The Imāmīs, in agreement with other anti-Umayyad writers, see in ʿUmar b. ʿAbd al-ʿAzīz the most shining example of virtue in the midst of evil. In a Shīʿī tradition, al-Bāqir prophesies that ʿUmar b. ʿAbd al-ʿAzīz will become caliph, will do his best to spread justice and will be honored by the people when he dies; at the same time al-Bāqir adds that the inhabitants of heaven will curse ʿUmar because, notwithstanding his good deeds, he sat on a throne to which he had no right.[42] ʿUmar is praised for having given the Hāshimīs large pensions, despite opposition from within his own family.[43] After al-Bāqir told ʿUmar to reign justly, the caliph is said to have ordered the return of Fadak to the Shīʿa.[44] A story is told about a meeting which ʿUmar held with a Khurāsānī scholar, who represented one hundred ʿulamāʾ of his country. The scholar proved to the caliph that the Umayyad dynasty was illegitimate, and was based neither on naṣṣ, nor on ijmāʿ (the Khurāsānians, for instance, were never consulted), nor on inheritance from the forefathers. ʿUmar acknowledged the correctness of these assertions and said that he only agreed to rule in order to rectify some of the injustice perpetrated by his predecessors.[45]

The only Umayyad personage who is completely acceptable to the Shīʿa seems to be Saʿīd (or Saʿd), a son of ʿAbd al-Malik by a slave mother, who is known as Saʿīd al-Khayr.[46] When Saʿīd started to weep in the belief that he belonged to the family referred to in the Qurʾān as "the cursed tree," al-Bāqir is said to have comforted him by telling him, "You do not belong to them; you are an Umayyad who is one of us, the ahl al-bayt."[47] The reason for this high praise appears to lie in Saʿīd's personal devotion to al-Bāqir.

II

The problems which arose with regard to relations between the imams and the Umayyad rulers are reflected in the issues which are raised by the Imāmīs in their polemics with representatives of other Shīʿī currents in the Umayyad period.

To begin with, let us take supporters of the imamate of Muḥammad Ibn al-Ḥanafiyya. Here the Imāmī aim is to demolish the claim of these supporters--Kaysānīs and others--that Ibn al-Ḥanafiyya was the only legitimate imam of his generation. This is done by one of two methods: it is either asserted that Ibn al-Ḥanafiyya neither claimed the imamate for himself, nor called on anyone to accept him as imam;[48] or else it is acknowledged that Ibn al-Ḥanafiyya did originally regard himself as imam, but that he subsequently realized his error and recognized the imamate of Zayn al-ʿĀbidīn. The story which is often recounted in this context tells of a dispute between

Ibn al-Ḥanafiyya and Zayn al-ʿĀbidīn concerning the identity of the imam, as a result of which the two agreed to go to Mecca and put their case before God. When the Black Stone pronounced that Zayn al-ʿĀbidīn was the only rightful imam, Ibn al-Ḥanafiyya immediately renounced his own claims and declared his loyalty to Zayn al-ʿĀbidīn.[49] Former adherents of Ibn al-Ḥanafiyya, such as Abū Khālid al-Kābulī, followed their master in recognizing the fourth imam;[50] and two sons of Ibn al-Ḥanafiyya, Ibrāhīm and al-Ḥasan, are mentioned in Imāmī texts among those who transmitted from Zayn al-ʿĀbidīn.[51]

The outcome of the alleged confrontation between Zayn al-ʿĀbidīn and Ibn al-Ḥanafiyya not only establishes Zayn al-ʿĀbidīn's superiority over his rival; it also confers a much-needed stamp of legitimacy on Zayn al-ʿĀbidīn's imamate. The validity of that imamate is more problematic than that of most other imams. It seems that Zayn al-ʿĀbidīn, unlike his two immediate successors, did not play any role in the development of Imāmī law. The reason appears to be that he was recognized as imam by the Imāmiyya only in the days of Jaʿfar al-Ṣādiq, when the dispute with Zayd b. ʿAlī made it imperative to buttress the doctrine that the imamate passes from father to son.[52] Until that time it was not uncommon for Shīʿīs to switch allegiance from one member of the <u>ahl al-bayt</u> to another.[53] Even Imāmī traditionists could not disregard the difficulties inherent in Zayn al-ʿĀbidīn's position: whereas al-Ḥasan and al-Ḥusayn were said to have been explicitly designated by Muḥammad himself, not all Shīʿīs acknowledge such a <u>naṣṣ</u> for Zayn al-ʿĀbidīn.[54] The later Imāmīs account for this by claiming that the relevant <u>naṣṣ</u> traditions enjoyed only a limited circulation because, following Karbalāʾ, the Shīʿīs were persecuted and so were unable to spread their traditions.[55]

An even greater challenge to the Imāmiyya than that posed by Ibn al-Ḥanafiyya stems from the revolt, in 122/740, of al-Bāqir's brother Zayd b. ʿAlī. No Imāmī disputes the correctness of the information provided by the historians on the occurrence of such a revolt; the polemics against the Zaydiyya concern instead Zayd's personality and the nature of his uprising.

Zayd himself is usually presented in a positive light as a devout, knowledgeable, generous and courageous person, who was surpassed in excellent qualities only by the imams themselves.[56] His revolt is seen as an attempt to free the Shīʿīs from the Umayyad yoke and to re-establish the rightful leaders.

The crucial point in the Imāmī version is that Zayd did not seek the imamate for himself, but instead regarded Jaʿfar al-Ṣādiq as the legitimate imam. Had his revolt succeeded, he would have called on Jaʿfar to take up his duties as ruler.[57] The reason why many ignorant Kūfan Shīʿīs believed that Zayd was the imam is that he took up the sword and called for al-riḍā min āl Muḥammad (i.e. a member of Muḥammad's family who would be acceptable to all). That call was erroneously interpreted as referring to himself; but in fact he knew that his brother al-Bāqir was entitled to the imamate, and that al-Bāqir had passed the imamate on to Jaʿfar al-Ṣādiq.[58] In a rebuttal of Zaydī claims that Jaʿfar recognized Zayd as the imam,[59] the Imāmīs maintain that Zayd regarded Jaʿfar as the only true imam of his generation.[60] Zayd, in fact, is presented as having adopted precisely those tenets which distinguish the Imāmiyya from the Zaydiyya: he cursed the shaykhān (i.e. Abū Bakr and ʿUmar) and recognized the imamate of the twelve imams.[61]

In justifying Zayd's rebellion the Imāmīs make the following points: first, Zayd was predestined for that role: Muḥammad prophesied that one of his offspring, called Zayd, would die as a martyr. It is reported that when Zayn al-ʿĀbidīn saw his son on the day he was born, he immediately realized that Muḥammad's prophecy referred to him, and he therefore called him Zayd.[62] Secondly, Zayd's revolt occurred with the imam's permission.[63] Thirdly, as mentioned before, Zayd did not fight for personal gain, but in order to defeat an evil rule and restore justice. Jaʿfar al-Ṣādiq is quoted as saying in this context: "I and my Shīʿa will remain in a state of well-being so long as there is a member of the family of Muḥammad who rebels."[65] At the same time, the famous theologian Muḥammad Bāqir al-Majlisī (died 1110/1700) is quick to point out that armed revolt by a member of the ahl al-bayt is in itself no proof that that member has any valid claim to the imamate.[66]

Al-Majlisī's remark need not be construed as expressing disapproval of Zayd. Such disapproval is, however, evident in some Imāmī traditions. In several sources, Zayd is reported to have thought of himself as the imam and to have been disabused of that notion only by the Shīʿī mutakallim Muʾmin al-Ṭāq.[67] In other words: throughout the lifetime of Zayn al-ʿĀbidīn, Zayd was kept in the dark concerning the identity of the imam and of his appointed successor, even though these were Zayd's own father and brother. What were the motives which prompted

Zayn al-ʿĀbidīn to conceal such crucial information from his son? One Imāmī theory is that this was a precautionary measure designed to protect Zayd, since no one who knew the identity of the imam could feel safe from the imam's enemies.[68] A second explanation is based on the principle that a person to whom the identity of an imam is divulged becomes an unbeliever if he refuses to acknowledge that imam; Zayn al-ʿĀbidīn kept his own counsel because he did not wish to expose Zayd to such a daunting eventuality.[69] A third, even less flattering, explanation is that Zayn al-ʿĀbidīn feared that Zayd would plot against al-Bāqir once he discovered that al-Bāqir was to be the next imam.[70] In an Imāmī tradition, al-Bāqir is said to have warned that Zayd would lay claim to something to which he had no right, by calling on the people to accept him as their ruler.[71] When al-Bāqir advised his brother not to act precipitously, Zayd reportedly answered: "He who stays at home with his curtain lowered and refrains from jihād is not our imam."[72] Al-Bāqir reminded Zayd that God ordered the imam not to go on a jihād before the appointed time; only if Zayd was completely convinced of the justice of his cause should he rebel.[73] Though later Imāmī scholars attempted to play down the significance of these and similar anti-Zayd traditions,[74] there is no doubt that they reflect the opposition which Zayd's revolt engendered among the less militant members of the Shīʿa.

Even Zayd's harshest critics from among the Imāmiyya stress, however, that he died as a shahīd, and that Jaʿfar al-Ṣādiq was deeply shaken by the news of Zayd's cruel death and donated considerable sums of money to the families of those who fell while fighting for Zayd.[75] Moreover, Zayd's rebellion and martyrdom are seen by the Imāmiyya as having driven the last nail into the Umayyad coffin: God's wrath at the outrageous manner of his death was so great that He immediately thereafter decreed the collapse of the Umayyad regime.[76] In a different formulation, this idea is extended to the revolt of Zayd's son Yaḥyā (died c. 125-6/743-4): there were three murders, says a Shīʿī tradition, which together brought about the end of the Umayyads: the murder of al-Ḥusayn by the Sufyānīs, of Zayd b. ʿAlī by Hishām and of Yaḥyā b. Zayd by al-Walīd b. Yazīd.[77]

The last Shīʿī group to which I should like to refer are the Ḥasanids. The rivalry between Ḥasanids and Ḥusaynids erupted at various times in the Umayyad period, and occasionally resulted in litigation before the caliphs' court.[78] At the beginning of the

ʿAbbāsid period, this rivalry took a more serious turn when some Ḥasanids rose against the reigning caliphs and eventually adopted the Zaydī doctrine, according to which an imam may be of Ḥasanid, and not only Ḥusaynid, stock.

As in the case of Zayd, Imāmī scholars adopt a somewhat ambivalent attitude towards the Ḥasanids. On the one hand, it is stressed that none of al-Ḥasan's sons rose against the Umayyads or claimed to be the imam; Zayd b. al-Ḥasan, for instance, carried the practice of taqiyya so far that he even accepted a governorship on behalf of the Umayyads.[79] He is also quoted as acknowledging the imamate of the first five of the twelve imams.[80] Imāmī traditionists contend that any criticisms which the Ḥasanids voiced against the imam sprang out of taqiyya,[81] and that where genuine disagreements did arise, they are to be regarded as family quarrels, which do not detract from the high esteem enjoyed by al-Ḥasan's offspring.[82] There was no jealousy of the Ḥasanid branch, say the Imāmīs, only a conviction that their revolts were futile. This conviction was based on various books in the possession of the imams (such as Kitāb ʿAlī, Kitāb Fāṭima), in which the names of all future rulers were inscribed. These names did not include any of the Ḥasanids.[83] This explains why Jaʿfar al-Ṣādiq voiced his misgivings when he was told about the secret meeting at al-Abwāʾ, at which the Hāshimīs decided to recognize Muḥammad b. ʿAbdallāh, "The Pure Soul," as the future caliph;[84] it also explains why, some years later, Mūsā al-Kāẓim refused to support the revolt of Ḥusayn b. ʿAlī "Ṣāḥib Fakhkh" against the ʿAbbāsids.[85] Furthermore, the Imāmīs maintain that the Ḥasanids had no aspirations of their own, and that those who rebelled did so in order to install the rightful (that is, Ḥusaynid) imam.

In contrast to this benevolent attitude, other Imāmī traditionists refer to the Ḥasanids as enemies from within the ahl al-bayt who know the truth, yet are driven by jealousy into ignoring it and claiming the imamate for themselves.[86] The falsity of their claim is symbolized by a conversation allegedly held between two Zaydīs and Jaʿfar al-Ṣādiq. The Zaydīs claimed that the Prophet's sword was held by ʿAbdallāh b. al-Ḥasan, a great-grandson of al-Ḥasan b. ʿAlī; al-Ṣādiq replied that ʿAbdallāh had never even laid eyes on the sword, since it was in his (i.e. Jaʿfar's) possession and had been in the possession of the imams before him.[87] The Imāmiyya rejects Ḥasanid claims by putting forward the doctrine that after the transfer of the imamate from al-Ḥasan to al-Ḥusayn, all subsequent imams must, by God's decree, be of Ḥusaynid stock.[88] As a further argument, Imāmī traditionists point out that al-Bāqir represents both Ḥasanids and Ḥusaynids, since his mother was a daughter of al-Ḥasan.[89] The Ḥasanids, therefore, have no reason to feel discriminated against.

The challenge of confrontation with Umayyad power and with different Shīʿī movements in the Umayyad period impelled the Imāmiyya to formulate its views on a number of key issues. The passivity displayed by most of the imams, which originally stemmed from political and tactical considerations, led to the elevation of <u>taqiyya</u> to the level of a doctrinal tenet, to a growing sophistication in the Imāmī theory of <u>jihād</u>, and to the spread of deterministic notions; the claims of extremist Shīʿīs, of Zayd b. ʿAlī and of the various Ḥasanid pretenders contributed to the shaping of the doctrine of an imamate which passes from father to son and whose charisma is restricted to the Ḥusaynid branch; and the persecutions suffered at the hands of the Umayyads opened the way for a future-oriented religion, in which feelings of present despair were assuaged by expectations of future recompense.

9

ON THE ORIGINS OF ARABIC PROSE: REFLECTIONS ON AUTHENTICITY

G.H.A. Juynboll

The study of the origins and earliest history of Arabic prose has occupied a multitude of scholars in East and West. Among the latest, two deserve to be mentioned, inasmuch as their hypotheses form appropriate starting points for discussion. These two scholars are Nabia Abbott and Fuat Sezgin.

Nabia Abbott, of the University of Chicago, has devoted many years of her life to the study and publication of Arabic papyri.[1] These papyri can be considered as the most ancient records of Arabic literature. To the texts Abbott has published she has added detailed studies on the origins of Arabic prose literature. In these studies, which eloquently show her acquaintance with the sources in print as well as in manuscript, she has formulated a few theories. The most important of these is that, contrary to the generally accepted theory of oral transmission, the writing down of extensive pieces of text in Arabic, regardless of their contents, must have started even before the Prophet's death and was practised thereafter on a gradually increasing scale.

Sezgin's main theory[2] corroborates that of Abbott, expanding it though with considerations about the taḥammul al-ʿilm, the transmission of knowledge, in early Islam. These considerations offer even more abundant evidence for the assumption that the Arabs had already started writing down what they heard and knew during the life of the Prophet. Although the Arabs have always claimed that they had strong memories, they resorted to writing, as soon as it dawned upon them that memories are fallible, whereas written records are destined to survive longer.

References to the recording of material in pre-Islamic Arabic are very rare,[3] and it is, therefore, feasible to assume that the activities of Muḥammad's secretaries may have set an example readily followed by all those who had mastered the art of writing and who had material at their disposal to write on. This material was, at first, hard to come by and it appears from the sources that, at one time or other, literally anything was used to write on, even parts of the human body.[4] The oldest materials that have come down to us are pieces of parchment and papyri, until paper was introduced from China.[5]

What did early Arabic prose consist of? The following six items may comprise all the genres that deserve to be listed under this heading:

I. The Qur'ān; it falls, I think, outside the scope of this paper to discuss the historical circumstances under which its compilation was finally realized. It is true, a few years ago a study was published in which this very issue forms the basis of a theory of --to put it mildly--debatable tenor.[6] I think, however, that this study should not concern us here. Summarizing the history of the Qur'ān, it suffices to point out that its first compilation was made a few decades after the Prophet's death, a compilation which may be considered as, at least, the skeleton of the text which initiated the activities of later Qur'ān scholars.

II. Philological material; this comprised Qur'ān text studies and exegesis, grammatical, and lexicographical studies, or, put in a more general way, the numerous writings produced by those philologians who eventually constituted the schools of Baṣra and Kūfa.

III. Historical material; this requires a more elaborate description. One part of this material, for instance, was the result of a natural continuation of that widely spread pre-Islamic pastime, the telling of stories, in which were related fictitious or (allegedly) historical data about tribal ancestors. A few of these pre-Islamic narratives, such as remnants of the ayyām al-ʿarab genre, eventually emerged in sources such as the Kitāb al-aghānī. Whereas that which may be considered as the Islamic counterparts of those pre-Islamic narratives formed part of the ḥadīth, the tradition literature, and akhbār, that is the historical literature. Furthermore, genealogical writings constituted other historical material.

IV. Khuṭbas; the sermons of Islamic preachers and administrators preserved in sources such as Jāḥiẓ's Kitāb al-bayān wa 'l-tabyīn.

V. Early writings on kalām and mysticism.

VI. The writings of the kuttāb, the official scribes of the administration. The first material in this genre was produced when the Umayyad era drew to a close.

After this rough sketch of what the prose literature of the first one and a half centuries of Islam consisted of, the people who produced it should be scrutinized.

Again we can skip item number one, the Qur'ān. The only point that might be mentioned here is that I have developed the theory that knowledge of the Qur'ān among the early Muslims should not be overrated. Those people known as qurrā', who emerge in the sources for the first time in the year A.H. 4 and who play such a significant political role in the conflict between the Syrian and Iraqi parts of the Islamic empire, may not at all have been experts on the Qur'ān as the name they are known by seems to indicate.[7]

Items IV, V and VI need not detain us here either. The Islamic preachers of item IV, few of whose sermons have been preserved, have played only a minor part as a group. They can hardly be described as the protagonists of a neatly defined genre. If at all, they are known for other activities such as the transmitting of traditions. J. Pedersen has dealt with the preachers of Islam in some detail.[8] Furthermore item number V, the writings concerning kalām and mysticism, have been dealt with by Van Ess. Finally, item number VI concerns basically no more than the prose attributed to ʿAbd al-Ḥamīd al-Kātib (died 132/750) and Ibn al-Muqaffaʿ (died 139/756). I should like to confine myself to pointing out that the style in which they wrote foreshadows later adab prose, and was introduced into Islam by members of the conquered people with whom I should like to deal in more detail in items number II and III to which we shall now turn.

II. Philological material. In early Islam this material was collected mostly by mawālī. This activity, born out of necessity, was soon also fanned by another incentive: their curiosity as to the exact contents and meaning of the Holy Scripture of their conquerors and the intricacies of the language in which it was written. Arabic was officially introduced as the administrative language under ʿAbd al-Malik b. Marwān who reigned from 65/685 until 86/705. There are numerous references in the sources to the deficient knowledge of Arabic among the conquered people.[9] It must have taken several decades before the last traces of defective pronunciation and grammar had disappeared.

Pellat has given a lively description of the exchange of knowledge in the market, the Mirdās, of Baṣra, where poetry and grammar, akhbār and ḥadīth were bought and sold.[10] Tafsīr was initially almost purely linguistic, something which shows once more how difficult it must have been for the earliest Muslims, mawālī just as much as Arabs, to understand what the Qur'ān said. The first lively interest in tafsīr was curbed, though, by pious men such as ʿUmar, who wanted it to be restricted to explanations of linguistic and lexicographical nature. Only many years later, in the course of the second half of the second century, did the tafsīr al-mutashābihāt, the obscure passages, gain recognition, when it was thought that sophisticated isnād criticism would guarantee the authenticity of the material.[11] As will appear below, I do not set store by isnād criticism per se, but in a few respects it has been successful. At any rate, many of the most fantastic explanations were barred from orthodox tafsīr literature. That the public was enamoured of these stories is proved by the following anecdote about Muqātil b. Sulaymān (died 150/767), one of the earliest mufassirūn to try his hand at the mutashābihāt, and who was not averse to answering questions that had no bearing on the Qur'ān whatsoever. Once he was asked by someone: "If the people ask me about the colour of the dog of the Seven Sleepers, what shall I answer?" Muqātil said: "Tell them it was spotted. No one will try to refute it."[12]

All the material concerning Qur'ānic exegesis, linguistic and historical (for instance qirā'āt and asbāb al-nuzūl), as well as all other philological material, was transmitted in the same way as ḥadīth and akhbār. An appraisal of this transmission method will be given in the next and final item which concerns the historical literature.

III. Historical material. One genre and its authors should be mentioned first, genealogy. This genre was practised after the advent of Islam as it had been before. But to the aims underlying it was added one important new one. It sought to gather information on the way certain forefathers had reacted to Islam, and it sought to establish the coveted status of Companion or Successor. Also whether or not certain people had been present at certain crucial battles, so as to become eligible for state pensions and the like, was something of increasing importance. On the whole, genealogists were highly valued during their days as historians but they were mostly considered poor transmitters of ḥadīth. Suffice it to mention here Muḥammad b. al-Sā'ib al-Kalbī (died 146) and his son Hishām (died

204). Because of the genealogists delving into the past life histories of people, they may well be considered as the precursors of what are later called the faḍā'il and mathālib genres discussed below.

On the whole, the Arabs' sense of history has guaranteed a never-flagging interest in the past, a past which, for emotional reasons, was very often depicted as more glorious than the actual facts would warrant. The pre-Islamic tribesmen gathered around the campfire at night--at the so-called samar (nocturnal conversation)--and told each other stories. These stories were mostly orally transmitted from generation to generation. The people who proved to be most expert in the art of storytelling enjoyed a special reputation. This class of people, the quṣṣāṣ, did not die out upon the advent of Islam. No, Islam provided them with sheer inexhaustable material to continue their activities. But, among other reasons, because of Muḥammad's policy that all Muslims were equal before God, the contents of the stories changed: tribal rivalry--which otherwise really never disappeared--ceased to be the main topic of the qiṣaṣ. The storytellers tended to focus attention on the Prophet, the miracles ascribed to him, his conquests, and those of his followers. The names of many quṣṣāṣ have been preserved. There is evidence that their ranks were infiltrated by mawālī in the course of time, but only gradually, and on a scale much less than in other realms of Arabic prose. It seems as if the mawālī, who must have lacked this predilection for typically Arab storytelling,[13] preferred to take a less romantic view of the past. After all, it was not their own past. It was in the ranks of the serious muḥaddithūn and akhbāriyyūn that we see a rapidly increasing percentage of mawālī participating in preserving for posterity the exploits of the first Islamic community.

The quṣṣāṣ played such an important role in early Islam that a closer scrutiny seems justified. As pointed out above, Islam did not stop their activities, but their reputation gradually declined. However, those quṣṣāṣ, who were at the same time Companions of the Prophet, came to be considered as reliable transmitters because of the criterion formulated at about the end of the third century A.H.[14] that all Companions were deemed equally trustworthy and would never put lies into the mouth of Muḥammad. As examples of these early quṣṣāṣ can be mentioned Abū Hurayra in Medina,[15] al-Aswad b. Sarī' in Baṣra and Ḥudhayfa b. al-Yamān in Kūfa. They were often attached to mosques as imām and/or Qur'ān reciter.[16]

Sometimes they are called quṣṣāṣ in one source, whereas other sources name them as belonging to the ʿibād, which may perhaps be rendered as "pious servants of God."[17] Under ʿUmar b. ʿAbd al-ʿAzīz, who ruled from 99/717 until 101/720, they still enjoyed a favourable reputation.[18] During the generation of the Successors the number of unreliable quṣṣāṣ increased with time and was, on the whole, much higher than that of reliable ones. Also a few mawālī were described as quṣṣāṣ, the most famous example having been al-Ḥasan al-Baṣrī (died 110).[19] Generally speaking, allegedly reliable quṣṣāṣ disappeared from the sources at the end of the first century A.H., their places being taken by others who were thought untrustworthy. But they never died out. For example, Abū Bakr al-Hudhalī (died 167) was known for his knowledge of the ayyām al-ʿarab, but also as a liar in ḥadīth.[20] Especially interesting seem those quṣṣāṣ who combined their storytelling with the function of qāḍī. One Shaqīq al-Ḍabbī, a Successor, was qāṣṣ in Kūfa as well as a judge known for his innovative ideas.[21] Al-Ḥasan al-Baṣrī, in his turn, was known as the greatest faqīh of his time. He was qāḍī of Baṣra for several years and one of its celebrated quṣṣāṣ.[22] Muslim b. Jundab exercised the function of qāḍī without receiving wages and was at the same time an eloquent qāṣṣ.[23] When the traditionists are dealt with below, the qāḍīs of early Islam will again appear to have played a memorable part.

As pointed out above, the mawālī soon invaded the ranks of those who gathered historical material. Reading through Ibn al-Nadīm's Fihrist it appears that the vast majority of early akhbāriyyūn were mawālī. The theory seems tenable that, rather than collecting the fanciful accounts of quṣṣāṣ, they recorded the reports of eyewitnesses to certain events. Thanks to the studies of Abbott and Sezgin it has now been established with a reasonable degree of certainty that the transmission of this material was predominantly carried out in the form of written records. I cannot help comparing these records with "dossiers" or "files" on certain major events, or courses of events, such as the ridda, ʿUmar's shūrā, the killing of ʿUthmān, and battles such as those of al-Jamal and Ṣiffīn. All the "files" on one event compiled by different akhbāriyyūn did not necessarily contain identical material, but all of them were eventually referred to by the same titles in, for instance, the Fihrist. On the basis of their literary activities it seems safe to conclude that mawālī had a mentality different from that of their conquerors. The mawālī were keen on forming a clear idea of the political and ideological background of this new religion which they had recently been compelled to embrace.[24] They were not so much concerned with the hyper-romantic view which the purely Arab tribesmen, who had subjugated them, tried to make them adopt through the glowing accounts of their quṣṣāṣ. Perhaps it seems a little bit too apodictic to impute to all the mawālī this--what we might call --more scholarly approach of history. Therefore, it may be justified to consider this approach as perhaps also born out of discontent and frustration with the all too little challenged "superiority" of the Arab overlords, whose words had to be taken for granted without dispute.

The questions that should always be asked when dealing with early Arabic literature are those concerning its authenticity and historical reliability. Recent publications such as Abbott's papyri editions[25] and, especially, R.G. Khoury's edition of two very early papyri attributed to Wahb b. Munabbih (died 110)[26] have thrown new light on the dark period that elapsed between the compilation of the Qur'ān and the first literary remains preserved to us, such as Ibn Isḥāq's Sīra, Wāqidī's Maghāzī and Ibn A'tham's Kitāb al-futūḥ. Furthermore, Abbott's arguments in favour of the authenticity of the Kitāb fī akhbār al-Yaman by ʿAbīd b. Sharya who died shortly after Muʿāwiya, as against Krenkow's scepticism, seem most convincing.[27]

On the whole, there do not seem to be cogent reasons for doubting the authenticity of early composed works as preserved in secondary sources such as Ṭabarī's Annals, the Sharḥ nahj al-balāgha by Ibn Abī 'l-Ḥadīd, or, in fact, many others.

When dealing with isnāds the following consideration should be taken into account. Evidence based on a scrutiny of isnāds supporting texts which are not over-tendentious is more acceptable than evidence gleaned from isnāds supporting texts clearly showing religious and/or political bias.

As regards stylistic considerations, it may be pointed out that the overall terseness of style in early Arabic prose is a valid criterion. It should, however, be handled with caution.[28]

On the other hand, the historical reliability of the earliest extant histories is something much more complicated to assess. Of late a few young German scholars have undertaken the task of analyzing anew certain texts belonging to Umayyad historiography. They have reached rather surprising conclusions which modify, or are diametrically opposed to, the theories set forth by Wellhausen, theories which remained almost unchallenged for more than half a century.[29]

In my opinion, students of early Islamic history have to develop a keen sense for what seems true and what false. Some people are more successful in this than others. On the other hand, subjecting the contradictory material to minute analysis in an endeavour to arrive at a passable harmonization may lead, in some cases, to satisfactory results. But, in my eyes, this "sixth sense" as I should like to call it, which distinguishes true from false, remains in the final analysis an indispensable criterion.

At this point I venture to introduce two new criteria describing the historicity of early Islamic texts. For the sake of argument I should like to divide the sources roughly into two categories, those that represent predominantly the storyteller's approach to history and those that represent predominantly the mawālī's approach to history. I am well aware of the fact that a few sources seem to belong to both categories, such as Ibn Isḥāq's Sīra and Wāqidī's Maghāzī. Both are compiled by mawlās on the one hand but, on the other hand, neither is void of fanciful legends. However, both mawlās lived many years of their lives in Medina, the cradle of Islam, and both dealt with a subject which, more than any other, seems to have turned historiography into hagiography. But if one compares Wāqidī's Maghāzī with that of Wahb b. Munabbih, the difference is such that applying the above-mentioned criteria does not seem too inappropriate.[30]

What has been said about early Arabic historiography and the participation of the mawālī in gathering and transmitting is also valid for ḥadīth literature. It appears from perusing the biographical lexica of transmitters that the role played by mawālī in collecting ḥadīth gradually grew in importance. I think that, on the whole, historical material about the political upheaval wrought by Islam roused the interest of mawālī collectors in much the same way as information on the ideology that motivated the conquerors. But it is safe to assume, it seems to me, that the ḥadīth collected by the mawālī will have mainly been concerned with basic doctrine and legal matters, rather than anything else.

During the first century after the Hijra ḥadīth material slowly increased. That we should not visualize the ḥadīth in those early days as anything remotely resembling the later canonical collections in bulk, may be demonstrated by the following piece of evidence.

When Zuhrī (died 124/742) had recorded everything on which he could lay hands roughly 100 years after the Prophet's death, all his material[31] amounted to no more than 2,000 to 2,200 traditions.[32] How many of these were legal traditions is difficult to estimate. But, in view of the abundance of reports dealing with, for example, maghāzī and tafsīr already in circulation, the legal traditions cannot have been very numerous. As Zuhrī's material is described in Ibn Ḥajar's Tahdhīb,[33] it consisted of sunnā māḍiya[34] (i.e. ḥalāl wa-ḥarām), targhīb, tafsīr, and ansāb. Only the first of these four rubrics contains legal traditions and, because of the spreading of the use of isnāds by that time, quite a few must have had identical or nearly identical matns supported by different isnāds.

Furthermore, the theory that legal traditions took a long time to be taken into account, especially in certain areas of the Islamic empire, can be corroborated by a report about al-Naḍr b. Shumayl, who died about 200 years after the Prophet. It is alleged that he was the first to propagate the Sunna in Marw and all of Khurāsān.[35] The Umayyad administration was, on the whole, not very much concerned with accounts of the Prophet's behavior and that of his Companions.[36] ʿUmar II is here an exception.[37] It is true, Abbott has gathered sufficient evidence for her surmise that the Umayyads were more interested in ḥadīth than they are generally given credit for, but that does not mean that traditions, especially legal ones, were collected--or, the case so being, conveniently fabricated--to meet a standing need. It seems to me that, during the beginning of the Umayyad caliphate, tradition collectors must have come across a gradually increasing body of traditions reflecting, more than anything else, the bias of the then operating political factions in the empire, such as the Shīʿites, Khārijites, Murjiʾites and Qadarites. On purpose I have mentioned the latter two in one breath with the former, since I believe that purely doctrinal considerations entered the minds of those people--and of their respective opponents--only after all political points at issue had either ceased to exist or had foundered under the unyielding rule of the Umayyads, their governors, and, later, the ʿAbbāsids. Muḥaddithūn who were experts on ḥalāl wa-ḥarām were rare, as appears clearly from Ibn Ḥajar's Tahdhīb.

I propose to scrutinize one muḥaddith closely. Maybe it is possible to draw some inferences from this scrutiny. I have selected a Successor, because it is during their generation that ḥadīth experienced its first major growth. And it is also in their time that wholesale fabrication of ḥadīth began. It will appear that this Successor may almost be considered as a prototype of a first century muḥaddith.[38]

ʿAmr b. ʿAbdallāh b. ʿUbayd, mostly called Abū Isḥāq al-Sabīʿī, from the tribe Hamdān, was a muḥaddith who lived in Kūfa. He was born in 29 or 32 and died between 126 and 129, which makes him at least 91 or at most 97 years of age when he died. At this point the question is justified: why select such a long-lived traditionist? The answer is simple: because there are hardly any transmitters who did not die at a ripe old age. In a recent study the average age of early Islamic scholars was fixed at 78 lunar years, that is 75 or 76 solar years.[39] One of the very rare transmitters who died at an age corresponding with what we might expect to be the average life span of males in those days in that part of the world --namely at about 50--was the famous Ibrāhīm al-Nakhaʿī. The vast majority of transmitters, dying at such advanced ages, may have pretended to be much older than they were in reality in order to establish at least the probability that they could have met certain masters. In so doing, they were able to claim the coveted status of Successor rather than that of Successor of a Successor.[40]

It is my conviction that by means of this age trick a large number of Successors under the traditionists undeservedly enjoyed the privileges that went with this status. In a great many tarājim the status of late Successors depends on their having met certain Companions who died late such as Abū Hurayra (died c. 58) and, especially, Anas b. Mālik (died 93 or even later). Abū Isḥāq, the Successor whose activities are studied here, is no exception. He claimed that he had received traditions from ʿAlī (died 40/661) and al-Mughīra b. Shuʿba (died c. 49). If he really heard from ʿAlī, something which is doubted in any case, he must have been only eight or at most eleven years old. Furthermore, Ibū Isḥāq transmitted from forty more masters,[41] twenty-two of whom had also transmitted from ʿAlī and/or were confirmed Shīʿites who fought at his side at Ṣiffīn and Nahrawān. Most of these masters were lesser known Companions and Successors from Kūfa. Among them were very few mawālī. Only one was known as a qāṣṣ.[42]

Thirty-nine people are listed as having received traditions from Abū Isḥāq. Six of them were sons and grandsons,[43] but these relatives are not mentioned as having had Shīʿite sympathies. Among the other transmitters only six were known as Shīʿites. In comparison with the twenty-two Shīʿites among Abū Isḥāq's masters one is almost inclined to draw the inference that he was not successful in what may be called his "political campaigning" for the Shīʿa. That he was well-known for his Shīʿite sympathies appears from a remark of a certain al-Jūzajānī[44] who said that, together with al-Aʿmash, Manṣūr b. al-Muʿtamir, Zubayd b. al-Ḥārith and others, Abū Isḥāq was one of those confirmed Shīʿites who were the "leaders of the traditionists of Kūfa."[45] The percentage of mawālī among his pupils is considerably higher than that among his masters, but it is difficult to give accurate figures, inasmuch as the information whether or not someone is a mawlā is not always given.

As was the case with the master himself, quite a few of Abū Isḥāq's pupils did not enjoy good reputations as reliable transmitters either. They were accused of the usual faults such as muddle-headedness later in life, tadlīs (tampering with isnāds), and undesirable political or heretical inclinations. Only three of his masters were deemed equally unreliable, but it should not be forgotten that one third of them were Companions. The most frequently recurring blemish on the reputation of a transmitter of, say, before A.H. 150 is that his claim to have heard traditions from certain long-lived Companions was proved false. Gradually, when the older Successors have all disappeared, false claims of samāʿ disappear also. Abū Isḥāq and most of his contemporaries are recorded in far from impeccable tarājim in the Tahdhīb, but no matter how disreputable they are as transmitters, among their pupils there emerge all the names of the truly great muḥaddithūn. Another remarkable feature is that the later the muḥaddith, the fewer are the references to party bias.

Summing up, Abū Isḥāq was a controversial transmitter who, like his masters, and, especially, like his pupils, was not unanimously deemed absolutely trustworthy. Even so his traditions are found in all six canonical collections; so are those of most of his pupils.

On the whole, one can say that in the majority of isnāds, which are deemed reliable and which, consequently, emerge in the canonical ḥadīth collections, the links formed by Successors and Successors of Successors are the weakest by far. Classical Muslim isnād criticism has not been as foolproof as orthodox circles, and in their wake many scholars in the West, have always thought. At first this may seem a rather sweeping statement. Let me, therefore, mention the following arguments.

Apart from the age trick referred to above,[46] I should like to deal briefly with the internal rivalry between ḥadīth centres. This rivalry was, among other things, also due to political considerations. One transmitter, al-Ḥārith b. Ḥaṣīra, spread faḍā'il traditions about the ahl al-bayt in Kūfa, but transmitted traditions of a general tenor in Baṣra.[47] Sometimes a transmitter operated in more than one centre and, subsequently, the traditions spread in the one centre are considered more reliable than those spread in the other(s).[48] Apart from the rivalry between schools, there is also rivalry between the individual members of one school. The innumerable reports on the faḍā'il, or mathālib, of transmitters are frequently contradictory. If, for example, transmitter A in his tarjama is preferred to B, often B, in his own tarjama, is preferred to A. To Yaḥyā b. Ma'īn are ascribed various sayings in which he enumerated the most learned of Zuhrī's pupils. Not one is identical with the other.[49] Yet, on the basis of this highly erratic material, transmitters were cleared or rejected.

The study of transmitters, the so-called 'ilm al-rijāl, came into being relatively late. Shu'ba b. al-Ḥajjāj (died 160) was reputedly the first traditionist who scrutinized transmitters in Iraq,[50] and who rejected the weak. "If it had not been for Shu'ba," it says in his tarjama, a saying ascribed to Shāfi'ī,[51] "the ḥadīth would not have been known in Iraq." A spurious saying perhaps, but nevertheless a very relevant one. Another great rijāl expert was the same Yaḥyā b. Ma'īn (died 233) already referred to above. He was very meticulous in screening transmitters. He even went so far as to write down forged traditions in order to preserve the names of the forgers for posterity. Yet, many times I have come across sayings of his, in which certain transmitters are declared trustworthy who had been decried as forgers, or at least weak, by others. The only inference to be drawn from this, it seems to me, is that even the experts did not know. There had elapsed too long a time between the beginning of ḥadīth fabrication and their own days. What we now call ḥadīth fabrication was, at first, surely no more than an on the spot inventing of pseudo-significant precedents set by the oldest members of the Islamic umma. It seems to me that it must have started immediately after the conquests with the advent of the first Muslim administrators, be it on a limited scale in the beginning.

As appears from the detailed scrutiny of the earliest qāḍīs of Islam--a study which I shall publish elsewhere--at first they improvised or, differently put, they resorted to ra'y. In the course of the second century A.H. the percentage of qāḍīs who were known forgers of ḥadīth increased, and this in Iraq much more so than in other regions of the Islamic empire. Since they, through their activities in ḥadīth, were also known as muḥaddithūn, they are all listed in the biographical lexica of transmitters.[52] For example, Wāqidī, who used to be qāḍī in Bagdad, once transmitted a tradition in which there was no ḥīla (legal device). It seems as if that was expected from him.[53] Sharīk b. ʿAbdallāh, one of the foremost pupils of Abū Isḥāq dealt with before, was qāḍī in Wāsiṭ. There he transmitted bawāṭīl traditions, a word which may be rendered as "null and void." After he had laid down his function his traditions became confused. He resorted to his own judgment when his knowledge failed. He was by disposition ad rem and, therefore, he found it awkward if he was at a loss for words. He was a specialist in Kūfa traditions and, besides, an extreme Shīʿite. He was deemed a very unreliable transmitter, and at least one innovative legal maxim was attributed to him. Even so, his traditions occur in five of the six canonical collections.[54] But also a man like ʿAbdallāh b. Muḥarrar, qāḍī of al-Jazīra, was said to be a liar who confused isnāds.[55] In the same way I could mention many, many more.

It is feasible that qāḍīs were selected for their knowledge of fiqh (if that term was already in use by that time). It is alleged that a great many people had insight in fiqh but were still declared to be unreliable traditionists.[56] Just like the qāḍīs, a good faqīh need not necessarily be a reliable muḥaddith either. It was Mālik b. Anas (died 179) who was the first to rely solely on fuqahā' that were at the same time thiqa.[57] This is one more argument in favor of my surmise that isnād criticism came into being relatively late, so late, in fact, that it could not longer be established with incontrovertible certainty whether or not an isnād was sound. Moreover, references to wholesale isnād fabrication--in contrast to that of matns--are numerous.[58] Whether the matns of forged isnāds were objectionable in content is, then again, an entirely different matter.

Until here, I have only dealt with isnād criticism. That does not mean that I underestimate the extent to which *matns* were criticised. But inasmuch as we have but a few collections of forged traditions (*mawḍūʿāt*), such as that of Ibn al-Jawzī (died 597/1200), and a great many very big collections of allegedly sound ones, it is hard to tell how many obvious forgeries were discarded and, consequently, never compiled. The fantastic figures of several millions of traditions, from which the great collectors compiled their works containing a mere few thousand, may indicate that sifting true from false may have occurred also by means of textual criteria. Be that as it may, it is not generally known that during, or slightly prior to, the time of Muslim, who died only a few years after Bukhārī in 261/875, *isnād* criticism was considerably slackened. In the introduction to his *Ṣaḥīḥ Muslim* hotly argued in favor of the admissibility of a transmitter into an *isnād* when *samāʿ* in a general sense had been established between him and his spokesman, whereas the anonymous opponent of Muslim had expressed himself in favor of the necessity of establishing *samāʿ* between transmitters in the case of every single tradition. I cannot help thinking that, if this opponent's approach had become the rule in tradition criticism, the tradition literature would have looked decidedly different. It would certainly have measured no more than a fraction of its present bulk.

Summing up, *isnād* criticism is not conclusive in my opinion. Even if an *isnād* seems sound by the most severe standards, it is still possible that it was forged in its entirety. Therefore, in evaluating traditions we must again rely on our sixth sense, and ask ourselves whether the *matn* is historically plausible. *Vaticinationes post eventum* can be discarded automatically. The majority of *faḍā'il* and *mathālib* traditions that go back to the Prophet can also be rejected.[59] Legal traditions present a much more difficult problem. Schacht's criterion, the more deficient the *isnād*, the older the tradition, is an effective tool but should be handled with caution. Religious practices as described in historical sources should be adduced when dating traditions dealing with those practices. Traditions of the *targhīb wa-tarhīb* genre are, fortunately, not of crucial importance for a better understanding of early Islam. Whether genuine utterances of the Prophet or second century fabrications of pious Muslims, they reflect a mentality which is, in the final analysis, purely Islamic. Most of these traditions are constructed with care and it is very difficult to be sure about their authenticity.[60] On the whole, it is our sixth sense that should pass the final judgment. Only extensive and repeated reading can develop this sense.

10

SOME CONSIDERATIONS CONCERNING THE PRE-ISLAMIC AND THE ISLAMIC FOUNDATIONS OF THE AUTHORITY OF THE CALIPHATE

H.M.T. Nagel

I

In recent decades research on the origins of the Muslim community and its early history has tended to stress the importance of the non-Muslim pre-Islamic environment as one of the main elements on which the structure of Islam was erected. Understanding the ancient Arab society, its customs, and its institutions, means to assess fairly the work of the Prophet and his first adherents: this is the principal idea of writers like W. Montgomery Watt and M.J. Kister, to name just two outstanding scholars in this field.

A study which is concerned with the evolution of the main elements of Islamic authority during the first decades after Muḥammad's death certainly has to follow the same principal idea. How can we explain the authority the Prophet exercised over his followers, particularly in the Medinan period of his life? Are there any phenomena in the ancient Arab society which are similar to the Muslim community of Medina? The Islamic historical tradition seems to recognize that the "state" of Medina can be compared with other forms of community and government extant in pre-Islamic Arabia. "O God, Ibrāhīm pronounced Mecca inviolable and thus he declared it a sacred territory within the two narrow passes (of <u>ʿayr</u> and <u>thawr</u>) so that there might be no bloodshed and nobody might bear arms for fighting and beat trees for other purposes than (for gathering the leaves for) fodder,"[1] the Prophet is reported to have proclaimed.[2] In a short paper R.B. Serjeant has called attention to the fact that an institution which might be compared to the <u>ḥaram</u>-type mentioned in the Prophet's proclamation has survived in some remote districts of southern Arabia. In these sacred enclaves--today called ḥawṭa--the tribesmen can meet safely for trade or for negotiations; there are ḥawṭas where the cutting of trees is forbidden. Often a holy man is considered to have founded the ḥawṭa, and later on his tomb may become a place of pious veneration. There may also be some tribes who make agreements with the representative of the sacred territory; they bind themselves to "assist him (i.e. the representative) against those tribes who do not abide by their agreements with him, and to help him to use the threat of force to execute a judgement."[3]

Such tribal confederations are called lummiyya, "a word semantically linked with umma."[4] Serjeant points to the striking analogy between the ḥawṭa and the early Medinan community, an analogy which is borne out further if one reads the "Constitution of Medina"; the emigrants of Quraysh and their Medinan supporters are considered one umma, which has to defend its joint interests and which is ready to accept the Prophet's judgment.[5] The assumption that Muḥammad's actions after his emigration to Yathrib were quite in keeping with the customary law of his time seems to be not too far from the truth; he founded a ḥaram according to the pattern he knew from Mecca and perhaps from other examples throughout the Arabian Peninsula.

Immediately after the Prophet and his followers had settled down in Yathrib, they engaged in warfare against the rival ḥaram of Mecca. Soon after the first great victory Muḥammad turned against the Jews of Yathrib. In the course of a few years they were either expelled from their abode or even slaughtered. Economical and political reasons have been adduced to explain this course of events, which are supposed to prove a new orientation of Muḥammad's thought. Mecca and its sanctuary, of which the ʿAbd Manāf clan of Quraysh was in charge, are said to have become the main objects of the Prophet's deliberations and actions. Ibrāhīm was now credited with the foundation of the Holy House; Muḥammad therefore came to consider him to be his most prominent precursor. But a new inquiry into the subject has brought to light the fact that it was already towards the end of the Meccan period that the Prophet started to propagate the image of Ibrāhīm the "arch-monotheist" in order to denounce the unbelief of the pagan Meccans.[6] This means that from the very beginning of his Medinan career Muḥammad hoped to return to Mecca to establish Islam there.

The events which followed the Prophet's victory at

Badr made it quite clear that the Medinans would never conquer Mecca through military action. Muḥammad was compelled to attempt to reconcile his interests with those of the leading Meccan aristocracy. The lines of this policy became visible in the spring of 628, when Muḥammad left Medina on an expedition, which he had organized for cutting off the communications between Mecca and Syria in order to strike a serious blow at the trade of Quraysh. For various reasons the Prophet and his opponents decided to avoid fighting and to settle the points at issue by means of negotiation. In the famous agreement of Ḥudaybiya, which was then concluded, the Meccans acknowledged Muḥammad's position as a leader of a community equal to their own.[7] In the period after Ḥudaybiya, members of the noblest clans of Quraysh left Mecca to join Muḥammad. Among them we find ʿAmr b. al-ʿĀṣ and Khālid b. al-Walīd; al-ʿAbbās b. ʿAbd al-Muṭṭalib embraced Islam in March 629, when the Prophet was on his way to his native town to perform the pilgrimage granted to the Muslims in the Ḥudaybiya covenant.[8]

One cannot doubt that the Meccan aristocrats, who had become converts to Islam under these circumstances, must have represented a new element in the Muslim community. Many of them belonged to ʿAbd Manāf, a clan which had played the leading part in Mecca and whose authority had been based on its wealth[9] and on the religious office it held at the sanctuary.[10] ʿUthmān and ʿAlī, who was a very young man in those days, were the only prominent early Muslims from ʿAbd Manāf.[11] Now the noble newcomers enjoyed Muḥammad's special respect notwithstanding their late conversion and although one could not be quite sure whether they were altogether wholehearted Muslims. Some of them quickly rose to high positions in the Medinan community; e.g. Khālid b. al-Walīd is reported to have been one of the Muslim leaders at Mu'ta (629), and one year later he conquered Dumāt al-Jandal;[12] then he succeeded in curbing the Banū 'l-Ḥārith b. Kaʿb of Najrān.[13] The ascendancy of the old Meccan aristocracy over Medinan affairs caused a great deal of tension within the community, but the incontestable authority of the Prophet kept the centrifugal forces under control. To a certain extent this must have been due to the Prophet's singular political success. In the last years of his life many tribes formally acknowledged Muḥammad's supremacy. Furthermore, the trade, which had been nearly interrupted by the Meccan-Medinan hostilities, could now be restored and continued on an even larger scale. The Meccan "commonwealth" expanded beyond its former boundaries; it was transformed into a Muslim "commonwealth" the foundations of which were not altogether alien to pagan Arab institutions.[14]

II

But the economic and political point of view, essential as it is, must not be over-emphasized. Islam meant more than just a re-establishment of pagan patterns of organization. Muḥammad was indeed convinced that Islam was not a new religion, but he was no less convinced that Islam was the true religion, which had been revealed by God to abrogate Arab paganism.[15] Proceeding on the assumption that pre-Islamic customs and institutions were vanishing only gradually to become covered by a layer of Islamic ideas and ideals, and that paganism could not be superseded totally, but survived in many forms, one will not find one single cause owing to which the history of the Muslim community might have evolved. On the one hand, it is very likely that Muḥammad's first actions in Yathrib were fully in keeping with the old ḥaram conception; on the other hand, his authority was no less derived from the religious message he had been chosen to preach.

Even his Meccan opponents had already felt that the God of Muḥammad's revelation was of a quality other than the gods they were worshipping in the Kaʿba. Therefore they demanded from the Prophet a change in his teaching so that the traditional deities could be retained.[16] Allāh, as experienced by the Prophet, was a threat to the pagan way of life, and the community which was rallying round Muḥammad at Mecca seems to have known a special act of initiation, muslim meaning "the one who performed the act of islām," i.e. the ritual turning of one's face from west to east, to Allāh.[17] Through carrying out this rite, which later on was replaced by the shahāda to be pronounced in the presence of witnesses, the believer entered a new community, which was more than a counterpart of any of the social formations common in Arab paganism. For this islām incorporated the converted people in the body politic of Allāh, the One God; the fore-runners of this new body politic, which had emerged at Mecca and was rapidly evolving at Medina, were the communities of Nūḥ, Mūsā and particularly Ibrāhīm; their alleged achievements had fallen into decay.

There is little doubt that the Prophet had

recourse to the traditional institution of <u>ḥaram</u> after he had emigrated to Yathrib. This is borne out by the evidence cited above. Apparently the <u>umma</u> he founded was closely related to other types of institutions current at his time. But we must not forget that the authority of the Prophet was not so much based on his affiliation to the influential Meccan clan of ʿAbd Manāf, as on his being the Messenger of God. Why then should he have demanded that all points of controversy were to be referred to "God and to Muḥammad"?[18] The community of the Prophet, the community of the believers, as it was called almost without exception till Muḥammad's death and even thereafter,[19] was very similar to any other type of body politic at that time and place, if regarded from outside, but its development was determined by principles of a different kind, if considered from within. Owing to these principles, it was soon to disrupt the old structures.

The <u>umma</u> of a <u>ḥaram</u> was composed of sundry tribes, who paid allegiance to a person of high esteem or to its representative, as several tribes had done to the sons of ʿAbd Manāf.[20] The believers and those who joined them submitted themselves to the Judgment of the Prophet, through whom God himself was speaking, i.e. they owed allegiance to the Creator Himself. Therefore the act of <u>islām</u> was equal to an irrevocable conversion,[21] because it was impossible to forsake the one community on earth which was--through Muḥammad--governed by Allāh, the one and single God. For this God had promised Paradise to the obedient and Hell to the disobedient. Insubordination to the leaders of the ʿAbd Manāf clan and the Meccan <u>ḥaram</u> could have meant war, insubordination to Allāh and Muḥammad meant condemnation in addition to war. The religious foundation of the authority peculiar to the Prophet here becomes obvious.

Simultaneous with the political success of the community of the believers a deeper comprehension of their role in human history began to evolve. The word <u>umma</u> gradually disappeared from the sources, especially from the Qurʾān. The believers now were referred to as the community (<u>jamāʿa</u>) in general, as the single "party of God" (<u>ḥizb Allāh</u>)[22] compared to which all other "parties" were of inferior significance. This feeling of superiority and exclusiveness is reflected in a revelation which prohibited marriage between Muslims and pagans; this law is said to have been proclaimed shortly after the conclusion of the Ḥudaybiya covenant.[23] The believers, guided by their Prophet, had come to consider themselves the ideal community.[24]

The feeling of solidarity among the believers must have been strengthened not only by political success, but also by the supreme authority Muḥammad claimed for his orders, which were, as we have stated above, tantamount to the Creator's will. This was taken so far as laws of general applicability were concerned. But even in matters of everyday policy the Prophet would resort to God. When ʿAbdallāh b. Ubayy had deserted the camp of the believers shortly before the battle of Uḥud, the following verses were revealed: "What befell you (i.e. Muḥammad) . . ., was by the permission of God, and in order that He might know the believers and in order that He might know those who played the hypocrite; they were asked to come and fight in the way of God or to defend (themselves), but they said: 'If we knew ought of fighting, we would follow you.' They were that day nearer to unbelief than to belief . . .; but God knoweth what they conceal . . .[25]--It was God Himself who consoled His Messenger and who blamed Ibn Ubayy and his party for their treacherousness. And again it was by God's order that Muḥammad reprimanded the 'hypocrites', among them those Medinans who had not taken part in an expedition to Tabūk: "O thou Prophet, strive with the unbelievers and the hypocrites, and be rough with them; their resort is Gehenna, a bad destination . . . So if they repent, it will be better for them, but if they turn away, Allāh will punish them with a painful punishment in this World and the Hereafter; they have not in the land a friend or a helper."[26]

It is the Creator who guides the community; it is He who is responsible for the history of mankind and who engages personally in the affairs of the body politic of His followers. The personal involvement of the Creator in the history of Islam renders the Muslim community different from all other communities in ancient Arabia and invests the Prophet with an authority hitherto unknown to his pagan environment.[27]

III

One can easily imagine that Muḥammad's death must have seriously threatened the further existence of his work. His authority, which had been deeply rooted in the convictions of the Muslim community, could not be bestowed on any other person; apparently there was nobody to claim his authority. Moreover, could prophethood be granted to anybody after the decease of the Prophet? The doctrine of the "Seal of the Prophets" began to emerge; in the Qur'ān there is only one verse which perhaps can be related to this concept.[28]

In this situation the centrifugal forces reasserted themselves. The conflicting interests of the anṣār on the one side and of the "Meccan aristocracy" on the other side were a menace to unity. Since the Ḥudaybiya covenant had been concluded, the influence of the Meccans had begun to eclipse the reputation of the Medinan "helpers"; nevertheless their opposition never grew into a significant political movement during Muḥammad's lifetime. But once the unrivalled leader was dead, the anṣār decided to throw off what some of them might have considered a Meccan yoke. The sources relate unanimously that some prominent representatives of the Khazraj met in the Saqīfa Banī Sā'ida to discuss the recent developments, and finally agreed that Sa'd b. 'Ubāda, a man of outstanding talent, should be recognized as their amīr, i.e. as the (military?) leader of the Medinan helpers, not of the community as a whole. Meanwhile the close relatives of the Prophet were busy preparing for the funeral ceremonies so that they could not take part in the struggle for power, a fact often emphasized in historiography in order to explain why the "Family of the Prophet" failed to carry through their alleged interests. At this moment 'Umar is reported to have rushed to the assembly of the anṣār, accompanied by Abū 'Ubayda b. al-Jarrāḥ and Abū Bakr. At 'Umar's instigation Abū Bakr was proclaimed a candidate for the leadership of the whole community. After a great deal of debating, the anṣār were ready to swear an oath of allegiance to Abū Bakr.[29] It is not improbable that the proclamation of Abū Bakr had been finally favored by the anṣār, because they did not want to revive the dangerous strife between Aws and Khazraj, Sa'd b. Ubāda's tribe.[30] The oath of allegiance made to Abū Bakr was a compromise, which not only the anṣār had to comply with, but which the noble Meccan clans of Quraysh also had to accept. This they did hesitatingly. 'Alī b. Abī Ṭālib, Ṭalḥa, and Zubayr are said to have refused to join the majority for six months.[31]

For a better understanding of these events and the ensuing consequences, we must throw a cursory glance at the socio-political alignments prevailing in the Muslim community at that time. First of all there is one important, even striking fact: the body politic founded by Muḥammad in Yathrib is always said to have been of a character which would dissolve the ancient tribal structure of society and amalgamate the different traditional entities into one new society based on Islam, the party of God (ḥizb Allāh). The fraternization (mu'ākhāt) which Muḥammad effected between his Meccan followers and the anṣār is sometimes regarded as a symbol of such a line of social development. But if one peruses the extant sources, one arrives at the surprising conclusion that the anṣār and the emigrants often acted jointly in politics, but in reality did not grow into one homogeneous community. There is clear evidence that the prominent Meccan refugees did not marry into the Medinan clans of Aws and Khazraj. The list of the wives of the Prophet furnished by Ibn Saʿd has no name which belongs to either of these two clans. Muḥammad married three women from the tribes of Banū Muṣṭaliq, Banū Naḍīr and Banū Qurayẓa, after these had been defeated by the Muslims; those three ladies had been part of the booty which fell to Muḥammad's share.[32] The only famous Meccan companions of the Prophet who actually married into anṣār families were ʿUmar b. al-Khaṭṭāb, his brother Zayd, and, perhaps at a later date, Abū Bakr. ʿUmar espoused Jamīla bint Thābit from the clan of ʿAmr b. ʿAwf,[33] Zayd married her sister Ḥabība.[34] ʿUmar had a second wife from the same clan.[35] Jamīla and Ḥabība are mentioned among those women who took the oath of allegiance to Muḥammad.[36] Abū Bakr was married to Ḥabība bint Khārija b. Zayd; Muḥammad is related to have linked her father with Abū Bakr in mu'ākhāt; Ḥabība's name is to be found among the women who became converts to Islam under Muḥammad's guidance.[37] Umm Kulthūm, her first child, was born shortly after Abū Bakr's death.[38]

While intermarriage between the anṣār and the muhājirūn was a rare occurrence, the bonds of kinship among the emigrants were strengthened through marriages. As is well-known, Fāṭima, Muḥammad's daughter, became ʿAlī's wife; ʿUmar married their daughter Umm Kulthūm when he had succeeded Abū Bakr in the leadership of the faithful. ʿĀ'isha, Abū Bakr's daughter, was Muḥammad's wife. Muḥammad married Ḥafṣa, ʿUmar's daugher, when her first husband had died. Asmā' bint Abī Bakr was married to Zubayr, her sister Umm Kulthūm to Ṭalḥa. ʿUthmān was the husband of two daughters of the Prophet, Ruqayya and Umm Kulthūm. ʿAlī married Umāma, daughter of Abū 'l-ʿĀṣ b. Rabīʿ from ʿAbd Shams and Zaynab, the first daughter of the Prophet.[39] ʿAlī's daughters were married to members of Quraysh without exception, among them descendants from Hāshim and ʿAbd Shams likewise.

When the Meccans had come to terms with Muḥammad and were ready to embrace Islam, the old feeling of solidarity, which had prevailed among the descendants of ʿAbd Manāf,[40] the noblest line of Quraysh, apparently did not cease to exist, but rather reasserted itself. There is much evidence pointing to this. Muḥammad wanted to make use of the political skill and experience the Meccans had in dealing with various powerful tribes. For instance, some time after the expedition to Mu'ta the Prophet sent ʿAmr b. al-ʿĀṣ, a recent convert to Islam, with some fighters from the anṣār and the muhājirūn against a group of rebels from the tribes Quḍāʿa and Balī. ʿAmr had been made leader of this expedition because his mother belonged to Balī, and Muḥammad hoped to reconcile the rebels much more easily if they saw a kinsman appealing to them. Nevertheless ʿAmr had to call for support, and the Prophet sent some more troops, most of them early emigrants. Abū ʿUbayda b. al-Jarrāḥ, one of Muḥammad's earliest companions, a member of the Qurashī clan of al-Ḥārith b. Fihr, was in command of them. When Abū ʿUbayda reached ʿAmr b. al-ʿĀṣ, he demanded to be recognized as the supreme chief of the united forces; the early emigrants supported Abū ʿUbayda's claim, but ʿAmr maintained that the leadership was his. Finally Abū ʿUbayda complied with ʿAmr's demand. The historical tradition about this expedition tends to stress the paradoxical fact that Muḥammad had taught his followers to perform the Islamic rites, but never to aspire to leadership. Furthermore, ʿAmr failed to observe the ritual commandments during this expedition, and it was just through leadership granted by the Prophet that people like ʿAmr acquired wealth and great prestige.[41] Even if one might discover here some traces of later transformation aiming at the denigration of the Banū ʿAbd Shams, the story as a whole remains indicative of the tensions provoked by Muḥammad's favorable attitude towards his former enemies. As a result of this policy the community became divided into three groups: the anṣār; the early emigrants who did not belong to ʿAbd Manāf; and the Meccan aristocrats, most of them recent converts, and their partisans.

This is clearly borne out by historical tradition concerning the role of Abū Bakr and ʿUmar. Not only Hāshim, the clan of the Prophet, had been opposed to the proclamation of Abū Bakr, but also Abū Sufyān, a leading member of the ʿAbd Shams. He pointed to the humble origin of Muḥammad's first successor.[42] Khālid b. Saʿīd b. al-ʿĀṣ, a grandson of ʿAbd Shams and one of the first Muslims,[43] refused for two months to swear allegiance to Abū Bakr and criticized the ʿAbd Manāf clan, particularly ʿAlī and ʿUthmān, because they had disclaimed their right.[44] A similar reaction is ascribed to Abū ʾl-ʿĀṣ b. Rabīʿ from the ʿAbd Shams clan: he sided with ʿAlī.[45]

Khālid b. al-Walīd from the powerful and respected Meccan clan of Makhzūm, one of the most successful enemies of the believers at Uḥud, paid little attention to Abū Bakr's orders during the <u>ridda</u> wars. When Khālid had embraced Islam, Muḥammad had sent him on military expeditions because he was fully aware of his talent. Now Khālid, engaged in warfare against the apostates, did not wait for Abū Bakr's detailed instructions. The <u>anṣār</u> among Khālid's troops mutinied and stayed behind, but later rejoined him. Khālid attacked Mālik b. Nuwayra, the chief of Banū Yarbūʿ, who had been reconciled to Islam after apostasy, killed him and slaughtered many of his clansmen. ʿUmar is said to have tried to incite Abū Bakr against Khālid, when this news reached Medina, but Abū Bakr forgave him, knowing that he could not do without him.[46] Some months later another strange event took place. Khālid had conquered al-Ḥīra and some adjacent parts and had defeated some joint Iranian and Byzantine forces at al-Firāḍ, when he secretly left his troops, who were retiring to al-Ḥīra, and hurried to Mecca to perform the pilgrimage. Abū Bakr was very angry, when he heard about Khālid's unauthorized act, the meaning of which is not quite clear. Back in al-Ḥīra, Khālid was ordered to go to Syria to reinforce the Muslim troops there.[47] During Abū Bakr's reign Khālid b. Saʿīd, ʿAmr b. al-ʿĀṣ, Walīd b. ʿUqba, and Yazīd b. Abī Sufyān, four outstanding members of ʿAbd Shams, led the operations in the Syrian battlefield; soon Muʿāwiya, Yazīd's brother joined them. Shuraḥbīl b. Ḥasana and Abū ʿUbayda b. al-Jarrāḥ were the only important figures on the scene who did not belong to ʿAbd Shams. ʿUmar is said to have warned Abū Bakr against Khālid b. Saʿīd,[48] but the influence of those whose allegiance to Medina was open to suspicion was somewhat strengthened when Khālid b. al-Walīd arrived there.

The Muslims had just won their first and decisive victories in Syria, when Abū Bakr suddenly died. ʿUmar became his successor. According to historical tradition, he had been nominated by Abū Bakr. Nevertheless we do not know how ʿUmar could have asserted himself. In any case, opposition to him was very weak at Medina, perhaps because of the involvement of the ʿAbd Shams clan in Syrian affairs. ʿUmar wanted to carry through a policy which aimed at regaining full command of the events taking place within the conquered territories. Therefore one of his first decisions was to remove Khālid b. al-Walīd from his post and to appoint Abū ʿUbayda instead.[49] There is no other interpretation of this action than to see it as ʿUmar's intention to support the interests of the non-ʿAbd Manāf muhājirūn and the anṣār in order to reduce the power of the Meccan aristocrats, who--since the Ḥudaybiya covenant--had set about appropriating the lion's share of the spoils.

The establishment of the dīwān is indicative of the same policy: ʿUmar wanted to distribute the booty (which must have been very copious in those early days of the conquests) among the believers according to their merits in furthering Islam. Those clans and people who had been influential and highly respected before they had submitted to the rule of Islam should not automatically retain their favorable position.[50] Of course ʿUmar met with serious opposition, which was not easily to be overcome. For instance, when he took measures to secure the constant influx of revenue from the provinces to the Medinan treasury, the arbitrary ʿAmr b. al-ʿĀṣ, who had entered Egypt without paying heed to ʿUmar's orders, mocked at the low origin of the Commander of the Faithful: "God damn the day on which I became one of ʿUmar b. al-Khaṭṭāb's governors! I saw (my father) al-ʿĀṣ b. Wā'il clad in brocade studded with gold buttons, while al-Khaṭṭāb b. Nufayl was carrying firewood on a donkey!"[51]

ʿUmar, of humble origin, but one of the earliest Muslims and related to the anṣār by bonds of marriage, was, no doubt, the best man to establish a homogeneous community based on the principles of Islam. Besides the dīwān, he inaugurated the Muslim calendar,[52] which starts from the hijra, the birthday of the community of the believers; he declared the pilgrimage to Mecca obligatory on every Muslim, and he took the necessary measures to restore and enlarge the ḥaram sanctuary. With his permission stations were erected along the road from Medina to Mecca.[53] Finally he is related to have prohibited non-Muslims from dwelling in the Arabian Peninsula.[54] The important rival ḥarams in Arabia had ceased to exist before and during the ridda wars, their idols had been destroyed, and now there should be only one ḥaram, the Islamic one; its authority should cover the whole Peninsula.

Referring to the measures just mentioned, one may

call ʿUmar the second founder of the Islamic state, or rather of an Islamic type of a ḥaram confederation. But he was in no case the founder of the supra-national Islamic empire, which came into being through the rapid expansion of the conquests following the first raids into Sasanian and Byzantine territories. Though ʿUmar is reported to have visited Jābiya on the Jawlān heights,[55] one cannot be sure that he was interested in expanding the territory of Islam beyond the borders of Arabia. The caliph's warning against crossing a river, a common topos in the historical traditions on the conquests, seems to be a faint echo of his fear of getting involved in events which he could not control.[56] It was only for interrupting the annual raids the Sasanians waged against southern Iraq that ʿUmar permitted Kūfan and Baṣran troops to penetrate into Iran.[57]

ʿUmar did not succeed in enforcing his policy of an Islamic Arabia upon the noble Quraysh in Syria. This land had become their uncontested stronghold after Abū ʿUbayda had died of pestilence at ʿImwās.[58] In A.H. 23 an assassin wounded ʿUmar with a dagger. Before the caliph died a few days later, he appointed a committee which would decide who was to be his successor. The members of this committee were without exception old Meccan muhājirūn; the second pillar on which the Medinan regime was resting in those days, the anṣār, was not represented at all. The one-sidedness of this committee was perhaps not quite in accordance with ʿUmar's intentions; some sources say he feared lest the anṣār's vote would be taken into consideration. Be that as it may, after thorough discussions the committee arrived at a compromise, which cannot be called unwise if one takes into account the political circumstances prevailing in those days. ʿUthmān was proclaimed Caliph. He had been one of the earliest companions of the Prophet and had married two of his daughters, but in addition to that he belonged to ʿAbd Shams, that noble family of the ʿAbd Manāf clan, which was making a fortune out of the Islamic expansion. One could hope that ʿUthmān would be able to relieve the political tension between the early muhājirūn and the Meccan aristocracy, at the cost of the anṣār, no doubt. The results of ʿUthmān's policy are too well-known to be expounded in detail here. Ḥasan al-Baṣrī says that ʿUmar did not permit the prominent Qurashī muhājirūn to take part in the expeditions except for well defined ends and for a limited time.[59] Shaʿbī (died about 725), another renowned transmitter of historical traditions, points to the same fact and tells us that ʿUthmān was no longer able to keep the Quraysh back in Medina. "Now (the Quraysh) made trouble in the (distant) regions, and people became attached to them . . . ."[60] This means that ʿUthmān willy-nilly allowed the Quraysh to control the provinces. Thus the problem of how to keep the distant regions under the command of the Medinan government had become still more urgent than it had been during ʿUmar's reign. ʿUthmān tried to solve it by appointing close relatives as governors. This was ʿUthmān's ill-famed nepotism.[61] Nevertheless there is no doubt concerning ʿUthmān's sincere intentions. For he ordered that his governors and those people who wanted to complain about ill-treatment should come during the pilgrimage to talk frankly with him.[62]

ʿUthmān came of one of the wealthiest clans of Quraysh and it is reported that he did not scorn good food and clothing as ʿUmar had done. Nevertheless, ʿUthmān saw to it that the Islamic prescriptions concerning alcoholic drinks and gambling were observed. In the eighth year of his rule he had to appoint a person to take action against such prohibited amusement in Medina.[63] The caliph did not shrink from punishing Walīd b. ʿUqba, his Kūfan governor, for drinking wine. Our sources know many other events which gradually alienated ʿUthmān even from members of the ʿAbd Shams clan. Furthermore, a pious opposition had come into being which was critical of the luxury in which many Qurashīs and other famous believers were living. The main body of his critics finally comprised the anṣār (probably from the beginning of his reign), the Medinan bon-vivants, many of the provincial governors and their followers, and the pious opposition.

A great deal has been written about the events which preceded and followed the murder of ʿUthmān,[64] and we will not attempt a reassessment of the conflicting political and religious currents, which in those crucial days were determining the course of Islamic history.[65] It must be stressed, however, that rivalry among the clans and tribes played an important, if not decisive, part in the tragedy. There was mutual animosity, inherited from pre-Islamic times, embittered by new and far-reaching interests which, in turn, were kindled by the unexpected conquests. For instance, Ṭalḥa b. ʿUbaydallāh is depicted as one of ʿUthmān's most ruthless enemies.[66] Ṭalḥa was actually leading the ritual prayer when people besieged the caliph's house.[67]

There is little doubt that Ṭalḥa considered himself a candidate for the leadership of the community. His ambitions seem to be of a rather early date. We know that he opposed ʿUmar, when Abū Bakr wanted to nominate the latter as his successor,[68] and it is interesting that ʿAlī was protesting against Abū Bakr's decision together with Ṭalḥa.[69] But after the events which led to the murder of ʿUthmān, Ṭalḥa rigidly refused to pay allegiance to ʿAlī. It must be noted that Ṭalḥa belonged to the Taym clan of Quraysh, the same clan as Abū Bakr's, and Ṭalḥa's relationship to Abū Bakr's family must have been very close even in pre-Islamic times. It was Abū Bakr who made Ṭalḥa embrace Islam; Ṭalḥa is reported to have taken care of Abū Bakr's family during the emigration from Mecca.[70] Later on Ṭalḥa married Abū Bakr's daughter Umm Kulthūm, and after the Prophet's death he even wanted to marry ʿĀʾisha.[71] There are some other traditions which point to Ṭalḥa's ambitions and to a certain rivalry between him and ʿAlī. For instance it was generally noticed that Ṭalḥa gave his children the names of the prophets prior to Muḥammad,[72] while he blamed ʿAlī for having given one of his children the name Muḥammad and the Prophet's kunya Abū ʾl-Qāsim.[73] Furthermore Ṭalḥa had married into the clan of ʿAbd Shams. So it is not surprising that he supported ʿUthmān after ʿUmar's death, but was one of ʿAlī's opponents after ʿUthmān had been murdered. Muʿāwiya later on seems to have been aware of Ṭalḥa's standing among the Quraysh, and of the political power of his supporters in the region of Baṣra; in order to win them over Muʿāwiya wanted to engage his son Yazīd to Ṭalḥa's daughter Umm Isḥāq, but unfortunately these plans came to nothing.[74] Nevertheless the antagonism between ʿAlī and Ṭalḥa did not originate in the days of Islam, but much earlier.[75] One of Ṭalḥa's ancestors had had the right of supplying food to the foreign pilgrims who were visiting Mecca;[76] later on the sons of ʿAbd Manāf claimed this privilege.[77]

Political power, derived from ancient nobility and from special relationship to single tribes or to confederations of tribes, remained the most important source of authority throughout ʿAlī's caliphate. The anṣār, excluded from leadership for about twenty-five years, now rose to high positions.[78] Those groups whose interests had been neglected during ʿUthmān's reign rallied round ʿAlī's flag. Recent inquiries into these events have revealed the heterogeneity of this coalition. Owing to these circumstances the history of ʿAlī's caliphate is nothing but the history of the collapse of his coalition.[79] While ʿAlī, who had lost his reputation in the arbitrators' agreement, had to engage in a long and more or less abortive war against some of his former supporters, Muʿāwiya, since the days of the plague of ʿImwās the unrivalled master of the Syrian region, became the only remarkable political power within the boundaries of the emerging Muslim empire. It was due to his finesse politique (ḥilm) that he succeeded in stabilizing the community from within and in launching new attacks against the infidels.[80] There can be no doubt that the basis of his authority was the high esteem his family had enjoyed since pre-Islamic times. Muʿāwiya did not refrain from full assertion of the nobility inherited from his ancestors. He declared his very talented governor Ziyād to be his brother in order to enhance and strengthen the latter's position among the unruly inhabitants of Mesopotamia.[81] When Muʿāwiya had died, his son Yazīd had some difficulties concerning the acknowledgement of his rights. After his short reign anarchy and internal strife almost did away with the Umayyad dynasty, but finally Marwān and his son ʿAbd al-Malik defeated their enemies and re-established Umayyad rule throughout the empire. It was under the caliphs of the Marwānid line, and particularly under ʿAbd al-Malik, that Umayyad power reached its apogee.

IV

We have dwelt on these details because they are indicative of one of the dimensions of authority as exercised in the early Islamic state: the dimension of nobility, ascribed to a certain clan or family, nobility which has little or even nothing to do with the history of Islam, but is a heritage from the infidel ancestors. A great deal of the political conflicts within the early Muslim community cannot be explained but by analyzing the material which has been transmitted concerning the pre-Islamic history of the clans and tribes, and there is still much to be done in this field of research.

The Islamic dimension of authority, which ʿUmar seems to have claimed as a basis for his rule, was not commonly accepted during his time; it was still too vague to defy the ancient concept of power, to which even the Prophet had to adjust himself at the end of his career. ʿUthmān's reign was the turning point at which the ancient concept of authority came to reassert itself on a large scale, but it is in those years, too, that particularly Islamic concepts of authority begin to evolve, which express the ideas and dreams of heterogeneous movements opposing the caliphate. I shall give a rough outline of these concepts at the end of this study. But firstly we must say a little more about the ideology of the ruling dynasty.

Since the days of Muʿāwiya the Umayyads are referred to as kings (mulūk). One of the characteristics of their kingship (mulk) was that it could be transferred by heritage. Ḥasan al-Baṣrī, one of the boldest critics of the dynasty, blamed Mughīra b. Shuʿba for having extorted the oath of allegiance to Yazīd from the Iraqis, when Muʿāwiya was still alive.[82] Although later on denounced as a degradation of the prophetic rule, the concept of mulk had not been alien to the Arabs in the first decades of Islam. Of course they knew the kings of al-Ḥīra and the Banū Ghassān; everybody heard the tales about Imru 'l-Qays and the Kindite dynasty. Members of some of these pre-Islamic dynasties used to perform the pilgrimage to Mecca.[83] Furthermore, even petty rulers were called kings. For instance ʿAmr b. Iṭnāba of Khazraj, who had been appointed by Nuʿmān b. Mundhir as his representative at Yathrib, was referred to as king.[84] On his way to Tabūk Muḥammad met the king of Aylat, who presented some gifts to the Prophet.[85] Four kings, descendants of the Kindite dynasty, came to Muḥammad together with al-Ashʿath b. Qays, embraced Islam, and returned to their countries. "They were called kings, because each of them was in possession of a valley (wādī) and of everything therein."[86] Such a kingdom was similar to a ḥaram, as can be inferred from the following tradition concerning ḥalāl and ḥarām and recommending that one should not get involved in actions of doubtful character: "Whosoever lets (his cattle) graze next to a protected region (ḥimā), almost makes them graze inside it; every king has a protected area (ḥimā), and God's protected areas are His prohibitions (maḥārim)."[87] The close relation between kingship and holy, protected regions, which were common in Arabia, becomes obvious. Therefore it is not surprising that the rule of the ʿAbd Manāf clan over Mecca is called a mulk.[88] Even the Medinan community of the believers could be called by this term.[89]

The Umayyad rulers and their entourage were proud of their kingship, which they pretended to have inherited from ʿUthmān, or through him from ʿAbd Manāf. It is God Himself who made the sons of Umayya the rulers over the community. According to an idea which is often stressed, God entrusted the earth to

His khalīfa, who guides the believers and is the pillar of Islam "as the earth has mountains for its pillars."[90] In this line of thinking a second, new connotation of kingship is elaborated, which is also alluded to in the aforementioned ḥadīth: The true king is God alone. This idea is expressed several times in the Qur'ān.[91] God has revealed Himself to the Prophet as the only One who has the course of history under His control; He bestows kingship according to His supreme will.[92] The Umayyad ruler is a malik, who can claim incomparably less authority than God, but because kingship has been entrusted to him by the Creator, his authority is far beyond the power of any pre-Islamic king. Zuhrī, one of the most important historians of the Umayyad period, relates that one day Muʿāwiya was told that ʿAbd-allāh, the son of ʿAmr b. al-ʿĀṣ, declared that there would be a king from Qaḥṭān. Muʿāwiya answered that this was a false statement, wrongly ascribed to the Prophet: "I heard the Prophet say: The kingship belongs to Quraysh; whosoever wants to contend with them for it, will be cast down on his face by God, as long as (Quraysh) holds on to religion!"[93] The assertion of a kingship bestowed by the Creator on the north Arab clan of Quraysh, against the claims of the "south party," which had become powerful in Zuhrī's lifetime, is the actual reason for this statement.[94]

Beside the aspect of clanship and nobility, whether purely pre-Islamic or enhanced through the alleged election by God, we come across a second aspect of authority which at first sight is more deeply rooted in the Islamic faith, though it also has its relations with pre-Islamic society. It is a well-established fact that Muḥammad had been called al-amīn (the trustworthy one) by his Meccan compatriots; he had a good head for managing the commercial affairs of the wealthier people and was renowned for his honesty.[95] The trustworthy (amīn) treasurer, ". . . a man who performs what he has been ordered, his soul agreeing with (the order) . . .," is a widespread topos in Muslim tradition.[96] Again the term amīn is connected with commercial or financial activities. The Meccan Abū 'l-ʿĀṣ b. Rabīʿ from ʿAbd Shams was called al-amīn; he enjoyed a high reputation for his wealth, honesty (amāna) and commercial acumen (tijāra); he was one of those who used to accompany the caravans of Quraysh,[97] the same job Muḥammad is said to have done. The trustworthy merchant is alleged to be of the same rank as a prophet.[98] In the Qur'ān Muḥammad is referred to as an honest (amīn) messenger,[99] and the prophet Hūd says to his people: "I bring you a message from my Lord, I am to you a sincere and trustworthy (amīn) adviser" (7:67). Do we go too far if we suppose that the term amīn, when applied to Muḥammad, acquires a peculiar connotation which suggests that he is honestly transmitting and performing God's orders, just as he was performing the orders of the wealthy merchants? One day ʿAlī sent a piece of gold from Yaman to the Prophet, who decided to distribute it among four noblemen who had been his enemies. Some of his old followers and a few of the anṣār blamed Muḥammad for this, but he asked how they could do so, while he was the "amīn of the One who is in heaven," receiving his orders immediately from God.[100]

The Prophet himself used to charge some of his companions with duties, and these persons are sometimes called amīn. For instance a certain Mirdās b. Marwān was Muḥammad's amīn in charge of the shares of Khaybar.[101] But it was Abū ʿUbayda b. al-Jarrāḥ who was considered as the outstanding amīn of the community. The Prophet had sent him to Yaman to teach Islam to the people. On another occasion a delegation from Najrān asked Muḥammad to send to them an authorized representative. It was Abū ʿUbayda to whom this honorable mission was entrusted. In this connection again the word amīn is used.[102] After Muḥammad's death Abū ʿUbayda was one of the candidates for the leadership. When ʿUmar was about to die from his wounds, he is alleged to have said: "If Abū ʿUbayda were still alive, I would have appointed him (my successor) and would not have held counsel. If someone had asked me with respect to him, I would have answered that I had appointed the amīn Allāh wa-amīn rasūlihi",[103] i.e. Abū ʿUbayda was Muḥammad's trustworthy representative teaching Islam in his name in places the Prophet did not visit personally, and he could have been the representative of God after Muḥammad's death. It is clearly borne out by evidence that amīn Allāh was one of the titles of the leaders of the community after Muḥammad. A certain Abū 'l-Mukhtār Yazīd b. Qays complained to ʿUmar that the governors in Mesopotamia and the adjacent territories were wasting the booty on luxuries. He asked ʿUmar to extort half of their wealth from them. Yazīd b. Qays starts as follows: "Send a message to the Amīr al-Mu'minīn: You (ʿUmar) are God's amīn so far as prohibiting and enjoining are concerned, you are God's amīn among us, and whosoever is an amīn of the Lord of the Throne, my heart will turn to him."[104] Furthermore, there is a ḥadīth which deals with the fitna: The Prophet recommends siding with the amīn and his party when internal strife jeopardizes the unity of the believers. In this connection ʿUthmān is the amīn.[105]

Unfortunately our source material is too meagre to give an adequate idea of the functions the amīn was expected to carry out. With respect to the tradition concerning Abū ʿUbayda, one may venture the suggestion that the amīn was responsible for temporal and spiritual guidance in general, as the Prophet himself had been. However the title amīn must have been superseded very early by two other ones: the amīr al-mu'minīn and the khalīfa. Amīr as used in the maghāzī traditions--if I am right, the word does not occur in the Qur'ān--seems to denote a military leader, imāra being the command over an expedition.[106] The title amīr al-mu'minīn came into use under ʿUmar and seems to point to his--for the most part abortive --attempts at keeping the military actions and the conquests under central control; it expresses ʿUmar's claim to be the supreme commander.[107] In fact, Abū Bakr did not act as a military commander when he was in charge of the community, and he did not interfere seriously with the actions of the Muslim military leaders, as ʿUmar did later on.

Abū Bakr was called khalīfat rasūl Allāh, i.e. he who acts in the place of the messenger of God.[108] When Muḥammad had to leave Medina on an expedition, he would appoint (istakhlafa) someone who was in charge of the ritual prayer;[109] this khalīfa performed a very important duty, because through common prayer the further existence of the community of the believers was demonstrated in Muḥammad's absence. Mostly this task had been entrusted to the early Meccan companion Ibn Umm Maktūm;[110] other names, in particular those of anṣārīs, are of rare occurrence with regard to this duty. It was only during the days of quarrel about the expedition to Tabūk that a similar function was entrusted to Abū Bakr.[111] And again Abū Bakr had to perform this duty, when the Prophet had fallen ill a few days before his death. After Muḥammad's decease Abū Bakr became his khalīfa, and the function which is defined by this word must have comprised the same as that of the previous khalīfas. The further history of the term khalīfa was determined by two factors: 1. ʿUmar's policy to secure the control of the Medinan khalīfa over the military actions of the community, a policy which was tantamount to the addition of new and important aspects to his functions; 2. the expression amīn Allāh pointed to the idea that the authority of the

Commander of the Faithful was sanctioned by God. Therefore it is not surprising that one came to consider the Medinan khalīfa no longer as the khalīfa of the Prophet, but as the khalīfa of God. Probably the occurrence of the expression khalīfat Allāh in the Qur'ān was instrumental in this process of transformation. Thus the concept of God's Caliph was emerging, and the Umayyads did not shrink from making use of it for their own sake.

V

Since the time of ʿUthmān the authority of the Commander of the Faithful was based firstly on his noble origin and secondly on the claim that Allāh, the Lord of human history and the One and personal God of Islam, had sanctioned the caliph's reign. The terms malik/mulk and khalīfa were interpreted according to these ideas. One can imagine that a regime like this will tend to assume an autocratic character; allegedly its deeds are in accordance with God's will.[112]

For this reason, powerful, but heterogeneous, movements opposing Umayyad rule were assailing the caliphs. The policy of the caliphs could not satisfy everybody. Those who were discontented with them were looking for forms of government whose autocratic character was mitigated by some other religious or political foundations. For the Umayyad caliphate, they maintained, was a degradation of what government should be in Islam; true Islamic government had been a reality only in the Prophet's lifetime.[113] Now there was nothing left but mulk, un-Islamic tyranny.

The thinking of the politico-religious movements opposing the Umayyads was developing along three main lines:[114] 1. The Khārijite groups wanted to evade autocracy by applying the revelation to all affairs of government. They hoped to check the alleged tyranny by means of the Qur'ānic laws and commandments. Their extremist wing even thought that one could do without any permanent ruler. 2. The Shīʿa movement longed for a charismatic leader whose orders, legitimated through constant divine inspiration, were able to satisfy the religious and worldly desires of the faithful. 3. The Sunnis were convinced that strict application of the standards which were sanctioned by the Prophet's and his Companions' deeds and sayings would procure the salvation of the Muslim community. With the exception of ʿUmar II, who accepted the ideas of Sunnism, the Umayyad caliphs were not able to amalgamate these new trends with their concept of government.[115]

NOTES

Chapter 1

1. For a bibliographical survey, see my "Syriac sources for seventh-century history," Byzantine and Modern Greek Studies 2 (1976): 17-36. In the present article I use the following abbreviations for frequently cited sources: BH = P. Bedjan, Gregorii Barhebraei Chronicon Syriacum (Paris: 1890) (English translation in E.A.W. Budge, The Chronography of Barhebraeus (Oxford: 1932); pp. 89-105 of vol. 1 covers the seventh century); Chr. 1234 = J.B. Chabot, Chronicon ad annum 1234 pertinens 1 (C.S.C.O., Scr. Syri 36: 1920) (Latin translation in C.S.C.O., Scr. Syri 56: 1937); MS = J.B. Chabot, Chronique de Michel le Syrien, 4 (Paris: 1899-1924; reprint 1963) (French translation in vol. 2); PsD = J.B. Chabot, Incerti auctoris chronicon pseudo-Dionysianum vulgo dictum 2 (C.S.C.O., Scr. Syri 53: 1933) (French translation by Chabot, Chronique de Denys de Tell-Mahre, quatrième partie (Paris: 1895); pp. 4-11 cover the seventh century).

2. J. Assfalg, Verzeichnis der orientalischen Handschriften in Deutschland, V: Syrische Handschriften (Wiesbaden: 1963), no. 5.

3. Ed. H. Usener, in Rheinisches Museum, n.F. 41 (1886), p. 508 (compare p. 515, for hope of recovery).

4. Ep. 14 (Patrologia Graeca 91, col. 540).

5. Ed. N. Bonwetsch, Doctrina Jacobi nuper baptizati (Abhandlungen der Gesellschaft der Wissenschaften zu Göttingen, phil.-hist.Kl. n.F.12, 3: 1910), p. 63.

6. F. Macler, Histoire d'Héraclius par l'évêque Sebeos (Paris: 1904), pp. 104-5 (section 32, cf. 34); cf. W.E. Kaegi, "Initial Byzantine reactions to the Arab Conquest," Church History 38 (1969): 139-49.

7. See note 1.

8. Cf. R. Abramowski, Dionysius von Tellmahre (Abhandlungen für die Kunde des Morgenlandes 25.2: 1940), pp. 14 ff.

9. Daniel 5:19

10. Chr. 1234, pp. 236-7; MS 2: 412-3 = 4: 410. They go on to add that the change of rule was

advantageous even though they did not regain control of their churches confiscated under Heraklios, seeing that the Arabs simply maintained the status quo in this matter.

11. R.H. Charles, The Chronicle of John, Bishop of Nikiu (London: 1916), 121.2: "all said . . . the victory of the Muslims was due to the wickedness of the emperor Heraklios and his persecution of the orthodox through the patriarch Kyros."

12. Patrologia Graeca 89, col. 1156.

13. Kaegi, "Initial Byzantine Reactions . . .," p. 142 wrongly tries to identify the Biblical name "Amalek" as a corruption of ʿAmr b. al-ʿĀṣ or ʿAbd al-Malik.

14. Ed. S.P. Brock in Analecta Bollandiana 91 (1973): 299-346 (section 23).

15. BH, p. 97; Elias of Nisibis, Opus Chronologicum (ed. E.W. Brooks, C.S.C.O., Scr. Syri 21), Part I, pp. 126-30.

16. MS 2: 403 = 4: 405; Chr. 1234, pp. 227-8.

17. Cf. BH, p. 97: rejection of idolatry would lead to God giving the Arabs "that land of promise"; compare also Sebeos (see Note 6) section 20, and Vardan (J. Muyldermans, La domination arabe en Arménie (Louvain and Paris: 1927), p. 41 (text) = p. 74 (translations)).

18. MS 2: 404 = 4: 406 (MS wrongly has "Law and prophets"); Chr. 1234, p. 229. In BH several anachronistic statements have crept in; e.g. (p. 98) the attribution to the Prophet of the institution of Ramaḍān (contrast Elias of Nisibis (ed. Brooks, p. 131), who credits it to ʿUmar, under the year A.H. 14).

19. Ed. F. Nau, "Un colloque du patriarche Jean avec l'émir des Agaréens," Journal asiatique 11 ser. 5 (1915): 225-79 (sections 2, 4). Nau dated the conversation to 639, but 644 is preferred by Lammens (Journal asiatique 11 ser. 13 (1919): 97-110).

20. Chr. 1234, p. 240: "When you enter that land, kill neither old man, nor child nor woman; do not force the stylites to come down from their columns, do not harm the solitaries, because they have set their lives apart to worship God. Do not cut down any tree or lay waste cultivated land, and do not hamstring any domesticated animals, whether cattle or sheep. Establish a covenant with every city and people who receives you, give them assurances and let them live according to their laws and the practices they had before our time. Let them pay tribute in accordance with the sum fixed between you, and let them practise their own religion where

they live. Those, however, who do not receive you, you are to fight, conducting yourselves carefully in accordance with the ordinances and upright laws transmitted to you from God, at the hands of our prophet, so that you do not anger God."

21. MS 2: 431 = 4: 421; cf. Chr. 1234, p. 260; Sebeos section 31.

22. Chr. 1234, p. 261.

23. Chr. 1234, p. 261.

24. BH, pp. 96-7.

25. Also found in the anonymous Nestorian chronicle composed between 670 and 680, ed. I. Guidi, *Chronica Minora* I (C.S.C.O., Scr. Syri 1), p. 38: "The victory of the sons of Ishmael, who overpowered two strong empires, came from God." Cf. C. Cahen, "Note sur l'accueil des chrétiens d'Orient à l'Islam," *Revue de l'histoire des religions* 166 (1964): 51-8.

26. See below, p. 16.

27. Syriac life of Maximos (see note 14), 18; the term probably means little more than non-Christian here, and should not be taken as implying the hostile attitude that becomes prevalent in later Byzantine writers (on whom see S. Vryonis, "Byzantine attitudes towards Islam during the late Middle Ages," *Greek, Roman and Byzantine Studies* 12 (1971): 263-86).

28. MS 2: 421-2 = 4: 416-17; Chr. 1234, pp. 246-7; BH, p. 101.

29. Scholia on Gregory Nazianzen's *Invective* 1, no. 33 (attributed to Nonnus), in *Patrologia Graeca* 36, col. 1004 (English translation of the Syriac version in S.P. Brock, *The Syriac Version of the Pseudo-Nonnus Mythological Scholia* (Cambridge: 1971), pp. 97-8).

30. "Prophet": PsD, p. 149; Chr. 1234, pp. 240, 254, 275; *Apocalypse of John the Less* (see note 66), p. 18; Elias of Nisibis (see note 15), p. 126. "Apostle": PsD, p. 149; Chr. 1234, p. 227.

31. E.g. List of Arab "kings," ed. J.P.N. Land, *Anecdota Syriaca* 2 (Leiden: 1868), p. 11 of addenda; French translation by F. Nau in *Journal asiatique* 11 ser. 5 (1915): 226 note 1.

32. Iohannan b. Penkaye (ed. A. Mingana, *Sources Syriaques* 1 (Leipzig: 1907), p. 146*; Chr. 1234, pp. 227, 238. In a late sixth century text it is used of the initiator of a heresy: S.E. and J.S. Assemani, *Bibliothecae Apost. Vaticanae . . . Catalogus*, 3: 65. In the Harklean New Testament (616) *haddi* translates *hodēgein*.

33. Chr. 1234, p. 277: *taḥlupa da-nbiyeh d-alaha*; ʿUthmān is also addressed as *amira da-mhaymne*.

34. Ed. R. Duval, Isho'yahb Patriarchae III Liber Epistularum (C.S.C.O., Scr. Syri 11 (translation: 12)), p. 226; the anonymous Nestorian Chronicle (ed. Guidi, see note 25), pp. 30, 31-2) uses mdabbrana, "leader," of both Muḥammad and his successors.

35. E.g. in the conversation between the patriarch John and the unnamed emir (see note 19).

36. E.g. Isho'yahb, Liber Epist., p. 97; Chr. 1234, p. 238; colophon of BM Add. 14666, dated A.H. 63; Patriarch Athanasius apud A. Vööbus, Syrische Kanonessammlungen 1 (C.S.C.O., Subsidia 35; 1, p. 200).

37. MS 2: 418, 423 = 4: 414, 416.

38. E.g. colophon of BM Add. 14666 (A.H. 63).

39. Eccl. Hist. 6: 38.

40. For the date, see J.M. Fiey, "Isho'yaw le grand," Orientalia Christiana Periodica 36 (1970): 7.

41. Cf. Fiey, pp. 30-33, 43; also W.G. Young, Patriarch, Shah and Caliph (Rawalpindi: 1974), pp. 85-99.

42. Liber Epist., p. 251; compare note 25.

43. Liber Epist., pp. 248 ff.

44. Liber Epist., p. 97.

45. Ed. Mingana (see note 32), p. 144*.

46. Liber Epist., p. 237.

47. Liber Epist., p. 266.

48. A. Mingana, "Timothy's Apology for Christianity," in Woodbrooke Studies 2 (Cambridge: 1928), pp. 59, 62.

49. Compare Chr. 1234, p. 240.

50. Compare the story in MS 2: 422 = 4: 417.

51. Ed. Mingana (see note 32), p. 141*.

52. Ed. Mingana, p. 147*.

53. Ed. Mingana, p. 147*.

54. Ed. Mingana, p. 155*.

55. Ed. Mingana, pp. 165 ff; Isho'yahb (Liber Epist., p. 249) already wonders whether the mass apostasies in Mazon (Oman) did not portray the arrival of the "man of sin." Compare even earlier Maximos, in Patrologia Graeca 91, col. 540. According to Sebeos section 35 the Ishmaelite "chief" is the "grand ally of Antichrist."

56. Ed. Mingana, p. 167*; see also p. 157* for the "captives."

57. Vat. syr. 58, ff. 118b-137a, of 1584. For other Syriac extracts see my "Syriac sources . . ." (note 1), p. 34. On the background, see the literature cited by I. Shahid, in Le Muséon 89 (1976): 174-6.

58. Thus in the title, f. 118b.

59. Ff. 126a-133b.

60. Ff. 134a-136a.
61. Ff. 123b-126a.
62. F.136a.
63. The starting point will be the Hijra, and not the conquest of Iraq, as most scholars have supposed; The Hijra dating is already used for the Nestorian synod of 676 (J.B. Chabot, Synodicon Orientale (Paris: 1902), p. 216 (text) = p. 482 (translation)); likewise John of Phenek (ed. Mingana, p. 160*): A.H. 67.
64. F.129a-b.
65. PsD, p. 154 (on this muddled passage, see D.C. Dennett, Conversion and Poll Tax in Islam (Cambridge, Massachusetts: 1950), pp. 45-6).
66. Ed. J.R. Harris, The Gospel of the Twelve Apostles (Cambridge: 1900), pp. 34-9 (translation), 15*-21* (text).
67. Cf. A. Vasiliev, "Medieval ideas of the end of the world: west and east," Byzantion 16 (1942/3): 473 f.
68. Cf. J. Meyendorff, "Byzantine views of Islam," Dumbarton Oaks Papers 18 (1964): 118; on John of Damascus, see in general D.J. Sahas, John of Damascus on Islam (Leiden: 1972).
69. Isaac of Nineveh was translated into Greek in the ninth century.
70. Cf. Kaegi, "Initial Byzantine reactions . . ." (note 6), p. 149.

Chapter 2

1. This formulation, of course, implies that there was a sanctuary at Mecca before the Muslim sanctuary was established there. Theoretically, any discussion of the origins of the Muslim sanctuary would need to begin by allowing for the possibility that the Meccan sanctuary owes its origins completely to Islam. I have not overlooked this possibility, but think that the evidence which will be presented in this paper justifies expressing the question in these terms.
2. I wish to thank Prof. P.M. Holt and M.A. Cook for reading versions of this paper and suggesting improvements.
3. See e.g. al-Azraqī, apud Die Chroniken der Stadt Mekka, ed. F. Wüstenfeld (Leipzig: 1858-61), Vol. 1 passim; Ibn al-Kalbī, Kitāb al-Aṣnām, ed. W. Atallah (Paris: 1969), pp. 3 ff.
4. J. Wellhausen, Reste arabischen Heidenthums (3rd edition, Berlin: 1927), especially pp. 68 ff.; H. Lammens "Les sanctuaires préislamites . . .," MUSJ 11: 41-73; idem, "Le culte des bétyles,"

L'Arabie occidentale avant l'hégire (Beirut: 1928).

5. See e.g. A.J. Wensinck, "The navel of the earth," Verhandelingen der Koninklijke Akademie van Wetenschappen te Amsterdam, Afdeeling Letterkunde, Nieuwe Reeks, 17, No. 1: 13, discussing the association between the sanctuary and the idea of "high places" in Islam and elsewhere.

6. Substantial parts of Snouck Hurgronje's work are available in a French translation by G.-H. Bousquet: "Le pèlerinage à la Mecque," Selected works of C. Snouck Hurgronje, ed. and trans. G.-H. Bousquet and J. Schacht (Leiden: 1957), pp. 171-213; "La légende qorânique d'Abraham . . .," Revue Africaine 95 (1951): 273-288; see too "Ibrāhīm," EI, 2 (R. Paret).

7. For general summaries, see: C. Snouck Hurgronje, Mekka (The Hague: 1889-90), 1: 2 ff.; M. Gaudefroy-Demombynes, Le pèlerinage à la Mekke (Paris: 1923), pp. 27-41; "Kaʿba," EI, 1 (A.J. Wensinck).

8. Azraqī, passim.

9. Ibid., pp. 271 ff.

10. See "Zamzam," EI, 1 (B. Carra de Vaux).

11. Ibid., "Al-Masdjid al-Ḥaram" (A.J. Wensinck).

12. Azraqī, pp. 105-9, 140-5.

13. Cf. especially the accounts of the fire which damaged the Kaʿba in Azraqī, pp. 105-6, with the fire which destroyed al-Qallīs as reported in the Persian trans. of Ṭabarī, ed. H. Zotenberg, 2: 198; note the role of the wind in each case.

14. On the bi'r (or jubb) al-Kaʿba, see Azraqī, pp. 169 ff.

15. M.J. Kister, "Maqām Ibrāhīm, a stone with an inscription," Le Muséon 84 (1971): 477-91.

16. Wellhausen, p. 76; Gaudefroy-Demombynes, p. 103; Lammens, "Sanctuaires préislamites," p. 56.

17. For a summary, see Kister, p. 479, notes 8, 9.

18. Kister, p. 480; however, Kister also cites here al-Rāzī, Mafātīḥ al-ghayb (Cairo: 1327), 1: 473, where the phrase "ittakhadhtu min fulānin ṣadīqan" is cited as an analogy to the Qur'ānic phrase. Rāzī's analogy, and others of a similar sort which he gives, is hardly convincing evidence that the use of "min" in the Qur'ānic verse is normal if the Maqām Ibrāhīm there indicates the sacred stone at Mecca (in the Būlāq 1289 ed. the passage is in 1:719). Cf. Qur'ān 2:63: "a-tattakhidhunā huzu'an" ("do you make us an object of derision?").

19. Ibn Hishām, Sīra (Cairo: 1955), 1: 314 (= Ṭabarī, Ta'rīkh (Leiden: 1879 ff.), 1: 1188): "ʿAbd Allāh b. Masʿūd ran . . . to the Maqām . . .

and Quraysh were in their 'groups' (?andiya) . . . and he stood by (ʿinda) the Maqām and said . . ."; Gaudefroy-Demombynes, p. 103; Lammens, "Sanctuaires préislamites," p. 105, n. 1. Because of the nature of the reference, it is not possible to say for sure what preposition would be used for "in."

20. Ibn Hishām, 1: 175[7], 151[9]; Lammens, "Sanctuaires préislamites," p. 105, n. 1.

21. Ibid.

22. Dīwān, ed. P. Schwartz (Leipzig: 1909), no. 91.

23. Azraqī, p. 273.

24. Ibid., p. 278.

25. Cf. ibid., p. 105 with p. 108.

26. Maqdisī, "Descriptio imperii moslemici," BGA 3, no. 2 (1906): 72; Wellhausen, p. 74; "Kaʿba," EI, 1.

27. E.g. Ibn Hishām, 1: 5 (= Azraqī, p. 220); Ibn Saʿd, Kitāb al-ṭabaqāt, ed. E. Sachau et al., 1, part 1: 25. Yāqūt, Muʿjam al-buldān, ed. F. Wüstenfeld, 2: 208, mentions only the tomb of Hagar in al-Ḥijr, not that of Ishmael, and various other locations are sometimes given for Ishmael's tomb (e.g. al-Harawī, p. 86[13]: between Zamzam and al-Rukn). Other traditions associate al-Ḥijr with Hagar and Ishmael in other ways: it was a cattle pen for Ishmael's animals (Azraqī, p. 31[13-14]); it was the place where Abraham left his concubine and son when he settled them in the wilderness (Ṭabarī, Tafsīr, new Cairo ed., 3: 62).

28. Lammens, "Sanctuaires préislamites," p. 44, n. 2; Gaudefroy-Demombynes, pp. 37, 328.

29. Ibn Hishām, 1: 661.

30. E.g. Ṭabarī, Taʾrīkh, 2: 222, 233 ("wa-Ibn al-Zubayr bi-hā qad lazima al-Kaʿba"); Balādhurī, Ansāb al-ashrāf (Jerusalem: 1938), 4b: 13[20] ("lazima jāniba al-Kaʿba").

31. Ibn ʿAsākir, Taʾrīkh Dimashq (Damascus: 1951 ff.), 7: 410.

32. Ibn Ḥanbal, Musnad (Cairo: 1313), 6: 290.

33. Ṭabarī, Taʾrīkh, 1: 2995, 3112.

34. E.g. Ṭabarī, Tafsīr, Būlāq ed., 15: 3 f.; Ibn Hishām, 1: 397.

35. Ibn Hishām, 1: 110, 142 (= Azraqī, p. 284); Yaʿqūbī, Taʾrīkh (Beirut: 1970), 1: 246.

36. "Bétyles," p. 147, n. 7. But cf. idem, "Sanctuaires préislamites," p. 107, where he argues that Muḥammad was not practising incubation when he was taken on the Night Journey--an argument made necessary by Lammens's desire here to prove that al-Masjid al-Ḥarām generally refers to all of the ḥaram.

37. Azraqī, pp. 145 ff.; Ṭabarī Ta'rīkh, 2: 854.

38. Azraqī, pp. 142, 218-19, 222; Ṭabarī, Ta'rīkh, 2: 537; Balādhurī, Ansāb, 4B: 55-6; Ibn Sa'd, 1, part 1: 94-5.

39. Azraqī, p. 219; according to another tradition, ibid., "Ā'isha said that she did not mind whether she prayed in the Ka'ba or in al-Ḥijr ("mā ubālī ṣallaytu fi'l-Ḥijr aw fi'l-Ka'ba"). The association, in the traditions, of 'Ā'isha with al-Ḥijr (she takes refuge there, she prays there, she is the supposed source of the ḥadīth justifying its inclusion in the bayt) is striking.

40. Muḥibb al-Dīn Ṭabarī, al-Qirā (Cairo: 1948), p. 465.

41. Azraqī, pp. 219-20: "fa-awḥā Allāh (ilā Ismā'īl) innanī aftaḥu laka bāban min al-janna fi'l-Ḥijr."

42. Maqdisī, p. 72.

43. Azraqī, p. 267; Yāqūt, 2: 290; Lane, Lexicon, s.v.; R. Burton, Personal narrative of a pilgrimage . . . (memorial ed., London: 1893), 2: 305; Wellhausen, p. 74; "Ka'ba," EI, 1.

44. "Bétyles," p. 149.

45. Wellhausen, p. 74, n. 1; Bukhārī, Manāqib al-anṣār, Chapter 27 (ed. Krehl, 3: 20).

46. Ṭabarī, Ta'rīkh, 1: 3464; Wellhausen, p. 74.

47. Wellhausen, p. 74.

48. Lammens, "Bétyles," p. 148, n. 1.

49. See e.g. Azraqī, p. 225[11], where Sa'īd b. Jubayr is said to have put his sandals "on the wall of al-Ḥijr" ("'alā jadr al-Ḥijr"). If al-Ḥaṭīm was commonly used as a designation of this wall, as some sources say, it might be wondered why Azraqī's tradition does not use it here.

50. See e.g. Ibn al-Kalbī, pp. 3 f. where this is clearly and succinctly stated.

51. Azraqī, pp. 306-19; Balādhurī, Futūḥ, ed. M. de Goeje, p. 46; Muḥibb al-Dīn Ṭabarī, p. 607; Lammens, "La Mecque à la veille de l'hégire," MUSJ, 8 (1922), passim; "al-Masdjid al-Ḥarām," EI, 1.

52. The formula usually used in the historical works says that Muḥammad changed the qibla from Bayt al-Maqdis to the Ka'ba (e.g. Balādhurī, Ansāb (Cairo: 1959), 1: 271; Ṭabarī, Ta'rīkh, 1: 1279; Ya'qūbī, 2: 42). Ṭabarī's Tafsīr on the qibla verses (new Cairo ed., 3: 177 f.) consists largely of traditions which debate the question of which part of the Ka'ba is the exact qibla. For Ṭabarī, it would seem, the question why the Qur'ān uses al-Masjid al-Ḥarām instead of al-Ka'ba does not arise. Cf., however, the Tafsīr of al-Bayḍāwī, ad loc., which

goes to some trouble to explain, not very convincingly, the Qur'ānic usage here. It is probable that the formula "al-Kaʿba qiblat ahl al-masjid wa'l-masjid qiblat ahl al-ḥaram wa'l-ḥaram qiblat ahl al-arḍ" (Azraqī, pp. 264-5) is also a response to this question.

53. Azraqī, pp. 39-40, 301; Ṭabarī, Tafsīr, new Cairo ed., 7: 21; Bukhārī, Anbiyā', chapters 10, 40; Muḥibb al-Dīn Ṭabarī, p. 606.

54. Ibn Hishām, 1: 402 (= Ṭabarī, Tafsīr, Būlāq, 15: 3).

55. Azraqī, p. 301; Muḥibb al-Dīn Ṭabarī, p. 607; Ṭabarī, Tafsīr, Būlāq, 15: 3 (all of the ḥaram is a masjid).

56. Ṭabarī, Tafsīr, new Cairo ed., 14: 190 f. (all of the ḥaram is a masjid and a qibla).

57. For a good example of the possible variants, cf. Balādhurī, Ansāb, 4B: 56 ("wa-jaʿala Ibn al-Zubayr al-ḥajar al-aswad fī tābūt . . . thumma sattara al-rukn bi-thawb wa-radda al-ḥajar"), Azraqī, p. 143 ("jaʿala al-rukn fī tābūt"), and Ṭabarī, Ta'rīkh, 2: 537 ("jaʿala al-rukn al-aswad fī tābūt"). "Kaʿba," EI, 1 says that the arkān are the four corners of the Kaʿba and that the Black Stone is called al-Ḥajar al-Aswad. Wellhausen, p. 74: "Der schwarze Stein heisst schlechthin die Ecke (alRukn) als gäbe es kein andere heilige Ecke."

58. Lammens, "Sanctuaires préislamites," pp. 51-2, 80; "Bétyles," pp 145-7. For the wiping (annointing? masḥ) of the arkān see Azraqī, p. 49; Fāsī, Shifā', p. 192. Cf. the lapis pertusus of the Jerusalem sanctuary which, says the Bordeaux Pilgrim (PPTS 1: 21-2), the Jews annointed with oil.

59. See note 57 above.

60. Azraqī, pp. 143, 220.

61. Azraqī, p. 143.

62. Ibid., pp. 42-3; Ibn Hishām, 1: 195-6; Ṭabarī, Tafsīr, new Cairo ed., 3: 61.

63. Al-zabūr is usually, of course, translated by "the Psalms," and it could be that the tradition is saying that the text was found in "one of the Psalms." The context, however, seems to require something else, and M.A. Cook pointed out to me that the dictionaries have the expression zabara al-bi'r (he lined the well with stone) and the noun zabr (stone, casing of a well; see Lane, Lexicon, s.v.). Given the mention of stones and wells in other traditions, it could be that al-zabūr here means something like "the well lining."

64. Pèlerinage, p. 32, n. 4, citing Masʿūdī, Murūj, ed. A.J.-B. Pavet de Courteille and A.C.

Barbier de Meynard, 1: 120.

65. Cf. al-Ḥalabī's account of the burial of the sanctuary objects by the last Jurhumī chief of Mecca (Sīra (Būlāq: 1280), 1:43) with that of Ibn Isḥāq (Sīra, 1:114): where Ibn Hishām's Sīra says that the ḥajar al-rukn was among the things which were buried, Ḥalabī's Sīra refers to al-ḥajar al-aswad.

66. Ibn Hishām 1: 114 (= Tabarī, Ta'rīkh, 1: 1132-4). Azraqī's version (p. 52) does not refer to the ḥajar al-rukn. Note that Fāsī, pp. 191-2, has two variants of the tradition as it is found in Ibn Hishām which may be significant. One mentions the burial of al-ḥajar in a place other than in Zamzam, the other attributes the burial of al-rukn to B. Iyād ibn Nizār, also in a place other than Zamzam.

67. Caetani, Annali, 1:62; cf. Gaudefroy-Demombynes, p. 48.

68. Ibn Saʿd, 1, part 1, 25[22-27].

69. D. Sidersky, Les origines des légendes musulmanes . . . (Paris: 1933), pp. 53-4, no. 15.

70. Genesis, 18:22 ff.; the Targums, both on this verse and on 19:27, gloss "standing" as "praying" (English trans. W. Etheridge (London: 1862), 1, Genesis and Exodus).

71. See above, pp. 30-1.

72. E. Landau, Die dem Raume entnommenen Synonyma für Gott in der Neuhebräischen Literatur (Zürich: 1888), pp. 30 ff.; S. Schechter, Rabbinic theology (London: 1909), p. 27, n. 1; L. Ginzberg, The legends of the Jews (Philadelphia: 1911 ff.), 1: 349, n. 130, for bibliography. Lammens, "Sanctuaires préislamites," p. 104, n. 4, suggests that in the Qur'ān maqām means sometimes "quelque chose comme l'essence divine."

73. On the sakīna in Islam: A. Geiger, Was hat Mohammed aus dem Judenthume aufgenommen? (2nd edition, Leipzig: 1902), pp. 53-55, English trans. Judaism and Islam (Madras: 1898), pp. 39-40; I. Goldziher, "La notion de la sakîna chez les mohamétans," RHR 28 (1893), reprinted in Gesammelte Schriften, 3: 296-308

74. On the difficulties caused to the exegetes by the apparent variation in the number of Abraham's visitors in the Genesis account, see J. Bowker, The Targums and Rabbinic literature (Cambridge: 1969), p. 210.

75. E.g. the Targum of Ps. Jonathan, ad loc.; Ginzberg, 1: 349.

76. B. Schrieke, "Die Himmelsreise Muhammads," Isl., 6 (1916): 12.

77. See above, p. 34.

78. Ibn Hishām, 1: 399-400.
79. Wensinck, pp. 24-5.
80. Ginzberg, 1: 351.
81. Ishmael, Muḥammad and ʿAbd al-Muṭṭalib seem to take, in the Muslim traditions, the place assigned to Jacob in the Jewish. M.A. Cook has suggested that the designation al-ḥujar for the burial place of Muḥammad in Muslim tradition (explained as the 'rooms' of the Prophet's wife) may be related to the designation al-Ḥijr for Ishmael's burial place.
82. Ginzberg, 1: 349 and note 141.
83. Azraqī, p. 143.
84. The traditions about the two supposedly different events frequently use the same or similar words and phrases.
85. Azraqī, p. 232; Fāsī, 1: 168.
86. Azraqī, p. 32, cf. pp. 227 ff. Ibn Saʿd, 1, part 1: 12, "The Black Stone (al-ḥajar al-aswad) shone like the moon for the people of Mecca until the pollution of impure people caused it to go black." For a discussion of various questions which arise in connection with the tradition that the Stone's blackness is to be ascribed to sin, see Muḥibb al-Dīn Ṭabarī, p. 261.
87. Ginzberg, 1: 12-13.
88. Ibid.; Fāsī, 1: 168.
89. See above, pp. 39-40.
90. See above, p. 40.
91. See e.g. al-Ḥarbī, Kitāb manāsik al-ḥajj (Riyāḍ: 1969), p. 483.
92. Ginzberg, 1: 349 and note 141.
93. E.g. Azraqī, pp. 42-3; Ṭabarī, Tafsīr, new Cairo ed., 3: 61; Ibn Hishām, 1: 196. According to the expert whose opinion on the inscription on the Maqām Ibrāhīm is reported by Fākihī, the first line of the inscription, translated into Arabic, reads: "innanī anā Allāh lā ilāh illā anā" (Kister, p. 485; see too the 3 texts found, according to the tradition given by ʿAbd al-Razzāq, in the Maqām Ibrāhīm, each of which begins: "innanī Allāh Dhū Bakka"; ibid., p. 486, note 48).
94. Fākihī, Muntaqā (MS Leiden Or. 463, fol. 335a ff.); text and translation in Kister, pp. 485 ff. For a reproduction of the foreign inscription given by Fākihī, see Dozy, Israeliten, appendix. The maqām is mentioned by name as the place of the inscription also in Ibn Hishām, 1: 196 (Arabic text given, no mention of it being in a foreign script), and in Azraqī, p. 42[12] (also gives Arabic text with no mention of a foreign script). Maqām Ibrāhīm is named as the place of 3 ṣufūḥ in ʿAbd al-Razzāq

(Jāmiʿ, MS Feyzullah Ef. 541, fol. 134a), given by Kister, p. 486 note 48.

95. Kister, p. 489.

96. See above, pp. 39-40

97. Azraqī, p. 43[16] = Ibn Hishām, 1: 196.

98. Kister, p. 486. Fākihī explains al-Barābī as "ancient Egyptian writing on stones" ("Kitāb fi'l-ḥijāra bi-miṣr min kitāb al-awwalīn"), apparently, therefore, hieroglyphics. M.A. Cook has pointed out, however, that barābī is the plural form of barbā, from Coptic p'erpe, the word for an ancient Egyptian temple; see Dozy, Supplément, s.v.

99. Kister, p. 491.

100. Ibid., pp. 481-2; note 22 for sources.

101. E.g. Azraqī, pp. 25 ff. The parallels here are very striking. In some traditions Abraham builds until he comes to the place of the rukn, and he then sends Ishmael off to find a suitable stone. In others Abraham builds until the walls become too high, and he then sends Ishmael off to find a stone for him to stand on.

102. Kister, p. 482, n. 23 for sources.

103. My first thought was that the whole tradition of the inscription on the stone called Maqām Ibrāhīm was to be explained as a development from the tradition about the inscription found on the stone beneath the sanctuary. But as M.A. Cook argued with me, Fākihī's account is circumstantial and seems to be based on fact. I now think it likely, therefore, that Fākihī did see an inscription on the Maqām Ibrāhīm, but that the interpretation which he and others give is derived from the tradition about the stone beneath the sanctuary.

Bibliography to Chapter 3

Adams, R.M., The Evolution of Urban Society (Chicago: 1966)

al-ʿAlī, Sāliḥ, al-Tanẓīmāt al-ijtimāʿiyya wa'l-iqtiṣādiyya fī'l Baṣra (Baghdad: 1965)

Altheim, F. and Stiehl, R., Die Araber in der alte Welt (Berlin: 1964-8)

Arberry, A.J., The Koran Interpreted (London: 1955)

al-Balādhurī, Futūḥ al-Buldān (Leiden: 1866), trans. P.K. Hitti and E.C. Murgotten, The Origins of the Islamic State (New York: 1916-1924)

Beeston, A.F.L., "Kingship in Ancient South Arabia," JESHO 15 (1972): 256-268

Bell, Richard, The Origin of Islam in its Christian Environment (London: 1926)

Bellah, R., "Religious Evolution," American Sociological Review 29 (1964): 358-374

Bousquet, G.H., "Observations sur la nature et les causes de la conquête arabe," Studia Islamica 6 (1956): 37-52
Caskel, W., Die Bedeutung der Beduinen in der Geschichte der Araber (Cologne: 1953)
——"The Bedouinization of Arabia," American Anthropologist, Memoirs 76 (1954): 36-46
Chelhod, J., Introduction à la Sociologie de l'Islam (Paris: 1958)
——Le Sacrifice chez les Arabes (Paris: 1955)
——Les Structures du Sacré chez les Arabes (Paris: 1964)
Dussaud, René, Les arabes en Syrie avant l'Islam (Paris: 1907)
Eikelman, Dale, "Musaylima," JESHO 10 (1967): 17-52
Eisenstadt, S.N., The Political Systems of Empires (New York: 1969)
Encyclopedia of Islam, new ed. articles: al-ʿArab, Badw, Djazīrat al-ʿArab
Fahd, T., La Divination arabe (Leiden: 1966)
——Le Panthéon de l'Arabie Centrale à la veille de l'Hégire (Paris: 1968)
Faris, N.A., The Arab Heritage (Princeton: 1944)
Gabrieli, F., ed. L'Antica Società Beduina (Rome: 1959)
Goldziher, Ignaz, Muhammedanische Studien, trans. S.M. Stern, Muslim Studies, vol. 1 (London: 1967)
von Grunebaum, G., "The Nature of Arab Unity before Islam," Arabica 10 (1963): 4-23
Kamerer, A., Pétra et la Nabatène (Paris: 1929)
Kawar, Irfan, "The Arabs in the Peace Treaty of A.D. 561," Arabica 3 (1956): 181-213
Kister, M.J., "Al-Ḥīra: some notes on its relations with Arabic," Arabica 11 (1968): 143-169
——"Mecca and Tamim," JESHO 8 (1965): 113-163
——"Some Reports Concerning Mecca from Jāhiliyya to Islam," JESHO 15 (1972): 61-93
Lammens, Henri, La Mecque à la veille de l'hégire (Beirut: 1924)
——L'Arabie occidentale avant l'hégire (Beirut: 1928)
——Le berceau de l'Islam (Rome: 1914)
Lattimore, Owen, Inner Asian Frontiers of China (New York: 1940)
Levi Della Vida, G., "Pre-Islamic Arabia," in Faris, N.A. (ed.), The Arab Heritage (Princeton: 1944), pp. 24-57
Massignon, L., "Explication du plan de Basra," Westostliche Abhandlungen R. Tschudi, 1954, pp. 157-174
——"Explication du plan de Kufa," Mélanges Maspéro 3 (1940): 337-360
Montagne, R., La Civilisation du Désert (Paris: 1947)

Nöldeke, T., Die ghassânischen Fürsten aus dem Hause Gafna (Berlin: 1887)
Obermann, J., "Islamic Origins: A Study in Background and Foundation," in N.A. Faris (ed.), The Arab Heritage (Princeton: 1944), pp. 58-120
Olinder, Gunnar, The Kings of Kinda of the Family of Ākil al-Murār (Lund: 1927)
Pellat, C., Le milieu Baṣrien et la formation de Ǧāḥiẓ (Paris: 1953)
Pigulevskaya, N., "Les Rapports Sociaux a Nedjrān," JESHO 4 (1961): 1-14
Rodinson, Maxime, "L'Arabie avant l'Islam," Encyclopédie de la Pléiade (Paris: L'Histoire Universelle, 1957)
——"The Life of Muhammad and the Sociological Problem of the Beginning of Islam," Diogenes 20 (1957): 28-51
Rothstein, Gustav, Die Dynastie der Laḥmiden in al-Ḥīra (Berlin: 1899)
Ryckmans, G., "Les religions préislamiques," L'Histoire générale des religions (Paris: 1960)
Ryckmans, J., L'Institution monarchique en Arabie méridionale avant l'Islam (Louvain: 1951)
Shahid, Irfan, "Pre-Islamic Arabia," Cambridge History of Islam, vol. 1 (Cambridge: 1970), pp. 3-29
Shoufani, Elias, Al-Riddah and the Muslim Conquest of Arabia (Toronto: 1972)
Torrey, Charles C., The Jewish Foundations of Islam (New York: 1933)
Watt, W.M., Muhammad at Mecca (Oxford: 1953)
——Muhammad at Medina (Oxford: 1956)
——"The Tribal Basis of the Islamic State," Dalla tribu allo state (Rome: 1962), pp. 154-160
Wellhausen, Julius, Reste arabischen Heidenthums (2nd edn., Berlin: 1897, 3rd edn., Berlin: 1961)
——Skizzen und Vorabeiten (6 vols.) (Berlin: 1884-99)
Wolf, E.R., "The Social Organization of Mecca and the Origins of Islam," Southwestern Journal of Anthropology 7 (1951): 329-356

Chapter 4

1. Before going any further the author feels compelled to recognize his debt to the scholarship and inspiration of Professors C.E. Bosworth, C. Cahen, R. Frye, A.K.S. Lambton, I. Lapidus, and M.A. Shaban among others whose contributions are indicated in the footnotes.

2. Balādhurī, Kitāb futūḥ al-buldān (Leiden: 1866), p. 313.

3. Ṭabarī, Ta'rīkh al-rusul wa'l-mulūk (Leiden:

1879), 1: 3449.

4. C.E. Bosworth, *Sīstān under the Arabs* (Rome: 1968), pp. 23, 26; Ibn ʿAbd Rabbih, *al-ʿIqd al-farīd* (Cairo: 1367/1948), 4: 167.

5. M.A. Shaban, *The ʿAbbasid Revolution* (Cambridge: 1970), pp. 100, 110.

6. Bosworth, p. 47.

7. Bosworth, p. 61; Masʿūdī, *Murūj al-dhahab* (Beirut: 1966), 2: 251; Ṭabarī, 1: 2543, 2708-9, 3432, 2: 989.

8. Narshakhi, *History of Bukhara* (Cambridge: 1954), p. 37. In 683-4 we find these Bukhārans in the company of the armed *mawālī* of ʿAbd al-Malik ibn ʿAbdallāh ibn ʿĀmir ibn Kurayz at Baṣra (Ṭabarī, 2: 464), and this unit was settled at Wasit by Ḥajjāj (Balādhurī, *Futūḥ*, p. 376).

9. Narshakhi, pp. 40-1.

10. Ṭabarī, 1: 3350.

11. Narshakhi, pp. 44-5.

12. Ibid., p. 30.

13. Balādhurī, *Futūḥ*, pp. 391-2.

14. Ibid., pp. 308, 392

15. Ibid., p. 329

16. Ibid., p. 314.

17. A.K.S. Lambton, "An Account of the Tārīkhi Qumm," *BSOAS* 12 (1948): p. 596.

18. The *Sūq al-Ṣughd* was one of the oldest quarters of Marv (M.A. Shaban, "Khurāsān at the time of the Arab conquest," *Iran and Islam* (Edinburgh: 1971), p. 487).

19. Balādhurī, *Futūḥ*, p. 314.

20. Yaʿqūbī, *Les pays* (Cairo: 1937), pp. 65-68.

21. Balādhurī, *Futūḥ*, p. 326.

22. Balādhurī, *Ansāb al-Ashrāf* (Cairo: 1959), 1: 494; Bosworth, pp. 5, 23-4. There had been a *hirbadh* at Darabjird at the time of the conquest (Balādhurī, *Futūḥ*, p. 403).

23. B. Spuler, *Iran in früh-islamischer Zeit* (Wiesbaden: 1952), p. 190.

24. B.M. Tirmidhi, "Zoroastrians and their fire temples in Iran and adjoining countries from the 9th to the 14th centuries as gleaned from the Arabic geographical works," *Islamic Culture* 24 (1950): 282.

25. Ibid., p. 274.

26. A. Houtum-Schindler, *Eastern Persian Irak* (London: 1898), p. 76. There had been seven fire-temples at Jamkaran in the seventh century.

27. Bosworth, p. 23.

28. Ṭabarī, 2: 586. Under the year A.H. 65 (A.D. 684-5) Magians in Khurāsān are accused of marrying their mothers, sisters, and daughters.

29. M. Boyce, The Letter of Tansar (Rome: 1968), p. 68.
30. Bosworth, p. 23; R. Frye, "Zurvanism Again," Harvard Theological Review 52 (1959): 65-8; Spuler, pp. 186-7
31. Tirmidhi, pp. 275, 282.
32. Bosworth, pp. 4-5; Tirmidhi, p. 282.
33. Bosworth, p. 23; Mas'ūdī, 2: 405; Spuler, pp. 190-2; Tirmidhi, pp. 271-84.
34. Tirmidhi, p. 281.
35. Narshakhi, pp. 20-21.
36. C. Wendell, "Baghdād: Imago Mundi, and other Foundation-Lore," IJMES 2 (1971): 126-7.
37. R.C. Zaehner, Hindu and Muslim Mysticism (London: 1960).
38. It is worth noticing that Mukhtār appointed Yazīd b. Mu'āwiya al-Bajalī governor of Iṣfahān, Qumm and their districts (Dīnawarī, Kitāb al-akhbār al-ṭiwāl (Leiden: 1912), p. 300).
39. Ishō'yahb III, Corpus Scriptorum Christianorum Orientalium (Louvain: 1955), 11: 248, 12: 179-80.
40. Narshakhi, pp. 47-9.
41. Balādhurī, Futūḥ, p. 329.
42. Dīnawarī, p. 138.
43. Balādhurī, Futūḥ, p. 306.
44. Ṭabarī, 1: 2903.
45. Ibid., 2: 1635-7.
46. Tārīkh-i Sīstān (Tehran: 1314/1935), p. 106.
47. Bosworth, p. 57.

Chapter 5

1. 'Abd al-Razzāq, al-Muṣannaf, ed. Ḥabīb al-Raḥmān al-A'ẓamī (Beirut: 1392/1972), 11: 291, no. 20569 (= Jāmi' Ma'mar b. Rāshid: ". . . an yu'mala bi-rukhaṣihi"); Ibn Balbān, "al-Iḥsān fī taqrīb ṣaḥīḥi bni Ḥibbān," MS. Br. Mus., Add. 27519, fol. 90a; al-Suyūṭī, al-Durr al-manthūr fī l-tafsīr bi-l-ma'thūr (Cairo: 1314), 1: 193; Abū Nu'aym, Ḥilyat al-awliyā' (Beirut: 1387/1967, reprint), 6: 191 inf., 276, 2: 101 inf. (". . . an tuqbala rukhaṣuhu"); al-Māwardī, "al-Amthāl wa-l-ḥikam," MS Leiden, Or. 655, fol. 87b (". . . an yu'khadha bi-rukhaṣihi kamā yuḥibbu an yu'khadha bi-farā'iḍihi"); al-Mundhirī, al-Targhīb wa-l-tarhīb, ed. Muḥammad Muḥyī l-Dīn 'Abd al-Ḥamīd (Cairo: 1379/1960), 2: 261, no. 1541 (and see ibid. no. 1539: ". . . an tu'tā rukhaṣuhu kamā yakrahu an tu'tā ma'ṣiyatuhu"; another version: ". . . kamā yuḥibbu an tutraka ma'ṣiyatuhu"); al-Munāwī, Fayḍ al-qadīr, sharḥ al-jāmi' al-ṣaghīr (Beirut: 1391/1972), 2:292, no. 1879, 293, no. 1881 (". . . an tuqbala rukhaṣuhu

kamā yuḥibbu l-ʿabdu maghfirata rabbihi"; 2: 296, no. 1894: ". . . kamā yakrahu an tuʾtā maʿṣiyatuhu"); al-Daylamī, "Firdaws al-akhbār," Chester Beatty 4139, fol. 53a; al-Khaṭīb al-Baghdādī, Mūḍiḥ awhām al-jamʿ wa-l-tafrīq (Hyderabad: 1379/1960), 2: 10 (". . . an tuʾtā mayāsiruhu kamā yuḥibbu an tuʾtā ʿazāʾimuhu"); cf. al-Kulaynī, al-Kāfī, ed. Najm al-Dīn al-Āmulī (Tehran: 1388), 1: 208-209, no. 4.

2. al-Shaybānī, al-Iktisāb fī l-rizqi l-mustaṭāb, Talkhīṣ Muḥammad b. Samāʿa, ed. Maḥmūd ʿArnūs (Cairo: 1357/1938), p. 81: ". . . fa-ṣāra l-ḥāṣilu anna l-iqtiṣara ʿalā adnā mā yakfīhi ʿazīmatun, wa-mā zāda ʿalā dhālika min al-tanaʿʿumi wa-l-nayli min al-ladhdhāti rukhṣatun, wa-qāla ṣallā llāhu ʿalayhi wa-sallam: inna llāha yuḥibbu an yuʾtā bi-rukhaṣihi . . ."

3. Abū ʿUbayd, Kitāb al-amwāl, ed. Muḥammad Ḥāmid al-Fiqī (Cairo: 1353), pp. 84-85; cf. al-Bayhaqī, al-Sunan al-kubrā (Hyderabad: 1356), 9: 140-1: ". . . bāb man kariha shirāʾa arḍi l-kharāj . . .," followed by "bāb man rakhkhaṣa fī shirāʾi arḍi l-kharāj . . ." And see the traditions against buying of kharāj land: Ibn Zanjawayh, "al-Amwāl," MS. Burdur 183, fols. 29b-32a (and see e.g. ibid., fol. 30a, inf., ". . . samiʿa l-ḥasana yaqūlu: man khalaʿa ribqata muʿāhidin fa-jaʿalahā fī ʿunuqihi fa-qad istaqāla hijratahu wa-wallā l-islāma ẓahrahu wa-man aqarra bi-shayʾin min al-jizyati fa-qad aqarra bi-bābin min abwābi l-kufri").

4. al-Shawkānī, Nayl al-awṭār, sharḥ muntaqā l-akhbār min aḥādīthi sayyidi l-akhyār (Cairo: 1372/1953), 1: 299; Ibn Abī Shayba, al-Muṣannaf, ed. ʿAbd al-Khāliq Khān al-Afghānī (Hyderabad: 1386/1966), 1: 109-110; ʿAbd al-Razzāq, 1: 290-296, nos. 1116-1136; al-Fākihī, "Taʾrīkh Makka," MS. Leiden Or. 463, fol. 421a; al-Mundhirī, 1: 118-122, nos. 267-278; al-Sharīshī, Sharḥ maqāmāt al-Ḥarīrī, ed. Muḥammad ʿAbd al-Munʿim Khafājī (Cairo: 1372/1952), 3:74; al-Muttaqī l-Hindī, Kanz al-ʿummāl (Hyderabad: 1381/1962), 9: 231-234, nos. 1978-2010; cf. al-Ḥākim, Maʿrifat ʿulūm al-ḥadīth, ed. Muʿaẓẓam Ḥusayn (Cairo: 1937), p. 98.

5. See e.g. al-Munāwī, 2: 54, no. 1311: ". . . uffin li-l-ḥammām . . .," enjoins husbands to forbid their wives to enter baths, stresses the filthiness of their water and confines the entrance of men to those wearing the maʾāzir; cf. al-Ṭayālisī, Musnad (Hyderabad: 1321), p. 212, no. 1518: ʿĀʾisha reproaches the women from Ḥimṣ for entering baths. And see Nūr al-Dīn al-Haythamī, Majmaʿ al-zawāʾid

wa-manbaʿ al-fawāʾid (Beirut: 1967, reprint), 1: 277-278 (the prohibition for women to enter baths; and see ibid., p. 114: the bath is the abode of the Devil); al-Ṭabarī, Dhayl al-mudhayyal (Cairo: 1358/1939), p. 116; al-Tirmidhī, Ṣaḥīḥ (Cairo: 1353/1934), 10: 246; al-Dhahabī, Mīzān al-iʿtidāl, ed. ʿAlī Muḥammad al-Bajāwī (Cairo: 1382/1963), 3: 631, no. 7889; al-Daylamī, MS. Chester Beatty 3037, fol. 90b (the prohibition to enter baths by women is preceded by a prediction of the Prophet that the Muslims will conquer the lands of the ʿajam and will find there "buildings called baths"; a concession at the end of the ḥadīth is granted to women who are ill, or after confinement). And see al-Kattānī, "Juzʾ," MS. Chester Beatty 4483, fol. 9b (". . . biʾsa l-bayt al-ḥammām"; the Prophet permitted, however, men to enter the bath wearing the maʾāzir, after being told of the importance of the bath for the cleanness of the body and the treatment of the sick). Cf. Aḥmad b. Ḥanbal, al-ʿIlal wa-maʿrifat al-rijāl, ed. Talât Koçyiğit and Ismail Cerrahoğlu (Ankara: 1963), 1: 266, no. 1716 (the prayer in a bath is disliked), 271, no. 1745 ("al-arḍu kulluhā masjidun illā l-ḥammām wa-l-maqbara"). And see the story of Ibn ʿUmar who was shocked when he saw the naked men in the bath (Ibn Saʿd, Ṭabaqāt (Beirut: 1377/1957), 4: 153-154); and see the various Shīʿī traditions in Yūsuf al-Baḥrānī's al-Ḥadāʾiq al-nāḍira fī aḥkām al-ʿitra al-ṭāhira, ed. Muḥammad Taqiyy al-Ayrawānī (Nadjaf: 1378), 5: 528-540.

6. See al-Khaṭīb al-Baghdādī, 2: 311, 11.4-5; Ibn al-Sunnī, ʿAmal al-yawm wa-l-layla (Hyderabad: 1358), p. 85: "niʿma l-bayt al-ḥammām yadkhuluhu l-rajulu l-muslim . . ."; al-Daylamī, MS. Chester Beatty 3037, fol. 174b; al-Waṣṣābī al-Ḥabashī, al-Baraka fī faḍli l-saʿyi wa-l-ḥaraka (Cairo: n.d.), p. 268; Nūr al-Dīn al-Haythamī, 1: 279 (a bath was built on the spot approved of by the Prophet). The tradition that the Prophet used to frequent the bath is vehemently refuted by al-Qasṭallānī, as recorded in al-Zurqānī's Sharḥ al-mawāhib al-laduniyya (Cairo: 1327), 4: 214. Al-Qasṭallānī, quoting the opinion of Ibn Kathīr, states that there were no baths in the Arabian peninsula in the time of the Prophet. Al-Khaṭīb al-Baghdādī discussing the tradition of Umm al-Dardāʾ about her entering a bath in Medina (Mūḍiḥ 1: 359) states that there were no baths in Medina in the period of the Prophet; in that period baths existed only in Syria and Persia (Mūḍiḥ 1: 362-364). Cf. al-Suyūṭī, al-Ḥāwī li-l-fatāwī, ed. Muḥammad Muḥyī l-Dīn ʿAbd al-Ḥamīd (Cairo: 1378/1959),

1: 526-528; Ibn ʿAsākir, Ta'rīkh (Tahdhīb) (Damascus: 1329), f. 3: 380; Murtaḍa al-Zabīdī, Itḥāf al-sāda al-muttaqīn bi-sharḥ asrār iḥyā' ʿulūm al-dīn (Cairo: 1311)(reprinted Beirut), 2: 400. On the building of baths in Baṣra in the early period of Islam and the profits gained from them see al-Balādhurī, Ansāb al-ashrāf, 1, ed. Muḥammad Ḥamīd-ullah (Cairo: 1959): 502; al-Thaʿālibī, Thimār al-qulūb, ed. Abū l-Faḍl Ibrāhīm (Cairo: 1384/1965), p. 318, no. 476.

7. See Ibn Abī Shayba, 1: 107-108; ʿAbd al-Razzāq, 1: 295-298 (see e.g. the answer of Ibn ʿAbbās, "innamā jaʿala llāhu l-mā'a yaṭahhiru wa-lā yuṭahharu," ibid., no. 1142; and see the answer of al-Shaʿbī when asked, on leaving the bath, whether one is obliged to perform the ghusl (to clean oneself) from the water of the bath: "So why did I enter the bath?", ibid., no. 1146); and see the outspoken answer of Ibn ʿAbbās when he entered a bath in the state of iḥrām: "Mā yaʿba'u 'llāhu bi-awsākhinā shay'an," al-Bayhaqī, al-Sunan al-kubrā, 5: 63 inf.

8. al-Suyūṭī, al-Durr al-manthūr, 3:234.

9. Abū Ṭālib al-Makki, Qūt al-qulūb (Cairo: 1351/1932), 2: 46

10. Ibn ʿAbd al-Barr, Jāmiʿ bayān al-ʿilm wa-faḍlihi (al-Madīna al-munawwara: n.d., reprint), 2:36: "innamā l-ʿilmu ʿindanā l-rukhṣatu min thiqatin; fa-ammā l-tashdīdū fa-yuḥsinuhu kullu aḥadin."

11. Abū Nuʿaym, 6: 217.

12. See Ibn Abū l-Dunyā, Majmūʿat al-rasā'il (Cairo: 1354/1935), pp. 39-72: "kitābu ḥusni l-ẓanni bi-llāh."

13. Ibid., p. 45, no. 29; Abū Nuʿaym, 3: 31.

14. ". . . al-tathqīlu lladhī kāna fī dīnihim . . . al-tashdīdu fī l-ʿibādati . . . al-shadā'idu llatī kānat ʿalayhim . . . tashdīdun shuddida ʿalā l-qawmi, fa-jā'a Muḥammadun (ṣ) bi-l-tajāwuzi ʿanhum."

15. al-Suyūṭī, al-Durr al-manthūr, 3: 135; al-Ṭabarī, Tafsīr, ed. Maḥmūd and Aḥmad Shākir (Cairo: 1958), 13: 167-168; al-Qurṭubī, Tafsīr, (Cairo: 1387/1967), 7: 300; Hāshim b. Sulaymān al-Baḥrānī al-Tawbalī al-Katakānī, al-Burhān fī tafsīri l-qur'ān (Qumm: 1393), 2: 40, no. 3.

16. al-Suyūṭī, al-Durr al-manthūr, 1: 193.

17. al-ʿĀmilī, al-Kashkūl, ed. Ṭāhir Aḥmad al-Zāwī (Cairo: 1380/1960), 1: 221.

18. See Ibn Balbān, fol. 90a-b, the headings: ". . . dhikru l-ikhbāri ʿammā yustaḥabbu li-l-mar'i min qubūli mā rukhkhiṣa lahu bi-tarki l-taḥammuli

ʿalā l-nafsi mā lā tuṭīqu min al-ṭāʿāti . . .; al-ikhbāru bi-anna ʿalā l-marʾi qubūla rukhṣati llāhi lahu fī ṭāʾatihi dūna l-taḥammuli ʿalā l-nafsi mā yashuqqu ʿalayhā ḥamluhu . . .; . . . mā yustaḥabbu li-l-marʾi l-taraffuqu bi-l-ṭāʿāti wa-tarku l-ḥamli ʿalā l-nafsi mā lā tuṭīqu . . .; al-amru bi-l-qaṣdi fī l-ṭāʿāti dūna an yuḥmala ʿalā l-nafsi mā lā tuṭīqu."

19. See ʿAbd al-Razzāq, 11, no. 20549. The authenticity of the story of the woman who was put in Hell because she caused the death of a cat, was questioned by ʿĀʾisha. She asserted that the woman was an unbeliever, a kāfira. The believer is more respected by God ("akramu ʿinda llāhi") than that He would chastise him because of a cat, she argued. She rebuked Abū Hurayra, the transmitter of the ḥadīth, and bade him to transmit the tradition more accurately. See al-Zarkashī, al-Ijāba li-īrādi mā stadrakat-hu ʿĀʾishatu ʿalā l-ṣaḥāba (Cairo: n.d.), p. 61; Nūr al-Dīn al-Haythamī, 1: 116; and see Ibn ʿAbd al-Ḥakam, Futūḥ miṣr, ed. C. Torrey (Leiden: 1920), p. 292; Hannād b. al-Sariyy, "Kitāb al-zuhd", MS. Princeton, Garret 1419, fol. 101a, inf.-101b.

20. See ʿAbd al-Razzāq, 11: 282-288, nos. 20546; 20559 ("Bāb al-rukhaṣ wa-l-shadāʾid") and 11: 290-292, nos. 20566-20574 ("Bāb al-rukhaṣ fī l-ʿamal wa-l-qaṣd").

21. al-Munāwī, 2: 296-297; and see ibid., pp. 292-293 (see the commentary: the ʿazīma, injunction, order, has an equal standing with the rukhṣa. According to the circumstances the ordained wuḍūʾ is as obligatory as the rukhṣa of tayammum). And see ibid., p. 293: the concessions have to be carried out according to the circumstances for which they were given.

22. Abū Ṭālib al-Makkī, 1:111.

23. al-Munāwī, 2: 51, no. 1300; al-Daylamī, MS. Chester Beatty 4139, fol. 94b.

24. Ibn ʿAbd al-Ḥakam, p. 292; al-Munāwī, 6: 225, no. 9031; al-Daylamī, MS. Chester Beatty 3037, fol. 158b.

25. al-Suyūṭī, al-Durr al-manthūr, 1: 193; Ibn ʿAbd al-Ḥakam, p. 265; Aḥmad b. Ḥanbal, Musnad, ed. Shākir (Cairo: 1368/1949), 8: 238, no. 5392; al-Dhahabī, 2: 483; Ibn Kathīr, Tafsīr (Beirut: 1385/1966), 1: 382; cf. al-Ṭabarī, Tafsīr 3: 461-469 (see p. 460: "al-ifṭāru fī l-maraḍi ʿazmatun min allāhi wājibatun wa-laysa bi-tarkhīṣ"; and see p. 464: "al-ifṭāru fī l-safari rukhṣatun min allāhi taʿālā dhikruhu, rakhkhaṣahā li-ʿibādihi wa-l-farḍu l-ṣawmu . . ."); Ibn Balbān, fol. 90b, sup.;

al-Sha'rānī, Lawāqiḥ al-anwār (Cairo: 1381/1961), pp. 716-717; al-Mundhirī, 2: 258-262; Ibn Qutayba, Ta'wīl mukhtalif al-ḥadīth (Cairo: 1326), pp. 307-308; al-Zurqānī, Sharḥ al-muwaṭṭa' (Cairo: 1381/1961), 2: 415-420.

26. al-Ṭabarī, Tafsīr, 3: 500 ult., 508; Ibn Kathīr, Tafsīr, 1: 390, line 5 from bottom; al-Suyūṭī, al-Durr al-manthūr, 1: 199, line 1.

27. See al-Ṭabarī, Tafsīr, 3: 230-246; al-Qurṭubī, 2: 182 (and see ibid., about the reading: "fa-lā junāḥa 'alayhi an lā yaṭṭawwafa"); al-Majlisī, Biḥār al-anwār (Tehran: 1388), 99: 235, 237-8, 239 line 2; al-Zarkashī, al-Ijāba, pp. 78-9; al-Fākihī, fols. 374b-380a; al-Bayhaqī, al-Sunan al-kubrā, 5: 96-8; Amīn Maḥmūd Khaṭṭāb, Fatḥ al-malik al-ma'būd, takmilat al-manhal al-'adhb al-mawrūd, sharḥ sunan abī dāwūd (Cairo: 1394/1974), 1: 243-50, 2: 15-16.

28. al-Ḥākim, al-Mustadrak (Hyderabad: 1342), 1: 203; al-Khaṭīb al-Baghdādī, Mūḍiḥ, 2: 12 sup.; al-Zajjājī, Amālī, ed. 'Abd al-Salām Hārūn (Cairo: 1382), p. 181 (". . . wa-kadhālika al-naq'u: raf'u l-ṣawti bi-l-bukā'i; wa-hādhā kāna manhiyyan 'anhu fī awwali l-islāmi--a'nī l-bukā'a 'alā l-mayyit, thumma rukhkhiṣa fīhi . . ."; al-Rāghib al-Iṣfahānī, Muḥāḍarāt al-udabā' (Beirut: 1961), 4: 506; Ibn Abī Shayba, 3: 389-395; al-Ṭabarānī, al-Mu'jam al-ṣaghīr, ed. 'Abd al-Raḥmān Muḥammad 'Uthmān (al-Madīna al-munawwara: 1388/1968), 2: 82 (noteworthy is the report of Ibn Abī Shayba 3: 391 about the faqīh Abū l-Bakhtarī: ". . . kāna rajulan faqīhan wa-kāna yasma'u l-nawḥ"; and see the discussion on this subject: Maḥmūd Muḥammad Khaṭṭāb al-Subkī, al-Manhal al-'adhb al-mawrūd, 8: 281-4; al-Zarkashī, al-Ijāba, pp. 34, 50-1.

29. Ibn Qutayba, pp. 305-6.

30. al-Ḥāzimī, al-I'tibār fī bayāni l-nāsikh wa-l-mansūkh min al-akhbār (Hyderabad: 1359), pp. 130-1, 228; al-Fākihī, fol. 478b, 479 penult.

31. Ibn Daqīq al-'Īd, al-Ilmām bi-aḥādīthi l-aḥkām, ed. Muḥammad Sa'īd al-Mawlawī (Damascus: 1383/1963), p. 244, no. 592; al-Zurqānī, Sharḥ al-muwaṭṭa', 2: 428-30; al-Ḥāzimī, pp. 137-42.

32. al-Ṭaḥāwī, Sharḥ ma'ānī l-āthār, ed. Muḥammad Zuhrī l-Najjār (Cairo: 1388/1968), 2: 88-96; Ibn Abī Shayba, 3: 59-64; al-Bayhaqī, Ma'rifat al-sunan wa-l-āthār, ed. Aḥmad Ṣaqr (Cairo: 1969), 1: 21 sup.; Ibn Qutayba, pp. 308-9; al-Dhahabī 2: 398 sup.; Abū Nu'aym, 7: 138; al-Zarkashī, al-Ijāba, p. 54; al-Zurqānī, Sharḥ al-muwaṭṭa', 2: 410-15; 'Abd al-Razzāq, 4: 182-94, nos. 8406-8456. See e.g. nos.

8412, 8418; kissing during the fast was considered as *rukhṣa*; against the rigid prohibition to look at a woman (see e.g. nos. 8452-8453) there are traditions permitting much more than kissing (see e.g. no. 8444 and the extremely permissive tradition no. 8439); and see Abū Nuʿaym, 9: 309 ("kullu shayʾin laka min ahlika ḥalālun fī l-ṣiyāmi illā mā bayna l-rijlayn"); and see this tradition al-Daylamī, MS. Chester Beatty 3037, fol. 120b, l.1; al-Muttaqī l-Hindī, 8: 384-5, nos. 2787-2793; Ibn Daqīq al-ʿĪd, pp. 243-4, nos. 590-1; al-Kattānī, MS. Chester Beatty 4483, fol. 3a; al-Shafiʿī, *al-Umm* (Cairo: 1321 reprint), 2: 84 sup.; Maḥmūd Muḥammad al-Subkī, *al-Manhal al-ʿadhb al-mawrūd, sharḥ sunan abī dāwūd* (Cairo: 1390), 10: 109-13, 115-16; Ibn Abī Ḥātim, *ʿIlal al-ḥadīth* (Cairo: 1343 reprint), 1: 47, no. 108.

33. Ibn Abī Shayba, 1: 44 ("man qāla: laysa fī l-qubla wuḍūʾ"), 45 ("man qāla: fīhā l-wuḍūʾ"); ʿAbd al-Razzāq, 1: 132-6, nos. 496-515; al-Ḥākim, *al-Mustadrak*, 1: 135; al-Shawkānī, *Nayl*, 1: 230-3; al-Zurqānī, *Sharḥ al-muwaṭṭaʾ*, 1: 129-30; Ibn Abī Ḥātim, 1: 48, nos. 109-110, 63 no. 166.

34. al-Suyūṭī, *al-Durr al-manthūr*, 2: 109 inf.

35. Ibn ʿAsākir, 6: 218: ". . . fa-ataw l-umarāʾa fa-ḥaddathūhum fa-rakhkhaṣū lahum, wa-aʿṭawhum fa-qabilū minhum . . ."; al-Qāḍī ʿIyāḍ, *Tartīb al-madārik*, ed. Aḥmad Bakīr Maḥmūd (Beirut: 1387/1967), 1-2, 616 (Saḥnūn): ". . . wa-balaghanī annahum yuḥaddithūnahum min al-rukhaṣ mā yuḥibbūna, mimmā laysa ʿalayhi l-ʿamalu . . ."; al-Dhahabī, 1: 14 inf.: ". . . ilā kam tuḥaddithu l-nāsa bi-l-rukhaṣi? . . ."; and see al-Suyūṭī, *al-Durr al-manthūr*, 3, 139.

36. Abū Nuʿaym, 3:32; al-Rāghib al-Iṣfahānī, 1: 133: ". . . man akhadha bi-rukhṣati kulli faqīhin kharaja minhu fāsiq." And see Aḥmad b. Ḥanbal, *ʿIlal*, 1: 238, no. 1499: Mālik, asked about the *rukhaṣ* of singing granted by some people of Medina, said: "In our place the libertines behave in this way."

37. Muṣʿab b. ʿAbdallāh, "Ḥadīth," MS. Chester Beatty 3849/4 (*majmūʿa*), fol. 44b, inf.-45a (the text: "antum idhan antum"); al-Muttaqī al-Hindī, 5: 405 inf., no. 2414 (the text: "antum idhan antum idhan").

38. ʿAbd al-Malik b. Ḥabīb, "Taʾrīkh," MS. Bodley. Marsh. 288, p. 167: ". . . wa-qāla abū jaʿfarin al-manṣūru li-māliki bni anasin ḥīna amarahu bi-waḍʿi muwaṭṭaʾihi: yā abā ʿabdi llāhi ttaqi shadāʾida bni ʿumara wa-rukhaṣa bni ʿabbāsin wa-shawādhdha bni masʿūdin wa-ʿalayka bi-l-amri

l-mujtama'i 'alayhi."

39. al-Ḥākim, al-Mustadrak, 1: 75.

40. al-Ṭaḥāwī, Sharḥ ma'ānī, 2: 215-218.

41. al-Bayhaqī, al-Sunan al-kubrā, 1: 86-87.

42. al-Balādhurī, Futūḥ al-buldān, ed. 'Abdallah and 'Umar al-Ṭabbā' (Beirut: 1377/1958), p. 58, l.3.

43. Abū 'Ubayd, Gharību l-ḥadīth (Hyderabad: 1384/1965), 2: 54; al-Ṭaḥāwī, Sharḥ ma'ānī, 3: 49-50; al-Zurqānī, Sharḥ al-mawāhib, 4: 325 inf.-326; al-Fasawī, "al-Ma'rifa wa-l-ta'rīkh," MS. Esad Ef. 2391, fol. 32a, sup. ("an ibni mas'ūdin annahu kariha nihāba l-sukkar").

44. al-Ṭaḥāwī, Mushkil al-āthār (Hyderabad: 1333), 2: 166-179; Nūr al-Dīn al-Haythamī, 5: 147-151; al-Bayhaqī, al Sunan al-kubrā, 1: 28-30.

45. al-Ḥākim, Ma'rifat 'ulūm, p. 196 sup.; al-Ḥāzimī, pp. 228-230.

46. Ibn Wahb, Jāmi', ed. J. David-Weill (Cairo: 1939), pp. 103-106; al-Ṭaḥāwī, Sharḥ ma'ānī, 4: 326-329; Nūr al-Dīn al-Haythamī, 5: 109-114; al-Zurqānī, Sharḥ al-muwaṭṭa', 5: 348-350; idem, Sharḥ al-mawāhib, 7: 68-82; al-Waṣṣābī, al-Baraka, pp. 268-270; Ibn Qayyim al-Jawziyya, al-Ṭibb al-nabawī, ed. 'Abd al-Ghanī 'Abd al-Khāliq, 'Ādil al-Azharī, Maḥmūd Faraj al-'Uqda (Cairo: 1377/1957), pp. 127, 131 inf.-147; idem, Zād al-ma'ād (Beirut: n.d.), 3: 116-125; al-Damīrī, Ḥayāt al-ḥayawān (Cairo: 1383/1963), 2: 139-140; al-Tha'ālibī, Thimār al-qulūb, pp. 126, no. 672, 431, no. 690.

47. al-Suyūṭī, al-Durr al-manthūr, 4: 133.

48. On the tamattu' pilgrimage see e.g. Ibn Ḥazm, Ḥajjat al-wadā', ed. Mamdūḥ Ḥaqqī (Beirut: 1966), pp. 49, 89, 90, 102; Nūr al-Dīn al-Haythamī, 3: 236; al-Bayhaqī, al-Sunan al-kubrā, 5: 15-26.

49. See on him al-Fāsī, al-'Iqd al-thamīn fī ta'rīkhi l-baladi l-amīn, ed. Fu'ād Sayyid (Cairo: 1384/1965), 4: 49-52; Naṣr b. Muzāḥim, Waq'at Ṣiffīn, ed. 'Abd al-Salām Hārūn (Cairo: 1382), index; Ibn Ḥajar, al-Iṣāba, ed. 'Alī Muḥammad al-Bajāwī (Cairo: 1392/1972), 2: 24-26, no. 1602.

50. Ibn 'Abd al-Barr, Jāmi' bayān, 2: 30; cf. al-Zurqānī, Sharḥ al-muwaṭṭa', 3: 52 (and see pp. 48-51); al-Muttaqī l-Hindī, 5: 83, no. 678, 88, no. 704.

51. Zād al-ma'ād, 1: 188-191, 203-18.

52. 'Abd al-Razzāq 1: 163-171 ("man qāla lā yutawaḍḍa'u mimmā massat al-nār"), pp. 172-174 ("mā jā'a fīmā massat al-nār min al-shidda"); Ibn Abī Shayba, 1: 46-52 ("man kāna lā yatawaḍḍa'u mimmā massat al-nār; man kāna yarā l-wuḍū'a mimmā ghayyarat al-nār"); al-Bayhaqī, al-Sunan al-kubrā,

1: 153-158; al-Ḥāzimī, pp. 46-52; Nūr al-Dīn al-Haythamī, 1: 248-249 ("al-wuḍū' mimmā massat al-nār"), pp. 251-254 ("tarku l-wuḍū' mimmā massat al-nār"); al-Ṭaḥāwī, Sharḥ ma'ānī, 1: 62-70; Aḥmad b. Ḥanbal, al-'Ilal, 1: 305, nos. 1984-1985, 317, no. 2062, 366, no. 2424; al-Shawkānī, Nayl, 1: 245-247, al-Fasawī, fol. 229a; Abū Yūsuf, Kitāb al-āthār, ed. Abū l-Wafā (Cairo: 1355), pp. 9-11, nos. 41-50; al-Ḥākim, Ma'rifat 'ulūm, pp. 30, 217; al-Bayhaqī, Ma'rifat al-sunan, 1: 401; Ibn Sa'd, 7: 158; al-Bukhārī, al-Ta'rīkh al-kabīr (reprint),I, 2 no. 1543, III,2 nos. 2361, 2805; Abū Nu'aym, 5: 363; Ibn 'Asākir, 6: 125, 174, 321; al-Khaṭīb al-Baghdādī, Ta'rīkh Baghdād (Cairo: 1351/1931), 13: 100; Ibn Ḥajar, al-Iṣāba, 3: 263, no. 3701, 8: 248, no. 12125; Ibn Ḥibbān, Kitāb al-majrūḥīn, ed. 'Azīz al-Qādirī (Hyderabad: 1390/1970), 2: 173.

53. Nūr al-Dīn al-Haythamī, 1: 252 inf.-253.

54. al-Dhahabī, 3: 234, no. 6270.

55. Ibn Abī l-Jawṣā', "Ḥadīth," al-Ẓāhiriyya, Majmū'a 60, fol. 64b.

56. al-Ṭaḥāwī, Sharḥ ma'ānī, 1: 65.

57. Nūr al-Dīn al-Haythamī, 1: 252; al-Bayhaqī, al-Sunan al-kubrā, 1: 157 inf.; 'Abd al-Razzāq, 1: 170-171, nos. 658, 663; al-Ṭaḥāwī, Sharḥ ma'ānī, 1: 69.

58. 'Abd al-Razzāq, 1: 168-169, nos. 653, 655-656; al-Bayhaqī, al-Sunan al-kubrā, 1: 158, lines 4-5, al-Ṭaḥāwī, Sharḥ ma'ānī, 1: 70 sup.

59. al-Bayhaqī, al-Sunan al-kubrā, 1: 141; Nūr al-Dīn al-Haythamī, 1: 252 ult.-253, line 1; al-Sharīf al-Murtaḍā, Amālī, ed. Muḥammad Abū l-Faḍl Ibrāhīm (Cairo: 1373/1954), 1: 395-396.

60. al-Ṭaḥāwī, Sharḥ ma'ānī, 1: 66, 68; al-Bayhaqī, al-Sunan al-kubrā, 1: 157; Nūr al-Dīn al-Haythamī, 1: 252, lines 12-15, 254, line 8 and line 18; Muḥammad b. Sinān al-Qazzāz, "Ḥadīth," al-Ẓāhiriyya, Majmū'a 18, fol. 2a; Muḥammad b. Aḥmad al-Qaṭṭān, "al-Fawā'id," al-Ẓāhiriyya, Majmū'a 18, fol. 24a inf.

61. al-Ṭaḥāwī, Sharḥ ma'ānī, 1: 69; al-Bayhaqī, al-Sunan al-kubrā, 1: 158 (Anas regrets his mistake and wishes he had not done it: "laytanī lam af'al"); 'Abd al-Razzāq, 1: 170, no. 659; al-Zurqānī, Sharḥ al-muwaṭṭa', 1: 88 inf.-89.

62. See 'Abd al-Razzāq, 1: 170, no. 659: ". . . mā hādhihi l-'irāqiyyatu llatī aḥdathtahā . . .?"

63. al-Shawkānī, Nayl, 1: 247; al-Ḥākim, Ma'rifat 'ulūm, p. 85; al-Bayhaqī, al-Sunan al-kubrā, 1: 156; al-Ṭaḥāwī, Sharḥ ma'ānī, 1: 67; al-Bayhaqī, Ma'rifat al-sunan, 1: 395, 401, lines 1-2; Ibn

ʿAsākir, 6: 321.

64. Ibn Abī Shayba, 1: 46-7; al-Ṭaḥāwī, Sharḥ maʿānī, 1: 70-1; al-Shawkānī, Nayl, 1: 237-9; al-Bayhaqī, al-Sunan al-kubrā, 1: 158-9; idem, Maʿrifat al-sunan, 1: 402-6; Ibn Qayyim al-Jawziyya, Iʿlām al-muwaqqiʿīn ʿan rabbi l-ʿālamīn, ed. Ṭāhā ʿAbd al-Raʾūf Saʿd (Cairo: 1973), 2: 15-16, 106; Nūr al-Dīn al-Haythamī 1: 250.

65. See al-Zurqānī, Sharḥ al-mawāhib, 4: 352 (". . . barakat al-ṭaʿām al-wuḍūʾ qablahu"; and see the interpretation).

66. See al-Zurqānī, Sharḥ al-mawāhib, 7: 247, lines 24-30 (". . . faʿaltuhu yā ʿumaru--yaʿnī li-bayāni l-jawāzi li-l-nāsi wa-khawfa an yuʿtaqada wujūbu mā kāna yafʿalu min al-wuḍūʾi li-kulli ṣalātin; wa-qīla innahu nāsikhun li-wujūbi dhālika, wa-taʿaqqaba bi-qawli anasin: kāna khāṣṣan bihi dūna ummatihi wa-annahu kāna yafʿaluhu li-l-faḍīla . . .").

67. Ibid., 7: 248, line 1 seq. Concerning the concept of Ṣufī rukhaṣ, cf. M. Milson, A Sufi Rule for Novices, Kitāb adab al-murīdīn (Harvard: 1975), pp. 72-82; and see his discussion on the subject in the Introduction, pp. 19-20.

68. ʿAbd al-Razzāq, 5: 496; al-Qasṭallānī, Irshād al-sārī (Cairo: 1323), 3: 173-4; al-Nasāʾī, Sunan, ed. Ḥasan al-Masʿūdī (Beirut: n.d.), 5: 222; al-Bayhāqī, al-Sunan al-kubrā, 5: 85; Yūsuf b. Mūsā al-Ḥanafī, al-Muʿtaṣar min al-mukhtaṣar (Hyderabad: 1362), 1: 174; al-Munāwī, 4:292-3, nos. 5345-5347; al-Muttaqī l-Hindī, 5: 24, nos. 220-222; cf. al-Azraqī, Akhbār Makka, ed. F. Wüstenfeld, p. 258; Muḥibb al-Dīn al-Ṭabarī, al-Qirā li-qāṣidi ummi l-qurā, ed. Muṣṭafā l-Saqā (Cairo: 1390/1970), pp. 306, 331; al-Taḥāwī, Sharḥ maʿānī, 2: 178 inf.

69. al-Azraqī, p. 258; al-Fākihī, fols. 292a, 296a; ʿAbd al-Razzāq, 5: 50, 52; al-Muttaqī l-Hindī, 5: 90, nos. 717-719, 722; al-Wāqidī, Maghāzī, ed. M. Jones (London: 1966), p. 1098; al-Bayhaqī, al-Sunan al-kubrā, 5: 84; Ibn Ẓuhayra, al-Jāmiʿ al-laṭīf (Cairo: 1357/1938), p. 124; Ibn Kathīr, Tafsīr, 1: 432-3.

70. See e.g. al-Fākihī, fol. 296a, sup. (The Prophet urges the people to praise God and to extol Him during the ṭawāf; and see ibid., similar reports about some Companions); al-Azraqī, pp. 259 inf.-260; ʿAbd al-Razzāq, 5: 51, nos. 8964-8965; al-Qasṭallānī 3: 170; al-Ḥarbī, al-Manāsik wa-amākin ṭuruqi l-ḥajj, ed. Ḥamad al-Jāsir (al-Riyāḍ: 1389/1969), pp. 431-3; Muḥibb al-Dīn al-Ṭabarī, pp. 305-6; al-Shawkānī, Nayl, 5; 53-4.

71. al-Fākihī, fol. 292a; ʿAbd al-Razzāq, 5: 50,

no. 8962.

72. al-Fākihī, fol. 292a-b; cf. Muḥibb al-Dīn al-Ṭabarī, p. 271.

73. al-Fākihī, fol. 292a, inf.

74. al-Zubayr b. Bakkār, "Jamharat nasab quraysh," MS. Bodley, Marsh 384, fol. 160b; al-Fākihī, fol. 292b; Muḥibb al-Dīn al-Ṭabarī, p. 270.

75. See on him Abū Nu'aym, 8: 140-61; al-Fāsī, al-'Iqd, 7: 417, no. 2678.

76. al-Azraqī, p. 259; Abū Nu'aym, 8: 155 (the tafakkuh is explained as talking about women and describing their bodies during the ṭawāf); Muḥibb al-Dīn al-Ṭabarī, p. 271.

77. al-Fākihī, fol. 292b.

78. See Muḥibb al-Dīn al-Ṭabarī, p. 271, line 1: ". . . wa-anna ḥukmahu ḥukmu l-ṣalāti, illā fīmā waradat fīhi l-rukhṣatu min al-kalām."

79. See e.g. al-Fākihī, fols. 311a-312a; 'Abd al-Razzāq, 3: 377, no. 6021.

80. al-Fākihī, fol. 296b; and see al-Azraqī, p. 257; Amīn Maḥmūd Khaṭṭāb, Fatḥ al-malik al-ma'būd, 1: 200-2; Ibn Abī Shayba, 4:96; al-Bayhaqī, al-Sunan al-kubrā, 5: 72-3.

81. al-Fākihī, fol. 296b.

82. al-Fākihī, fol. 296b.

83. al-Azraqī, p. 259; Muḥibb al-Dīn al-Ṭabarī, p. 273; al-Fākihī, fol. 293b, sup.

84. Nūr al-Dīn al-Haythamī, 3: 244.

85. See al-Fākihī, fol. 293a (the remark of Ḥusayn b. 'Alī about the buttocks of Mu'āwiya during the ṭawāf; and see fol. 294a: al-Sā'ib b. Ṣayfī and his talk with Mu'āwiya about Hind).

86. See on him Ibn Ḥajar, Tahdhīb, 6: 376-378, no. 716; al-Fāsī, al-'Iqd, 5: 480, no. 1856.

87. See on him al-Fāsī, al-'Iqd, 7: 218, no. 2469.

88. al-Azraqī, p. 260; Muḥibb al-Dīn al-Ṭabarī, p. 278.

89. al-Fākihī fol. 291b ("dhikru karāhiyati l-kalāmi bi-l-fārisiyyati fī l-ṭawāf"); see the tradition about 'Umar: 'Abd al-Razzāq, 5: 496, no. 9793; cf. al-Ṭurṭūshī, al-Ḥawādith wa-l-bida', ed. Muḥammad al-Ṭālibī (Tunis: 1959), p. 104.

90. Ibn Abī Shayba, 4: 10; al-Azraqī, p. 258; al-Fākihī, fols. 295b-296a; and see the survey of the different opinions: Ibn Ẓuhayra, pp. 129-30; al-Majlisī, 99: 209, no. 19.

91. al-Fākihī, fol. 307b.

92. al-Fākihī, fol. 307b.

93. al-Wāqidī, p. 736; Nūr al-Dīn al-Haythamī, 8: 130; al-Fākihī, fol. 307a; al-Muttaqī l-Hindī,

5: 95, no. 745.

94. al-Azraqī, p. 257; Ibn ʿAbd al-Barr, al-Istīʿāb, ed. ʿAlī al-Bajāwī (Cairo: 1380/1960), 1: 347; al-Fākihī, fol. 307b.

95. al-Fākihī, fol. 307b.

96. Maria Nallino, Le Poesie di an-Nābigah al-Ǧaʿdī (Rome: 1953), p. 137 (IX) (and see the references of the editor); al-Fākihī, fol. 307b inf.-308a.

97. al-Fākihī, fol. 307b; and see a different version of this verse Aghānī (Būlāq), 10; 12.

98. al-Fākihī, fol. 308a; and see the verses: Yāqūt, Muʿjam al-buldān, s.v. Amaj; and see Ibn Abī l-Dunyā, "Dhamm al-muskir," al-Ẓāhiriyya, Majmūʿa 60, fol. 8a (Saʿīd b. Jubayr changes the text of the verse from "wa-kāna karīman fa-lam yanziʿ" into "wa-kāna shaqiyyan fa-lam yanziʿ").

99. al-Fākihī, fol. 308a.

100. al-Fākihī, fols. 307b-310a.

101. al-Shāfiʿī, 2: 127; al-Azraqī, p. 260; al-Fākihī, fols. 296a-297a; Nūr al-Dīn al-Haythamī, 3: 219-20; Ibn Ẓuhayra, pp. 133 ult.-134.

102. al-Azraqī, pp. 265-6; al-Fākihī, fols. 299a ult.-299b; Muḥibb al-Dīn al-Ṭabarī, pp. 319-20; al-Qasṭallānī, 3: 172-3; Ibn Ḥajar, Fatḥ al-bārī, 3: 384-5; Ibn Ẓuhayra, p. 127; al-Fāsī, al-ʿIqd, 4: 273.

103. al-Fākihī, fol. 432a (and see ibid., fol. 439b, lines 5-7 and fol. 354b: "dhikru idārati l-ṣaffi fī shahri ramaḍāna wa-awwalu man faʿalahu wa-awwalu man aḥdatha l-takbīra bayna l-tarāwīḥi ḥawla l-bayti fī shahri ramaḍāna wa-tafsīru dhālika"); al-Zarkashī, Iʿlāmu l-sājid bi-aḥkāmi l-masājid, ed. Abū l-Wafā Muṣṭafā l-Marāghī (Cairo: 1385), p. 98; al-Fāsī, al-ʿIqd, 4: 272, 276 sup.; al-Shiblī, "Maḥāsin al-wasāʾil fī maʿrifati l-awāʾil," MS. Br. Mus., Or. 1530, fols. 38b-39a, 41b-42a.

104. al-Fākihī, fol. 443a; al-Fāsī, al-ʿIqd, 6; 151, no. 2050 (quoted from al-Fākihī); idem, Shifāʾ al-gharām (Cairo), 2:188 (quoted from al-Fākihī); Ibn Ẓuhayra, p. 300 inf. (quoted from al-Fākihī).

105. See on him Wakīʿ, Akhbār al-quḍāt, ed. ʿAbd al-ʿAzīz Muṣṭafā al-Marāghī (Cairo: 1366/1947). 1: 257-258; Ibn Ẓuhayra, p. 297.

106. al-Fākihī, fol. 443a; al-Fāsī, al-ʿIqd, 3: 247-8, no. 720 (quoted from al-Fākihī).

107. al-Fākihī, fol. 309b.

108. al-Muṣannaf, 4: 410; Lisān al-ʿArab, s.v. sh-w-f; Ibn al-Athīr, al-Nihāya, s.v. sh-w-f.

109. Ibn Abī Shayba, 4: 411 (ʿUmar remarks, however, that girls should not be compelled to marry ugly [or mean; in text dhamīm; but probably damīm] men; "the girls like in this matter what you like," he said); cf. Ibn Raʾs Ghanama, "Manāqil al-durar fī manābit al-zahar," MS. Chester Beatty 4254, fol. 19b: "qāla ʿumaru: lā yuzawwijanna l-rajulu bnatahu l-qabīḥa fa-innahunna yarghabna fīmā targhabūn."

110. See on him Ibn Ḥajar, Tahdhīb, 12: 260.

111. al-Fākihī, fol. 355b: "dhikru l-akli fī l-masjidi l-ḥarāmi wa-l-ghadāʾ fīhi", and see al-Ṭurṭūshī, pp. 106-8; al-Zarkashī, Iʿlām al-sājid, pp. 329-30.

112. al-Fākihī, fol. 355b.

113. See on him Ibn Ḥajar, Tahdhīb, 4: 228, no. 381.

114. See on him ibid., 2: 147, no. 249; al-Dhahabī, 1: 437, no. 1629.

115. al-Ṭurṭūshī, p. 105.

116. al-Zarkashī, Iʿlām al-sājid, p. 307; al-Ṭurṭūshī, p. 105; al-Marāghī, "Taḥqīq al-nuṣra bi-talkhīṣ maʿālim dāri l-hijra," MS. Br. Mus., Or. 3615, fol. 50a.

117. See on him al-Bukhārī, al-Taʾrīkh al-kabīr, 3[1], no. 430; Ibn Ḥajar, Tahdhīb, 5: 308, no. 524.

118. Cf. al-Ṭurṭūshī, p. 105.

119. "Taʾrīkh Makka," fol. 355b-356a; al-Zarkashī, Iʿlām al-sājid, pp. 306-8, 317-18; Muḥibb al-Dīn al-Ṭabarī, pp. 659-60, nos. 30-31; al-Majlisī, 99: 240, no. 1; about the odious impurity which causes bad smells see al-Fākihī, fol. 357b, ult.-358a ("dhikru irsāli l-rīḥi fī l-masjidi l-ḥarāmi"); al-Zarkashī, Iʿlām al-sājid, pp. 313-14; cf. about a superstitious belief current among common people in Egypt: ʿAlī Maḥfūẓ, al-Ibdāʿ fī maḍārr al-ibtidāʿ (Cairo: 1388/1968), p. 454.

120. al-Fākihī, fol. 297a; al-Azraqī, p. 261; ʿAbd al-Razzāq, 8: 457, no. 15895.

121. al-Fākihī, fol. 297b; al-Azraqī, p. 261; ʿAbd al-Razzāq, 8: 448, no. 15862; al-Bayhaqī, al-Sunan al-kubrā, 5:88; al-Qasṭallānī, 3: 173-4; al-Ḥākim, al-Mustadrak, 1: 460; Ibn Ḥajar, Fatḥ al-bārī, 3: 386-7; Muḥibb al-Dīn al-Ṭabarī, p. 319, no. 73.

122. al-Fākihī, fol. 297b; ʿAbd al-Razzāq, 8: 448, nos. 15860-15861, 11, 292, no. 20572; Lisān al-ʿArab, s.v. z-m-m, kh-z-m.

123. Fatḥ al-bārī, 3: 386.

124. al-Ṭaḥāwī, Sharḥ maʿānī, 3: 128-132; Yūsuf b. Mūsā al-Ḥanafī, 1: 260-2; al-Suyūṭī, al-Durr

al-manthūr, 1: 351-2; idem, *Ta'rīkh al-khulafā'*, ed. Muḥammad Muḥyī l-Dīn ʿAbd al-Ḥamīd (Cairo: 1371/1952), p. 99; al-Shāṭibī, *al-Iʿtiṣām* (Cairo: n.d.), 2: 52; Baḥshal, *Ta'rīkh Wāsiṭ*, ed. Gurguis ʿAwwād (Baghdād, 1387/1967), p. 231; Ibn Saʿd, 8: 470; al-Bayhaqī, *al-Sunan al-kubrā*, 10: 76; al-Fasawī, fol. 157b; Ibn ʿAbd al-Ḥakam, p. 294; al-Muttaqī l-Hindī, 5: 341, no. 2265, 449, no. 2507; Aḥmad b. Ḥanbal, *Musnad* 11: 7, no. 6714; al-Ṭayālisī, p. 112, no. 836; al-Ṭaḥāwī, *Mushkil al-āthār*, 3: 37-41; ʿAbd al-Razzāq, 8: 438, no. 15825, 448, no. 15863; al-Fākihī, fols. 315a-b; Ibn Daqīq al-ʿĪd, pp. 310-11, nos. 791-793. (And see al-Fākihī, fol. 511b: the story of the woman who vowed to perform the pilgrimage in silence if God would help to reconcile the fighting factions of her tribe. Abū Bakr, ordering her to discontinue her silence, remarked: "takallamī, fa-inna l-islāma hadama mā kāna qabla dhālika"); al-Ṭūsī, *Amālī* (Najaf: 1384/1964), 1: 369.

125. Ibn Abī l-Dunyā, "al-Tawba," MS. Chester Beatty 3863, fol. 17b; Baḥshal, p. 167; al-Khuwārizmī, "Mukhtaṣar ithārati l-targhīb wa-l-tashwīq ilā l-masājidi l-thalāthati wa-ilā l-bayti l-ʿatīq," MS. Br. Mus., Or. 4584, fol. 8a-b.

126. al-Fākihī, fols. 321b-322a ("dhikru l-mashyi fī l-ḥajji wa-faḍlihi"); al-Khuwārizmī, fol. 8b: "wa-li-l-māshī faḍlun ʿalā l-rākibi ka-faḍli laylati l-qadri ʿalā sā'iri l-layālī."

127. al-Fākihī, fols. 528a-529a ("dhikru ṣawmi yawmi ʿarafa wa-faḍli ṣiyāmihi; dhikru man lam yaṣum yawma ʿarafa makhāfata l-ḍuʿfi ʿani l-duʿā"); Ibn Abī Shayba, 4: 1-3, 21, 3: 104; al-Ṭaḥāwī, *Mushkil*, 4: 111.

128. al-Fākihī, fol. 528a, ult.; al-Mundhirī, 2: 236, no. 1463; Ibn Abī Shayba, 3: 97; al-Ṭaḥāwī, *Sharḥ maʿānī*, 2: 72; al-Bayhaqī, *al-Sunan al-kubrā*, 4: 283.

129. al-Fākihī, fols. 528a, inf., 528b; al-Ṭabarānī, 1: 255, 2: 71; Baḥshal, p. 276; al-Mundhirī, 2: 236;7, nos. 1461-1462, 1464-1465, 1467-1468; Muḥibb al-Dīn al-Ṭabarī, p. 403; Ibn Abī Shayba, 3: 96-7; al-Ṭaḥāwī, *Sharḥ maʿānī*, 2: 72; idem, *Mushkil*, 4: 112; al-Shawkānī, *Nayl*, 4: 267, no. 2; al-Bayhaqī, *al-Sunan al-kubrā*, 4: 283.

130. al-Mundhirī, 2: 237, no. 1466; al-Fākihī, fol. 528b; al-Suyūṭī, *al-Durr al-manthūr*, 1: 231 (another version: 1,000 years).

131. Muṣʿab b. ʿAbdallāh, "Ḥadīth," MS. Chester Beatty 3849/4, fol. 40a; Abū ʿUmar, Ghulām Thaʿlab, "Juz'," MS. Chester Beatty 3495, fol. 97a;

al-Fākihī, fol. 528b; al-Shawkānī, Nayl, 4: 267, no. 4; al-Bayhaqī, al-Sunan al-kubrā, 4: 283-4; al-Suyūṭī, al-Durr al-manthūr, 1: 231.

132. al-Bukhārī, al-Ta'rīkh al-kabīr, 3^2, no. 1600.

133. al-Fākihī, fol. 529a; Aḥmad b. Ḥanbal, al-ʿIlal, 1: 286, nos. 1849, 1852; al-Khaṭīb al-Baghdādī, Mūḍiḥ, 2: 338-9; al-Fasawī, fol. 61a; cf. Abū Nuʿaym, 7: 164; Muḥibb al-Dīn al-Ṭabarī, p. 404.

134. Abū ʿUbayd, Gharīb al-ḥadīth, 3: 4; al-Khaṭīb al-Baghdādī, Mūḍiḥ, 1: 434; al-Ṭaḥāwī, Sharḥ maʿānī, 2: 72; Muḥibb al-Dīn al-Ṭabarī, p. 404 (and see ibid., p. 405 inf.); al-Shawkānī, Nayl, 4: 268; al-Suyūṭī, al-Durr al-manthūr, 1: 231; Ibn Kathīr, al-Bidāya wa-l-nihāya (Beirut, al-Riyāḍ: 1966), 5: 174.

135. al-Ṭaḥāwī, Sharḥ maʿānī, 2: 72; idem, Mushkil, 4: 112; Abū Nuʿaym, 3: 347; al-Fasawī, fol. 32b; al-Shawkānī, Nayl, 4: 267, no. 3; al-Bayhaqī, al-Sunan al-kubrā, 4: 289; Yūsuf b. Mūsā al-Ḥanafī, 1: 152; al-Suyūṭī, al-Durr al-manthūr, 1: 231.

136. al-Fākihī, fol. 529a; cf. Muḥibb al-Dīn al-Ṭabarī, p. 405, lines 3-7 (fasting on the Day of ʿArafa is not favored for people performing the pilgrimage; it is however encouraged for people not performing the ḥajj. See the compromise-recommendations of al-Mudhirī, 2: 238: ". . . there is nothing wrong in fasting, if it does not weaken him in his duʿā' . . . for the pilgrims it is preferable to break the fast . . ." See the story of Ibn Wahb, who broke the fast at ʿArafa because he was occupied by the thought of breaking the fast: al-Qāḍī ʿIyāḍ, Tartīb al-madārik, 1, 430; and see on this subject: al-Shawkānī, Nayl, 4: 269).

137. See al-Quḍāʿī, "Ta'rīkh," MS. Bodley, Pococke 270, fol. 67b (quoted from al-Jāḥiẓ's Naẓm al-qur'ān); al-Qalqashandī, Ma'āthir al-ināfa fī ma'ālim al-khilāfa, ed. ʿAbd al-Sattār Aḥmad Farrāj (Kuwait: 1964), 1: 129; Muḥibb al-Dīn al-Ṭabarī, pp. 387 inf.-388 sup.; al-Fasawī, fol. 16a: ". . . ḥaddathanā abū ʿawāna, qāla: ra'aytu l-ḥasana kharaja yawma ʿarafa min al-maqṣūrati baʿda l-aṣri fa-qaʿada fa-ʿarrafa"; al-Bayhaqī, al-Sunan al-kubrā, 5: 117 inf.; see S.D. Goitein, Studies in Islamic History and Institutions (Leiden: 1966), p. 137.

138. al-Kindī, Wulāt Miṣr, ed. Ḥusayn Naṣṣār (Beirut:1379/1959), p. 72.

139. al-Mawṣilī, "Ghāyat al-wasā'il ilā maʿrifati l-awā'il," MS. Cambridge Qq 33(10), fol. 153a.

140. al-Suyūṭī, *al-Durr al-manthūr*, 1: 231 inf.
141. Ibn Kathīr, *al-Bidāya*, 9: 307; al-Ṭurṭūshī, pp. 115-16; al-Suyūṭī, *al-Durr al-manthūr*, 1: 231 inf.
142. al-Quḍā'ī, fol. 67b; al-Qalqashandī, 1: 129.
143. al-Ṭurṭūshī, pp. 116-17.
144. *Majmū'at al-rasā'il al-kubrā* (Cairo: 1323), 2: 57; Jamāl a-Dīn al-Qāsimī, *Iṣlāḥ al-masājid min al-bida' wa-l-'awā'id* (Cairo: 1341), p. 215 (from Ibn Taymiyya).
145. al-Muqaddasī, *Aḥsan al-taqāsīm*, ed. M.J. de Goeje (Leiden: 1906), p. 171, line 11.
146. Ibn Bābawayh, *Amālī l-ṣadūq* (Najaf: 1389/1970), pp. 126-7.
147. al-Fākihī, fol. 529a.
148. Muḥibb al-Dīn al-Ṭabarī, p. 403; al-Ḥākim, *al-Mustadrak*, 1: 464 inf.-465; al-Muttaqī al-Hindī, 5: 79, nos. 646, 648.
149. Muḥibb al-Dīn al-Ṭabarī, p. 417. Amīn Maḥmūd Khaṭṭāb, *Fatḥ al-malik al-ma'būd*, 2: 59 inf.-60, lines 1-7; al-Fākihī, fol. 531a, sup.
150. al-Suyūṭī, *Ta'rīkh al-khulafā'*, p. 200.
151. al-Shiblī, "Maḥāsin al-wasā'il," fol. 120a; al-Suyūṭī, *Ta'rīkh al-khulafā'*, p. 200.
152. al-Muttaqī al-Hindī, 5: 88, no. 708; al-Shiblī, "Maḥāsin al-wasā'il," fol. 119b (and see above notes 48, 50); and cf. the wicked innovations of al-Ḥajjāj: Abū Ṭālib al-Makkī, 2: 53-4.
153. al-Ḥākim, *al-Mustadrak*, 1: 251-2; Nūr al-Dīn al-Haythamī, 2: 59-62; al-Fākihī, fol. 481a inf.; al-Fasawī, fol. 217b; Ibn Abī Shayba, 1: 276-83; 'Abd al-Razzāq, 2: 9-38, nos. 2272-2396; al-Ṭaḥāwī, *Sharḥ ma'ānī*, 1: 458-64; al-Muttaqī l-Hindī, 8: 132-8, nos. 946-989; al-Zarkashī, *al-Ijāba*, pp. 66, 84.
154. Ibn Abī Shayba, 1: 285; 'Abd al-Razzāq, 2: 190-7, nos. 3024-3053; and see Ibn al-Athīr, *al-Nihāya*, s.v. q-'-a, '-q-b.
155. al-Ṭaḥāwī, *Sharḥ ma'ānī*, 1: 377-83; al-Shawkānī, *Nayl*, 2: 83-4; Ibn Abī Shayba, 1: 310-15.
156. Ibn Abī Shayba, 2: 389-91; Ibn Abī l-Ḥadīd, *Sharḥ nahj al-balāgha*, ed. Muḥammad Abū l-Faḍl Ibrāhīm (Cairo: 1964), 18: 164; and cf. Aḥmad b. Ḥanbal, *al-'Ilal*, 1: 325, no. 2122; Sa'īd b. Jubayr throws out the pebbles with which a woman counted her circlings during the *ṭawāf*.
157. Nāṣir al-Dīn al-Albānī, *Silsilat al-aḥādīth al-ḍa'īfa wa-l-mawḍū'a* (Damascus: 1384), no. 404.
158. Ibid., no. 412.
159. Ibid., no. 83.
160. al-Daylamī, MS. Chester Beatty 4139, fol.

27a (al-Daylamī adds: "wa-kāna ibrāhīmu l-taymī lā yuṣallī fī ṭāqi l-miḥrāb"); al-Suyūṭī, al-Khaṣā'iṣ al-kubrā, 3: 189; al-Munāwī, 1: 144-5, no. 153 reviews the different meanings of the work miḥrāb. And see the peculiar story of the Christian youth in the miḥrāb: al-Khaṭīb al-Baghdādī, Ta'rīkh Baghdād, 9: 45; al-Ṭurṭūshī, p. 94; al-Baḥrānī, 7: 281-5; Maḥmūd Mahdī al-Mūsawī al-Khawansārī, Tuḥfat al-sājid fī aḥkām al-masājid (Baghdad: 1376), pp. 111-16. And see R.B. Serjeant, "Miḥrāb," BSOAS (1959): pp. 439-53.

161. al-Suyūṭī, al-Khaṣā'iṣ al-kubrā, 3: 188-9; Ibn Abī Shayba, 2: 59; and see the careful evaluation of this ḥadīth by Albānī, Silsila, no. 448.

162. ʿAbd al-Razzāq, 2: 412, nos. 3898-3902; the tradition about the altars of the Christians, no. 3903; Ibn Abī Shayba, 2: 59-60 (al-ṣalāt fī l-ṭāq, "man rakhkhaṣa l-ṣalāt fī l-ṭāq"); Aḥmad b. Ḥanbal, al-ʿIlal, 1: 64, no. 373.

163. al-Suyūṭī, al-Khaṣā'iṣ al-kubrā, 3: 56-7; Ibn Abī Shayba, 1:309; al-Suyūṭī, al-Durr al-manthūr, 3: 217 inf.; al-Shaybānī, pp. 77-8; Abū ʿUbayd, Gharīb al-ḥadīth, 4: 225; al-Shawkānī, Nayl, 2: 167-70; idem, al-Fawā'id al-majmūʿa ed. ʿAbd al-Wahhāb ʿAbd al-Laṭīf (Cairo: 1960), pp. 25-7; Abū Ṭālib al-Makkī, 2: 51 inf.; Ibn Abī Jamra, Bahjat al-nufūs (Beirut: 1972 reprint), 1: 183; al-Samarqandī, Bustān al-ʿārifīn (on margin of Tanbīh al-ghāfilīn) (Cairo: 1347), pp. 127-8; Yūsuf b. ʿAbd al-Hādī, Thimār al-maqāṣid fī dhikri l-masājid, ed. Asʿad Ṭalas (Beirut: 1943), pp. 166, 170; al-Baḥrānī, 7: 277 (162 cont.); al-Zarkashī, Iʿlām al-sājid pp. 335-8; Muḥammad Mahdī al-Mūsawī, pp. 87-92.

164. See ʿAbd al-Razzāq, 2: 414-16, nos. 3907-3913; al-Bayhaqī, al-Sunan al-kubrā, 3: 238; Abū Ṭālib al-Makkī, 2: 51 inf.; Ibn Saʿd, 7: 96.

165. Ibn Abī Shayba, 2: 46; al-Ṭurṭūshī, p. 97; al-Zarkashī, Iʿlām al-sājid, p. 337; cf. Yūsuf b. ʿAbd al-Hādī, p. 170.

Chapter 6

* This article preserves to a large extent the form of the paper read at the colloquium. Most of it is merely a summary of a few former publications of mine; the ideas will look new only to somebody who does not read German. As I cannot go far beyond these results for the moment, it would have been meaningless to go into detail again. Only where I refer to primary sources is new material--and perhaps a new interpretation--to be expected; wherever I simply repeat myself I will only refer to my own

publications. I apologise for this narcissism, but even so it seems the most honest solution. [This remark was written in 1976. Now, in 1980, reading the proofs, some of what I said in the article looks to me even more dated than at that moment. I have left, however, everything as it was; literature which was published after 1976 has not been incorporated.]

1. On the method of disputation in Muslim theology cf. my article "Disputationspraxis in der islamischen Theologie," in: REI 45 (1977): 23ff. for further references.

2. The history of these terms has still to be written. For fiqh, cf. the material brought together by I. Goldziher in EI[1], German edition, 2, 107b (= Handwörterbuch des Islam, 132b), and slightly enlarged by J. Schacht in EI[2], 2, 887b; the most notorious examples for its use in this sense are the titles of the Kitāb al-fiqh al-akbar and the Kitāb al-fiqh al-absaṭ attributed to Abū Ḥanīfa (cf. EI[2], 1, 123b f.). The relationship of these titles to each other shows, incidentally, that akbar and absaṭ have to be connected with kitāb and not with fiqh; they serve as a differentiation between two books of different importance and, perhaps, origin, not between two different kinds of fiqh. It is therefore unjustified to assume that al-fiqh al-akbar, in the sense of "the greater (more important) fiqh," meant theology in contrast to normal fiqh in the sense of jurisprudence (an error committed by D.B. MacDonald in EI[1], German ed. 2, 720a = Handwörterbuch des Islam, 261b, also by A.J. Wensinck in his Muslim Creed (Cambridge: 1932), p. VI, and taken up by myself in: Erkenntnislehre des ʿAḍūdaddīn al-Īcī (Wiesbaden: 1966), p. 14). Uṣūl al-dīn is attested, although in a slightly divergent form, by Ashʿarī's (died 324/935-6) Ibāna ʿan uṣūl al-diyāna; as a later Ashʿarite example we may mention ʿAbd al-Qāhir al-Baghdādī's (died 429/1037) Uṣūl al-dīn. For Ḥanbalī texts cf. Ibn Baṭṭa's (died 387/997) Ibāna ʿan uṣūl al-sunnā wal-diyāna and especially Abū Yaʿlā's (died 458/1066) Muʿtamad fī uṣūl al-dīn. The term was taken over by the Christians: Elias I, patriarch of the Nestorian church (died 1049), seems to be the author of a theological compendium with the title Uṣūl al-dīn (cf. Graf, GCAL, 2: 159 f.). The connotations connected with uṣūl al-dīn usually implied a certain antithesis to kalām: the style of these treatises tended towards greater neutrality and "objectivity." Theological differences were not passed over in silence, but sometimes simply

enumerated as in doxographical works, and even if they were refuted, the dialectical structure typical for kalām was avoided. This is at least true for the later texts; Ashʿarī's Ibāna still shows a dialectical style. But this work starts with a ʿaqīda into which the uṣūl al-diyāna, in their original sense as "principles of religion," are incorporated.

3. D. Gimaret in Studia Islamica 40 (1974): 71.

4. For the authenticity of the letter written by Ḥasan al-Baṣrī, cf. my summary of the arguments in: Anfänge muslimischer Theologie (Beirut: 1977), pp. 27 ff. for further references. For ʿUmar II's epistle against the Qadariyya, cf. my edition, translation, and commentary of the text, ibid., pp. 114 ff. and 43 ff. (of the Arabic text). For the material found in ḥadīth, cf. my Zwischen Ḥadīt und Theologie (Berlin: 1975).

5. For an analysis of the text, together with an edition and translation, cf. Anfänge, pp. 35 ff.; a preliminary account of its importance for the theological development in the first century A.H. is given in my article, "The Beginnings of Islamic Theology," in: J.E. Murdoch and E.D. Sylla, eds., The Cultural Context of Medieval Learning (Dordrecht: 1975), pp. 87 ff.

6. Cf. Anfänge, pp. 19 ff., "Beginnings," pp. 89 f.

7. Cf. my Erkenntnislehre des ʿAḍudaddīn al-Īcī, pp. 56 ff. for further references.

8. Testimony for anti-Muslim polemics in A r a b i c appears somewhat later. The oldest documents known up to now are two Egyptian papyri which may be dated to the time of Theodore Abū Qurra (circa 740-820), the disciple of John of Damascus. It seems significant that the first text is composed in the form of a fictitious dialogue, whereas in the second one the opponent is directly addressed in the second person (cf. F. Bilabel and A. Grohmann, Griechische, koptische und arabische Texte zur Religion und religiösen Literatur in Ägyptens Spätzeit (Heidelberg: 1934), pp. 9 ff. and 26 ff.).

9. Cf. REI 45 (1977): 26.

10. For the authenticity of the Dialexis, cf. H.G. Beck, Kirche und theologische Literatur im byzantinischen Reich (Munich: 1959), p. 478; and recently J. Sahas, John of Damascus on Islam (Leiden: 1972), pp. 99 ff. In any case the text belongs to the second sentury A.H.

11. Cf. Anfänge, pp. 22ff

12. Cf., e.g. Qur'ān 3: 30: "fa-in ḥājjūka fa-qul"; or Qur'ān 2: 111, 2: 135, 10: 38 etc. where "qul" is preceded by the explicit argumentation of

the opponents; Qur'ān 2: 142, 10: 20 etc. where it is preceded by a question, and Qur'ān 10: 15 where it is preceded by an invitation. Sometimes the structure is more complex; cf. Qur'ān 10: 31 where the argumentation develops in two steps ("qul: man yarzuqukum . . .fa-sayaqūlūna: Allāh, fa-qul . . .") or Qur'ān 10: 50 f. where two answers are given. A typical dilemma structure is found in Qur'ān 3: 20: "wa-qul li-lladhīna ūtū l-kitāba . . . fa-in aslamū fa-qad ihtadaw, wa-in tawallaw fa-innamā ʿalayka l-balāgh."

13. Even pre-Islamic poetry, in spite of its natural unsuitableness for "prosaic" structures, may come rather close to formulations appropriate to kalām; there is, e.g., a passage in a qaṣīda by Zuhayr where alternatives are listed and pondered (cf. Dīwān with commentary by Thaʿlab (Cairo, Dār al-kutub: 1363/1944), pp. 74 f.; with commentary by Shantamarī, ed. C. de Landberg, Primeurs arabes, 2: 159 f.).

14. We should not understimate the importance of religious disputations with non-Muslims in this respect (cf. the material collected in my article in REI 45 (1977): 28 ff.). On the other hand, we must not overlook the fact that there is nothing directly corresponding to a kalām treatise in early Christian literature. There are lots of dialogues and erotapocriseis, but no texts composed in the impersonal style typical of kalām (cf. ibid., p. 59, with respect to the case of Iunilius' Instituta regularia divinae legis).

15. For the problems connected with his person cf. my article "maʿbad al-Ǧuhanī" in Islamwissenschaftliche Abhandlungen Fritz Meier zum sechzigsten Geburtstag (Wiesbaden: 1974), pp. 49 ff.

16. Cf. the summary in my Anfänge, pp. 12 ff., with references to the passages in the text itself.

17. Heikki Räisänen, The Idea of Divine Hardening (Helsinki: 1972).

18. Cf. my Zwischen Ḥadīṯ und Theologie, especially pp. 68 ff, pp. 184 f., and 192 f.

19. Cf. Anfänge, pp. 14 ff.

20. Cf. Zwischen Ḥadīṯ und Theologie, p. 183.

21. Cf. Zwischen Ḥadīṯ und Theologie, pp. 183 f. and 218; Anfänge, pp. 154 ff. It is interesting to see that Pharaoh was also discussed in Byzantine theology in connection with predestination; cf. Hildebrand Beck, Vorsehung und Vorherbestimmung in der theologischen Literatur der Byzantiner, Orientalia Christiana Analecta, Vol. 114 (1937), p. 120.

22. Cf. Anfänge, pp. 232 ff.; ibid., pp. 177 ff., for a detailed analysis of the scattered reports about Ghaylān al-Dimashqī. For the political program of Yazīd III, cf. my article "Les Qadarites et la Ġailānīya de Yazīd III," in Studia Islamica 31 (1970): 269 ff.

23. Cf. Kaʿbī, Maqālāt al-islāmiyyīn in Faḍl al-iʿtizāl wa-ṭabaqāt al-Muʿtazila, ed. Fu'ād Sayyid (Tunis: 1974), p. 117,-7 ff.: they wore ṣūf!

24. For the Ibāḍiyya, cf. the excellent article by T. Lewicki in EI^2, 3, 648 ff. and the literature mentioned in my article in ZDMG 126(1976): 25 ff. and 127(1977):*1* ff.

25. Cf. Zwischen Ḥadīt und Theologie, pp. 61 ff. and 189 ff. for further references.

26. An analysis of these phenomena has recently been given by W.F. Tucker in his Ph.D. thesis Revolutionary Chiliasm in Umayyad Iraq (Bloomington: 1971), parts of which have been printed separately in Arabica 22 (1975): 33 ff., MW 65 (1975): 241 ff., and Der Islam 54 (1976): 66 ff.

27. Cf. my edition of the text in Arabica 21 (1974): 20 ff.; also the summary in "Beginnings," pp. 93 ff. For Ḥasan b. Muḥammad b. al-Ḥanafiyya's biography cf. Anfänge, pp. 1 ff. and 277, also my forthcoming article "Ḥasan b. Muḥammad b. al-Ḥanafiyya" in EI^2, Supplement, for further references.

28. The analysis of the Kitāb al-fiqh al-akbar (I) given by Wensinck in his Muslim Creed, pp. 102 ff., remains valuable in many points; cf. now W.M. Watt, The Formative Period of Islamic Thought (Edinburgh: 1973), pp. 132 ff. and index s.v. Later examples of this simplistic and unitarian trend in Murji'ī/Ḥanafī thought are the ʿAqīdat al-uṣūl by Abū Layth al-Samarqandī (died 373/983), ed. A.W.T. Juynboll in: Bijdragen tot de Taal-, Land- en Volkenkunde van Nederlandsch Indië, ser. IV, vol. 5 (1881): 215 ff. and 267 ff., which became famous among the Muslims in Indonesia and Malaysia, the ʿAqīda by Najm al-Dīn al-Nasafī (died 537/1142) translated, together with Taftazānī's commentary, by E. Elder, A Commentary on the Creed of Islam (New York: 1950), and the ʿAqīda al-lāmiyya (Bad' al-amālī) by ʿAlī b. ʿUthmān al-Ūshī (died 575/1179) ed. Kemâl Edîb Kürkçüoğlu in: Ilah. Fak. Dergisi 3 (1954): 1 ff. We must not, however, create the impression that elaborate kalām had not originated in the same milieu. Already the Kitāb al-fiqh al-absaṭ attributed to Abū Ḥanīfa is composed in the form of a manual for dialectical discussion; cf., e.g. p. 43, 7 ff. of the edition by Muḥammad Zāhid al-Kawtharī

(Cairo: 1368). Wensinck even assumed that the Fiqh al-akbar was extracted from the Fiqh al-absaṭ (cf. Muslim Creed, p. 123. The hypothesis is not very convincing; it seems easier to suppose that we are dealing with a "more important," akbar, and a "more extended," absaṭ, presentation of the same tenets). Good examples of later kalām works in Ḥanafī environments are the Kitāb al-tawḥīd by Māturīdī, ed. Fatḥallāh Khulayf (Beirut: 1970) and the Kitāb tabṣirat al-adilla by Abū l-Muʿīn al-Nasafī (died 508/1114).

29. Cf. the edition by Muḥammad Zāhid al-Kawtharī (Cairo: 1368), p. 37, ult. f.: Abū Ḥanīfa seems to refer to the usage of the term Murji'a in Baṣra where ʿUthmān al-Battī lived. ʿUthmān b. Sulaymān al-Battī (died 143/760; cf. GAS 1: 418) was a famous jurist there who did not adhere to Abū Ḥanīfa's school; the Ḥanafīs were proud of the fact that Zufar b. al-Hudhayl al-ʿAnbarī (110/728-158/775), a famous disciple of Abū Ḥanīfa, had succeeded in alienating some of his pupils (cf. Kawtharī, Lamaḥāt al-naẓar fī sīrat al-Imām Zufar (Cairo: 1368), p. 18, 8 ff.). This was not so easy: Yūsuf b. Khālid al-Samtī, another pupil of Abū Ḥanīfa and addressee of one of his Waṣiyyas (cf. GAS 1: 417, no. VI) had been thrashed by the Baṣrans when he had pointed to the diverging views of Abū Ḥanīfa (cf. Kawtharī, ibid.).

30. Cf. Abū Ḥanīfa's Kitāb al-ʿālim wa l-mutaʿallim (Hyderabad: 1349), p. 20, -4 ff. and the English summary by J. Schacht in: Oriens 17 (1964): 111: "al-manzila al-thālitha hum al-muwaḥḥidūn naqifu ʿalayhim lā nashhadu ʿalayhim annahum min ahl al-nār wa-lā min ahl al-janna walākinnā narjū lahum wa-nakhāfu ʿalayhim." Also my remarks in Arabica 21 (1974): 50.

31. Cf. Abū Hilāl al-ʿAskarī, Kitāb al-awā'il, ed. Muḥammad al-Miṣrī and Walīd Qaṣṣāb (Damascus: 1975), 2: 134, 9 ff. and the German translation of the passage by S. Pines, Beiträge zur islamischen Atomenlehre (Berlin: 1936), pp. 126 f. (where the reading of the text is corrupt at the end). We should, however, take into consideration that the parallel in Qāḍī ʿAbd al-Jabbār, Faḍl al-iʿtizāl, p. 234, 17 ff. mentions khāṣṣ and ʿāmm just in the reverse sequence and therefore does not allow the interpretation we give to the passage.

32. That the discussion about ʿāmm and khāṣṣ has frequently to be interpreted in this context is made clear by Ashʿarī in the relevant chapter of his Maqālāt al-islāmiyyīn, ed. H. Ritter (Istanbul: 1927 ff.), p. 144, 7 ff. Cf.also the parallel material

in my article in Recherches d'Islamologie. Recueil d'articles offert à G.C. Anawati et L. Gardet (Brussels: 1977), pp. 340 f.

33. Cf. Yāqūt, Irshād al-arīb, ed. D.S. Margoliouth (GMS, No. 6), 7: 225, 11 f. Wāṣil died before Abū Ḥanīfa (in 131/748) but at a rather young age. For him cf. the recent article by Abū l-Wafā al-Taftazānī in: Dirāsāt falsafiyya muhdāt ilā l-duktūr Ibrāhīm Madkūr (Cairo: 1974), pp. 39 ff.

34. The rapid expansion of the Ḥanafī school of law can be nicely observed in the list of early Ḥanafīs given by al-Kardarī in his Manāqib Abī Hanīfa (Hyderabad, 1321), 2: 219 ff.

35. Cf. ʿAbdallāh-i Balkhī, Fażā'il-i Balkh, ed. ʿAbdulḥayy Ḥabībī (Tehran: 1348 sh./1969), p. 28, pu. ff. The dominating figure there during the first generation was Abū Muṭīʿ al-Ḥakam b. ʿAbdallāh al-Balkhī (died 199/814) who seems to be responsible for the redaction and composition (?) of the Kitāb al-fiqh al-absaṭ (cf. GAS 1: 414, no. II).

36. Cf. Anfänge, pp. 108 f.

37. This is the hypothesis proffered by R.M. Frank in his article "The Neoplatonism of Ǧahm ibn Ṣafwān," Le Muséon 78 (1965): 395 ff. The article is the most thorough contribution to the understanding of Jahm's ideas as such.

38. I am thinking of theologians like Muḥammad b. Nuʿmān, known as Shayṭān (or Mu'min) al-Ṭāq, Hishām b. Sālim al-Jawālīqī, ʿAlī b. Mītham, and, with certain modifications, Hishām b. al-Ḥakam. Their theory of an immanent and "corporeal" God has been treated by W. Madelung in a paper entitled "The Shīʿite and Khārijite contribution to pre-Ashʿarite kalām," which he read at the conference in honor of H.A. Wolfson at Harvard in 1971. It is due to appear in a collection of studies entitled Islamic philosophical theology to be edited by P. Morwedge at the State University of New York Press.

39. For him cf. the Ph.D. thesis by M.M. al-Sawwaf, "Muqātil ibn Sulaymān, an early Zaydī theologian, with special reference to his Tafsīr," (University of Oxford: 1968). He died in 150/767 in Baṣra; the material on his biography has been collected by al-Sawwaf, pp. 29 ff.

40. Perhaps we should not be too sceptical. Balkh was the old capital of the Bactrian empire; Tirmidh, the place where Jahm used to teach, seems to owe its name to the Greek prince Demetrios, the son of Euthydemos of Bactria (cf. W.W. Tarn, The Greeks in Bactria and India (Cambridge: 1938), pp. 118 f.). The Neoplatonic ideas which were introduced into

Islam by Fārābī (died 339/950) two centuries later, may have stemmed from Central Asia where they were developed at the same time, or perhaps even somewhat earlier, by Ismā'īlī circles, especially al-Nasafī who was executed in 331/942.

41. Cf. Dhahabī, Mīzān al-i'tidāl, ed. Bajāwī, 4: 173, 13ff.

42. We should expect traces of it in his exegetical works (cf. GAS 1: 36f.), but there seems to be almost nothing of this kind. It is true that he interpreted the "hand" of God in its literal sense (in Qur'ān 5: 64 and 38: 75; cf. now the recent edition of Muqātil's Kitāb al-wujūh wal-naẓā'ir fī l-Qurān al-karīm by 'Abdallāh Maḥmūd Shaḥḥāṭa (Cairo: 1975), p. 321, 11 ff.), but this does not automatically make him an anthropomorphist--and even this was eliminated by Abū l-Faḍl Ḥubaysh b. Ibrāhīm al-Tiflīsī (died 588/1192) in his Persian redaction of the same Kitāb al-wujūh (cf. p. 316, 3 ff. of the edition by Mahdī Muḥaqqiq in Intishārāt-i Dānishgāh-i Ṭahrān, no. 720 (Tehran: 1340 sh./1961), where God's hand is understood as His power and His generosity or as His action). Several problems come together here: the relevant texts are not yet edited (al-Sawwaf's thesis contains an edition of Muqātil's Tafsīr khamsimi'at āya); their transmission--with all its possibilities of later changes and additions --is rather complicated, and the judgments on Muqātil are normally pronounced in a polemical context. We should not forget that, in his period, the positions concerning anthropomorphism were probably different from later on. 'Abdallah b. 'Abbās, the great founder of Qur'ānic exegesis, seems to have naively assumed a m e t a p h o r i c a l interpretation of the anthropomorphisms in the Qur'ān. This is at least what may be learnt from early Ibāḍī sources like the Musnad by Rabī' b. Ḥabīb who preserved a direct connection with Ibn 'Abbās through his pupil Jābir b. Zayd al-Azdī (cf. my remarks in ZDMG 126 (1976): 32 ff and 127 (1977): 1*). Jābir b. Zayd equally rejected a literal exegesis in such cases (which is, of course, the reason why he preserved these reports about Ibn 'Abbās, whereas they were suppressed in the later "orthodox" tradition). This attitude was thus not a bid'a of the Mu'tazilīs, but probably rather the normal position of Qur'ānic scholars in early Islam. If Muqātil reacted against this it would be easy to understand why his opponents called him an "anthropomorphist." In any case, his tashbīh has nothing to do with the ideas of the Iraqi Shī'īs mentioned

above. The attribute "Zaydī" which is sometimes applied to him (cf. the title of al-Sawwaf's thesis), does not point in this direction; what it means in connection with him remains unclear anyway.

43. See above, n. 35.
44. Ed. Kawtharī, p. 49, 1 f.
45. He was also a mufassir (cf. GAS 1: 36).
46. Cf. Ṭabarī, Ta'rīkh, 2: 1918, 13ff.
47. Cf. p. 52, 2.
48. Cf. Wensinck, Muslim Creed, 104, paragraph 10.
49. Cf. GAS 1: 92 f.
50. Cf. M.T. Mallick in: Journal of the Pakistan Historical Society 24 (1976): 5 after Ta'rīkh Baghdād, 6: 107, 16 f.
51. This title may be hidden behind the so-called mashyakha preserved in the manuscript Ẓāhiriyya, maj. 107 (fol. 236-255) where the title has been added by a later hand (cf. Mallick, 29).
52. Cf. Tahir Mallick, "A Study of the Manuscript known as al-Djuz' al-auwal wa-t-ṯānī min mashyakhat Ibrāhīm b. Ṭahmān, a traditionist of the 2./8. century," (Ph.D. thesis Tübingen 1973). The text was published in RIMA 22 (1976): 241 ff.
53. Cf. my article in: Der Islam 43 (1967): 271 f. and 279. The attack against the Jahmiyya in the Kitāb al-fiqh al-akbar may point to an earlier usage of the term in Iraq, if the Kitāb al-fiqh al-akbar is of Iraqi origin.
54. Ibid., 273 f. They were also the first to talk about an "influence" (cf. Bishr b. al-Mu'tamir in: Khayyāṭ, Kitāb al-intiṣār, ed. A. Nader, p. 98, 8). Ḍirār himself rather intended to develop a theological concept of his own in contrast to Jahm, especially with regard to his determinism.
55. Cf. Der Islam 44 (1968): 30 ff. This geographical transfer may explain, to a certain extent, the mystery of the "Jahmiyya" (cf. Watt, The Formative Period, pp. 143 ff.).
56. Cf. for a detailed and well-balanced analysis, W. Madelung in: Orientalia Hispanica. Studia F.M. Pareja octogenario dicata (Leiden: 1974), 1: 504 ff. For the later development cf. Jan Peters, God's Created Speech (Leiden: 1976).
57. The best information about them is given in several articles by Watt; cf. his Formative Period, pp. 9 ff. and the literature mentioned in the notes.
58. Cf. the remarks by Madelung in: Orientalia Hispanica, pp. 505 f.
59. For Ḥarīth b. Sa'īd, cf. D.M. Dunlop in: Studies in Islam (New Delhi: 1964), 1: 12 ff. and my Anfänge, pp. 228 ff. A lot of valuable information

on pseudo-prophets in early Islam is found in the fifth chapter of Abū l-Maʿālī's Bayān al-adyān (which was long considered to be lost and is only found in the most recent edition of the work by Hāshim Rāẓī (Tehran: 1342 sh./1963), pp. 49 ff.). On Shīʿī pretenders, cf. the Ph.D. thesis by W.F. Tucker mentioned above, note 26. Even among the Ibāḍīs a certain Yazīd b. Unaysa expected a new prophet who was supposed to be a non-Arab abrogating the law brought by Muḥammad (cf. Watt, Formative Period, p. 34). The most interesting figure outside Islam during this period was the Jewish pretender Abū ʿĪsā (= ʿObadyā) al-Iṣfahānī who recognized Muḥammad as a Prophet before him and who presented himself, in correspondence with the ideal developed for Muḥammad, as an ummī who performs miracles (cf. the report in Qirqisānī, Kitāb al-anwār, ed. L. Nemoy (New York: 1939-43), pp. 283 ff.; also Friedländer in: JQR, NS 2 (1911-12): 240 ff. and Encyclopedia Judaica², 2: 183 f. s.n.). All this shows, of course, that the expression "seal of the Prophets" (Khātam al-nabiyyīn) applied to Muḥammad in the Qur'ān was not understood by everybody in the sense of his being the last prophet, as was the case in later times. But this is a problem which needs further investigation.

60. Cf. the poem by Ṣafwān al-Anṣārī translated by W.M. Watt/P. Cachia in: Islamwissenschaftliche Abhandlungen Fritz Meier zum 60. Geburtstag (Wiesbaden: 1974), pp. 310 f.; for ṣūf, cf. above no. 23 (in connection with Bashīr al-Raḥḥāl who did not belong to Wāṣil's duʿāt, but was only one generation--or even less--younger than he).

61. Cf. Ṣafwān, pp. 310 f.; also Kaʿbī, Maqālāt al-islāmiyyīn, p. 67. 4 and Qāḍī ʿAbd al-Jabbār, Faḍl al-iʿtizāl, p. 237, 5 ff. and p. 241, 1 ff. (both texts edited together by Fu'ād Sayyid, Tunis: 1974).

62. Cf. Lewicki in EI², 3, 650 b.

63. Cf. my Zwischen Ḥadīṯ und Theologie, p. 63.

64. This in spite of the fact that he was a Qadarī (cf. ibid., pp. 63 and 217).

65. Cf. Jāḥiẓ, al-Bayān wal-tabyīn, ed. ʿAbd al-Salām Muḥammad Hārūn (Cairo: 1380/1960), 1: 33, 2 ff.

66. Cf. Lewicki in EI², 3, 648 b and in: Cahiers d'histoire mondiale 13 (1971): 74 f.

67. Cf. Jāḥiẓ, Bayān, 1: 33, 6, in an anonymous poem.

68. Cf. Abū Hilāl al-ʿAskarī, Awā'il, 2: 137, 9 ff.; Jāḥiẓ, Bayān, 1: 33, 9 f.; Mubarrad, Kāmil, ed. Zakī Mubārak (Cairo: 1356/1937), p. 921, ult. ff.; Ibn al-Nadīm, Fihrist, ed. Reżā Tajaddud (Teheran:

1393/1973), p. 202, -7 f. etc. That weaving belonged to the low professions is a well-known, although not easily explicable, fact (cf. R. Brunschvig in: Studia Islamica 16 (1962): 51 ff., now reprinted in: Etudes d'Islamologie (Paris: 1976) 1: 154 ff.).

69. Cf. Kaʿbī, Maqālāt al-islāmiyyīn, p. 67, 6 ff.; Qāḍī ʿAbd al-Jabbār, Faḍl al-iʿtizāl, p. 237, 11 ff.; Ibn al-Murtaḍā, Ṭabaqāt al-Muʿtazila, p. 32, 9 ff. (Wilzer).

70. The middle class origin of the early Muʿtazilīs has been stressed in an interesting article--though hard to obtain--by Muḥammad ʿImāra in: al-Shūrā 2, no. 4 (1975): 74 ff.

71. For the history of the Muʿtazilī mission in the Maghrib, cf. the remarks in ZDMG 126 (1976): 51 n.

72. Cf. ibid., p. 58, n. 59.

73. Cf. Qāḍī ʿAbd al-Jabbār, Faḍl al-iʿtizāl, p. 251, 11.

74. The same is true, at least to a certain extent, for ʿUthmān al-Ṭawīl. In a non-Muslim environment he would not have needed to introduce himself by delivering fatwās (see above, p. 121).

75. Cf. ZDMG 126 (1976): 50.

76. Cf EI[2], 3, 224 b.

77. Cf. my Anfänge, p. 20.

78. Cf. Lewicki in: Cahiers d'histoire mondiale 13 (1971): 88. For some time I thought that we possess an early eastern parallel for this, too: Ibn al-Muqaffaʿ mentions in his Risāla fī l-ṣaḥāba "many mutakallimūn" among the commanders of Manṣūr's army (cf. ZDMG 126 (1976): 51 f. and Anfänge, p. 20, n. 1). But in the meantime I convinced myself, through C. Pellat's translation of the text (Ibn al-Muqaffaʿ, mort vers 140/757, "Conseilleur" du Calife (Paris: 1976), p. 24, paragraph 12), that this passage does not suit my purpose. The mutakallimūn among Manṣūr's generals are obviously simply those who "make statements" by giving orders. Also my translation of al-mubāyana li-ahl al-hawā found in the same context was wrong (compare ZDMG 126 (1976): 52 with Pellat, p. 32 ff., paragraph 25).

79. Cf. S. Pines in: Israel Oriental Studies, 1, 1971, 228.

80. Cf. Anfänge pp. 6 ff.; "Beginnings," p. 101.

81. Cf. Anfänge, pp. 124 f.

82. Cf. N. Abbott, Arabic Papyri, 2 (Chicago: 1967), pp. 14 f.; also C. Pellat in EI[2], 4, 734 a, s.v. "Ḳāṣṣ."

83. Cf. J. Pedersen in: Goldziher Memorial Volume, 1 (Budapest: 1948), p. 232, with examples

from the battle of the Yarmūk and of the Khawārij.

84. In Egypt they seem to have persisted even as an institution far beyond the Umayyad period (cf. Pedersen, p. 233 f. after Maqrīzī).

85. I know that this formulation is too undifferentiated. Muʿtazilīs seem to have become court theologians in a larger number only under the Barmakids and from the caliphate of al-Ma'mūn onward; Hārūn al-Rashīd still persecuted them. In Baṣra the theologians were connected rather with the local bourgeoisie and with independent intellectuals like physicians (for instance cf. the story of the physician Maʿmar b. al-Ashʿath who had among his ghulāms at least four mutakallimūn: the Muʿtazilīs Abū Bakr al-Aṣamm and Muʿammar, the predestinarian Ḥafṣ al-Fard and the Murji'ī Abū Shamir; in Ibn al-Nadīm, Fihrist, p. 113, 17ff.). The question needs further investigation.

Chapter 7

1. Accounts of early Ibāḍī history based on the writings of the sect may be found in the numerous articles of T. Lewicki, notably in EI, 2, "al-Ibāḍiyya"; Sālim b. Ḥamad al-Ḥārithī, al-ʿUqūd al-fiḍiyya fī uṣūl al-Ibāḍiyya (Dār al-Yaqẓa: 1974?); and in the first part of an interesting Ph.D. thesis (which I have only seen since more or less completing this article) by an Ibāḍī from North Africa, A.K. Ennami, entitled "Studies in Ibādism" (University of Cambridge: 1971). For an extreme opposite point of view rejecting any relationship at all between the North African and Omani Ibāḍiyya and dismissing the whole history of the Baṣran organization as a fabrication of many centuries later, see M.A. Shaban, Islamic History A.D. 600-750 (A.H. 132) (Cambridge: Cambridge University Press: 1971), in particular pp. 96-8, 104 and 150-2.

2. Cf. the author's articles "Bayāsirah and Bayādīr," in Arabian Studies, 1, fn. 10, and "Biobibliographical background to the crisis period in the Ibāḍī imamate of Oman (end of ninth to end of fourteenth century)," ibid., 3.

3. Shaban, p. 76.

4. Muḥammad b. Ibrāhīm al-Kindī (late 5th/11th century) "Bayān al-sharʿ," 68, chapter 17, Muscat Ministry of National Heritage MS.1029; (N.B. references given hereafter as Muscat MS. are to this new collection: few manuscripts are paginated and many, as yet, do not have an acquisition number): the oath of allegiance as given in the Bāb al-imāma of the 12/18th century of Sālim b. Saʿīd al-Ṣā'ighī's "Kanz

al-adīb,"Cambridge U.L. Add. 2896, agrees generally with the earlier author but does not state that the various responses must be repeated three times.

5. Ibn Ḥazm, Jamharat ansāb al-ʿarab, ed. Lévi-Provençal, p. 401.

6. M. Hinds, "Kufan political alignments," IJMES 2 (1971), cf. pp. 347-8.

7. Virtually all major Ibāḍī fiqh works contain a book or lengthy chapter devoted to this subject. It is further discussed in the author's article "The Ibāḍī Imāma," BSOAS 39 (1976), and in chapter 6 of Ennami's thesis.

8. The details of these arguments may be found in Muḥammad b. Saʿīd al-Qalhātī's Kitāb al-kashf wa'l-bayān, an early 7/13th century work of the Milal wa niḥal type based on early sources: a summary is provided by M. Kafafi in Bulletin of the Faculty of Arts, University of Cairo 14 (1952).

9. It is perhaps relevant to note that there are certain common features in Ibāḍī and Shīʿī doctrine whose origins might profitably be investigated; so, for example, the rules of taqiyya and kitmān which govern relationships with jabābira. That this relationship did not pass unobserved by outsiders is perhaps indicated by one of the problems posed to Abū Saʿīd Muḥammad b. Saʿīd al-Kudamī (late 4th century A.H.) in "Kitāb al-jāmiʿ al-mufīd aḥkām/jawābāt al-Shaykh A. Saʿīd" (two MSS in Muscat Min. Nat. Heritage collection): "If someone says the dīn of the Ibāḍīs is Shīʿī . . ?"

10. Qalhātī, B.M. MS. Or. 2606 p. 197: in fact it probably arises from the name of the Rustamid ʿAbd al-Wahhāb b. ʿAbd al-Raḥmān whose succession gave rise to the Nukkār schism: all Omanis are Wahbiyya.

11. The obvious fiddling with Rāsib genealogy is clear from the details of the 6/12th century "Kitāb ansāb al-ʿarab" by the Omani Salma b. Muslim al-ʿAwtābī (two MSS cited hereafter, that of the Bib. Nat. Paris MSS. arabes 5.019 and that in the private possession of Professor T.M. Johnstone of S.O.A.S.).

12. Ṭabarī, 1: 3430-9, mostly Abū Mikhnaf (ibid. pp. 3179-80 is also interesting for understanding the Banū Nājiyya position in Baṣra); Yaʿqūbī, Ta'rīkh, ed. Houtsma, 2: 227-8.

13. MJ. Kister, "Mecca and Tamim" JESHO 8 (1965).

14. Cf. the author's Water and Tribal Settlement in South-East Arabia (Oxford, Clarendon Press, 1977) and "Arab-Persian land relationships in late Sasānid Oman," Proceedings of the Seminar for Arabian Studies (1972) (held at Institute of Archeology, London, Sept. 1972 and published under the imprint Seminar

for Arabian Studies, 1973).

15. Muʿāwiya in Ṭabarī, 1: 2911-12; Ibn Qiriyya and al-Aṣmaʿī quoted Ibn Faqīh 92, 104.

16. ʿAbd al-Raḥmān b. Rustam . . . b. Kisrā, cf. Shammākhī, Kitāb al-siyar, p. 138; Abū Zakariyyā al-Warajlānī, Chronique (new French trans. by R. Le Tourneau in Revue Africaine 104, notably pp. 100-9); and also relevant is Kashf al-ghumma (attr. Sirḥān b. Saʿīd), chapter 32.

17. It was the support of this local population gained by remitting their tax which accounted for the success of these secessions to Ahwāz. Abū Bilāl only had about 40 followers when he left Baṣra but he was able to defeat an army of 2,000 sent against him by ʿUbaydallāh thanks to remitting the tax worth 100,000 dinars of the inhabitants of the Bāsak area, keeping only the ʿaṭā' due to his followers (Abū Sufyān Maḥbūb b. al-Raḥīl in chapter 31 of the Kashf; for slight variants cf. Shammākhī, p. 63 ff.). Similarly Nāfiʿ b. al-Azraq only started with 350 (Balādhurī, Ansāb al-ashrāf, 11: 80).

18. Kashf, chapter 31; Shammākhī, p. 62; al-Mubarrad, Kāmil, p. 581.

19. Barrādī, Kitāb al-jawāhir, pp. 155-6. In this connection it is worth noting that Abū Sufyān (Kashf, chapter 31) emphasizes that Abū Bilāl did not call for a hijra nor claim that his followers were the only true believers ("lā yadʿūna hijratan wa lā yantaḥilūnahā"), he did not intimidate other Muslims, take the ghanīma from them or enslave them etc.; he treated them as Ahl al-Qibla. This is a fundamental principle of Ibāḍī doctrine which distinguishes them from their "Khawārij" opponents. Details may be found in Abū l-Ḥawārī's letter to the Ḥaḍramī Ibāḍīs in the third century A.H. (Muscat MSS collection).

20. There are many such lists, but here for convenience I have used that of Muḥammad b. Yūsuf Aṭfayyash in his Risāla as translated by P. Cuperly, IBLA 130 (1972): 292-3.

21. Baghdādī, al-Farq bayn al-firaq (Cairo: 1328), pp. 92-3. For his career in Khāriji sources cf. al-Mubarrad, Kāmil, pp. 532-3; ʿAwtābī, Johnstone MS. fol. 125 v ff.; Kashf, chapter 31; and Shammākhī, pp. 62, 77-8.

22. E.g. Ibn Saʿd 7, 1: 130-3. Ennami, thesis, argues strongly against this but I find his arguments can be reversed against him.

23. Cf. the statement by Abū Sufyān's son, Abū ʿAbdallāh Muḥammad b. Maḥbūb (died 260/873): "kān Jābir afqah mina 'l-Ḥasan al-Baṣrī wa-afḍal minhu

walākinna 'l-Ḥasan li'l-ʿāmma wa-Jābir li'l-qawm," quoted in Jumayyil b. Khamīs al-Saʿdī, Qāmūs al-sharīʿa (Zanzibar edition) 8: 213. In this connection it is worth noting that the Ibāḍīs take a position of reservation (wuqūf) with regard to al-Ḥasan al-Baṣrī (Salma b. Muslim al-ʿAwtābī, in "Kitāb al-ḍiyā'," vol. 3, Muscat MSS nos. 113 and 160).

24. This incident, along with much of the biographical information, may be found in Jābir's biography in Shammākhī, pp. 70 ff. All Ibāḍī sources have something to say about Jābir and it is not possible to give detailed references here. Most of the main non-Omani sources will be found quoted in the works cited in note 1 above.

25. Abū Sufyān succeeded Abū Ayyūb Wā'il b. Ayyūb al-Ḥaḍramī to the Baṣran "imamate" fairly soon after the imamate was established in Oman (c. A.H. 177). He was actively involved in the "schismatic" disputes which reached a head during Muhannā b. Jayfar's Imamate (226-237/841-851) cf. ʿAbdallāh b. Ḥumayd al-Sālimī, Tuḥfat al-aʿyān (Cairo: 1961 edition), 1: 157-8; also the letters of Maḥbūb b. al-Raḥīl to the people of Oman and to the people of Ḥaḍramawt concerning Hārūn b. al-Yamān and Hārūn's letter to Muhannā b. Jayfar in a collection of documents entitled "Jawhar al-Muqtasir" (?), an unnumbered MS in the Muscat Min. of Nat. Heritage collection described by the writer in Arabian Studies 4 (1978). Abū Sufyān seems eventually to have retired to Oman (Jumayyil b. Khamīs, 8: 304).

26. Abū Sufyān in Shammākhī, pp. 76 and 81. Significantly the early Omani sources make absolutely no mention of this tradition.

27. Cf. al-Rabīʿ b. Ḥabīb al-Farāhīdī (died A.H. 170) at the end of Book 2 of al-Jāmiʿ al-ṣaḥīḥ in the Tartīb of Abū Yaʿqūb al-Warajlānī, ed. ʿAbdallāh b. Ḥumayd al-Sālimī (Damascus: 1968), p. 193: "Abū ʿUbayda states that . . . Anas (b. Mālik) and Jābir b. Zayd died in the same week, that is in the year A.H. 93."

28. Abū Sufyān, in his Sīra to the Ḥaḍramīs, quite categorically states that by far and away the most important of Abū ʿUbayda's teachers was Ḍumām; the emphasis is placed on the other two in Shammākhī, pp. 79 and 81.

29. For details of this Dīwān see Lewicki, "al-Ibāḍiyya," E.I.2, and A.K. Ennami, thesis; for the others, cf. Ennami, "A description of new Ibāḍī manuscripts from North Africa," J.S.S. 15 (1970): items 1-1 and 1-2; J. van Ess, "Untersuchungen zu einigen ibāḍitischen Handschriften," ZDMG 126 (1976):

nos. 1 to 3.

30. Cf. ʿAbdallāh b. Ḥumayd al-Sālimī, "al-Lumʿa al-marḍiyya . . .," in Majmūʿ sittat kutub (Tunis: n.d.), p. 78. It must be admitted that no one knew this work better than al-Sālimī (died 1914). He collated the Omani MSS (all of which are similar; an example may be found in Ibn Ruzayq's "al-Ṣaḥīfa al-qaḥṭāniyya," Rhodes House, Oxford, MSS. Afr. S. 3. fols. 182r-239v) with the copy sent him by his great Maghribi contemporary Muḥammad b. Yūsuf Aṭfayyash to produce the edition cited in note 27 above; he also produced a major commentary to it. An examination of the Musnad in its Tartīb by Abū Yaʿqūb al-Warajlānī shows it divides into four books. The first two, containing 742 ḥadīths, are Abū ʿUbayda's transmissions, always direct from Jābir followed by the full chain: here Rabīʿ's contribution is minimal. At the end of the second volume, interspersed with ḥadīths 741 and 742, comes the following information deriving from Rabīʿ: the ḥadīths of ʿĀʾisha are 68, Anas b. Mālik 40, Ibn ʿAbbās 150, Abū Saʿīd al-Khudrī 60, Abū Hurayra 72; the marāsīl transmissions from Jābir are 184, and from Abū ʿUbayda 88. The arranger then goes on to say that according to Rabīʿ there are 654 ḥadīths to be found in these two parts (Rabīʿ also adds the tradition that there are 4,000 ḥadīths in total, 900 concerning uṣūl, the rest ādāb and akhbār related by 900 men and one woman, ʿĀʾisha); the balance, the arranger presumes, are Rabīʿ from Abū Ayyūb, ʿUbāda Ibn al-Ṣāmit or Abū Masʿūd (sic; read ʿAbdallāh b. Masʿūd). None of this, of course, adds up, as the Allāh aʿlam clearly indicates, but it does give an idea of the content and is confirmed by my own sample taken from Book 3 of al-Sālimī's commentary which shows (figures in %) Ibn ʿAbbās 55, ʿĀʾisha 13, Abū Saʿīd al-Khudrī 13, Anas b. Mālik and Abū Hurayra 3 each (total 78%).

Book 3 (nos. 743-882) is much more heterogeneous and is basically Rabīʿ's own contribution of ḥadīths and of comments thereon by distinguished Companions; some of this is of particular interest for the development of Ibāḍī doctrine e.g. qadariyya (nos. 796-820), and the section wilāyat Quraysh waʾl-ṭāʿa liʾl-amīr (this may be compared with Jābir's own transmissions on wilāya and al-imāra in Book 1, chapter 7.

Book 4 is post-Rabīʿ transmission and brings the total up to 1,005; it consists of miscellaneous transmissions via Abū Sufyān, a Ziyāda by his contemporary, the Maghribi imam Aflaḥ b. ʿAbd al-Wahhāb (first half of the third century A.H.) based on Abū

Ghānim al-Khurāsānī (the author of the Mudawwana) and of various books (such as that of Yazīd al-Khwārizmī) which Aflaḥ's father had probably collected (cf. Sālimī, "Lum'a," p. 75): finally the maqāṭi' traditions of Jābir (i.e. Jābir-Prophet; nos. 924-end).

In concluding this brief survey of the Musnad, it must be emphasized that Rabī' himself never knew (adrak) Jābir, as claimed by Abū Sufyān's son Abū 'Abdallāh (cf. Jumayyil b. Khamīs, 8: 313): it is also most unlikely he knew Ḍumām b. Sā'ib, as Sālimī in his introduction to the Tartīb points out (the passage in Shammākhī, p. 104 which seems to state that Rabī''s three main teachers were Ḍumām, Abū 'Ubayda and Abū Nūḥ is, in fact, slightly ambiguous and forms, in my opinion, part of the Āl Raḥīl's deliberate manipulation of evidence concerning their predecessors).

31. Murūj, 2: 461-2.

32. "Jāmi' Abū 'l-Ḥasan" ('Alī b. Muḥammad al-Bisyawī, mid 5/11th century), Muscat MS. 361.

33. Muḥammad b. Ibrāhīm al-Kindī, "Bayān al-shar'," vol. 3.

34. Ziyāda to Jāmi' Abū 'l-Ḥasan: only part of the argument is indicated here.

35. Letters of Ibn Ibāḍ to 'Abd al-Malik b. Marwān. These are reproduced in many Ibāḍī works: for an Italian translation see R. Rubinacci, "Il califfo 'Abd al-Malik b. Marwān e gli Ibāḍiti," AIUON 5 (1953).

36. This could well be an ex post facto statement. It would be a considerable mistake to view this "mission" to Damascus as a sort of Kissinger visitation: much more likely is that amongst the throngs milling about the caliph's majlis seeking admission to discuss their complaints were some proto-Ibāḍīs (as witness the fact that they remained there a year). There is divergence between the Omani sources (e.g. Jumayyil b. Khamīs, 8: 301-3 and Kashf, chapter 39) and Shammākhī (pp. 79-80) over the names of the "delegation," but all sources agree that the sticking point was that 'Umar was not prepared to renounce 'Uthmān. Amongst the reforms that 'Umar carried out which would have pleased the Ibāḍīs were: (a) financial reform, including possibly the withdrawal of the limitations on the Gulf merchants (cf. H.A.R. Gibb, "The Fiscal Rescript of 'Umar II," Arabica 2 (1955): notably clause 9); (b) reform of the oppressive central government regime imposed by Ḥajjāj in Oman ('Awtābī, Johnstone MS. fol. 168; Balādhurī, Futūḥ, p. 78); (c) the removal from office of Yazīd b. al-Muhallab who was much too personally

ambitious and favored the old form of government, so long, of course, as he benefited; (d) a pro-Yamani policy (in Shaban's sense).

Even Mukhtār b. ʿAwf in his famous sermon (when the Ibāḍīs took the Holy Cities) in which he lashes into the Umayyads, whom he collectively characterizes as financially corrupt, spares ʿUmar II as well-intentioned; but then comes the "fāsiq Yazīd . . ."

37. This patronymic would certainly seem to have been used by Abū Jaʿfar Mansūr (cf. Shammākhī, pp. 91 and 109). It is perhaps worth noting here (as does Lewicki in E.I., 2, drawing on the first of these passages) that the ʿAbbāsid caliph may have been initially well disposed towards the Ibāḍīs. Was it possible that the Ibāḍīs had pinned hopes on the ʿAbbāsid revolution and perhaps even helped them? If so they were soon to be disappointed.

38. This is clear from a dispute in Ḍumām's majlis concerning the status of a particular person, quoted both in the "Jawābāt" of Abū Saʿīd al-Kudamī and the "Bayān al-Sharʿ," 3.

39. Abū ʿAbdallāh Muḥammad b. Maḥbūb in Jumayyil b. Khamīs, 8: 312, has a particularly important passage for clarifying the relationship between these early figures.

40. Shammākhī, pp. 83 and 91. Abū Zakariyyāʾ al-Warajlānī's statement that Abū ʿUbayda died in ʿAbd al-Raḥmān's imamate (A.H. 160 or 162-168: cf. Le Tourneau's translation, p. 131; Masqueray's translation has led Lewicki to believe that it was in that of his successor ʿAbd al-Wahhāb, A.H. 168-208) should be treated with suspicion, not just because this is after Abū Jaʿfar's death (A.H. 158) but because he states that al-Wārith b. al-Kaʿb was imam in Oman. Not only are the latter's dates 179-192, but from the history of the events preceding his election it is clear that Abū Ayyūb was imam in Baṣra. I think if we place Abū ʿUbayda's death towards the end of the 150s we will not be far out.

41. For Ḥājib's organization and details of individual merchants see in particular Shammākhī, pp. 83, 85, 90-2, 106, 112-15 and corresponding bibliographical sections in Omani sources; Lewicki has discussed two of these in his article "Les premiers commerçants arabes en Chine," Rocznik orientalistyczny 9 (1935). Also of considerable interest in explaining their influence in forming the new states is the non-Ibāḍī source Ibn Ṣaghīr (he visited Tāhert and recorded at first hand the traditions of the Rustamid State about A.H. 290) who describes the visit of the Baṣran merchant delegation

to ʿAbd al-Raḥmān b. Rustam; cf. Chronique d'Ibn Ṣaghīr ed. and trans. A. de C. Motylinski in Pt. 3, of the XIV Int. Or. Congress, Algiers 1905 (Paris: 1908).

42. That is the area of outwash fans with considerable grazing and groundwater resources (exploited by qanāt) at the foot of the mountains extending towards the desert proper. For details of the early Omani settlement pattern and political relationships see the appendix to the author's Water and Settlement, and his D. Phil. thesis (Oxford: 1969) "Arab settlement in Oman: the Origins and Development of the Tribal Pattern and its Relationship to the Imamate."

43. It is particularly difficult to work out the names of the early Azd leaders in Baṣra due to rationalization by the sources. But for the earliest period from the period of Ibn al-ʿĀṣī's campaigns to the Battle of the Camel see in particular ʿAwtābī, Paris MS. fol. 223 ff.; Ṭabarī, 1: 3179, 3195, 3203; Ibn Durayd, Ishtiqāq (Cairo: 1958 edition), pp. 483, 511; and Ibn al-Kalbī, copy of the Escorial MS. in B.M. (add. 22.376), fol. 68r.

44. Balādhurī, Ansāb al-ashrāf, 4b: 103; Ṭabarī, 2: 440. For the origins of the obligation cf. Ṭabarī, 1: 3412 ff.

45. Ibn Durayd (who was an Omani, Ishtiqāq, p. 502); but ʿAwtābī (Paris MS. 222v-223r, Johnstone MS. 159v) has three further versions of who Muhallab's mother was, Ḥuddān, ʿAbd al-Qays, and ʿAmr b. Bakra!

46. Apart form the standard sources for studying Muhallabite history there is an extremely valuable biography of the early members of the family given by ʿAwtābī under the ʿAtīk (Paris MS. fols. 222v ff.). A careful study of this, along with other passages by the same author, reveals Abū Ṣufra's true early history and shows the weaknesses of the Muhallabite pedigree: this writer is inclined to believe what their Tamīm and other contemporary enemies said about their origins (e.g. as quoted in Yāqūt, Muʿjam al-buldān, art. Kharāk.)

47. Cf. one of the replies in Abū Saʿīd al-Kudamī's "Jawābāt". Obviously the Muhallabites were fully conversant with the views of the unitarian Khawārij and were sympathetic to them, but their personal conduct was incompatible with strict Ibāḍī principles.

48. Conversion of female members of the family is striking; four, at least, are mentioned in the sources.

49. These should not be confused with the four later missionaries to the non-Azd tribes organized by al-Rabīʿ b. Ḥabīb and who were active in Oman during the period leading to the establishment of the full Omani imamate, in the second half of the second century.

50. Cf. the author's article, "The Julandā of Oman," *Journal of Omani Studies* 1 (1975).

51. Abū Zakariyyā' al-Warajlānī, p. 100.

Chapter 8

1. Berlin: 1901. (Abhandl. d. kön. Gesellsch. d. Wissenschaften zu Göttingen. Philolog.-histor. Kl. Neue Folge, Bd. 5, no. 2.) Now available in an English translation entitled *The religio-political factions in early Islam* (North Holland Publishing Co.: 1975).

2. Ed. H. Ribber (Istanbul: 1931), p. 23.

3. al-Mufīd, *Mas'ala fi l-naṣṣ al-jalī*, in *Nafā'is al-makhṭūṭāt*, ed. Muḥammad Ḥasan Āl Yāsīn, 5 (Baghdad: 1375), 5:56; al-Sharīf al-Murtaḍā, *Tanzīh al-anbiyā'* (Najaf: 1380), pp. 170-1.

4. Ibn Bābawayhi, ʿIlal al-sharā'iʿ (= *ʿIlal*), ed. Muḥammad Ṣādiq Baḥr al-ʿUlūm (Najaf: 1966), p. 211, *cit*. Muḥammad Bāqir al-Majlisī, *Biḥār al-anwār* (= *Biḥār*) (Persia: 1305-15), 10: 101; al-Faḍl b. al-Ḥasan al-Ṭabarsī, *Iʿlām al-warā* (= *Iʿlām*), ed. Muḥammad Mahdī al-Khursān, (Najaf: 1970), pp. 426-427, *cit*. *Biḥār*, 10: 104; Ahmad b. Abī Ṭālib al-Ṭabarsī, *al-Iḥtijāj* (= *Iḥtijāj*) (Najaf: 1966), 2: 9-10, *cit*. *Biḥār*, idem.

5. Different versions of this tradition are recorded in Muḥammad b. Ibrāhīm al-Nuʿmānī, *Kitāb al-ghayba* (Tehran: 1318), p. 24; *ʿIlal*, pp. 171-2; Muḥammad b. al-Ḥasan al-Ḥurr al-ʿĀmilī, *Ithbāt al-hudāt bi-l-nuṣūṣ wa-l-muʿjizāt* (Qumm: 1378-9), 2: 257-9; Ibn Maʿṣūm, *Talkhīṣ al-riyāḍ* (a commentary on the *Ṣaḥīfa* ascribed to ʿAly Zayn al-ʿĀbidīn) (Tehran: 1381), 1: 17. The fact that al-Bāqir was told to speak out may be seen as an exhortation against too rigid an application of *taqiyya*.

6. *Iʿlām*, pp. 426-7, 453; *Iḥtijāj*, 2: 9-10 (both quoted in *Biḥār*, 10: 104); al-Fayḍ al-Kāshānī, *al-nawādir fī jamʿ al-aḥādīth* (Tehran: 1960), p. 150.

7. Muḥammad b. Yaʿqūb al-Kulīnī, *al-Kāfī* (= *Kāfī*), ed. ʿAlī Akbar al-Ghaffārī (Tehran: 1375-7), 8: 4-5.

8. *ʿIlal*, pp. 241-3; *Iḥtijāj*, 2: 287-8 (both quoted in *Biḥār*, 10: 162).

9. *ʿIlal*, p. 211, *cit*. *Biḥār*, 10: 101 (agreements with the Banū Ḍamra and the Banū Ashjaʿ, and with the Meccans at Ḥudaybiyya). Cf. *Kitāb Sulaym b. Qays*,

cit. Iḥtijāj, 2: 8, cit. Biḥār, 10: 105.

10. Sa'īd b. Hibat Allāh al-Rāwandī, Kitāb al-kharā'ij (Bombay: 1301), p. 88, cit. Biḥār, 10: 110.

11. al-Mufīd, Kitāb al-irshād (Najaf: 1962), p. 189, cit. Biḥār, 10: 110; Ibn Shahrāshūb, Manāqib āl Abī Ṭālib, ed. by a committee of Najaf scholars (Najaf: 1956), 3: 195.

12. al-Mufīd, Kitāb al-irshād, cit. Biḥār, 10: 111; I'lām, p. 205.

13. al-Sharīf al-Murtaḍā, Tanzīh, pp. 215-9, cit. Biḥār, 10: 106. According to another Shī'ī account, al-Ḥasan asked his men whether they were prepared to fight and even die in the cause of justice, or whether they would rather live and put up with evil; the entire camp opted for the second alternative (al-Daylamī, I'lām al-dīn, cit. Biḥār, 10: 105).

14. al-Mufīd, al-Ikhtiṣāṣ (Najaf: 1971), p. 55, cit. Biḥār, 10: 126 (where the two men are identified as Sufyān b. Abī Laylā al-Hamdānī and Ḥudhayfa b. Usayd al-Ghiffārī).

15. al-Sharīf al-Murtaḍā, Tanzīh, p. 219, cit. Biḥār, 10: 107.

16. al-Sharīf al-Murtaḍā, Tanzīh, p. 107, cit. Biḥār, 10: 107.

17. 'Ilal, p. 219, cit. Biḥār, 10: 103.

18. 'Ilal, pp. 212-3, cit. Biḥār, 10: 102.

19. 'Ilal, p. 218, cit. Biḥār, 10: 103. See also Aḥmad b. Yaḥyā al-Balādhurī, Ansāb al-ashrāf, 4/1, ed. M. Schloessinger and M.J. Kister (Jerusalem: 1971), p. 138; Ibn Abī l-Ḥadīd, Sharḥ nahj al-balāgha, ed. Muḥammad Abū l-Faḍl Ibrāhīm, 5 (Cairo: 1959), 5: 98.

20. Tanzīh al-anbiyā', pp. 221-6.

21. This particular point is made by al-Mufīd in his Kitāb al-irshād, pp. 199-200. Cf. also 'Ilal, p. 219, cit. Biḥār, 10: 103. I'lām, p. 217.

22. Ibn Ma'ṣūm, 1: 17-18.

23. (Najaf: 1968), pp. 116-17.

24. Muḥsin al-'Āmilī, A'yān al-shī'a (= A'yān) (Damascus: 1935 ff.), 4/1: 450.

25. Ibid., 4/1: 450-1.

26. For the snake as a symbol of bravery see Abū Manṣūr al-Tha'ālibī, Thimār al-qulūb, ed. Muḥammad Abū l-Faḍl Ibrāhīm (Cairo: 1965), pp. 422 ff. I owe this reference to Prof. M.J. Kister.

27. Iḥtijāj, 2: 39. Cf. Ibn Shahrāshūb, 3: 309. According to a non-Imāmī version on the authority of Abū Mikhnaf, it was not Zayn al-'Ābidīn who was challenged to fight Khālid but rather 'Amr, a young son of al-Ḥasan b.'Alī and a survivor of Karbalā'. See Muḥammad b. Jarīr al-Ṭabarī, Ta'rīkh, ed. M.J.

de Goeje et al. (Leiden: 1879-1901), 2: 378.

28. Biḥār, 11: 27.

29. Probably the Meccan traditionist ʿAbbād b. Kathīr al-Thaqafī al-Baṣrī (died between 140-50/757/67). See Ibn Ḥajar al-ʿAsqalānī, Tahdhīb al-tahdhīb (Hyderabad: 1325-7) 5: 100-2.

30. Kāfī, 5:22; Iḥtijāj, 2: 44-5; Ibn Shahrāshūb, 3: 298 (the latter two quoted in Biḥār, 11: 33, Aʿyān, 4/1: 482).

31. Aʿyān, 4/2: 107.

32. Kāfī, 8: 341, cit. Biḥār, 11:80.

33. See in general al-Kishshī, Rijāl (Najaf: n.d.), index; ʿAbbās al-Qummī, Safīnat al-biḥār (Najaf: 1352-5), 1: 226, 2: 260.

34. These points are discussed further in my articles, "Some Imāmī Shīʿī views on taqiyya," JAOS 95, no. 3 (1975): 395-402, and "The development of the Imāmī Shīʿī doctrine of jihād," ZDMG, 126, no. 1 (1976): 64-86. Cf. also Kāfī, 8:16; Ibn Bābawayhi, Faḍā'il al-shīʿa (Tehran: n.d.), p. 12.

35. Kāfī, 5: 21; Ibn Maʿṣūm, 2: 245. See also Abū l-ʿAbbās al-Ḥimyarī, Qurb al-isnād (Najaf: 1950), pp. 200-1.

36. al-Farazdaq, Dīwān (Beirut: 1960) 2: 178-81; al-Kishshī, pp. 118-21; al-Mufīd, al-Ikhtiṣāṣ, pp. 187-90 (the latter two quoted in Biḥār, 11: 37); Abū Nuʿaym al-Iṣfahānī, Ḥilyat al-awliyā' (Cairo: 1932-8) 3: 139, cit. Aʿyān, 4/1: 474-5; al-Rāwandī, p. 29; Ibn Shahrāshūb, 3: 306, cit. Biḥār, 11: 36; Ibn al-Ṣabbāgh, al-Fuṣūl al-muhimma (Persia: 1302), pp. 218-20; C. van Arendonk, Les débuts de l'imāmat Zaidite au Yémen, trans. J. Ryckmans (Leiden: 1960), p. 14 (in the original paging); D.M. Donaldson, The Shiʿite Religion (London: 1933), p. 110.

37. Kāfī, 8: 120-2; al-Mufīd, Kitāb al-irshād pp. 264-5; Iḥtijāj, 2: 59-60.

38. Ibrāhīm b. Muḥammad al-Bayhaqī, Kitāb al-maḥāsin wa-l-masāwī, ed. F. Schwally (Giessen: 1902), pp. 498-504, whence Aʿyān, 4/2: 54-9.

39. Kāfī, 8: 51-2; cf. ʿAlī b. Ibrāhīm al-Qummī, Tafsīr, ed. Ṭayyib al-Mūsawī al-Jazā'irī (Najaf: 1386-7) 2: 68 (ad Qur'ān 21: 68).

40. Quoted in Biḥār 11: 78-9 from ʿUyūn al-muʿjizāt (probably by Ḥusayn b. ʿAbd al-Wahhāb, a contemporary of al-Sharīf al-Murtaḍā; its attribution to al-Sharīf al-Murtaḍā himself is disputed by Āghā Buzurg al-Ṭihrānī in his al-Dharīʿa ilā taṣānīf al-shīʿa (Najaf: 1936-8, Tehran: 1941 ff.), 15: 383).

41. al-Ṣaffār al-Qummī, Baṣā'ir al-darajāt (Tehran: 1285), p. 116, cit. Biḥār, 11: 34; Ibn

ʿAbd Rabbihi, al-ʿIqd al-farīd (Cairo: 1361) 4: 385; al-Rāwandī, p. 26. Cf. J. van Ess, Anfänge muslimischer Theologie (Beirut: 1977), p. 7.

42. al-Rāwandī, p. 31, cit. Biḥār, 11: 71. A similar prophecy is attributed to Zayn al-ʿĀbidīn. See al-Ṣaffār al-Qummī, p. 45, cit. Biḥār, 11: 94.

43. al-Ḥimyarī, p. 72, cit. Biḥār, 11: 92.

44. Ibn Bābawayhi, Kitāb al-khiṣāl (Najaf: 1971), pp. 100-1; Ibn Shahrāshūb, 3: 337-8 (both quoted in Biḥār, 11: 94). Cf. Muḥammad b. Ḥasan Ibn Isfandiyār, Ta'rīkh-i Ṭabaristān, ed. ʿAbbās Iqbāl (Tehran: 1941), pp. 53-4; L. Veccia Vaglieri, "Fadak," E.I.2.

45. al-Daylamī, Iʿlām al-dīn, cit. Biḥār, 11; 97a. According to a non-Imāmī source, ʿUmar b. ʿAbd al-ʿAzīz often disagreed with the Shīʿīs and emphasized his competence in rebutting their arguments. See J. van Ess, "The beginnings of Islamic theology," ed. J.E. Murdoch and E.D. Sylla, The Cultural Context of Medieval Learning (Dordrecht: 1975), pp. 89 f.

46. Cf. al-Ṭabarī, 2: 1174, 1462, 1831 ("wa-kāna ḥasan al-sīra").

47. al-Mufīd, al-Ikhtiṣāṣ, pp. 81-2, cit. Biḥār, 11: 97b. The text of several epistles sent to Saʿīd (or Saʿd) al-Khayr by al-Bāqir is recorded in Kāfī, 8: 52-57. At one point (ibid., p. 56) the imam addresses Saʿīd as "my brother."

48. al-Sharīf al-Murtaḍā, al-Fuṣūl al-mukhtāra min al-ʿuyūn wa-l-masā'il (Najaf: n.d.), 2: 95.

49. al-Ṣaffār al-Qummī, p. 147; Kāfī, 1: 348; Iʿlām, pp. 258-9; Iḥtijāj, 2: 46-7, cit. Biḥār, 11:32; al-Rāwandī, p. 27; Ibn Shahrāshūb, 3: 288, cit. Aʿyān, 4/2: 437; Muḥammad b. Rustam al-Ṭabarī, Dalā'il al-imāma (Najaf: 1963), pp. 89-90.

50. See al-Kishshī, pp. 111-12, and the discussion in J. van Ess, Frühe Muʿtazilitische Häresiographie (Beirut: 1971), pp. 29-31.

51. Ibn Shahrāshūb, 3: 312, cit. Biḥār, 11: 38. See also Abū Jaʿfar al-Ṭūsī, Kitāb al-rijāl, ed. Muḥammad Ṣādiq Āl Baḥr al-ʿUlūm (Najaf: 1961), pp. 82, 86.

52. Cf. W. Madelung, Der Imam al-Qāsim ibn Ibrāhīm und die Glaubenslehre der Zaiditen (Berlin: 1965), p. 44.

53. M.A. Shaban, The ʿAbbāsid revolution (Cambridge: 1970), p. 149; idem, Islamic History A.D. 600-750 (A.H. 132): A new interpretation (Cambridge: 1971), p. 179.

54. Iʿlām, p. 257.

55. Ibid.

56. Ibid., p. 262; Aʿyān 33: 37 ff. (quoting various sources).

57. Ibn Bābawayhi, Amālī, ed. Muḥammad Mahdī al-Khursān (Najaf: 1970), pp. 311-12, cit. A'yān, 33: 53. Cf. in general A'yān, 33: 46 ff.

58. al-Mufīd, Kitāb al-irshād, p. 268, cit. Biḥār, 11: 52; I'lām, p. 262; A'yān, 33: 43, 70. See also Quṭb al-Dīn al-Lāhijī, Maḥbūb al-qulūb (MS Princeton, N.S., no. 1979), p. 617

59. Cf. Van Arendonk, p. 35, n. 1; Madelung, p. 160.

60. Ibn Bābawayhi, Amālī, pp. 486-7, cit. Biḥār, 11: 48; A'yān, 4/2: 101-2.

61. al-Khazzāz al-Rāzī, Kifāyat al-athar (Persia: 1888), pp. 327-8, cit. Biḥār, 11: 56, 57, A'yān, 33: 71; Aḥmad b. Muḥammad Ibn 'Ayyāsh, Muqtaḍab al-athar, cit. Biḥār, 11: 48.

62. Muḥammad b. Idrīs al-Ḥillī, al-Sarā'ir, cit. Biḥār, 11: 53; A'yān, 33: 39-40.

63. Muḥammad b. Makkī al-'Āmilī, al-Qawā'id wa-l-fawā'id, cit. A'yān, 33: 42.

64. Muḥammad b. Idrīs al-Ḥillī, cit. Biḥār, 11: 47.

65. al-Khazzāz al-Rāzī, p. 327, cit. Biḥār, 11: 56-7, A'yān, 33: 73 (in the original text Zayd refers to Ja'far as "my brother" rather than "my nephew"). This tradition is also quoted in Zaydī literature. See e.g. Aḥmad b. Yaḥyā Ibn al-Murtaḍā, Kitāb al-baḥr al-zakhkhār (Cairo: 1947-9), 5: 385.

66. Biḥār, 11: 56.

67. On whom see e.g. Ibn al-Nadīm, Fihrist, ed. Riḍā Tajaddud (Tehran: 1971), p. 224; al-Kishshī, pp. 163-9.

68. Iḥtijāj, 2: 140-1.

69. al-Kishshī, p. 165, cit. Biḥār, 11: 54.

70. Biḥār, 11: 53.

71. A'yān, 33: 46.

72. Kāfī, 1: 356-7, cit. Biḥār, 11: 58-9, A'yān, 33: 63-4.

73. Ibid. Zayd is also said to have been warned by both al-Bāqir and Ja'far al-Ṣādiq not to rebel; they reminded him that all the offspring of Fāṭima who rebel before the coming of the Sufyānī would be killed, and prophesied that he would be crucified on the walls of Kūfa. See al-Rāwandī, p. 31, cit. Biḥār, 11: 52, A'yān, 4/2: 26; Ibn al-Ṣabbāgh, p. 231. Zayd's mother is said to have claimed that Ja'far's warning sprang from his jealousy of her son. See al-Lāhijī, p. 615.

74. See e.g. the commentary (quoted from al-Wāfī of al-Fayḍ al-Kāshānī) to Kāfī, 1: 357; in general A'yān, 33: 66.

75. Ibn Bābawayhi, Amālī, p. 299, cit. Biḥār,

11: 47, A'yān, 33: 113; al-Mufīd, Kitāb al-irshād, p. 269, cit. A'yān, 33: 113.

76. Abū Bakr al-Khwārizmī, Risāla (to the Shī'a of Naysābūr), cit. A'yān, 33:81; see also Biḥār, 11: 59. Cf. Kāfī, 8: 161.

77. Ibn Bābawayhi, Thawāb al-a'māl (Najaf: 1972), p. 220, cit. Biḥār, 11: 50-1.

78. Cf. Van Arendonk, p. 25, n. 6.

79. al-Mufīd, Kitāb al-irshād, pp. 195-7; Ibn al-Ṣabbāgh, p. 173.

80. I'lām, p. 266. Zaydī historians, on the other hand, maintain that al-Ḥasan b. al-Ḥasan b. 'Alī (died 96/714) rose against the Umayyads during 'Abd al-Malik's reign, then had to go into hiding, and was finally poisoned by the caliph's emissaries; the Imāmī claim about Ḥasanid quiescence is thus refuted. See e.g. Ismā'īl b. al-Ḥusayn Jaghmān, "al-Simṭ al-ḥāwī l-muttasi' majāluhu li-l-rāwī," MS. Br. Mus., Or. 3898, fol. 181b. It should be noted that while some Zaydī authors consider al-Ḥasan b. al-Ḥasan as the fourth Zaydī imam, others claim that the imamate passed directly from al-Ḥusayn b. 'Alī to Zayd b. 'Alī. See R. Strothmann, Das Staatsrecht der Zaiditen (Strasbourg: 1912), p. 107; cf. Madelung, p. 174.

81. Biḥār, 11: 195-6.

82. Cf. Kāfī, 8: 84-5; Ibn Bābawayhi, Ma'ānī l-akhbār (Najaf: 1971), p. 373.

83. al-Ṣaffār al-Qummī, p. 45, cit. Biḥār, 7: 313; 'Ilal, pp. 207-8, cit. Biḥār, 7: 243; cf. Van Arendonk, p. 42.

84. Abū l-Faraj al-Iṣfahānī, Maqātil al-ṭālibiyyīn, ed. Aḥmad Ṣaqr (Cairo: 1368), pp. 205 ff., 253 ff., whence al-Mufīd, Kitāb al-irshād, pp. 276-7, I'lām, p. 278, A'yān, 4/2: 103-6; Van Arendonk, pp. 41-2.

85. Cf. Kāfī, 1: 366; L. Veccia Vaglieri, "al-Ḥusayn b. 'Alī Ṣāḥib Fakhkh," E.I.2.

86. Iḥtijāj, 2: 137-8, cit. Biḥār, 11: 50.

87. al-Ṣaffār al-Qummī, pp. 46-7; al-Mufīd, Kitāb al-irshād, pp. 274-5, cit. A'yān, 4/2: 40; I'lām, pp. 285-6.

88. Biḥār, 7: 241-2 (quoting various sources).

89. Ibn Shahrāshūb, 3: 338, cit. Biḥār, 11: 61.

Chapter 9

1. Cf. her Studies in Arabic literary papyri, vol. 1, Historical texts (Chicago: 1957), vol. 2, Qur'ānic commentary and tradition, (Chicago: 1967) and vol. 3, Language and literature (Chicago: 1972).

2. Fuat Sezgin, Geschichte des arabischen

Schrifttums (abbr. GAS), vol. 1 (Leiden: 1967), pp. 53-84.

3. Cf. R. Blachère, Histoire de la littérature arabe, vol. 1 (Paris: 1952), pp. 58-65.

4. Cf. Ibn Saʿd, Kitāb al-ṭabaqāt al-kabīr, ed. E. Sachau a.o. (Leiden: 1905-17), 6: 174, line 15 (wall), p. 179, line 9 (hands); cf. GAS, 1: 63, for more references.

5. The oldest Arabic manuscript extant written on paper is Abū ʿUbayd's "Gharīb al-ḥadīth," dated A.H. 252 (Or. 298) preserved in Leiden University Library.

6. Günter Lüling, Kritisch-exegetische Untersuchung des Qur'āntextes, Erlangen ± 1970.

7. Cf. JESHO, 16: 113-29; JSS, 19: 240-51 and ZDMG, 125: 11-27.

8. J. Pedersen, "The Islamic preacher: wāʿiẓ, mudhakkir, qāṣṣ," Ignace Goldziher memorial volume, part 1 (Budapest: 1948), pp. 226-51.

9. E.g. Ibn Ḥajar al-ʿAsqalānī, Tahdhīb al-tahdhīb (abbr. Tahdhīb)(Hyderabad: 1325-7), 10: 292; 1: 292; 11: 130; Ibn al-Nadīm, Fihrist (Cairo: n.d.), pp. 66, 141. The famous Shuʿba b. al-Ḥajjāj is reported to have said: "Learn Arabic, because it will increase your brain power," cf. Tahdhīb, 4: 346.

10. Le Milieu baṣrien et la formation de Ǧāḥiẓ (Paris: 1953), p. 11.

11. For an excellent and concise account of the development of tafsīr literature, see Abbott, Studies, 2: 106-13.

12. Tahdhīb, 10: 282.

13. This was certainly not the case with all mawālī; think of ʿIkrima, the mawlā of Ibn ʿAbbās.

14. Cf. G.H.A. Juynboll, The Authenticity of the Tradition Literature. Discussions in modern Egypt (Leiden: 1969), p. 79.

15. Although Abū Hurayra is never called a qāṣṣ as such, his activities in the field of preserving memories of the Prophet eloquently point in that direction. Also Ibn Ḥajar al-ʿAsqalānī mentions his qiṣaṣ as part of his output, cf. Fatḥ al-bārī (Cairo: 1959), 5: 46, lines 21 f.

16. E.g. ʿUbayd b. ʿUmayr al-Laythī (died 68) in Mecca (Tahdhīb, 6: 71); Muslim b. Jundab (died 106) in Medina (Jāḥiẓ, al-Bayān wa 'l-tabyīn, ed. ʿAbd al-Salām Muḥammad Hārūn (Cairo: 1947-50), 1: 367); ʿAdī b. Thābit served in the mosque of the Shīʿites in Kūfa (Tahdhīb, 7: 165 f.)

17. E.g. Ibrāhīm b. Yazīd al-Taymī (died 94), Tahdhīb, 1: 176; Muṭarrif b. ʿAbd Allāh (died 87 or 95), ibid., 10: 173.

18. ʿUmar II was taught by a qāṣṣ in Medina (Tahdhīb, 10: 124); he had the qāṣṣ Muḥammad b. Qays in his service (Tahdhīb, 9: 414).

19. Cf. Jāḥiẓ, Bayān, 1: 367. Furthermore, e.g. ʿAṭā' b. Yasār (died 103, Tahdhīb, 7: 217 f.) and Salmān al-Agharr (Tahdhīb, 4: 319 f.).

20. Tahdhīb, 12: 45 f.

21. Ibn Ḥajar al-ʿAsqalānī, Lisān al-mīzān (abbr. Lisān) (Hyderabad: 1329), 3: 151.

22. Tahdhīb, 2: 265 f.

23. Tahdhīb, 10: 124; Bayān, 1: 367.

24. E.g. Wāqidī, the well-known mawlā historian, is reputed to have known all about Islam but not to have done any work in matters regarding the Jāhiliyya, cf. al-Khaṭīb al-Baghdādī, Ta'rīkh Baghdād (Cairo: 1931), 3: 5.

25. Cf. note 1 above.

26. Der Heidelberger Papyrus PSR Heid Arab 23. Leben und Werk des Dichters (Wiesbaden: 1972), 2 vols. Cf. M.J. Kister in: BSOAS, 37: 545-71.

27. Cf. Studies, 1: 11-16.

28. For a description of this early style, see G. Widengren, "Oral tradition and written literature among the Hebrews in the light of Arabic evidence with special regard to prose narratives," Acta orientalia, 23: 201-62, especially pp. 232 ff., which, in turn, refers often to W. Caskel, "Aijām al-ʿarab. Studien zur altarabischen Epik," Islamica, 4: 1-99.

29. E.g. Ursula Sezgin, Abū Miḥnaf. Ein Beitrag zur Historiographie der Umaiyadischen Zeit (Leiden: 1971); Miklos Muranyi, Die Prophetengenossen in der frühislamischen Geschichte (Bonn: 1973); H.M.T.Nagel, Untersuchungen zur Entstehung des abbasidischen Kalifates (Bonn: 1972); idem, Studien zum Minderheitenproblem im Islam 2. Rechtleitung und Kalifat. Versuch über eine Grundfrage der Islamischen Geschichte (Bonn: 1975); Albrecht Noth, "Iṣfahān-Nihāwand. Eine quellenkritische Studie zur frühislamischen Historiographie," ZDMG 118: 274-96; idem, Quellenkritische Studien zu Themen, Formen und Tendenzen frühislamischer Geschichtsüberlieferung, Teil 1: Themen und Formen (Bonn: 1973); idem, "Der Charakter der ersten grossen Sammlungen von Nachrichten zur frühen Kalifenzeit," Der Islam 71: 168-99; Gerd-Rudiger Puin, Der Dīwān von ʿUmar ibn al-Ḫaṭṭāb. Ein Beitrag zur frühislamischen Verwaltungsgeschichte (Bonn: 1970); Gernot Rotter, Die Stellung des Negers in der Islamisch-arabischen Gesellschaft bis zum XVI. Jahrhundert (Bonn: 1967); idem, "Zur Ueberlieferung einiger historischer Werke Madā'inīs in Ṭabarīs Annalen," Oriens, 23-24: 103-33;

idem, "Abū Zurʿa ad-Dimašqī (st. 281/894) und das Problem der frühen arabischen Geschichtsschreibung in Syrien," Die Welt des Orients 6: 80-104.

30. Cf. GAS, 1: 305 where Yāqūt is quoted as having called Wahb: "al-akhbārī ṣāḥib al-qiṣāṣ."

31. The primitive material on which all this was written down may have accounted for the bulk of Zuhrī's library as described in a.o. Ibn Saʿd, 2/2: 136.

32. Half of this material went back to the Prophet, 200 were of doubtful provenance and about some 50 there was difference of opinion; cf. Tahdhīb, 9: 447 f.

33. Ibid., 9: 447 ff.

34. Cf. M.M. Bravmann, The Spiritual Background of Early Islam; Studies in Ancient Arab Concepts (Leiden: 1972), pp. 139-49, for various connotations of these terms.

35. Tahdhīb, 10: 437 f.

36. The way the Umayyads dealt with Saʿīd b. al-Musayyab (Tahdhīb, 4: 87), by repute the greatest expert in the sunna and jurisdiction of the Prophet and his successors, bespeaks their lack of interest.

37. It was ʿUmar II who ordered Zuhrī and others to start collecting ḥadīth (cf. Abbott, Studies, 2: 22-6) and who ordered ʿAṣim b. ʿUmar b. Qatāda to go and sit in the mosque of Damascus and relate to the people the Prophet's maghāzī and the merits of the Companions, cf. Tahdhīb, 5: 54.

38. Most of the following information is gleaned from Tahdhīb, 8: 63-7. In Ibn Saʿd's Ṭabaqāt a non-committal tarjama (6: 219 f.) is devoted to him.

39. Cf. Richard W. Bulliet in: JESHO, 13: 200; also A.J. Arberry in: Islamic Quarterly, 13: 169 ff. and 14: 20; cf. also JESHO, 14: 130, note 1.

40. Cf. also J. Van Ess, Zwischen Ḥadīṯ und Theologie. Studien zum Entstehen prädestinatianischer Überlieferung (Berlin and New York: 1975, p. 129. In Ibn Saʿd, 6: 35, lines 7-10, a Companion is mentioned who, according to Kūfan traditionists, was older than the traditionists of Medina said he was.

41. For the sake of expediency I have limited myself here to the pupils of Abū Isḥāq as listed in his own tarjama in the Tahdhīb, the collecting of the names of all his alleged pupils from their respective tarājim being a far too time consuming task.

42. Abū ʾl-Aḥwaṣ ʿAwf b. Mālik, cf. Tahdhīb, 8: 169.

43. One of his grandsons, Isrāʾīl b. Yūnus, is recorded as having stolen ḥadīth from others (Tahdhīb, 1: 263), an accusation one occasionally

encounters also in the tarājim of others, cf. Tahdhīb, 6: 315.

44. Abū Isḥāq Ibrāhīm b. Ya'qūb al-Jūzajānī (died 256) was a traditionist who lived in Damascus. He had Khārijite inclinations and was a fervent member of the traditionist school of Damascus. He had a violent dislike of 'Alī and detested traditionists who spread pro-'Alī traditions. Even so, his remarks concerning Abū Isḥāq al-Sabī'ī are probably historically reliable and should be taken at face value. If his remarks had been too extremely anti-'Alī, Ibn Ḥajar would have mitigated them in a comment in the same tarjama, a custom he ordinarily resorts to, when opinions expressed about certain transmitters are unreliable or, simply, too apodictical. Cf. Tahdhīb, 1: 181 ff.

45. Tahdhīb, 8: 66.

46. The following information adds to the evidence already given. The technical term 'ulūw is used to indicate the vast difference in age between master and pupil; this was a highly considered feature of the links of isnāds. When Aḥmad b. Ḥanbal came to Kūfa to collect traditions, his attention was especially drawn to the oldest living traditionist of the time, one al-Muṭṭalib b. Ziyād, cf. Tahdhīb, 10: 177.

47. Tahdhīb, 2: 140.

48. E.g. cf. Tahdhīb, 1: 278 and Lisān, 6: 145 (Baṣra/Kūfa); Tahdhīb, 6: 172 (Medina/Baghdad); 1: 478 (Syria/Ḥijāz and Iraq); 1: 323 (Syria/Iraq and Syria/Ḥijāz); 6:279 (Medina/Baṣra/Kūfa); 9: 186 (Syria/Kūfa).

49. Cf. Tahdhīb, 10: 244, 4: 400, 11: 451 and 10: 8.

50. Tahdhīb, 4: 345.

51. Tahdhīb, 4: 344.

52. E.g. Tahdhīb, 3: 330; 2: 304-8.

53. Tahdhīb, 9: 364.

54. Tahdhīb, 4: 333-7.

55. Tahdhīb, 5: 389 f.

56. E.g. Tahdhīb, 2: 146, 3: 464 f.

57. Tahdhīb, 10: 9; cf. 3: 465.

58. E.g. Lisān, 4: 414 f.; Tahdhīb, 11: 38 f, 183 ff; 9: 185.

59. Cf. a recent study of the faḍā'il genre: Ernst August Gruber, Verdienst und Rang. Die Faḍā'il als literarisches und gesellschaftliches Problem im Islam (Freiburg: 1975)

60. One tradition in Abbott, Studies, 2: 200 f., no. 12, going back to Abū Hurayra is a blatant forgery in my opinion, because what started as a tradition of a Companion suddenly turns into a

Prophetic tradition without the link between Abū Hurayra and the Prophet having been made clear. The forger is here caught red-handed. Examples such as this are rare though.

Chapter 10

1. There is much ambiguity in the sources as to the borders of Medinan territory; we cannot discuss this item here; see e.g. Yāqūt, Muʿjam al-buldān, s.v. thawr.
2. Samhūdī, Khulāṣat al-wafā (Medina and Damascus: 1972), pp. 46 ff., where different versions are discussed.
3. R.B. Serjeant, 'Ḥaram and Ḥawṭah," Mélanges Taha Husain (Cairo: 1962), p. 45.
4. Ibid., p. 49.
5. Ibid., pp. 47 ff.; for a translation of the "Constitution" see W.M. Watt, Muhammad at Medina, pp. 221 ff.
6. Fazlur Rahman, "Prefoundations of the Muslim Community in Mecca," SI 43 (1976): 18.
7. For details see Watt, Muhammad at Medina, pp. 46 ff.
8. Ibid., pp. 59 f.
9. M.J. Kister, "Mecca and Tamīm," JESHO 8 (1965): 116 ff.
10. Serjeant, p. 54.
11. Watt, Muhammad at Medina, pp. 171 and 174 (Hāshim, al-Muṭṭalib, Nawfal, and ʿAbd Shams were the sons of ʿAbd Manāf).
12. Watt, Muhammad at Medina, pp. 54, 115.
13. Ibn Hishām, Sīra, 4: 239 f.
14. M.A. Shaban, Islamic History 600-750 (Cambridge: 1971), pp. 14 f. Muḥammad reformed the rite of the Kaʿba; the idols of other sanctuaries were destroyed by Khālid and other Meccan leaders, see e.g. Wāqidī, Kitāb al-maghāzī, ed. Marsden Jones (London: 1966), pp. 969 ff.
15. When evaluating the deeds of the Prophet, Shaban is not always fully aware of this fact.
16. Rahman, pp. 8 f.
17. O. Spies, "Islam und Syntage," Oriens Christianus 57 (1973): 1-30; Muḥammad often changed the names of people who had become converts to Islam, see e.g. Zubayrī, Nasab Quraysh, ed. Lévi Provençal (Cairo: 1953), p. 88; Ibn Saʿd, Ṭabaqāt, ed. Mittwoch et al., 3/1: 190; 5: 7, 8, 36, 37; for ʿAbd al-Raḥmān b. Samura see Ibn Ḥajar, Iṣāba, No. 5134.
18. Watt, Muhammad at Medina, p. 223.
19. Spies, p. 7.
20. Kister, "Mecca and Tamīm," pp. 120 ff.

21. Islam cuts the bonds which tie a man to his past, Wāqidī, p. 749.
22. For an analysis of the expression ḥizb/aḥzāb see Rahman, pp. 13 ff.
23. Cf. Watt, Muhammad at Medina, pp. 235 ff.
24. Fazlur Rahman, p. 12.
25. Watt, Muhammad at Medina, p. 184 (Qur'ān 3: 166-167)
26. Watt, Muhammad at Medina, p. 190 (Qur'ān 9: 73-74; translated by Bell).
27. With the exception of Musaylima, who asserted that he was guided by the Merciful (raḥmān), see V.V. Bartol'd, "Museilima," Sočin'enija 6 (Moscow: 1966): 562.
28. H.M.T. Nagel, Rechtleitung und Kalifat (Bonn: 1975), pp. 23 f.
29. Ṭabarī, Annales, 1: 1817 sqq.; for a further interpretation of these events see below note 106.
30. Ibn al-Athīr, Kāmil (Beirut edition: 1965), 2: 331.
31. Ibid., 2: 325.
32. Ibn Sa'd, 8: 83, 85, 92.
33. Zubayrī, p. 349.
34. Ibid., p. 363.
35. Ibid., p. 350.
36. Ibn Sa'd, 8: 252.
37. Ibid., p. 262.
38. Zubayrī, p. 278; a grandson of the Qurashī Umayya b. Khalaf married a daughter of the Khazrajī Abū Dardā', Ibn Ḥazm, Jamharat ansāb al-'arab, ed. Lévi Provençal (Cairo: 1948), p. 342. The connection between the Zubayrīs and the Ḥāritha b. Ḥārith b. Khazraj (ibid., p. 321) dates from a later period.
39. Ibn al-Athīr, 2: 401; cf. Ibn Ḥajar, Iṣāba, s.v. Abū 'l-'Āṣ b. Rabī' (kunyas No. 682).
40. Cf. W.M. Watt, "God's Caliph," Iran and Islam, in memory of the late V. Minorsky, ed. C.E. Bosworth (Edinburgh: 1971), p. 573, n. 11.
41. Wāqidī, pp. 769 ff.; Zubayrī, pp. 409 f.
42. Ṭabarī, 1: 1827 ff; Abū Bakr's nickname Abū Faṣīl (bakr = a young vigorous he-camel; faṣīl = a newly born camel) was used by Abū Sufyān and by 'Uyayna b. Ḥiṣn, the noble chief of the Fazāra, whose daughter was married to 'Uthmān (Ṭabarī, 1: 1827; Balādhurī, Futūḥ, ed. de Goeje (Leiden: 1866), p. 96).
43. Ibn Ḥajar, Nr. 2168.
44. Ṭabarī, 1: 2079.
45. Ibn Ḥajar, No. 692.
46. Ṭabarī, 1: 1921 sqq.
47. Ṭabarī, 1: 2073; memories of the glorious expeditions led by Khālid b. al-Walīd into southern

Iraq were still alive among the Kūfan ahl al-ayyām in the days of Muʻāwiya. The ahl al-ayyām were contemptuous of all fighting which happened later on; Ṭabarī, 1: 2073, 2076, 2110.

48. Ṭabarī, 1: 2079 ff.

49. Ibid., pp. 2144 ff.; that ʻUmar was not considered equal in nobility to the ʻAbd Manāf families, can be inferred from the tradition recorded in Ibn Saʻd, 3/1: 300, lines 10 ff.

50. Cf. G-R. Puin, Der Dīwān von ʻUmar b. al-Ḫaṭṭāb (Bonn: 1970).

51. Ibn ʻAbd al-Ḥakam, Futūḥ Miṣr, ed. Torrey, p. 146; on ʻUmar's attitude towards the noble Quraysh cf. ʻAbdallāh b. al-Mubārak, Kitāb al-jihād, ed. Nazīh Ḥammād (Beirut: 1971), pp. 75, 85.

52. Ṭabarī, 1: 2749.

53. Ibid., pp. 2528 f.

54. W. Schmucker, Die christliche Minderheit von Nağran . . ., Studien zum Minderheitenproblem im Islam 1 (Bonn: 1973), pp. 250 sqq.

55. A. Noth, Quellenkritische Studien zu Themen, Formen und Tendenzen frühislamischer Geschichtsüberlieferung (Bonn: 1973), pp. 161 sq.

56. Ibid.

57. Ṭabarī, 1: 2634.

58. Khalīfa b. Khayyāṭ, Taʼrīkh, ed. Akram Ḍiyāʼ al-ʻUmarī (Najaf: 1967), p. 129.

59. Ṭabarī, 1: 3025.

60. Ibid., p. 3026.

61. Shaban, p. 66.

62. Ṭabarī, 1: 3027.

63. Ibid., p. 3027 sq.

64. Cf. M. Hinds, "The Murder of ʻUthmān," IJMES 3 (1972): 450 ff.

65. A very convincing analysis of these events was elaborated by Shaban, pp. 70 ff.

66. Ṭabarī, 1: 2979.

67. Ibid., p. 2989.

68. Ibn al-Athīr, 2: 425.

69. Ibn Saʻd, 3/1: 196.

70. Ibid., 8: 43.

71. Ibid., 8: 145.

72. Ibid., 3/1: 70; ʻUmar had prohibited this practice, ibid., 5: 50, 52.

73. Ibid., 5: 66.

74. Zubayrī, pp. 282 f.

75. Ṭabarī, 1: 3071.

76. Ibn Saʻd, 3/1: 152 (rifāda); cf. W. Caskel, Das genealogische werk des Hišām b. al-Kalbī (Leiden: 1966), 2: 582.

77. On the rise of the ʻAbd Manāf clan see

Muḥammad b. Ḥabīb, Kitāb al-munammaq, ed. Fāriq (Hyderabad: 1964), pp. 15 ff.

78. Cf. R. Vesely, "Die Anṣār im ersten Bürgerkriege," Arch. Or. 26 (1958): 36 ff.

79. Shaban, pp. 72 ff.

80. Ibid., pp. 79 ff.

81. Fariq, Ziyād b. Abīhi (Delhi and London: 1966), pp. 60 ff. gives a full account of the istilḥāq.

82. I. Goldziher, Muhammedanische Studien, 2: 32.

83. Kister, "Mecca and Tamīm," p. 138.

84. Kister, "al-Ḥīra--Some Notes on its Relations with Arabia," Arabica 15 (1968): 147 f.

85. Bukhārī, Ṣaḥīḥ, jizya 2.

86. Ibn Saʻd, 5: 7.

87. Ibn Ḥanbal, Musnad (Cairo 1313 edition), 4: 269 ff.

88. Ṭabrī, 1: 3071.

89. Ibn Ḥanbal, 1: 168.

90. Watt, "God's Caliph," pp. 569 ff.

91. God = malik: 20: 144; 23: 116 etc.; the earth is God's mulk: 25: 2; 39: 44 etc.

92. 3: 26.

93. Ibn Ḥanbal, 4: 94.

94. On this conflict and its economic and governmental implications, see the detailed analysis by Shaban, pp. 120 ff. ʻAbdallāh b. ʻAmr's refusal to accept Yazīd as Muʻāwiya's successor (Ibn ʻAbd al-Ḥakam, p. 234) is at the bottom of this ḥadīth. In Egypt the south Arabian element had been strong since the early days of Islamic occupation. There is a ḥadīth transmitted by ʻAbdallāh b. ʻAmr, which tells us that Ḥijaz and Yaman are the noblest parts of the world (ibid., p. 1).

95. Shaban, p. 11.

96. See A.J. Wensinck, Concordance, s.v. amīn; cf. Ibn Māja, Sunan, ṣadaqāt 7.

97. Ibn Ḥajar, kunyas No. 692.

98. Dārimī, Sunan, buyūʻ 8.

99. Qur'ān 26: 107 etc.

100. Ibn Ḥanbal, 3: 4.

101. Ibn Ḥazm, Jamharat, p. 339.

102. Ibn Saʻd, 3/1: 289 ff.

103. Ibid., 3/1: 300.

104. Balādhurī p. 384; Ibn ʻAbd al-Ḥakam, p. 147.

105. Zubayrī, p. 103; Ibn Ḥanbal, 2: 345.

106. In the light of this hypothesis a reassessment of the events in the Saqīfa Banī Sāʻida is possible. Perhaps the anṣār did not claim to share in the leadership of the community as a whole, but to share in the command of all the expeditions in order

to check the ascendancy of Quraysh over the warfare of the believers and to secure a fair share of the booty. It must be noted that Sa'd b. 'Ubāda, a most generous supporter of the early muhājirūn, and now claiming imāra for himself, was very hostile to the Meccan aristocrats and was critical of the Prophet's leniency towards them (e.g. Wāqidī, pp. 573, 651, 740, 821 f.). Sa'd was very angry with Muḥammad after the Hawāzin battle, because the Prophet had given the lion's share of the booty to his Meccan compatriots (qawmuhu, 'ashīratuhu, Wāqidī, p. 957). As must be inferred from the bad relations between Khālid b. al-Walīd and Medina (Abū Bakr, 'Umar), the growing influence of Quraysh was a source of serious conflicts. When amīr al-mu'minīn had become one of the titles of the caliph, the Muslim historians erroneously interpreted the traditions on the events in the Saqīfa as a struggle for the leadership of the whole community. 'Umar's policy of refusing military leadership to the Quraysh complied with the demands of the anṣār to some extent.

107. The interpretation of amīr as counsellor, suggested by Shaban, p. 57 and others, is not borne out by Arabic evidence, and I cannot understand why one should follow the Byzantine sources in this case.

108. Watt, "God's Caliph," p. 566.

109. There is a ḥadīth in which the function of the leader of an expedition is contrasted with the representative who stays behind with the noncombatant people, Ibn Ḥanbal, 1: 300 (khalīfa fī 'l-ahl).

110. Ibn Ḥajar, No. 5764; cf. Wāqidī, p. 7 f.

111. Ibn Sa'd, 2: 119; the same practice, described in the same terms, was still common in later years. For instance 'Abdallāh b. 'Amr was his father's khalīfa in Egypt; it was his duty to lead the prayer (Ibn 'Abd al-Ḥakam, pp. 174, 179).

112. This is the so-called doctrine of predestination, which the Umayyads are said to have espoused. Of course this doctrine was formulated when the effects of "autocratic" rule were felt among the believers, and not vice versa. Only then the opposition could come into being and could discuss how to counteract "autocracy," a discussion, which--given the theocratic character of the Islamic state--of course evolved as a "religious" or theological discussion. It is absurd to assume a "dispute about the relative authority of Scripture and men" similar to the conflicts within Judaism as the basis of the development of religious and political thought in Islam, as Hawting seems to suggest (BSOAS 39 (1976): 661).

113. According to the opposition the Prophet alone could claim true divine inspiration (*waḥy*) and the community had to suffer from the later rulers, because these had no *waḥy*, Nagel, *Rechtleitung*, pp. 32 f.

114. The sociological and economic implications of these movements are still unknown to a large extent. It is only on the early Khārijites that we have good information. See Shaban, and Juynboll, "The Qurrā' in early Islamic history," JESHO 16 (1973): 113 ff.

115. For a detailed discussion of these and some related questions see Nagel, *Rechtleitung*.

REFERENCES TO THE QUR'ĀN

GENERAL INDEX

N.B. Ibn (if not used as the first part of a name by which someone is usually best known), b., bint and al- have been discarded in the alphabetical order.